ENTICEMENTS

Enticements

Queer Legal Studies

Edited by

Joseph J. Fischel *and* Brenda Cossman

NEW YORK UNIVERSITY PRESS

New York

NEW YORK UNIVERSITY PRESS
New York
www.nyupress.org

Please contact the Library of Congress for Cataloging-in-Publication data.

ISBN: 9781479807598 (hardback)
ISBN: 9781479807611 (paperback)
ISBN: 9781479807635 (library ebook)
ISBN: 9781479807628 (consumer ebook)

This book is printed on acid-free paper, and its binding materials are chosen for strength
and durability. We strive to use environmentally responsible suppliers and materials to the
greatest extent possible in publishing our books.

Manufactured in the United States of America

10 9 8 7 6 5 4 3 2 1

Also available as an ebook

CONTENTS

Introduction

An Enticement

JOSEPH J. FISCHEL AND BRENDA COSSMAN

To *entice* is to lure, tempt, seduce.

An *enticement* sweetens an offer. *Buy this volume now and we'll throw in the answer key for free!* (Just kidding: All answers herein are provisional, revisable, context-dependent; more on legal realism anon.)

In Anglo-American criminal law, *enticement* and its family resemblances (*solicitation*, *inducement*) are often found lingering near the child, the *minor*: Enticing a minor into sexual or otherwise criminal activity is itself a crime.

In common law, *enticement* was a tort against a person who caused a married woman to stop performing her wifely duties. Under common-law lights, political lesbianism is an exemplary enticement.

So *enticement* registers something like an illicit appeal for an illicit object: The appeal eroticizes the object, and the out-of-boundness of the object (the answer key, the child, the lesbian) makes the appeal strange, suspect, or, in a word, queer.

Enticements: Queer Legal Studies invites you to break the law. Less provocatively, *Enticements* foregrounds queer engagements with law that collectively beseech us to reevaluate what we understand as *queer* and what we understand as *law*. Like queer theory (sans *legal*), queer legal studies, or at any rate the queer legal studies scholarship gathered in this volume, mostly breaks from the identity project of LGBT legal advocacy. In other words, rather than redressing LGBT-based injuries and inequalities as its departure point, the contributions of *Enticements* investigate a wildly proliferating assortment of genders, sexualities, and sex/gender discourses, questioning presumptive connections between identity, desire, gender, sex-as-in-assignation and sex-as-in-fucking. As

1

with *law*: While some chapters centralize watershed gay or antigay rights court cases, others look to prison diaries, legislative hearings, customary law, municipal ordinances or guidelines, and so forth. In fact, several of the chapters herein, like Ummni Khan's panegyric for the "kinky brat," or Evelyn Kessler's diagnosis of the discursive hyper-, hypo-, and asexualization of Chinese immigrants to the United States in the late nineteenth century, have no immediate connection to law. "Can work be regarded as queer," ask Janet Halley and Andrew Parker, "if it's not explicitly 'about' sexuality?" (2007, 422). We could likewise ask, *can work be regarded as queer legal theoretic, if it's not explicitly "about" law?* The answer to both questions must be yes, despite that whiff of intellectual imperialism you are smelling. We learned from Freud and Foucault alike(!) that sex is also where it isn't. Likewise, law is where it isn't, which does not mean law is everywhere. But our cultural representations, patterns of thought, and modes of intimacy (reconsider the conceptual drift of "consent" from modern political thought to sex law to sex politics to sex) are undoubtedly inflected by what we term the juridical imaginary, an imaginary of innocence and guilt, victim and perpetrator, the good, the wicked, and the *um*pirically neutral. In the juridical imaginary, something called justice is delivered and deliverable. The contributions of *Enticements* meditate on law, and with it the juridical imaginary, as variably constrictive, facilitative, and constitutive of our intimacies and sexualities. How have such intimacies and sexualities been regulated, criminalized, privileged, pathologized, exceptionalized, or even banalized by law, legal actors, and our juridical imaginary? While scholarship that later catalogued under the sign of "queer theory" launched during the terrifying heights of the HIV/AIDS epidemic, its wider appeal, intellectual sexiness, and institutionalization into university curricula occurred in the era of antiretrovirals, Ellen (DeGeneres), "Queer as Folk," and Clintonian liberalism. This is to say that by the early 2000s, queer theoretic targets became liberalism, same-sex marriage, gay respectability, and Lisa Duggan's neologism, "homonormativity" (2002). As this volume goes to press, homonormativity is the absolute least of our concerns. We find ourselves in fatally familiar, entirely unknown territory, in which right wing–stoked fears of white left-behindism are recircuited to undercut the freedoms, citizenship, and well-being of women, queer and transgender folks, and racial minorities. At the end of this introduction we submit that it is especially urgent, at a moment of terrorizing retrenchment ("when we live with the possibility of unthinkable destruction"; Rubin 1984) to collaboratively theorize a queerer juridical imaginary.

Enticements is a long overdue collection, loudly absent from the archive of legal theory and queer studies. In the 1990s, several important anthologies were published on critical race theory (CRT), an incisive, expansive critique of law as ameliorative of racial injustice. CRT scholarship has had enduring influence over the ways we understand law and legal theory as vehicles for justice and equality. Queer thought has had no similarly definitive moment in law and left legal scholarship, despite a handful of volumes on or proximate to law and sexuality (for example, Brown and Halley 2002; Fineman et al. 2009; Leckey and Brooks 2011; Otto 2018; Stychin 1995). The present volume is designed to—if not quite inaugurate—then consolidate and embolden queer legal studies as a critical, necessary field for the historical present.

One reason queer theory has never had the same cachet in legal thought as critical race or feminist legal theory is that the latter two modes of inquiry are *less* equivocal toward the standing of their nominal beneficiaries, racial minorities and women. From the outset, *queer* has designated projects that undermine and sometimes refuse the stability and cohesiveness of sexual identities. This fact presents a challenge for assimilating queer studies into and on behalf of liberal law's promises of anti-discrimination and equal treatment along identity lines. *Enticements* concentrates its analytic energies on questions of desire, sexuality, gender and sexual non-normativity, and erotic power, exploring the lives and afterlives of *queer* across jurisdictions and jurisprudence. To that end, the volume deploys *queer* as a way of imagining the legal regulation of, juridical preoccupations with, and cultural aversions/attractions to the "sexual." But, just as the *queer* of queer theory names a definitional ambivalence to its object (the "sexual"), so too do we leave the meaning of queer, or sexual, purposefully under-defined. Queer legal studies might be queer by virtue of its citational practices; its archival practices; its embrace of the affective and its foregrounding of materiality and embodiment; or even by its aesthetic or style, as intermittently irreverent, glamorous, daring, transgressive, camp, political, illicit, shocking, or even deceptively doctrinal or ordinary. *Enticements* entertains, hopefully revitalizes, many possibilities of *queer*.

Genealogies of Queer Legal Studies

Queer legal studies (QLS) draws upon multiple disciplines and interdisciplines and developed in response to two generations of cultural and political contestations over the regulation of sexuality, gender, reproduction, and the family. To narrativize an epistemic formation is to flatten and familiarize it—what could be any less queer?!—but here we relay two significant genealogies for QLS, one queer theoretic, the other critical legal theoretic. Under the expansive rubrics of "queer theory" and "critical approaches to law" are subfields, subgenres, and total disciplinary departures that have been influential for QLS.

Queer Theories

One version of queer theory's genesis begins with philosopher Michel Foucault's argument that sexuality is a discursive production rather than a natural condition (1978). Put too simply, *The History of Sexuality Volume 1* provocatively proposed that expert discourses, chief among them psychoanalysis, did not so much release a silenced sexuality from the grip of Victorian moralism, as they constituted the very object—sexuality—that they purported to describe. Sexuality, constructed as a deep and mysterious truth of the self, a truth with endless etiological power (*angry at your advisor? It might be Oedipal*) and endless taxonomic potential (*invert, hysterical woman, the precocious child, homosexual, sadist, pedophile, zoophile . . .*), inaugurates fields of science and expertise, systems of regulation and surveillance, and modern subjectivity itself. Consider, for example, when "homosexuals" became "gay," when the perverts invented Pride, or when heterosexuals self-identify, especially when they do so shamefully—*if only I could be gay!* (see Seresin 2019). Sexuality so historicized, Foucault bequeathed or at least underscored two lessons for theorizing power to future feminist and queer scholars, lessons perhaps hardest to digest for those scholars traveling in or adjacent to law. First, truth and knowledge do not stand outside power but are contingent upon, and consequences of, power relations (hence Foucault's provocative terms "regimes of truth"; 1975). To say (or scream, or identify as) "gay" in opposition to a "Don't Say Gay" law is not *simply* to speak truth to power, but to speak from a truth—gayness—that accreted into an identity form through medi-cal, criminological, psychological, and psychiatric discourses. Second, power is not only coercive, oppressive, repressive, dominating, and sovereign-emanating (modes of power Foucault shorthands as "juridi-cal"), but also productive, diffuse, multiply sourced, relational, and "capillary." While many self-proclaimed Foucauldians have focused their attention on state or statelike powers that subordinate homosexuals and superordinate heterosexuals, Foucault himself emphasized the powers that made homo-, and therewith hetero-, sexuality.

Foucault's *History of Sexuality* marked a groundbreaking shift in our understanding of sexuality, a promising counteroffer to essentialist and biological accounts of sexuality, as well as to some psychoanalytic or Marxist-psychoanalytic accounts of sexuality as repressed, oppressed, sublimated, or epiphenomenal. Scholars who would become founda-tional to queer theory followed Foucault's ideas around sexuality, power, and knowledge and deployed them to break with prevailing approaches to sexuality, albeit positivist or feminist.

Foucault was not alone in approaching sexuality as a site of power; feminists in the 1970s had begun to theorize the ways in which sexual-ity operated as a site of oppression for women (the feminist focus on sexuality as *power over* was un-Foucauldian yet a necessary corrective to Foucault; still, a shared conceit among Foucault and feminists is that power is an ingredient of, and not independent from, sexuality). Radi-cal feminism in particular reconstructed (hetero)sexuality as an oppres-sive institution for women. Queer theory would emerge alongside and against this feminism and its focus on gender-as-eroticized-hierarchy. In her field-defining essay, "Thinking Sex," anthropologist Gayle Rubin encouraged academics and activists alike to theorize sexuality, sexual injustice, and sexual stratification apart from gendered domination and submission. Rubin challenged feminism's claim on the sexuality field and argued that it was essential "to separate gender and sexuality ana-lytically to more accurately reflect their separate social existence" (1984, 308). For example, under some feminist analyses, pornography contrib-uted to the objectification of women. But pornography might also be a life-saving, world-making resource for queers and other sexual outsid-ers. It was time, declared Rubin, to develop an "autonomous theory and politics specific to sexuality" (308). Rubin's call to think of sexuality to the side of gender, and to the side of feminism, would be amplified by Eve Kosofsky Sedgwick in *Epistemology of the Closet*. "The study of sexuality," Sedgwick famously observed, "is not coextensive with the study of gender; correspondingly antihomophobic inquiry is not coextensive with feminist inquiry" (1990, 27). For Sedgwick, sexuality and gender represent two different analytic axes that could and should be productively imagined distinctively.

The break—albeit "analytic"—from feminism was a crucial move in the opening salvo of things queer. But it was not the only break, nor even queer studies' most significant one. Queer theory coalesced as a departure from LGBT identities. In 1991, Teresa de Lauretis coined the term "queer theory" as a provocation to unsettle the complacency of "gay and lesbian studies," with queer denoting "a certain critical distance" from the terms "lesbian and gay" (iv). Sedgwick took aim at the essentialism of the homo/hetero dichotomy, premised on the superiority of the former and the subordination of the latter (1990). Gay and lesbian identity was built upon a minoritizing discourse that reinforced this heterosexual/homosexual distinction and its homophobic subordination. Sedgwick's foundational intervention was anti- or at least ambivalently identitarian, shoring up how gay and lesbian identity may just as easily be put to the service of buttressing homophobia as dismantling it. Later in the 1990s, political scientist Cathy Cohen averred that sexualities are minoritized not only by object choice (e.g., men who like men), but also by state practices and dominant tropes of racialized respectability (1997). Cohen's intervention is a necessary one for this volume; several chapters diagnose how ostensibly heterosexual figures and heterosocial groups have been queered by state power or social norms. As David Halperin states plainly in *The War on Sex*: "The politics of sex cannot be reduced to a politics of identity" (2017, 12).

As queer theory migrated to law, or rather, as legal scholars imported queer theory to the analysis of law, these two breaks—untethering sexuality from gender, and untethering sex from modern taxonomic identity—would remain axiomatic. Nevertheless, it is worth reminding readers that, even from its literary origins, queer studies contested antigay laws and court decisions, censorship laws, and feminist reforms against pornography, not to mention the Law of the Father; in that sense, queer theory has always been queer legal theory or at least about law (and yet, stubbornly, "queer theory in the law schools has nothing like the éclat it still [still?] enjoys in literary study" (Halley and Parker 2007, 422–23).

The earliest scholarship that appeared under the sign of queer legal studies theorized sexuality as an analytically independent object of study and approached that object with dutiful skepticism toward the binary division, hetero/homo. If feminism and gendered dominance heretofore saturated our social theories about sexuality, then the homo/ hetero binary, as prepolitical and preordained, could just as easily, and just as mistakenly, crowd out better thinking about sex, power, and inequality. Law professor Janet Halley's scholarship forged both identitarian-skeptical and feminist-skeptical paths through queer legal thought. Halley's "Reasoning about Sodomy: Act and Identity in and after *Bowers v. Hardwick*" (1993) makes an array of stunning, field-defining interventions. Halley shows that despite the fact that most sodomy statutes in the United States were facially neutral—they applied to same-sex and different-sex sex alike—sodomy came to be identified with homosexuality. "Sodomy in these formulations is such an intrinsic characteristic of homosexuals, and so exclusive to us, that it constitutes a rhetorical proxy for us. It is our metonym" (1737). Halley reveals the unstable relationship between act and identity that underlies *Bowers v. Hardwick*, the much-derided Supreme Court opinion that held state anti-sodomy laws constitutional. She shows how the Court shuttles between act discourse and identity discourse to denigrate gays, to deny them constitutional protections, and to shield heterosexual sodomy from the juridical purview.

Ultimately, Halley emphasizes sex acts over sexual identities as the ground for coalitional sexual justice politics: There is a "political possibility of alliances along a register of [sex] acts" (1993, 1738–39). Such possibility entails both forging cross-identity coalitions premised on the sodomitical sex of which we all partake (or of which we would minimally appreciate the unpoliced option to partake) and, consequently, dethroning heterosexuality of its superordinated status by dissolving the fictional coherence of sexual identity outright. Identities are discursive placeholders for messy sexualities, and that messiness might be publicized and politicized rather than localized onto or on behalf of discrete (and formerly discreet) sexual minorities (1771–72).

While Halley's research on sodomy and sodomy proscriptions embodied queer legal studies' (intermittent) departure from LGBT identity, her later work, particularly *Split Decisions: How and Why to Take a Break from Feminism* (2006), exemplifies (and to a nontrivial degree establishes) queer legal studies' ambivalence to feminism. Critiquing a wide assortment of feminist and queer theories, Halley homes in on the dominance theory of feminist legal scholar Catharine MacKinnon, to advise that we dangerously overlook consequences of case law and legal decision-making if our interpretive analytic and political outlook begins and ends with the assumption of men's eroticized superordination over women (Halley 2006, 41–59). Feminist "wins" in law and politics (for example, sexual harassment as an actionable claim of sex discrimination), posits Halley, often come with costs: costs for men, but also costs for other sexual and gender minorities (290–303). Indeed, for Halley, the primary beneficiaries of a "break" from (governance) feminism would be queer people and queer sex.

A default analytic for measuring the queer reverberations of any particular law, administrative policy, or institutional norm ought to be assessing how such laws, policies, and norms constitute, constrain, or otherwise contour sex, gender, and sexuality in ways that exceed or subtend our modern taxonomy, L, G, B, or T. This does not mean, though, that estimating or documenting the effects of a new city zoning law on homeless transgender populations is an *un- or anti-queer* enterprise (Adler 2018). We do not territorialize *queer*. But the promise we see in a queer analytic is registering, in the foregoing example, how such a zoning law might delimit, redistribute, criminalize, or legalize opportunities for sex and intimacy; and how zoning laws give shape and value to what we think of, say, as "sex," or "sexual harassment," or even "a healthy relationship." These sorts of assessments may or may not calibrate to identitarian investigations (Cossman 2019, 25–27, 31–33).

Critical Approaches to Law

For us, queer legal studies interrogates laws and regulations—their codification and enforcement; their reforms; their social support, opposition, or indifference—with an interpretive prior, namely, that such laws effectuate sex, sexual hierarchy, and modes of intimacy for which antigayness is a too coarse, or a just incorrect, diagnosis. There is more to learn from even transparently homophobic sex laws and legal reforms than that the laws and reforms are transparently homophobic—and more to learn specifically about such laws and reforms' impacts on our sexual imaginaries, our sexuality, and our sex.

In addition to drawing from humanistic inquiry, queer legal studies builds on critical legal traditions that already approach law as a site of power and knowledge, of discursive production and unequal material distribution. Legal scholars who would deploy queer theory's insights were already well schooled in critical legal studies, feminist legal studies, and critical race theory. In this way, legal scholars influenced by queer theory developed a quite different, more textured analysis of law from scholars in other disciplines, whose approach to law, frankly, veered toward paranoid and kneejerk anti-regulatory. The queer theoretic flirtation with libertarianism has become all the more unsavory in the face of a global pandemic on the one hand, and ascendent, worldwide, right-wing, white supremacist movements on the other. There are many reasons to be skeptical and critical of criminal law, but that skepticism and criticism should not devolve into a categorical dismissal of law as a vehicle for social and sexual justice.

In this sense, there is then a third departure in what we think of as queer legal thought; that is, a break from the anti-regulatory impulse of much scholarship in queer studies. Consider Trevor Hoppe's and David Halperin's excellent collection *The War on Sex*, which explores the contemporary political and legal governance of sex (2017). The collection builds from a recognition that regulations on sexual expression and sexual conduct cannot be fully understood either in "m>f" (Halley 2006) or gay-negative (or gay-affirmative) terms. The collection examines the policing of sex acts, including, for example, legislative (and sometimes literal, physical) attacks on registered sex offenders, sex workers, and people living with HIV/AIDS to illustrate the extent that sex regulations, as well as the sexual regulatory imaginary (see Davis 2015 on the feminist regulatory imagination), reach beyond problems of identitarian injustice. Collectively, the essays in *The War on Sex* deliver a sustained polemic against the hyper-regulation of non-normative sex and sexuality. And so the collection tells us much more about what law should not do rather than what it should. In *The War on Sex*'s portrait of sexual regulation, a few sex laws are simply and summarily good (harm-prevention), most are bad (sex-repressive), "harm" is a self-evident category naturalized as physical imposition of force, and sex laws are justifiable if and only if they reduce harm so defined. It is an overly narrow conceptualization both of law and of the distributional consequences of legal regulation. Halperin's reflections on sex law symptomize what Eve Kosofsky Sedgwick called paranoid reading (and Janet Halley has argued that Sedgwick herself could not help but be paranoid about law) (Sedgwick 2003, 123–52; Halley 2017, 23–143). For Sedgwick, a paranoid reading is one in which the object of analysis (here, sex law) is understood either and only as threatening and dangerous or affirming and good. A paranoid reading—which is also often an accurate one—leaves little interpretive latitude, for the interpretation is always ultimately pegged to the political and psychical commitments of the interpreter: This law is homophobic or gay-affirmative; that law is sex-negative or assault-preventative. Too quickly, especially in proximity to sex, paranoid readings mutate into antinormative ones, in which *any* additional law, policy, or institutional practice is first and foremost perceived as buttressing or complicit in a gender- and sex-normative order we are not supposed to like.

Ours is not an anti-regulatory project; instead, it builds on the histories of critical interventions in law, which allow queer legal studies to paint a more complex picture of law than often represented by those outside of law. Queer theories' migration to law has many "in laws," critical traditions with which we share intellectual affinity and political orientation. One such in-law is American legal realism. A basic tenet of American legal realism is that the dichotomy between intervention and non-intervention is a false one, given the modern regulatory state and its vast social inequities (Adler 2018, 179–82; Hale 1923). "Homeless kids on the New York City subway are homeless not chiefly because we lack housing, but because trespassing violates tort law" (Carrillo 2014). In other words, homelessness is not an *empirical* problem of too many people and too few homes, but a *legal* problem of property distribution, ownership, and use. Feminist and queer theorists of law have picked up the point. As Jennifer Nedelsky points out in response to the anti-statist strands of Janet Halley's critiques (2011, 359–60), as Susan Appleton and Susan Stiritz point out in response to the anti-bureaucracy impulse of

Jeannie Suk Gersen and Jacob Gersen (2016, 49–65), as Libby Adler points out in response to free market ideologues (2018, 179–87), and as we have pointed out in response to Hoppe and Halperin's war on sex, the choice between intervention and nonintervention, along with its normative valence when it comes to sex (intervention = usually bad; nonintervention = usually better), is chimeric. Against so many inequalities, not just the sex and gender inequalities, and against such disparate modes of enculturation and education, sex is never "sex itself" (Halperin and Hoppe 2017, 19), but always shot through with norms, regulated, as it were, prior to regulation.

Critical legal studies implores us to consider the distributive consequences of legal interventions. How do particular laws redistribute social benefits and costs, power and status, material and discursive resources? Since all sex regimes bear costs, a central task for us to assess is: Which regimes bear the least cost for, or which regimes are most hospitable to, sexual and intimate flourishing? What combination of policies, procedures, enforcement patterns, and statutes contribute to a world that is least costly for gender and sexual pluralism? Not every queer theoretic law journal article or book must carry a brief for sexual pluralism or prescribe a particular law or doctrinal interpretation. But wherever readers may come down on the debate surrounding (non-legal) queer theory's normative or antinormative priors (Wiegman and Wilson 2015), law cannot help but be about the installation and (coercive) instantiation of norms. And so a queer theory of law must address the norms we want in code, the ones we do not, and the costs of winning. The answers to those inquiries will be local, contingent, and revisable, but the answer can never simply be: *Less is more*, or *no law is good law*, or *the state is "an evil empire"* (Halley 2017, 123).

And so another "in-law" of queer legal studies is critical race theory (CRT), a movement shamefully defamed by racist politicians and pundits in the 2020s, both to scale back the movement for Black lives and to censor speech and expression in public schools. The irony of that defamation is that CRT scholarship—by law professors like Charles Lawrence, Mari Matsuda, Kimberle Crenshaw, Gerald Torres, and Lani Guinier, to name a few—advance egalitarian and regulatory projects through institutional reform, while CRT's incendiary critics accuse CRT of broadstroking democratic institutions as interminably racist and therefore unsalvageable. That is, CRT (and we admit to broad stroking), in contrast to the thrust of critical legal studies, reconstructs rather than rejects law, rights, and courts as vehicles for social change. CRT is optimistic, neither cruelly nor utopically, about regulating better, and for antiracist futures. We think queer legal studies should follow suit. Indeed, this critical tradition cautions us against an overly restrictive notion of law, making room beyond traditional legal texts for the fluidity and messiness of law. Like CRT, the essays in *Enticements* embrace storytelling, "improper" objects of research, and unconventional methods and archives to critique law, law's subjects, and law's stakeholders. Some of the most elegant defenses of legal rights come out of the CRT tradition; still, CRT scholars have been avowedly skeptical that rights on paper, or watershed civil rights decisions like *Brown v. Board of Education*, ever fully deliver on their promises (Bell 1976; 1987). So too, CRT scholars have questioned otherwise unspoken costs of seemingly unassailable victories like affirmative action (for an alternative project to race-based affirmative action nevertheless anchored in the oppositional consciousness of people of color and led by racial minorities, see Guinier and Torres 2003, 67–107). While debating the best legal paths for Black freedom and equality, CRT never abandons its subjects; it carries a brief for Black people and racial minorities. As we noted above, at its theoretical core QLS is existentially ambivalent about carrying the brief for gays and lesbians, insisting as it does on the risks and rewards of consolidating sexuality into social identity. But to query sexual identity formations need not entail abandoning law, state, and regulation outright, even as we assess costs of winning.

Like CRT, queer legal studies is rich with critiques of the costs of winning. There is a robust scholarship critiquing *Lawrence v. Texas*, in which the US Supreme Court case invalidated state sodomy laws, and *Obergefell v. Hodges*, which established a constitutional right to same-sex marriage. But unlike CRT, appraisals on the costs of winning—a hallmark of queer legal studies—sometimes veers toward a hyperinflation of the queer costs of law; the writing borders on an overly paranoid/repressive reading, where the wins are actually losses and progay decisions are recoded as antigay. There is a fine line between registering or calculating costs and paranoid reading, but we think it is critical, politically and intellectually, to keep our cost-counting, from, again, collapsing into anti-everythingness, tossing out the queer baby with the x-normative bathwater (where x, at this point, could be any number of affronting prefixes). This sort of hyperinflation on the queer costs of law is probably nowhere more prevalent than in progressive laments over *Lawrence v. Texas*. Gender and sexuality legal scholars raced in front of each other to tell us just how assimilationist (Harcourt 2004; Ruskola 2005), privatizing (Franke 2004), racializing (Puar 2007), violence-authorizing (Huffer 2013; MacKinnon 2004; Spindelman 2004) and poorly written (Case 2003) was our victory. Some of these criticisms are instructive and generative. But at the end of the day, the *Lawrence* Court ruled that police could not criminalize us for privately performed, non-commercial, consensual sex. When Teemu Ruskola writes of *Lawrence*, "The Court, and the Constitution, will respect our sex lives, but on condition that our sex lives be respectable" (2005, 239), he is wrong (which he more or less admits; 242). We can tally up and speculate upon costs of sex law and legal reform without presupposing those costs are always, and only prohibitively, suffocatingly normative.

Our sensibility invites ambiguity and plurality to the readings of wins and losses, indeed to the reading of law itself, in order to open up possibilities for more reparative readings and subjunctive ones, of what was there and what could be. In countenancing what queer legal theory could be, we deploy the subjunctive from Saidiya Hartman, who describes it as "a grammatical mood that expresses doubts, wishes and possibilities" (2008, 11). While Hartman looks back to the archive, to the absences or distortions of the lives of Black women, to imagine what could have been, we look to the future, to what could be. It is a thinking of *queer* similarly inspired by José Esteban Muñoz's queer futurity: "Queerness exists for us as an ideality that can be distilled from the past and used to imagine a future. The future is queerness's domain" (2009, 1). Queer sensibilities, open and plural, can continue to reveal and disrupt narratives, discourses, institutions, and identities structured around sex, sexuality, and desire. But as Judith Butler warned, we need not be limited to such proper objects (1994). There are queer sensibilities that can explore affect, time, space, beyond the proper objects of sex and sexuality. Just as Lauren Berlant and Michael Warner opined that "queer theory is not the theory *of* anything in particular," queer legal theory ought not to be the theory of anything legal in particular (1995). In asking, *how do we do queer things in law?*, we need to remain open to unknown futures; futures that can, in Muñoz's words, imagine better possibilities. Queer, in its critique of heteronormativity, was and continues to be marshalled to identify the ways certain kinds of sex, stylizations of gender, and modes of intimacy are awarded gold-star status, while others are denigrated, abjected, shamed. This critical edge of queer/legal theory ought to be retained, but in a way that need not always go full tilt paranoid. Sedgwick, lamenting that paranoid readings had taken up all the oxygen in critical theory and queer studies, nonetheless recognized that such readings are good at some things (both diagnostic and prescriptive), just not all things. Queer legal futures are reparative, even nurturing, calling us to read with plentitude, to read beside rather than always beneath, behind, or beyond.

A Schema for Queer Enticements

Part one of our collection meditates on Queer Fictions or, Rewriting Gay Rights. The chapters in this section each reinvestigate the meanings of gay rights victories, asking—with care, not cynicism—what might be mystified, sanitized, or depoliticized by the dominant narrative of incremental LGBT triumph. If, as Zach Herz rightly presupposes in "The Epistemology of the Courthouse: Classical Antiquity in American LGBT-Rights Litigation," judges make for bad historians, how might good queer historians best support litigation advancing social and sexual equality? Not, Herz avers, by disinterring gay subjects out of the historical archive or by repackaging ancient beliefs and customs as gay-friendly. Herz argues that it is not simply judges' or historians' normative preferences that convolute the project of pressing history into the service of making doctrine. Rather, jurisprudence and historical inquiry are epistemologically incompatible. Herz reviews several landmark gay (and antigay) rights cases, along with the historico-political debates circulating through and around those cases, to evidence how both progay and antigay legal actors warp the queer and messy past to create a simple and justiciable present. By reconstructing a now infamous debate among philosophers about Platonic sexual morality and its bearing on Colorado law, Herz suggests that the task incumbent upon historians of sexuality is less to "correct the record" for the court than to shore up "correcting the record" as a double-edged mode of legal reasoning and a facile form of history.

In "The Sexual Subaltern and Law: Postcolonial Queer Imaginaries," Ratna Kapur retrieves forms of gendered and sexual subjectivity and subculture unassimilable either to colonial mandates or to LGBT legal advocacy, while cautious not to indulge in a precolonial nostalgia for the fantastically queer past. Kapur examines recent judgments of the Supreme Court of India on LGBT rights, as well as the political movements surrounding those judgments, to consider sexual dissidence and sexual subalternity foreclosed by queer victories, rights talk, and what she identifies as a stubbornly enduring "heterosexual presumption." Given both its Anglo-American preoccupations as well as its frequent single-axis focus on sexuality, Kapur argues that queer legal critique too often fails to disrupt either colonial or postcolonial narratives of sexual otherness or sexual modernism. But Kapur does not wish to abandon the insurrectionary potential of *queer*. Instead, Kapur closes her chapter by revisiting the Supreme Court of India's decision to permit women entry into a popular temple, and she locates in the legend of the temple's deity forms of sexuality and relationality beyond those dictated under liberal individualism, binary gender, and reproduction.

Matthew Waites complicates grand, unitary narratives of precolonial and colonial regulations of same-sex sex practices. His "Contesting Colonial Criminalization: Customary Law's Significance for Decolonizing Queer Analysis" shows us that underexamined bodies of customary law offer a granular and therefore more accurate account of how non-normative sex practices were penalized, not penalized, or unevenly penalized in colonial jurisdictions. An important upshot of Waites's research is that prior anticolonial reports on anti-sodomy laws largely overlook subnational regulatory apparatuses and dismiss customary legal systems as insignificant, thereby under accounting for the wide variety of responses to non-normative sex by local authorities. Waites reviews and critiques the literature on colonial criminalization of same-sex sex before introducing readers to customary law. Waites then closely reads British colonial surveys of customary law in Kenya, modeling how a queer legal studies engaging decolonial inquiry more finely captures sexual regulations and their enforcement patterns under colonialism.

In "Contamination to Congratulation: The Discursive and Legal Careers of the Homosexual in the United States and Cuba," Libby Adler historicizes the dialectic of homosexual advancement and antigay retrenchment in the United States and Cuba. Adler's comparative analysis is instructive on several fronts for scholars of law and sexuality. First, she shows how the codification of "liberal legal rights" is neither necessary nor sufficient for gay equality. Second, gay equality is not a telic, irreversible achievement, but waxes and wanes in accordance with broader transformations of political economy and state-building projects. At times, the homosexual is cast as a threat to the capitalist state, vulnerable to communist blackmail; at other times, the homosexual is the hero of neoliberalism, homophobia correspondingly reperceived as a relic of the uncivilized. As with socialism: The homosexual may personify decadent American indulgence or, alternatively, may be a harbinger of a progressive, fairer society. Third, Adler observes how rising economic inequalities in both Cuba and the United States diminish or deny the benefits of gay rights codification and homosexual advancement to more disadvantaged queer and trans populations: sex workers, racial minorities, young people, and poor people.

If the Queer Fictions of part one lubricate gay rights, they also tend to underdescribe histories, experiences, and regulations of gender pluralism and sexual diversity. The Queer Figures featured in part two capture contestations over sexual deviance and gender transgression to the side of antigay animus, sexism, or transphobia. Ummni Khan's kinky brat, Evelyn Kessler's Chinese immigrant, and Mary Anne Case's donorsexual are not *not* identity forms; in fact, the authors' essays in part labor to show how such identities come to cohere through (often sensationalist) media discourses, law, and public debate. Who is the queer now (or then), and how is that figure mobilized in the service of wide-ranging legal, political, and/or cultural agendas?

Ummni Khan goes to bat for the kinky brat. In "The Kinky Brat: Speak Pleasure to Power," Khan offers up the kinky brat as a complement, or a rival sibling, to Sara Ahmed's feminist killjoy (2017), in order to mobilize feminist practices of thinking, reading, looking, and politicking unanchored from a hermeneutics of misery. To make others unhappy while cultivating joy, Khan observes, is a noncontradiction, but she champions the latter, *pace* Ahmed, for living a feminist life. Khan redeems the attention-seeking, playful, rebellious, unapologetic kinky brat to personify an alternative epistemological and methodological approach to law, feminism, sexuality, and watching television. Khan extols the virtues of the kinky brat with a counter-reading of both *The Handmaid's Tale* as well as the controversy over the television show's signature red dress, briefly marketed as a sexy Halloween costume.

Evelyn Kessler's "Oversexed, Undersexed, 'No Sex': Queer Subjects and the Anti-Chinese Movement in the Age of Capital" renarrates the history of the anti–Chinese labor movement and the numerous, often contradictory ways Chinese immigrants were sexually othered. The racialized exclusion of Chinese immigrants was done, in part, through the fortification of sexual and gendered norms, whereby Chinese men and women were said to represent the excesses and deprivations of unfettered capitalism. Kessler demonstrates how these imagined subjects—along with their imagined bodies—served as negative referents for an idealized, white American gender and sexual regime that could be reconciled with industrial capitalist development. Queer theory is often considered or condemned as presentist and inattentive to political economy; Kessler's queer theory is a corrective, focalizing labor politics, social reproduction, and materialist fantasies of whiteness.

Mary Anne Case's "Donorsexuality after *Dobbs*" canvasses the legal embroilments and cultural contestations surrounding men who are "high-volume, non-commercial providers of fresh sperm" (one of whom identifies, suggested titularly, as a "donorsexual") for those seeking to become pregnant through artificial insemination. The phenomenon of the donorsexual, as Case evidences, solicits us to reinterpret watershed US Supreme Court cases involving sexual and reproductive rights that until now have been grounded in substantive due process. These rights constitutionally protect sexual freedom rather than sexual intimacy; put more colloquially, Supreme Court case law establishes our "right to fuck." But after *Dobbs* (2022), the right to fuck along with so many other substantive due process rights are in grave jeopardy. Therefore, Case contends that donorsexuals and the rest of us might look more to the Equal Protection Clause of the Fourteenth Amendment of the US Constitution than to its Due Process Clause, to wage and win battles for sexual and reproductive freedom and equality. Case proposes that *Skinner v. Oklahoma* (1942), decided under equal protection analysis, offers juridical inroads for donorsexuals and/as queers that may be less precarious than the line of substantive due process cases protecting sexual and reproductive rights.

The nineteenth-century Chinese immigrant, the kinky brat, and the donorsexual: Part of what queers these Queer Figures is that they are also fantasy structures, discursively designed or juridically constituted for varied purposes, inter alia, superordination, solidarity, projection, aversion, and arousal. The Policed Men of part three are fantastical too, even as flesh and blood men (sexed whatever at birth) are impacted and injured by the force of law, lawlike superintendence, and incarceration highlighted by the contributors herein. Men's sexual or sexualized conduct, outside hetero- (and sometimes homo-) normativity, is inconvenient or worse for social orders of all stripes. Whether sniffing poppers, fucking in a pandemic, writing sexually explicit letters from prison, or walking while trans in a gay bathhouse, queer men's insistent, unrepentant desires—the desire to get off, the desire to be desired, the desire for sociality, the desire for antisociality—trouble authorities. And so the chapters of part three concentrate on cultural and legal anxieties surrounding men having sex with men. An earlier queer theory was panned for focusing on the lives, identities, sexualities, and desires of gay men, or men who have sex with men. While we are cognizant of this criticism from one side and a #MeToo amplified criticism from another, it is nevertheless the case that predatory male desire, as a cultural specter, persistently structures zones of intimacy and zones of law, a social fact that several of our authors parse. The following chapters interrogate the ambivalences of risk, vulnerability, and pleasure in sexual spaces inhabited or presumptively inhabited by men.

"Flattening the [COVID-19] curve has flattened our sex lives," as Kyle Kirkup laments in "Queer Risk Knowledge: From HIV to COVID-19." But never fear: queers, queer activism, and queer risk assessment (along with queer assessments of "risk" as a fantasy of empiricism cleansed of moralism), salvaged safer sex from the wreckage. Kirkup reviews the literature on social and moral constructions of risk, and he is attentive as well to the emotive dimensions of risk discourse among state actors, queer activists, and safer sex educational projects. Kirkup diagnoses and then prescribes three tenets of what he calls "queer risk knowledge" that developed in response to the HIV/AIDS epidemic: first, a refusal to classify sexual behavior in strictly either/or terms (*x* is safe, *y* is dangerous); second, an abiding commitment to *sexual pleasure* as a nonfungible benefit in calculations of risk; and third, the rejection of both criminalization and incarceration as remedies for sex deemed dangerous. Kirkup surveys how queer risk knowledge mainstreamed during the COVID-19 pandemic, when several health departments and municipalities proffered outdoor, public, virtual, and glory hole sex as ways to reduce viral transmission.

Chris Ashford's "Queer Intimacies and Criminal Law: Queer Legal Praxis and the UK Poppers Ban" explores how the criminal law continues to interfere on the lives and sex practices of gay men, despite the dominant cultural narrative of social acceptance and legal recognition. In 1967, the UK Sexual Offences Act created the category of "homosexual" in the law of England and Wales, decriminalizing a narrow set of sex practices associated with the newfound legal identity. Ashford resists the narrative by which the Sexual Offences Act initiated the queer subject's journey from despised target of criminal law to celebrated beneficiary of civil law. Ashford examines the legislative and journalistic debates surrounding the passage of the 2016 Psychoactive Substances Act, and in particular the "poppers ban" seemingly embedded in the Act. When unwedded to love or marriage, gay sexual pleasure remains a persistent social problem for politicians, police, and pundits, Ashford discovered. Looking to what he terms "ephemeral encounters" among state actors, queers, and queer state actors over the benefits and the (mostly manufactured) risks of poppers, Ashford forges a "queer legal praxis" that unapologetically defends gay pleasure and its intensifications.

In "'I Would Kiss a Man Whenever I Want, Let Some Fucker Hit Me': Queering Narratives of Incarceration, Sexuality, and Offending," Matthew Ball draws on an archive of prison inmates' intimate correspondence to enrich our "understanding of the creation, maintenance, and performance of sexual subjectivities under conditions of carceral governance." Ball's findings are surprising and touching; they also point to the importance, methodologically and substantively, of archival material for queer criminology and criminology generally. The letters—between mostly gay- or bi-identified incarcerated men and one nonincarcerated man—undercut what we think we know about queer life and queer sociality in prison. Ball also shows how writing, reading, and researching these letters are or can be ways to express and experience sexual pleasure; alternately the letters also elicit feelings of empathy, repulsion, and indignation. Finally, Ball proposes that the inmates' epistolary accounts both of their offenses and of their feelings about their offenses invite scholars of queer criminology to rethink how self-understandings of sexual identity correspond to criminalized behaviors.

Popular debate over gender identification—from the International Olympic Committee to "bathroom bills" to, well, much of third wave feminism—too frequently distills down to the question *who is a woman?*. In "Trans Bodies, Gay Sexuality, Dysphoria: Sexual Freedom in the Bathhouse and Beyond," Ido Katri asks *who is a man?*, or more precisely, questions the question, asking why and for what purposes gay bathhouses police the boundaries of man-ness. Katri tours through gay bathhouses in Berlin, Tel Aviv, and Toronto, cataloguing both the varied criteria for men-only admission to venues for gay sex as well as the snide responses that he and his partner elicited from gay clientele. The sexual freedom famously associated with the gay bathhouse when it comes to sex is matched by an unforgiving gender austerity when it comes to embodiment. Katri ponders what accounts for this form of gay governance, governance that, under the credo of liberal inclusion, welcomes "ALL men"—except for the ones it doesn't. And why do boobs and makeup so distinctively disqualify one from the category *man*? Embracing more relational, dynamic conceptions of both (gay) sex and (gender) identity, Katri supposes that relaxing our attachments to the definitional criteria of regulatory fictions like *gay*, *gender*, and *transgender* will not only make for better policy but also for better sex.

In his encounters with gay bathhouses, Katri had some feels: frustration and rage, arousal and curiosity, and what we shorthand as political dysphoria. Katri depathologizes *dysphoria* by politicizing it, beseeching queer and trans folks to avow the power of sex and desire to disorient us from our orientations, defensively barricaded. Katri's chapter therefore segues us into the Queer Feels of part four. The contributions in this section foreground atmospheric affects and subjective feelings, queer or otherwise, in law, social movements, and lifeworlds. Care and refusal, hate and anger, righteousness and rectitude, optimism and love: These are some of the feels tracked—grokked, even—in the final three entries of the volume.

In "Thinking with Care: A Critique of Love across Interdisciplines," Jennifer Nash exposits what we might think of as the bivalence of *care* across the interdisciplines of Black studies and feminist studies. In the ongoingness of anti-Black violence, on the one hand, and against the racial and gendered inequalities exacerbated by the COVID-19 pandemic, on the other, Black studies scholars and many Black activists have reemphasized care as a political aspiration, collective ethic, and radical practice of self-love. Feminist theorists and activists, though, have long been wary of championing care, for *care* can mystify all the domestic, reproductive, sexual, monotonous, endless, and often filthy labor demanded of women. Nash troubles *care* carefully, cautious neither to romanticize nor junk the abstraction. Instead, she reconstructs *care*, as well as its political pitfalls and possibilities, by theorizing *care* alongside another popular keyword in Black studies, *refusal*. Nash then questions the geography of care, noting where and when the concept is rejected as exploitative and where and when it is heralded as emancipatory. Finally and boldly, Nash revisits the scholarship of critical race feminism in order to envision a "model of juridical care," a model unfavored or absented in contemporary Black studies' rejection of the US state as "fundamentally carceral" and anti-Black. Nash recalls that critical race feminists refused refusal, embedding their "visions of care" into our regulatory imaginary.

In "Sexual Innocence in Crisis Justice Movements: A Political Theology," Noa Ben-Asher uses a queer analytic to track rhetorics of childhood innocence in social movements on the political right and left. Despite polarization on policy issues such as reproductive rights, gun rights, immigration, climate change, LGBTQ rights, and pandemic measures, there are some surprising convergences between the political right and left when it comes to matters of ethics, morality, and affect. "Christian theology and its vision of sexuality," avers Ben-Asher, "underwrite contemporary crisis-justice politics." The chapter examines the "tales of justice" that emanate from the QAnon movement and Greta Thunberg's pursuit of climate justice. Both Thunberg and QAnon trope on the purity of children, wage an apocalyptic war of good versus evil, and represent themselves as truth-tellers in a world run amok by evil elites.

The final contribution takes a different format from the previous ones, an interview with Senthorun Sunil Raj about his book, *Feeling Queer Jurisprudence: Injury, Intimacy, Identity* (2021). Raj tracks how emotions like anger, hate, love, and disgust move in and around landmark LGBT rights cases and legislative reforms. He queries how some emotional landscapes cultivate respect for and legal protections of diverse sexual and gender identities and expressions, while others collapse possibilities for queer intimacies as well as for constructive debates about the regulation of those intimacies. Our interview with Raj invites him to extend his insights on the role of emotions in constituting and sometimes cabining identities, rights, strategies, and imaginaries.

Our volume closes with an afterword from Janet Halley, which, in our biased opinion, is luminous. As this introduction attests, Halley is a founding, foremost scholar in the interdiscipline of Queer Legal Studies, to whom our work and the work of the *Enticements* contributors are profoundly indebted. In her afterword, Halley retrieves reparative modes of critique from Eve Kosofsky Sedgwick—critiques Halley dubs "and others" and "chiasmatic"—to generatively reperceive and thereby synchronize *Enticements*' contributions. For Halley, and so for all of us, the many queer interventions of this volume envision "diacritical differences" anew and open out to "proliferating possibilities."

* * *

We began this collection before our world came to a screeching halt by a global pandemic; before the political violence of January 6, before the overturning of *Roe v. Wade*, and on, and on, and on. Nevertheless, this project materialized in a time of ascending homophobia, transphobia, and misogyny, nationally and internationally. Critical legal studies and critical race theory in particular teach us that times of progress are invariably followed by times of retrenchment, of attacks on the modest inroads made by the marginalized. We are in the midst of violent retrenchment. From the devastating attacks on abortion rights, voting rights, and environmental regulation as the world burns both literally and figuratively, to the undermining of the very democratic institutions on which rights struggles are predicated, it is an understatement to say that we are living in perilous and disorienting times, times that call for new ways of imagining what *could* be.

It is worth noting that our opponents on the far right have been reimagining—and relitigating—sex and gender formations for some time. From the revisioning of conservatism to the rise of the Federalist society and other conservative legal think tanks, those who are pushing back against sexual and gender diversity have been playing the long game (Anderson 2020; Cohen 2020). We too need to rethink our long game. We may have much to learn from what we might call the intersectional outlook of the far right. Mary Anne Case has observed, in describing the Vatican's war on gender—a unified attack on women's sexual and reproductive rights, sexual orientation and gender identity, and non-procreative, non-heteronormative sex—that feminists and sexual rights advocates too frequently operate in silos and along single axes of injustice (2017, 219). "We should strive more closely to resemble our opponents' vision of who we are and what we stand for" (218).

QLS may have only a modest role to play in rethinking and reimagining a coalitional politics for sex equality and sexual freedom. But its anti-identitarian—or at any rate, identitarian-skeptical—sensibility may help desilozation; its methodology of reparative renarration helps us to see differently, and its commitment to a queerer future help us to imagine things otherwise.

The world's horrors compel us to grasp at what is available, to think small, or at least in siloed terms: codify marriage to protect same-sex relationships; lobby employers to facilitate women's reproductive choices; prohibit discrimination against gender expression and gender identity at state levels. These efforts are as indispensable as they are insufficient. Several years after *Bowers v. Hardwick* and a decade before *Lawrence v. Texas*, Kendall Thomas enticed us to approach sexual politics generally, and violence against lesbian and gays specifically, in the idioms of power, embodiment, and "corporal integrity," rather than in the desiccated idiom of privacy (1992, 1476). Thomas urged gay rights activists, litigators, and scholars to reach "beyond the privacy principle," to relocate our strategy from "privacy to politics" in order to countenance how the US state undermines its democratic promise by authorizing or permitting violence against the bodies of its queer citizens (1509). The appeal to embodiment and state-sanctioned corporal violence was prescient: The post-*Dobbs* world is a threat to so many of our bodies and so also the "body politic" (Thomas 1992, 1515). Thomas's call was neither intersectional nor coalitional, exactly; and it was not post-identitarian for it could not afford to be. Yet Thomas foresaw that the "conceptual framework" of anti-sodomy litigation did not adequately address gay and lesbian claimants' "social interests" in civic participation, subcultural community-making, and, well, sex, free from state and nonstate violence perpetrated against their flesh and blood bodies (1435). This seems to us a crucial lesson for our present crises. What are the collective social and corporal interests of queers, girls and women, transgender and nonbinary communities, and racial minorities, and what might it take, beyond rearguard legislation, to realize those interests politically and juridically?

Like the contributions in this volume, we entice you to think sexuality—as a cultural formation, regulatory object, and axis for coalitional politics—queerly, anew and askew.

BIBLIOGRAPHY

Adler, Libby. 2018. *Gay Priori: A Queer Critical Legal Studies Approach to Law Reform.* Durham, NC: Duke University Press.

Ahmed, Sara. 2017. *Living a Feminist Life.* Durham, NC: Duke University Press.

Anderson, Kurt. 2020. *Evil Geniuses: The Unmaking of America: A Recent History.* New York: Random House.

Appleton, Susan Frelich and Susan Ekberg Stiritz. 2016. "The Joy of Sex Bureaucracy." *California Law Review* 7: 49–65.

Bell, Derrick. 1976. "Serving Two Masters: Integration Ideals and Client Interests in School Desegregation Litigation." *Yale Law Journal* 85: 470.

———. 1987. *And We Are Not Saved: The Elusive Quest for Racial Justice.* New York: Basic Books.

Berlant, Lauren and Michael Warner. 1995. "What Does Queer Theory Teach Us About X?" *PMLA* 110: 343–49.

Brown, Wendy and Janet Halley (eds.). 2002. *Left Legalism/Left Critique.* Durham, NC: Duke University Press.

Butler, Judith. 1994. "Against Proper Objects." *differences: A Journal of Feminist Cultural Studies* 6(2–3): 1.

Carrillo, Raúl. 2014. "Keeping It Real: Law, Coercion, and the Frontiers of Public Finance." *New Economic Perspectives,* June 25. https://neweconomicperspectives.org.

Case, Mary Anne. 2003. "Of 'This' and 'That' in *Lawrence v. Texas.*" *Supreme Court Review* 2003: 75–142.

———. 2017. "Seeing the Sex and Justice Landscape through the Vatican's Eyes: The War on Gender and the Seamless Garment of Sexual Rights." In *The War on Sex,* edited by David M. Halperin and Trevor Hoppe. Durham, NC: Duke University Press.

Cohen, Adam. 2020. *Supreme Inequality: The Supreme Court's Fifty Year Battle for a More Unjust America.* New York: Penguin Books.

Cohen, Cathy. 1997. "Punks, Bulldaggers, and Welfare Queens: The Radical Potential of Queer Politics?" *GLQ* 3: 437–65.

Cossman, Brenda. 2007. *Sexual Citizens: The Legal and Cultural Regulation of Sex and Belonging*. Stanford, CA: Stanford University Press.

———. 2019. "Queering Queer Legal Studies: An Unreconstructed Ode to Eve Sedgwick (and Others)." *Critical Analysis of Law* 6: 25–27, 31–33.

Davis, Adrienne. 2015. "Regulating Sex Work: Erotic Assimilationism, Erotic Exceptionalism, and the Challenge of Intimate Labor." *California Law Review* 5: 1202.

de Lauretis, Teresa. 1991. "Queer Theory: Lesbian and Gay Sexualities. *An Introduction.*" *Differences: A Journal of Feminist Cultural Studies* 3: iv.

Duggan, Lisa. 2002. "The New Homonormativity: The Sexual Politics of Neoliberalism." In *Materializing Democracy: Toward a Revitalized Cultural Politics*, edited by Russ Castronovo and Dana Nelson. Durham, NC: Duke University Press.

Fineman, Martha Albertson, Jack Jackson, and Adam Romero (eds.). 2009. *Feminist and Queer Legal Theory: Intimate Encounters, Uncomfortable Conversations* New York: Routledge.

Fischel, Joseph J. 2010. "Transcendent Homosexuals and Dangerous Sex Offenders: Sexual Harm and Freedom in the Judicial Imaginary." *Duke Journal of Gender Law and Policy* 17: 277–312.

Foucault, Michel. 1977. *Discipline and Punish: The Birth of the Prison*. New York: Vintage Books.

———. 1978. *The History of Sexuality, Volume I: An Introduction* (Robert Hurley, trans.). New York: Pantheon Books.

Franke, Katherine. 2004. "The Domesticated Liberty of *Lawrence v. Texas.*" *Columbia Law Review* 104: 1399–1426.

Guinier, Lani and Gerald Torres. 2003. *The Miner's Canary: Enlisting Race, Resisting Power, Transforming Democracy*. Cambridge, MA: Harvard University Press.

Hale, Robert. 1923. "Coercion and Distribution in a Supposedly Non-Coercive State." *Political Science Quarterly* 38: 3.

Halley, Janet. 1993. "Reasoning about Sodomy: Act and Identity in and after *Bowers v. Hardwick.*" 79 *Virginia Law Review* 1721: 1721–80.

———. 2006. *Split Decisions: How and Why to Take a Break from Feminism*. Princeton, NJ: Princeton University Press.

———. 2017. "Paranoia, Feminism, Law: Reflections on the Possibilities for Queer Legal Studies." In *New Directions in Law and Literature*, edited by Elizabeth S. Ankler and Bernadette Meyer, 123–43. Oxford: Oxford University Press.

Halley, Janet and Andrew Parker. 2007. "Intro to After Sex?" In Halley and Parker, ed., *After Sex: On Writing Since Queen Theory.*" Durham, NC: Duke University Press.

Halperin, David M. 2017. "The War on Sex." In Halperin and Hoppe, eds., *The War on Sex*. Durham, NC: Duke University Press.

Halperin, David M. and Trevor Hoppe (eds.). 2017. *The War on Sex*. Durham, NC: Duke University Press.

Harcourt, Bernard E. 2004. "'You Are Entering a Gay and Lesbian Free Zone': On the Radical Dissents of Justice Scalia and Other (Post-) Queers." *Journal of Criminal Law and Criminology* 94: 503–50.

Hartman, Saidiya. 2008. "Venus in Two Acts." SX26, 1.

Hoppe, Trevor. 2017. "Thinking Sex and Justice." In Halperin and Hoppe, eds., *The War on Sex*. Durham, NC: Duke University Press.

Huffer, Lynne. 2013. *Are the Lips a Grave? A Queer Feminist on the Ethics of Sex*. New York: Columbia University Press.

Leckey, Robert and Kim Brooks (eds.). 2011. *Queer Theory: Law, Culture, Empire*. New York: Routledge.

MacKinnon, Catharine A. 2004. "The Road Not Taken: Sex Equality in *Lawrence v. Texas*." *Ohio State Law Journal* 65: 1081–94.

Muñoz, José Esteban. 2009. *Cruising Utopia: The Then and There of Queer Futurity*. New York: New York University Press.

Nedelsky, Jennifer. 2011. *Law's Relations: A Relational Theory of Self, Autonomy, and Law*. Oxford: Oxford University Press.

Otto, Dianne (ed.). 2018. *Queering International Law: Possibilities, Alliances, Complicities, Risks*. New York: Routledge.

Puar, Jasbir. 2007. *Terrorist Assemblages: Homonationalism in Queer Times*. Durham, NC: Duke University Press.

Rubin, Gayle. 1984. "Thinking Sex: Notes for a Radical Theory of the Politics of Sexuality." In *Pleasure and Danger: Exploring Female Sexuality*, edited by Carole Vance. Boston: Routledge and Kegan Paul.

Ruskola, Teemu. 2005. "Gay Rights versus Queer Theory: What Is Left of Sodomy after *Lawrence v. Texas*?" *Social Text* 23: 235–49.

Sedgwick, Eve Kosofsky. 1990. *Epistemology of the Closet*. Berkeley: University of California Press.

———. 2003. *Touching Feeling: Affect, Pedagogy, Performativity*. Durham, NC: Duke University Press.

Seresin, Asa. 2019. "On Heteropessimism." *The New Inquiry*, October 9. https://thenewinquiry.com.

Spindelman, Marc. 2004. "Surviving *Lawrence v. Texas*." *Michigan Law Review* 102: 1615–67.

Stychin, Carl. 1995. *Law's Desire: Sexuality and the Limits of Justice*. New York: Routledge.

Thomas, Kendall. 1992. "Beyond the Privacy Principle." *Columbia Law Review* 92: 1431.

Wiegman, Robyn and Elizabeth A. Wilson. 2015. "Introduction: Antinormativity's Queer Conventions." *differences* 26: 1–25.

PART I

Queer Fictions, or, Rewriting Gay Rights

1

The Epistemology of the Courthouse

Classical Antiquity in American LGBT-Rights Litigation

ZACHARY HERZ

Judges make bad historians. What can good historians do about it? This chapter answers that question by considering the intellectual, ethical, and disciplinary hazards facing professional historians who discuss queer pasts in the context of litigation. For reasons that are arguably inherent to law as a form of normative reasoning, lawyers and judges require claims about the past to be stated with a certainty and determinacy that professional historians cannot abide.

While this problem is hardly unique to the LGBT sphere (Balkin 2013, 649–50), historical and legal-historical narratives around law and sexuality have diverged more sharply than those of other fields, for two reasons. First, historians of sexuality have long understood that it is hard to talk about queer pasts in ways that are both recognizable to modern audiences and true to the reality of the historical subject. Leaving aside Foucault's basic point about the tendency of sexual discourse to organize itself around a given set of narratives and then proclaim those narratives as biologic, universal, and socially repressed (Foucault 1978, 7–10), queer archives are often a disaster. Marginalized people cannot necessarily commemorate their lives as precisely or extensively as those with more normative social positions (Sedgwick 2005, 4–7), and queer history especially is so often a history of secret names, euphemisms, and code words (Dinshaw 2010, 11–12; Richlin 1993, 541–43). Working with these kinds of sources requires accepting an even greater level of indeterminacy or incoherence than do other kinds of historiographical work (which themselves require quite a lot).

Second, courts have debated the history of sexuality for a while now. Over the past fifty years, American LGBT civil rights advocates have used litigation as a key tool in enacting social change (Murdoch and Price 2001), and as a result much of our public discussion about LGBT people's lives takes place in the courtroom or with an eye toward its potential deployment there. Even as academic history increasingly reckons with the incoherence and idiosyncrasy of our subjects, a version of gay history appears in public that—shaped by law in ways even its promulgators often miss—casts queer people as a discrete and transhistorical minority, perfectly intelligible to modern sensibilities and legal doctrines.

This casting should worry us. Judges often care about history, but their understanding of the term differs from that of most professional historians in ways that are still undertheorized. By better understanding *why* queer history seems so different in and out of court, we can tell stories about our past that are more respectful and more true, while also making clearer arguments about who we are and what we deserve now.

This chapter will proceed in four parts. After explaining why law and historiography approach historical questions so differently, I consider two moments where claims about queer history were transformed by the distinctive pressures of American antidiscrimination law. I first explore how both judges and historians rewrote the history of sexual regulation in the transition from *Bowers v. Hardwick* (1986) (which upheld state bans on consensual sodomy as reflecting historical moral consensus) to *Lawrence v. Texas* (2003) (which struck down those same laws as novel infringements on sexual autonomy). I then discuss an argument about Plato's *Laws* that nearly derailed the Colorado antidiscrimination case *Romer v. Evans* (1996). I conclude by discussing the normative implications of these cases for both lawyers and historians.

Getting the Story Straight

You can't have law without a past. To be more specific, law courts necessarily apply preexisting normative heuristics to new facts. That temporal disjunction—in which the lawmaker develops a rule at T1 to be applied at T2—makes law an unavoidably historical enterprise. Aristotle, one of the first political theorists whose account of law as a moral practice survives, argues in the *Rhetorika*:

Most importantly of all, the judgment of the lawmaker (*nomothetou*) is not bounded, but concerned with the universal (*katholou*) and that which is yet to come (*mellontōn*), whereas the assemblyman or juryman cast judgment on specific and present matters which often implicate their loves, hates, and private interest. As a result, they can no longer properly reason their way to the truth, but instead their individual pleasure or pain casts a shadow on their judgment. (Arist. RH. 1354b)

Aristotle here contrasts the prospectivity of statutory law or *nomos* with the freewheeling, idiosyncratic decisional process of the assembly or jury court.[1] While the assemblyman or juror can employ whatever heuristic appeals to them at the moment of decision, Aristotle claims that a better system would remove that discretion and task legal actors with interpreting judgments made in the past with an eye toward the future. He argues that proper decision-making is impersonal, substituting decisions made at an earlier time without knowledge of individual circumstance for those made in the heat of the moment. In other words, Aristotle sees lawmaking as inherently prospective. This feature of law is sometimes associated with the natural-law tradition (for example Fuller 1969, 51–62), but even strict positivists like H.L.A. Hart see laws as "standing" or "persistent" in some way, and thus a mechanism by which choices made at one time bind later actors (Hart 2012, 23). The corollary to this argument, however, has garnered less notice. If making law is a prospective endeavor, applying law is a retrospective one, which necessarily entails interpreting past statements.

Certain definitional features of the law, however, set this interpretive project apart from other historical approaches. A judge's descriptive claims about the past—whether about the meaning of a case or of a statute—exist in the service of normative claims about what should happen in the future, and both sets of claims are made within an institutional framework that aims to produce specified and determinate legal outcomes. An academic text can highlight possibilities, subjectivities, or uncertainties when honest work requires, with few consequences beyond the professional; a judge whose writing has specified and determinate effects, however, will naturally incline to present that writing as informed by specified and determinate legal rules. A major theme of this volume and of critical work in law more generally is that legal processes enshrine rigid ways of knowing, ways that are often incompatible with the messy and contingent lives that legal subjects lead.[2]

Take the Supreme Court decision *Bostock v. Clayton County* (2020), which held that sexual orientation discrimination is forbidden by the Civil Rights Act of 1964. The author (Justice Gorsuch) claims to base his reasoning in part on that of the late Justice Antonin Scalia. First, Gorsuch quotes Scalia to rebut claims that Congress's later refusal to pass ENDA should bear on his reading of the Act: "[a]rguments based on subsequent legislative history . . . should not be taken seriously, not even in a footnote" (Bostock v. Clayton County 2020, 1747, quoting Sullivan v. Finkelstein 1990, 632, Scalia, J., concurring). Gorsuch next cites Scalia's guide to statutory interpretation, *Reading Law: The Interpretation of Legal Texts*, to argue that broad statutory language should be taken at face value (Bostock v. Clayton County 2020, 1749). The decision in fact builds on Scalia's writing even more than these citations suggest; one of the three major antidiscrimination decisions Gorsuch claims to follow (Bostock v. Clayton County 2020, 1743), *Oncale v. Sundowner Offshore Services, Inc.* (1998), was written by Scalia for a unanimous Court.

Justice Gorsuch supports his expansive reading of the Civil Rights Act by citing Scalia, then, but so do his interlocutors. Justice Alito's dissent in *Bostock* is profoundly—almost primarily—concerned with setting the record straight about Scalia's views. Alito claims that Gorsuch "attempts to pass off [his] decision as the inevitable product of the textualist school of statutory interpretation championed by our late colleague Justice Scalia, but no one should be fooled," and that his reasoning "represents . . . a theory of statutory interpretation that Justice Scalia excoriated"; most important for our purposes, he attacks Gorsuch's "effort to enlist Scalia in [his] updating project" (Bostock v. Clayton County 2020, 1773, Alito, J. dissenting). In a discursive mode that requires citation, the charge of "enlisting" is remarkable. It restates the basic work of legal citation in pejorative language, suggesting that Gorsuch has violated the spirit, if not the letter, of an unspoken interpretive code. Yet Alito never accuses Gorsuch of misquoting Scalia or misinterpreting specific language. Instead, he cites other books and other cases where Scalia made other claims, putting forward a different interpretive theory that would necessitate a different outcome (Bostock v. Clayton County 2020, 1825: "As Justice Scalia explained, 'the good textualist is not a literalist'"). The resulting argument feels theological, as the two judges quote contradictory holy texts at each other to establish what Scalia, and only secondarily the Civil Rights Act, really meant.

The project in which Gorsuch and Alito are engaged—an argument about what a dead man believed—is one familiar to most intellectual historians. But their argument here rests on very different premises. On the one hand, Alito is almost certainly right that, were Scalia still on the Court, he would have preferred the dissent's reading. In *Lawrence v. Texas*, Scalia suggested that homophobia was too "mainstream" to violate the Constitution and cited the lack of federal protection against antigay employment discrimination as proof of the claim (Lawrence v. Texas 2003, 602–3, Scalia, J., dissenting). On the other hand, this argument seems incompatible with Scalia's endorsement of cross-sex comparators to show sex discrimination in *Oncale* (Oncale v. Sundowner Offshore Services 1998, 80–81), to say nothing of his more general textualist commitments. This incompatibility should hardly surprise us, since people make contradictory statements all the time or offer general statements that become more nuanced in their application. The idea of Scalia, whose *Lawrence* dissent decried the Court's "anti-anti-homosexual culture" (Lawrence v. Texas 2003, 602), putting forward somewhat incoherent views in the service of protecting bans on consensual sodomy is perhaps less shocking than a Supreme Court justice holding such a narrow view of human cognition as to himself be shocked.

To be more specific: Alito takes Gorsuch's citations of Scalia to mean something very common in legal argumentation and very unusual everywhere else. Alito's argument presumes that there is a knowable and perfectly logical Scalian jurisprudence, and that individual statements appearing to contradict that jurisprudence are suspect as a result. He assumes that every opinion Scalia held was consistent with every other, and that Scalia would have endorsed the unbounded application of any general statement he made. This is obviously not how people think, but it is a necessary component of how common-law courts reason. Ronald Dworkin refers to these methodological assumptions as "integrity" and considers them necessary for the rule of law (1986, 225–75), but even critics of Dworkin would agree that the enterprise of precedential reasoning—of abstracting rules from court cases and applying them to new facts—requires treating precedents as idea-expressing agents in their own right with superhuman levels of coherence and rationality. What makes *Bostock* (and particularly Alito's dissent) so jarring is that it treats a person like a precedent, and assumes his logics and desires to be consistent, general, and immutable.

That assumption is incompatible with academic history. Even if our objects of study had lived by a coherent and unchanging set of beliefs, there is no reason to think our sources would reveal those beliefs to us.[3] The trouble is compounded for queer or otherwise marginalized historical subjects, who are excluded from records in ways that render them unintelligible to the historiographic lens (Chakrabarty 2008, 94; Spivak 2010, 249–62). Researchers might try to reconstruct those subjectivities in the face of an incomplete or hostile archival tradition, but even that reconstruction changes them in profound ways (Dinshaw 2010, 3–11).

This problem is one for historians of sexuality to worry about, and they have. My own commitments track best onto those of Laura Doan's "queer critical history," which begins by acknowledging "the unknowability and indeterminacy of the sexual past" (Doan 2013, 61). While Doan goes further than most in problematizing sexuality as a discrete category, her basic methodological point is broadly accepted in the historiography of sexuality. Contemporary erotics and erotic relations are structured by contemporary society; ancient ones are not (Dinshaw 2010, 12; Halperin 2002, 102–3). When we attempt to better understand those ancient ways of thinking for their own sake—to fit them into a historical, rather than a practical, past (Oakeshott 2004, 124–25)—this disjunct is a difficult hurdle that takes work to clear (Doan 2013, 51–52). But when law courts approach questions of premodern erotics, they do so with their own historiographic logic. As a result, when historical queers become legally salient, queer history starts to get weird. Courts that ask questions about the history of homosexuality expect to be answered in a certain argot: that of definitive statements, coherent socialities, transhistoricalism, and boundedness. That is not how our history speaks, and when queer stories are told in court or with an eye toward what happens there, those stories change. To show this disjunct between how law and history produce queer pasts, I will next describe two case studies in what happens when legal epistemology and queer history collide.

Ancient Sex on Modern Trial

Simon Cowell has a ghost problem. On April 14, 2019, *The Daily Mail* reported that Cowell—probably most famous in the United States for judging *American Idol*, but who continues to berate amateur performers in his native Britain—had unwittingly purchased a mansion haunted by the ghost of a "gay Roman god" (Bullock 2019). Specifically, the house had been possessed by the spirit of Antinous, a Greek-speaking boy who served as companion to the emperor Hadrian before suddenly dying in 130 CE and who was worshipped for centuries afterward. The *Mail* calls Antinous Hadrian's "gay lover" and the two of them a "pair" with a "special bond" that made other imperial subjects jealous (Bullock 2019). It then notes that Hadrian established a cult to Antinous after the boy's death, and that despite homophobic attempts to repress "the gay god," he is worshipped to this day.

This is, of course, bullshit. While our sources for the life of Antinous are late and somewhat sketchy (Vout 2005, 82–3), it is clear that the emperor Hadrian represented himself publicly as being close to the much younger Greek Bithynian; following Antinous' sudden death, Hadrian established cultic practices in his honor which became popular throughout the Greek-speaking cultures of the eastern Mediterranean. Hadrian appears in these accounts as an *erastēs*, or an older aristocratic man who mentors a young boy in exchange for erotic attention (Lear 2013). This type of relationship, which historians of Greek antiquity now call "pederasty," may well have seemed anachronistic even to Hadrian's audience; pederasty was most associated with Athenian elite practices that had been out of favor for hundreds of years by Hadrian's time. But Hadrian's public image was that of a Hellenophile with a particular interest in Greece's lost glory days (Opper 2008, 26), and this antiquated, ur-Greek social performance would fit that broader representational program without necessarily telling us anything about what happened in Antinous' bedroom or heart.

So, then, a British tabloid rendered a complicated, murky historical narrative in language that made it familiar to modern readers. *Quelle surprise.* But note how the *Mail* makes this story legible. While previous modernizations of Antinous focused on the boy himself as a symbol of eroticized youth (Waters 1995), here Antinous is Hadrian's boyfriend.

The *Mail*'s language emphasizes the domesticated and egalitarian, neglecting both the long history of pederasty that informed the couple's public image and the power imbalance that governed their lives. The *Mail* even ignores an ancient rumor that Hadrian sacrificed Antinous in order to gain eternal youth (Dio Cass. 69.11.2–3), which is not the sort of detail one expects a tabloid to omit. Instead, Hadrian and Antinous, the ancient world's most famous example of pederastic relations and a touchstone of Greek identity in a polyglot Mediterranean world, become a tragic story of doomed romantic love.

Going beyond real-estate ghost stories, the recent opera *Hadrian* (which premiered in Toronto in 2018) portrays the Hadrian/Antinous relationship as not only romantic but also sexually role-egalitarian. As one of its authors claimed, recalling Foucault's repressive hypothesis: "The mystery of why Hadrian's remarkable love for Antinous—underlined by his bottomless grief—has not been celebrated widely as a model of eros points to a fear of same-sex love that has changed little from his age to ours" (CBC News 2013). William Eskridge made a similar argument, that "the Emperor Hadrian's love for Antinous attained the status of legend, acclaimed for generations in sculpture, architecture, painting, coins, and literature" (1993, 1447).

On one hand there is nothing new about queers using stories of Hadrian and Antinous, or of other classical figures, to tell stories about themselves (Icks 2012; Waters 1995). But the content of those stories has changed. These two now appear as the paired, egalitarian subjects that theorists like Katherine Franke have identified as rewarded—or often constituted—by the litigative process (Franke 2008; see also Carpenter 2012). This romantic bond is visible nowhere in our ancient sources, but it appears frequently in the opening paragraphs of court cases. From Edie Windsor and Thea Spyer to John Lawrence and Tyron Garner, gay-rights plaintiffs have emphasized romance over power, pairs over groups, and "dignified" over tawdry ways of engaging with the world (Lawrence v. Texas 2003; U.S. v. Windsor 2013).

Civil litigation has changed our understanding of Classical antiquity,[4] but that history has also changed our understanding of civil rights. The first American challenge to the constitutionality of bans on same-sex marriage, *Baker v. Nelson* (1971), shows how ancient history works in court. *Baker* is a short decision that addresses multiple challenges, but its response to the petitioners' Fourteenth Amendment claim (the same one that would prevail in *Obergefell v. Hodges*, 2015) relies in its entirety on an uncritical invocation of past practice.

> The institution of marriage as a union of man and woman, uniquely involving the procreation and rearing of children within a family, is as old as the book of Genesis. Skinner v. Oklahoma ex rel. Williamson [. . .], which invalidated Oklahoma's Habitual Criminal Sterilization Act on equal protection grounds, stated in part: "Marriage and procreation are fundamental to the very existence and survival of the race." This historic institution manifestly is more deeply founded than the asserted contemporary concept of marriage and societal interests for which petitioners contend. (Baker v. Nelson 1971, 186)

We see here two very different historical claims. The court first makes sweeping and uncited claims about biblical marriage, which take "child-drearing" and "families" as transhistorical concepts with a fixed meaning intelligible both to nomadic herders living millennia ago and to a court clerk in 1970s Minneapolis-St. Paul.[5]

However, the next claim may explain Peterson's simplified reasoning. Peterson cites Justice Douglas's opinion in the Supreme Court case *Skinner v. Oklahoma* (1942), which struck down a mandatory sterilization law, for a single sentence suggesting that marriage and procreation are necessarily linked. If we take Peterson to make a claim about Douglas's own beliefs, that claim is flimsy; it is based on a single offhand statement not necessitated by the logic of *Skinner* itself, and no one would bat an eyelash if Douglas drew a distinction between opposing sterilization and penalizing infertile couples. Many people who consider marriage and procreation especially important activities would oppose linking them as firmly as Peterson does here, and this quote hardly forecloses the possibility of Douglas being among their number.

Justice Peterson is not discussing Justice Douglas's beliefs, however; he is interpreting Supreme Court case law and stands on firmer ground in doing so. The US Supreme Court had never squarely addressed same-sex marriage when *Baker* was written, and while the statement Peterson quotes is clearly dicta, he is arguably "justified" (in the specific hermeneutics of the common law) in taking it as guidance on this novel issue.

Common-law judges like Peterson are expected to make broad arguments about how strangers would have analyzed a given set of facts based on snippets of their writing. This expectation makes Peterson a careless reader of the history of institutions, but that speaks less to his own epistemic debilities than to the nature of the genre in which he works.

Of course, there are greater problems in *Baker v. Nelson* than an ahistorical approach to marriage. In particular, Justice Peterson looks to the Book of Genesis as a repository of American social traditions without acknowledging the Establishment Clause concerns one might raise in response.[6] Justifying a law on the basis of its accordance with tradition, when that tradition featured far greater entanglements of church and state than we claim to accept now, could vitiate the First Amendment; imagine a majority-Jewish municipality forbidding the consumption of pork by appealing to "tradition." In gay-rights cases, which often consider restrictions that accord with religious commitments, this accordance is a problem.

Classical antiquity, by contrast, gives judges an appealing thought experiment. What if there were a past civilization just like ours, except pagan? Someone inclined to look toward "western civilization" as an ideologically charged exemplar will struggle to find non-Christian governance in American or European history without going very far back. By contrast, Greek and Roman cultures are seen as sufficiently "civilized" (i.e., like our own) to merit respect, while also being presumed as secular. If Greeks or Romans did it, the logic goes, they must have had a good reason.

For example, consider *Bowers v. Hardwick*. *Hardwick* rejected a substantive due process challenge to consensual sodomy laws on the basis of, among other things, historical argument. Justice White specifically invoked the "ancient roots" of sodomy bans as a reason for upholding them, citing evidence from the common law and the nineteenth century (Bowers v. Hardwick 1986, 192–93). In a concurrence Chief Justice Burger goes further, stating that "[d]ecisions of individuals relating to homosexual conduct have been subject to state intervention throughout the history of Western civilization. Condemnation of those practices is firmly rooted in Judaeo-Christian moral and ethical standards. Homosexual sodomy was a capital crime under Roman law" (Bowers v. Hardwick 1986, 196).

Note the juxtaposition of these last two claims. In a case whose explicit reasoning privileges the moral sensibilities of the public as somehow immune from scrutiny (Bowers v. Hardwick 1986, 196), Burger almost acknowledges the religious character of those "Judaeo-Christian" sensibilities but takes a sharp left turn. Burger uses Roman law as a prophylactic, suggesting that another set of historical standards without "Christian" in the name might justify Georgians'—and presumably his own—distaste. Notably, there is no evidence for the regulation of sex between men until the fourth century CE, at which point Roman governance was effectively Christian. The specific law Burger cites, moreover, was promulgated by a Christian son of Constantine with a reputation for "unnatural vice."[7] Burger glosses over this history, and his brief reference to Roman law suggests a pre-Christian tradition of sexual regulation that insulates the moral sensibilities of a hostile majority from serious scrutiny.

This argument is striking for two reasons. First, Chief Justice Burger here juxtaposes an explicit descriptive claim—that "Romans" believed sex between men to be an appropriate object of state regulation—with an implicit normative one. Roman law only matters here because a political judgment is more likely to accord with the "ordered liberty" protected by the Due Process Clause (Palko v. Connecticut 1937, 325), and thus survive judicial review, if it can be placed within a historical framework. This particular use of history is a distinctive feature of substantive due process discourse, which views historically attested practice as especially deserving of the Clause's protection (Sunstein 1988); histories of sexuality were so important in gay-rights litigation precisely because of that doctrinal/historiographic nexus.

Second, Burger's history is wrong and badly so. Romans did not think of "sex between men" as a discrete legal category; what mattered instead was whether Roman men were having the kind of sex appropriate to their legal and economic status. In practice, this meant that a normative Roman man was expected to penetrate and specifically to penetrate his inferiors (along axes of gender, servility, citizenship, wealth *vel sim.*). Whether those penetrated people were men or women merited less concern (Walters 1997; Williams 1999).[8] Even the late codes Burger cites focus on effeminacy, prostitution, and men acting like women (specifically, on "arranging their male bodies in a womanly fashion"; *virile corpus muliebriter constitutum*), making it unclear whether they refer to homosexual sodomy, prostitution, masculine anal receptivity, or broader ecologies of gender deviance (Masterson 2014, 19–30). While I can speak with less confidence about the medieval and early modern restrictions Burger invokes, historians of those periods describe a wide variety of sexual and relational practices, many of which existed outside of legal scrutiny.[9]

As a result, *Hardwick* (most explicitly in Burger's concurrence, but also in the majority opinion) rests on an extreme oversimplification of the past, and its own logic suggests that falsifying that history would render its holding suspect. It should be no surprise, then, that both historians and activists began correcting the record. The 1980s and 1990s saw enormous advances in the study of historical queerness, from John Boswell's *Christianity, Social Tolerance, and Homosexuality* and *Same-Sex Unions in Premodern Europe* to Amy Richlin's and Bernadette Brooten's books on sexual nonconformity in Roman and Jewish contexts, to Froma Zeitlin's collection of essays on Classical Greek sexuality and performance, to Marilyn Skinner and Judith Hallett's pioneering volume *Roman Sexualities*, to Craig Williams's *Roman Homosexuality* (Boswell 1980, 1995; Brooten 1996; Hallett and Skinner 1997; Richlin 1992; Williams 1999; Zeitlin 1996). These texts complicated and temporized our notions of ancient sexuality, looking beyond etic categories of "gay" and "straight" to better understand how inhabitants of the ancient world conceived of their and their neighbors' erotic lives and gender presentations. I know this intellectual history best for Greece and Rome, but similar work was being written for other times and places; consider Bray's survey of homosexual subcultures in Renaissance England or Chauncey's *Gay New York* (Bray 1988; Chauncey 1994). As one of the most prominent courts in the English-speaking world based a widely condemned decision on an oversimplified account of historical sexual regulation, scholars whose own political commitments ran counter to *Hardwick*—and in many cases, whose freedom to have the sex they wanted was jeopardized by it—began courses of research that would produce evidence challenging *Hardwick's* claims.[10]

This connection between historiography and litigation would become explicit in 2003. In January of that year, ten prominent historians of sexuality submitted an amicus brief in *Lawrence v. Texas*, the case that overturned *Hardwick* and legalized sodomy in America. That brief aims directly at the so-called ancient roots that Justices White and Burger invoked, complicating their account of sexual regulation.

> *Amici*, as historians, do not propose to offer the Court legal doctrine to justify a holding that the Texas Homosexual Conduct Law violates the U.S. Constitution. Rather, *amici* believe they can best serve the Court by elaborating on two *historical* propositions important to the legal analysis: (1) no consistent historical practice singles out same-sex behavior as "sodomy" subject to proscription, and (2) the governmental policy of classifying and discriminating against certain citizens on the basis of their homosexual status is an unprecedented project of the twentieth century, which is already being dismantled. The Texas law at issue is an example of such irrational discrimination. (*Lawrence v. Texas* Brief, 1–2)

Some differences between *Hardwick*'s history and that of the brief are immediately apparent. The brief's signatories (afterwards "the historians")[11] are less interested in putting forward their own coherent account of sexual mores than they are in demonstrating the impossibility of such an endeavor; sodomy laws appear in the brief not as a tradition of regulating minority sexuality but as one of many expressions of shifting community norms. The brief complicates *Hardwick*'s narrative and renders the historical accounts on which it relies indeterminate; to borrow from Sedgwick, it reframes sodomy bans in universalizing, rather than minoritizing, terms.[12]

But while the historians claim to reject the epistemology of the courthouse, they cannot escape its shadow. The historians represent themselves as pointedly refusing to "offer . . . legal doctrine," but their claims are constrained by that doctrine in ways both acknowledged and not. First, the brief addresses a question that only a court would ask, and assimilates that court's historiographic methods in answering it. Outside of a court, the question "do restrictions on same-sex sex have ancient roots?" makes no sense. To be pedantic, these restrictions build on old traditions of state regulation of conduct and the historians do not argue otherwise; states have been outlawing things (like battery, or arson) for quite some time. On the other hand, Texas's law against "deviate sexual intercourse" (Texas Penal Code Ann. 2003 § 21.06(a)) innovated on those traditions in all sorts of ways (for example, in defining sodomy with reference to the participants' sex).[13] Texan lawmakers worked within established discursive and regulatory forms but adapted them to modern legislative practices and their own particular wants. In other words, they passed a new law with ancient roots.

The trouble is, everything is like this. Any law the historians could evaluate would adapt established legal frameworks (after all, the idea of a statute is an idea with a history) to a particular time, place, and regime. In appearing to claim otherwise, the historians responded specifically to the legal-historiographic claims of *Hardwick*, which were not so much that the restrictions themselves had ancient roots as that the disgust those restrictions claimed to vindicate had a long history and should be granted deference based on that history. Those claims rest on an idea—that policy motivations that have existed for a long time merit less scrutiny than recent ones—borrowed from law, and define "ancient roots" implicitly as the sorts of historical continuity that might be relevant in a substantive due process argument. The historians adopt this definition without ever saying so, and thus lend their historical expertise to an assertion (that bans on consensual sodomy "hold no legitimate place in our nation's traditions") that requires a law degree to fully parse. The stakes of this definitional incoherency, however, are low; *Lawrence* itself is no model of clarity (Case 2003; Cossman 2007, 28–31; Tribe 2004).

More frustrating, and perhaps more interesting, is the brief's historical narrative. That narrative perfectly fits the doctrinal needs of substantive due process jurisprudence. It describes consensual sodomy laws like the one at issue as suspiciously novel, replacing an earlier universalizing model of sexual regulation with one seeking to proscribe the sex had by a minority (*Lawrence v. Texas* Brief, 10). That minority, however, appears in oddly doubled vision. The historians argue that homosexuality was a discursive invention of the late nineteenth century that "would have been literally incomprehensible to the Framers of the Constitution" (Brief, 2) but they also invoke the pathos of subjects who "suffered under the weight of medical theories that treated their desires as a disorder, penal laws that condemned their sexual behavior as a crime, and federal policies and state regulations that discriminated against them on the basis of their homosexual status" (Brief, 20). The shift is subtle, but unmistakable; homosexuality is an invention, but the homosexual person

THE EPISTEMOLOGY OF THE COURTHOUSE | 43

(whose homosexual desires lead them to have homosexual sex) is not. The brief toggles between these two modes effortlessly:

> Proscriptive laws designed to suppress all forms of non-procreative and non-marital sexual conduct existed through much of the last millennium. Widespread discrimination against a class of people on the basis of their homosexual status developed only in the twentieth century, however, and peaked from the 1930s to the 1960s. Gay men and women were labeled "deviants," "degenerates," and "sex criminals" by the medical profession, government officials, and the mass media. (*Lawrence v. Texas* Brief, 2)

These two models are not a contradiction in terms, exactly. People can draw meaning and identity from a discursively constructed status, and hurting someone because they are gay is no less hurtful for that gayness being invented by Victorians. But they serve contradictory persuasive ends. The brief's rhetoric evokes transhistorical sympathies (between gay people facing historical discrimination and gay people in the Justices' own lives) in the service of an argument that other transhistorical sympathies (between moralizing publics of different periods in American history) are anachronistic and incoherent. This rhetorical tension may reflect litigative strategy; the historians are careful to describe sodomy bans in the language of classification and "animus," arming the Court to adopt an equal protection argument that would not require framing homophobic lawmaking as an innovation.[14] But it also reflects broader strategic concerns. Telling a court that the concepts with which it works would have been "literally incomprehensible" to earlier lawmakers is a frightening thing. One organizing fiction of judicial review is that courts interpret prior commitments (Solum 2015), and for that fiction to hold, the makers of those commitments must be familiar enough to be understood by judges without specialist training in the language and ideas of the periods in which they worked. Transhistoricism is as rhetorically seductive as it is doctrinally required.

The historians won. Justice Kennedy adopted their framework in his decision and noted that "early American sodomy laws were not directed at homosexuals as such but instead sought to prohibit nonprocreative sexual activity more generally" (Lawrence v. Texas 2003, 568–69). In this case, the historians' tendency to complicate and denarrativize accorded with their political ends. By showing the contingency of the ban at issue, and stopping the Court from neatly analogizing it to other regulations in other places and times, the historians could make a methodologically sophisticated argument for a normatively desirable regulatory shift. But when those two aims diverge, or when legal processes condition greater sexual or relational freedom on dodgier historical claims, historians run into trouble in court.

We see this trouble as we move from sodomy to marriage. American courts in the early twenty-first century had a number of plausible doctrinal paths to marriage equality; for example, one could argue that sex classifications are *ipso facto* unconstitutional (Koppelman 1994) or that relational choices ought to exist outside of state regulation (Franke 2008). But they consistently framed their decisions on marriage in minoritizing terms. As I have discussed elsewhere (Herz 2015) at greater length, US courts have imagined same-sex marriage as something that a discrete and biologically determined subgroup *naturally* wants to do, something so linked with membership in that group as to render its members' full personhood or dignity contingent upon its permissibility (Ben-Asher 2014; Clarke 2015). Foucault names the problem with this argument; our biologically determined and transhistorical desiring subjects only appear so from our specific vantage point. Neither desire nor sex are prediscursive (Butler 2011; Fischel 2016, 122), and reading historical marriage codes as oppressing a "species" (Foucault 1978, 43) whose existence they often predate requires drawing stronger transtemporal connections than the evidence always allows.

Enter Hadrian and Antinous. As I argued above, the emperor and his favorite appear in contemporary discourse as a new kind of subject: consensually paired, romantically (if not sexually) monogamous, and egalitarian. This kind of subject appears quite suddenly in classical historiography of the 1990s. It can perhaps first be identified in the writings of the earlier medievalist John Boswell, whose work claimed to isolate solemnized and accepted male-male marriages in a historical record that had been warped by the intolerance of later ages (Boswell 1980, 20–21; Boswell 1995, 190–98). But it was only later that large numbers of historians would take up (subtler versions of) his argument. Amy Richlin and Rabun Taylor described an endogamous subculture of sexually versatile homosexual men that was intuitively familiar to modern readers

(Richlin 1993; Taylor 1997), and Eva Cantarella's *Bisexuality in the Ancient World* described "passionate and romantic love" between men as common in a Roman milieu populated by desiring subjects analogous to the modern bisexual (Cantarella 1992, 127). This historiographical strain, controversial and contested within academic history (although by no means universally revoked), would be cited somewhat less critically by legal advocates. For example, Francisco Valdes would argue in the *Yale Journal of Law and Humanities* that Greco-Roman cultural leaders like Hadrian "exalted same-sex intimacy" before a shift toward procreative sexuality in the Christian era (Valdes 1996, 199–201, nn. 133–34). Similarly, William Eskridge's "History of Same Sex Marriage," published by the *Virginia Law Review*, built on Cantarella and Boswell to argue not only that Roman men married each other but also that those marriages "carried with them legal obligations and consequences" (Eskridge 1993, 1446).[15]

As a historical matter, these claims are weak. For example, Eskridge takes a scene in the *Second Philippic* in which Cicero refers to Marc Antony being swept up from prostitution "as if [Curio] had given you a wedding dress" as evidence of legally cognized male-male marriages.[16] Nevertheless, they do serious doctrinal work. By framing gays as a transhistorical minority who used to marry and who now cannot, classicizing arguments change marriage equality from a positive demand for recognition (a demand to which courts are generally hostile; Siegel 1997) into a negative demand for an end to discrimination or for equal treatment. There is no reason why one narrative should be preferred except for the vicissitudes of equal protection doctrine, but those vicissitudes make the stakes of queer history unusually high for the queer present, and they affect the ways we speak of both.

Reading gays into ancient history is bad ancient history, but it can also be bad law. Consider this snippet of oral argument from *Obergefell v. Hodges*, where the Supreme Court ultimately legalized same-sex marriage in all fifty states.

JUSTICE ALITO: Did they have same-sex marriage in ancient Greece?

Ms. BONAUTO: I don't believe they had anything comparable to what we have, Your Honor.

A: Well, they had marriage, didn't they?

B: Yes. They had some sort of marriage.

A: And they had same-sex relations, did they not?

B: Yes.

A: People like Plato wrote in favor of that, did he not?

B: In favor of?

A: Same-sex—wrote approvingly of same-sex relationships, did he not?

B: I believe so, Your Honor.

A: So their limiting marriage to couples of the opposite sex was not based on prejudice against gay people, was it?

B: I can't speak to what was happening with the ancient philosophers.

Oral Argument Transcript at 14–15, *Obergefell v. Hodges*, 576 U.S. 644 (2015) (edited for clarity)

Alito's reasoning is, unfortunately, sound. It is difficult to argue that same-sex marriages were recognized under Greek or Roman law. There is no evidence for it in our (extensive) legal sources (Williams 1999, 247–48), and even the literary evidence Richlin and Taylor marshal for same-sex marriage as a social practice suggests, at most, legally non-binding but nevertheless meaningful rituals performed by queer people living under unfriendly marriage regimes. Alito here shows how transhistorical gayness can be a double-edged sword, and can risk returning us to the "ancient roots" invoked in *Hardwick*. The best (to reveal my own normativity) critical work instead offers a break from history, and from the historicizing conservatism of law; it asks not how things have been but how they should be.

Affidavits of Daring

Some questions remain. What, exactly, is so different about academic and legal historiography? And what should historians and lawyers do about it? To address these questions, I here examine a famous case of "queer historiography gone wrong": the strange case of Martha Nussbaum and Amendment 2. Most readers will know Amendment 2, if at all, from the Supreme Court case *Romer v. Evans*, which found the amendment to reflect antigay prejudice and thus to lack the rational basis required under equal protection scrutiny. But the litigation around

Amendment 2 briefly hinged upon a variant of *Hardwick*'s imagined historical continuity, one that seems faintly silly now.

At trial, the plaintiffs argued that Amendment 2, which forbade Coloradan municipalities from protecting their inhabitants from antigay bias, was based on rank homophobia and lacked the rational basis required by the Fourteenth Amendment.[17] The state—particularly expert witnesses John Finnis and Robert George—took the same approach as Justice Burger and argued that Amendment 2 was based on "standards of morality" rather than prejudice (Defendants' Trial Brief at 56, Evans v. Romer, 854 P.2d 1270 (1993); Reply Brief at 23). Of course, invoking "morality" to get around the Fourteenth Amendment raises problems with the First, so the state again went hunting for "secular" authorities who might share their views. John Finnis, a philosopher at Oxford and expert witness in support of Amendment 2, invoked Classical Greek philosophy: "[A]ll three of the greatest Greek philosophers, Socrates, Plato and Aristotle, regarded homosexual conduct as intrinsically shameful, immoral and indeed depraved or depraving. That is to say, all three rejected the linchpin of modern 'gay' ideology and lifestyle" (Affidavit of John Finnis ¶ 35; Finnis 1994, 1055).[18] Another expert witness, Robert George of Princeton University, asserted (without citing evidence) that these three "tended to take the view that sexual pleasure should be sought only in the context of marriage" (Deposition of Robert George, at 225). The inference is clear enough; if Greek philosophers could disapprove of gay relationships without believing in Jesus, then we should assume that Colorado voters supported Amendment 2 on similarly secular grounds.

In response, opponents of Amendment 2 asked Martha Nussbaum to correct the record. Nussbaum—one of the world's foremost experts in classical philosophy and now a professor of philosophy and law at the University of Chicago—argued that Greek philosophical traditions were far less hostile to same-sex sex and love than Finnis and George alleged, and that their claims arose from (occasionally shocking) misreadings of ancient texts. As part of her argument, Nussbaum questioned Finnis's invocation of Plato's *Laws*, which describe homosexual sex as a *tolmēma*. While Finnis translated *tolmēma* as "enormity"—and followed a 1926 translation of Plato that referred to "those first guilty of such enormities" (Finnis 1994, 1058 n.19)—Nussbaum examined other uses of the word to show that it was nowhere near as pejorative as that translation implied, and meant something more like an "act of daring" (Nussbaum 1994, 1627–28). While she based her argument primarily on her own readings of classical texts, Nussbaum also (as is customary in the field) cited an academic Greek dictionary (the *LSJ*) to support her claim.

Pandemonium ensued. Nussbaum had cited an old edition of the *LSJ*, and while the material she examined had not changed between that one and the most recent version, she was nevertheless accused of perjury. Finnis later claimed (again, without evidence) that Nussbaum had intentionally misrepresented Plato's views in order to deceive the court (Finnis 1994, 1058).[19] The state court disagreed. It refused to issue criminal sanctions and simply washed its hands of the question; its final decision makes no reference to the claims raised by Finnis and George. The Nussbaum Affair was treated as a lurid sideshow at the time (Mendelsohn 1996; Rosen 1993), but is a useful example of what happens when academic questions come to court. Nussbaum's and Finnis's disagreement on the meaning of *tolmēma* seems so strange to us today, and the accompanying perjury accusations so overblown, because disputes about historical subjects work in a radically different epistemic mode than courts are used to.

To demonstrate how this mode works in practice, I will briefly discuss what I understand Plato to mean in the *Laws*. I do not expect anyone to take my claims as authority, but I aim to show how a serious philological argument would look and how it differs from the battle of dictionaries that Finnis and George wanted. The passage at issue reads, in full:

> Then regarding gymnasia and communal meals, while they now benefit cities in other respects, they are nevertheless dangerous in times of civil unrest, as the youths of Miletus, Boeotia, and Thurii demonstrate; moreover this institution appears to have corrupted the pleasures of love, which are customary and natural (*kata fusin*) not only for men but also for beasts. And one might first blame your cities for this, most of all those that employ gymnasia. And whether one argues earnestly or for sport, one must argue that, in the case of a female and male nature joining together in a bond of procreation, the pleasure which accompanies the act seems to derive from nature; it is contrary to nature (*para*

fusin), though, when male joins with male or female with female, and the *tolmēma* of the first (*tolmēma tōn protōn*) arose from a weakness of pleasure. (Pl. *Leg.* 636c)

Much hinges on *tolmēma*, a difficult word to define. Finnis and George tried to solve this problem by invoking dictionaries as a final authority, but Nussbaum is correct to respond that classical dictionaries are simply pieces of modern scholarship and not determinative in philological disputes (Nussbaum 1994, 1620; Halperin 2002, 62–63). Instead, we must look closely at other uses of the same word.

Tolmēma appears mostly in the elevated language of Greek drama, making it especially hard to gloss, but in those contexts denotes striking or unusual events without implying a moral stance. Consider, for example, Euripides' *Orestes* ll. 1063–4: "[Y]ou ought to imitate my *tolmēmata*" or Aristophanes' *Plutus* ll. 418–9: "I will wickedly destroy you wicked people, for you dare an unendurable *tolmēma*"). In each case, the authors provide context (that of wickedness or of imitability) that tells the reader how to morally evaluate the *tolmēma*. The term itself does not provide that information, and the two *tolmēmata* described here are meant to be evaluated quite differently. Finally, a passage from Thucydides' history of the Peloponnesian War explains that "the *tolmēma* of Aristogiton and Harmodius was undertaken because of an erotic entanglement" (Thuc. 6.54). Aristogiton and Harmodius were male lovers who killed the tyrant Hipparchus; while Thucydides argues they acted inappropriately (Thuc. 6.59; Meyer 2008, 19), the tyrannicides were widely admired in Athens for what they had done (Stewart 1997, 73). *Tolmēma* seems to denote actions that are brave and heedless, not good or bad per se (unlike the words "crime," "abomination," or "enormity," suggested as translations by experts testifying in support of Amendment 2).

The context surrounding its use in the *Laws*, however, is negative. Plato (or more precisely the character of the Athenian Stranger, who is hardly Plato's mouthpiece but does occasionally offer his views) describes same-sex sex as contrary to nature (*para fusin*) and suggests that the *tolmēmata* of the first people to engage in these acts were motivated by "the weakness of pleasure" (*akrateian hēdonēs*).[20] *Akrateia* is unambiguously pejorative, even if *tolmēma* is not. But Plato makes this claim as part of a broader political argument, one less about sex than about single-sex political institutions like the gymnasium that generate civil strife. Given Thucydides' use of the unusual *tolmēma* to denote tyrannicide borne of homoerotics, we should understand Plato—who mimics Thucydides' language to describe homoerotics destabilizing the state and who does so in the voice of an explicitly Athenian character—to reference Aristogiton and Harmodius quite directly here. Plato's *tolmēma*, then, indicates a specific confluence of recklessness, gay sex, and revolution.[21]

This reading complicates Nussbaum's claim that Plato simply describes same-sex sex as "intensely and powerfully pleasant" (Nussbaum 1994, 1632); while Plato spoke positively of same-sex erotics in the *Symposium* (an earlier work, and also one concerned with personal perfection rather than civic harmony), he disapproves of them here. But it devastates Finnis's. While Plato's invocation of "nature" (*fusis*) superficially accords with a Christian natural-law tradition, he nowhere suggests that "natural" human arrangements require legal support. Finnis claimed that disapproval of same-sex relationships *tout court* preceded Christianity, but Plato was specifically criticizing an elite homosociality that no longer exists. That makes him a useless authority here, unless Amendment 2 were meant to prevent gay couples from assassinating government officials in an erotic fugue.

I hope I have demonstrated why Plato is not a helpful authority on Colorado law. But more importantly, I hope I have shown what it takes to read Plato well, and why Judge Bayless was right not to try. Understanding a historical text does not mean substituting the correct English word for the Greek one; it means understanding the specific culture that produced a text's arguments, and knowing how different they look outside of their original milieux. Courts do not work that way. Legal interpretation requires abstracting transhistorically intelligible normative claims from a set of authorities, and thus assumes that such work is possible (Solum 2010, 96). One of the foundational commitments of queer theory is that people are different from each other (Sedgwick 2005, 22), and of queer history that the historical subject cannot be rendered neat or even truly legible (Dinshaw 2010, 12; Doan 2013, 51–52).[22] Here, these commitments remind us that Plato lived in, and wrote about, worlds that are not ours. In reducing a conflict about Platonic philosophy to a dispute over dictionary editions, Finnis and George asked the court to endorse claims about Plato that Plato would not have even understood well enough to condemn.

* * *

Nussbaum's own account of the Colorado litigation, *Platonic Love and Colorado Law*, makes clear that it was the defendants, and not she, who treated Plato as juridically cognizable (Nussbaum 1994, 1523 and n.24).[23] Nussbaum was there to poke holes in an oversimplified account of Platonic homophobia, and (whatever disagreements I might have with the positive vision of Plato offered in response) she was right in doing so. But when Nussbaum explains why Plato is so important to her, she makes a more transformative argument about historical and sexual difference. Nussbaum's most compelling argument for the relevance of historical material is that it shows us how "our own judgments are not the only judgments in the world" (Nussbaum 1994, 1598). In other words, history invites our epistemic humility. If humans with ethical worth can hold views so profoundly foreign to modern sensibilities, then those modern sensibilities might not reflect transhistorical or biologic truth. We cannot know how Plato would feel about Amendment 2, but instead of taking that unknowability as an obstacle to overcome, we should see it as a call to question the logics of a world that, not too far in the future, will seem as strange as that of Plato's assassins in love.

Conclusion

I have here provided a few examples of an underdiscussed phenomenon: of courts flattening out a complex historical sexuality to make it better fit their epistemic and discursive needs. My position on this flattening has not been subtle. When courts work in this mode they generate a popular history of sexuality that is often oversimplified in its particulars (Halperin 2002, 14–15), disrespectful to dead people who are remembered for passions and beliefs they would have found alien (Spivak 2010, 266–83), and dangerous for modern sexual subjects whose desires run counter to ideologically charged transhistorical narratives (Halperin 2002, 18–19). But—one more example of the historian's submission to legal discourse—I end this chapter with some calls for action.

Courts do not understand history as it is generally practiced by specialists. Because historians' approach to sources rests on assumptions that would make judicial work impossible, a court is not going to ask the sorts of questions to which contemporary historiography is amenable. This has some implications for how advocates should use histories in court, and for how historians should engage with that court's analytic processes. It would be pointless to opine on how the *Bowers* Court, the *Lawrence* Court, or the historians who involved themselves in each "should" have acted, but the questions these cases pose have not gone away. In particular, Justice Thomas's concurrence in *Dobbs v. Jackson Women's Health* (2022) states baldly that "in future cases, we should reconsider all of this Court's substantive due process precedents, including *Griswold* [*v. Connecticut* (1965), recognizing a constitutional right to access to contraceptives], *Lawrence*, and *Obergefell*" (Dobbs v. Jackson Women's Health 2022, slip op. at 3, Thomas, J., concurring in part and concurring in the judgment). While this view was rather pointedly rejected by the majority opinion (Dobbs v. Jackson Women's Health 2022, slip op. at 37–38), it is quite possible that the Supreme Court will soon revisit cases like *Lawrence* and *Obergefell* and in doing so will again ask queer litigants to reason from history in asking for some of their most basic freedoms.

I would not presume to tell those litigants what to do. The Supreme Court bar is a tawdry place, and an approach that aims to win the votes of Chief Justice Roberts, Justice Kavanaugh, and Justice Gorsuch will probably not be the one I prefer. But in flattering the originalists—in arguing from the past, even if it is a queer one—we risk denaturing our own history. We do not know how the historical subjects we invoke in court made sense of their own lives, at least not in the way that courts like to know things, and when we pretend otherwise we fail to do the history of sexuality well. We also risk teaching the public that takes our classes and (often) funds our work that history produces narratives to argue from, to the detriment of communities who do not live in ways most people understand.

Queer legal studies ought to hold these risks and rewards in tension. The lawyer in me evaluates the problems of originalism pragmatically, and sees how the benefits of such small historical indignities far outweigh their costs. But queer history calls us outside of structures that exchange indignity for benefit, in order that we might question them more sharply and imagine their alternatives more clearly. Similarly, the historian-as-expert-witness ought to use their platform not just to urge better outcomes but to question the epistemic framework within which they operate. The *Lawrence* brief did not just urge the Court to invalidate laws against sodomy; it noted the instability of the categories Burger had invoked and the difficulty of reasoning from the past. Martha Nussbaum did not just correct the record on Platonic sexual morality; she made it impossible for the court to ignore the weirdness, the foreignness, and the fundamental contingency of that morality. Rather than curate a history to meet particular doctrinal or political needs, these scholars used their expertise to show the radical inapplicability of arguments from history and called their audiences to think in different terms. That liberatory spirit has always been a part of academic history; as Bob Gordon argued in *Critical Legal Histories*, we examine the past to see how few guardrails really constrain human experience, to help us dream of better futures (Gordon 2017, 288–89, 320). But the queer legal historian is called to temper that radical vision with the pragmatics of the world we live in now and the judges who change it. This vision demands that we ask questions we do not answer, and that we surface more problems than we solve. But historians are not, by nature, problem solvers.

NOTES

1 On Athenian jury trials see Cohen 1995; Lanni 2006.

2 As Cossman and Fischel propose in the introduction to this volume, "Our sensibility invites ambiguity and plurality to the readings of wins and losses; indeed to the reading of law itself, in order to open up possibilities for more reparative readings and subjunctive ones, of what was there and what could be."

3 On the impossibility of the objective knowledge that these modes of reasoning presume, see Haraway 1988, especially 582–83.

4 This is disciplinary lingo—I use it to refer to the history of the cultures centered around the Mediterranean basin from approximately 500 BCE to 500 CE.

5 For example, Peterson ignores the very well attested practice of Israelite polygamy; see Goldfeder 2014, 245–54.

6 This claim was actually raised by petitioners, but Peterson dismissed it without comment; Baker v. Nelson 1971, 186 n.2.

7 See, for example, Eutr. 10.9.

8 While some have argued that an old Roman law called the *lex Scantinia* categorically forbade gay sex, it almost certainly was restricted to pederastic relationships involving free Roman boys; see Williams 1999, 119–24.

9   See, for example, Burger and Kruger 2001; Burgwinkle 2004; Dinshaw 2010. On the general incoherence of Justice Burger's conception of transhistorical sodomy, see Halley 1993, 1745–67.

10 For closer analyses of the *Hardwick* decision itself, see Halley 1993; Thomas 1993.

11 The brief was signed by ten academic historians: George Chauncey, Nancy F. Cott, John D'Emilio, Estelle B. Freedman, Thomas C. Holt, John Howard, Lynn Hunt, Mark D. Jordan, Elizabeth Lapovsky Kennedy, and Linda P. Kerber.

12 *Lawrence v. Texas*, Brief at 10 ("Over the generations, sodomy legislation proscribed a diverse and inconsistent set of sexual acts engaged in by various combinations of partners. Above all, it regulated *conduct* in which *anyone* (or, at certain times and in certain places, any male person) could engage"); see Case 2003, 88–92; Sedgwick 1990, 54.

13 Cf., for example, Georgia Code Ann. 1984 § 16-6-2. On the history of sodomy regulation in America, see Eskridge 2008.

14 See, for example, *Lawrence v. Texas*, Brief at 1, 3, 7, 10, 29; Lawrence v. Texas 2003, 581–82 (O'Connor, J., concurring in the judgment).

15 To be clear, Eskridge (1993) describes more practices and polities than Rome; I focus here for reasons of coherence and expertise.

16 Specifically, Eskridge focuses on Cicero's "legalistic advice" to Antony as evidence of the union's legal valence (1993, 1446). For Latinist approaches to the same passage see Fertik 2017; Sussman 1994.

17 See Cleburne v. Cleburne Living Ctr., 473 U.S. 432 (1985).

18 Finnis published his *Romer* affidavit nearly verbatim in the *Notre Dame Law Review*, and I rely on that account going forward.

19 "[T]o have quoted from the real 'authoritative dictionary' would have destroyed the fundamental contention of her oral evidence about Plato, while to have allowed the court to know the truth about the long-superseded nineteenth-century source of her lexicography would have deprived her testimony of the appearance of authoritative support which it so badly needed."

20 Others have taken *tōn proton* differently, as indicating "a *tolmēma* of the first order" *vel sim.*, but I agree with Nussbaum that it should be understood to refer instead to the first people who engaged in such acts. Nussbaum 1994, 1626–27.

21 On erotics in Athenian political culture, and particularly the importance of homoerotic bonds to Athenian conceptions of democracy, see Wohl 2002.

22 Respectively: "[Sex is] at least in part contingent on systems of representation, and, as such, [] fissured and contradictory" (Dinshaw 2010, 12); "No matter how many new words we invent, none will ever adequately capture the commonalities, contradictions, and confusions of sexual subjects" (Doan 2013, 51–52).

23 See also Nussbaum 1994, 1530 ("One may wonder what difference it makes whether Finnis got the Greeks right. Ultimately, his argument must stand or fall on its own merits, not by any such appeal to authority, as must the argument that rebuts it.").

BIBLIOGRAPHY

Baker v. Nelson. 191 N.W.2d 185 (1971).

Balkin, Jack M. 2013. "The New Originalism and the Uses of History." *Fordham Law Review* 82: 641–719.

Ben-Asher, Noa. 2014. "Conferring Dignity: The Metamorphosis of the Legal Homosexual." *Harvard Journal of Law and Gender* 37: 243–94.

Bostock v. Clayton County. 140 S. Ct. 1731 (2020).

Boswell, John. 1980. *Christianity, Social Tolerance, and Homosexuality: Gay People in Western Europe from the Beginning of the Christian Era to the Fourteenth Century.* Chicago: University of Chicago Press.

———. 1995. *Same-Sex Unions in Premodern Europe.* New York: Vintage Books.

Bowers v. Hardwick. 478 U.S. 186 (1986).

Bray, Alan. 1988. *Homosexuality in Renaissance England.* London: Alyson.

Brooten, Bernadette J. 1996. *Love Between Women: Early Christian Responses to Female Homoeroticism.* Chicago: University of Chicago Press.

Bullock, Andrew. 2019. "Simon Cowell's New £15m Mansion is 'Haunted by the Ghost of Antinous—the Gay Lover of Roman Emperor Hadrian.'" www.dailymail .co.uk.

Burger, Glenn and Steven F. Kruger. 2001. *Queering the Middle Ages.* Minneapolis: University of Minnesota Press.

Burgwinkle, William E. 2004. *Sodomy, Masculinity and Law in Medieval Literature: France and England, 1050–1230.* Cambridge: Cambridge University Press.

Butler, Judith. 2011. *Bodies That Matter: On the Discursive Limits of "Sex."* New York: Routledge.

Cantarella, Eva. 1992. *Bisexuality in the Ancient World.* New Haven, CT: Yale University Press.

Carpenter, Dale. 2012. *Flagrant Conduct: The Story of* Lawrence v. Texas. New York: W.W. Norton.

Case, Mary Anne. 2003. "Of 'This' and 'That' in *Lawrence v Texas.*" *Supreme Court Review* 2003: 75–142.

CBC News. 2013. "Rufus Wainwright and Daniel MacIvor Creating Hadrian Opera for COC." www.cbc.ca/.

Chakrabarty, Dipesh. 2008. *Provincializing Europe: Postcolonial Thought and Historical Difference.* Princeton, NJ: Princeton University Press.

Chauncey, George. 1994. *Gay New York: Gender, Urban Culture, and the Makings of the Gay Male World, 1890–1940.* New York: Basic Books.

Clarke, Jessica A. 2015. "Against Immutability." *Yale Law Journal* 125: 2–102.

Cleburne v. Cleburne Living Ctr., 473 U.S. 432 (1985).

Cohen, David. 1995. *Law, Violence, and Community in Classical Athens.* Cambridge: Cambridge University Press.

Cossman, Brenda. *Sexual Citizens: The Legal and Cultural Regulation of Sex and Belonging.* Stanford, CA: Stanford University Press.

Dinshaw, Carolyn. 2010. *Getting Medieval: Sexualities and Communities, Pre- and Post-modern*. Durham, NC: Duke University Press.

Doan, Laura. 2013. *Disturbing Practices: History, Sexuality, and Women's Experience of Modern War*. Chicago: University of Chicago Press.

Dworkin, Ronald. 1986. *Law's Empire*. Cambridge, MA: Harvard University Press.

Eskridge, William N. 1993. "A History of Same-Sex Marriage." *Virginia Law Review* 79: 1419–1513.

———. 2008. *Dishonorable Passions: Sodomy Laws in America, 1861–2003*. New York: Viking.

Evans v. Romer. 854 P.2d 1270 (Colo. 1993).

Fertik, Harriet. 2017. "Sex, Love, and Leadership in Cicero's Philippics 1 and 2." *Are-thusa* 50: 65–88.

Finnis, John M. 1994. "Law, Morality, and Sexual Orientation." *Notre Dame Law Review* 69: 1049–76.

Fischel, Joseph J. 2016. *Sex and Harm in the Age of Consent*. Minneapolis: University of Minnesota Press.

Foucault, Michel. 1978. *The History of Sexuality*. Translated by Robert Hurley. New York: Pantheon Books.

Franke, Katherine M. 2008. "Longing for Loving." *Fordham Law Review* 76: 2685–2708.

Fuller, Lon. 1969. *The Morality of Law*. New Haven, CT: Yale University Press.

Goldfeder, Mark. 2014. "The Story of Jewish Polygamy." *Columbia Journal of Gender and Law* 26: 234–315.

Gordon, Robert W. 2017. *Taming the Past: Essays on Law in History and History in Law*. Cambridge: Cambridge University Press.

Griswold v. Connecticut. 381 U.S. 479 (1965).

Hallett, Judith P. and Marilyn B. Skinner (eds.). 1997. *Roman Sexualities*. Princeton, NJ: Princeton University Press.

Halley, Janet E. 1993. "Reasoning about Sodomy: Act and Identity in and after *Bowers v. Hardwick*." *Virginia Law Review* 79: 1721–80.

Halperin, David. 2002. *How to Do the History of Homosexuality*. Chicago: University of Chicago Press.

Haraway, Donna. 1988. "Situated Knowledges: The Science Question in Feminism and the Privilege of Partial Perspective." *Feminist Studies* 14: 575–99.

Hart, H. L. A. 2012. *The Concept of Law*. Oxford: Oxford University Press.

Herz, Zachary. 2015. "The Marrying Kind." *Tennessee Law Review* 83: 83–160.

Icks, Martijn. 2012. *The Crimes of Elagabalus: The Life and Legacy of Rome's Decadent Boy Emperor*. Cambridge, MA: Harvard University Press.

Kelly, Alfred H. 1965. "Clio and the Court: An Illicit Love Affair." *Supreme Court Review* 1965: 119–158.

Koppelman, Andrew. 1994. "Why Discrimination against Lesbians and Gay Men Is Sex Discrimination." *New York University Law Review* 69: 197–287.

Lanni, Adriaan. 2006. *Law and Justice in the Courts of Classical Athens*. Cambridge: Cambridge University Press.

Lawrence v. Texas. 539 U.S. 558 (2003).

Lear, Andrew. 2013. "Ancient Pederasty." In *A Companion to Greek and Roman Sexualities*, 102–27. Hoboken, NJ: John Wiley & Sons.

Masterson, Mark. 2014. *Man to Man: Desire, Homosociality, and Authority in Late-Roman Manhood*. Columbus: Ohio State University Press.

Mendelsohn, Daniel. 1996. "The Stand: Expert Witnesses and Ancient Mysteries in a Colorado Courtroom." http://linguafranca.mirror.theinfo.org.

Meyer, Elizabeth. 2008. "Thucydides on Harmodius and Aristogeiton, Tyranny, and History." *CQ* 58: 13–34.

Murdoch, Joyce and Deb Price. 2001. *Courting Justice: Gay Men and Lesbians v. the Supreme Court*. New York: Basic Books.

Nussbaum, Martha C. 1994. "Platonic Love and Colorado Law: The Relevance of Ancient Greek Norms to Modern Sexual Controversies." *Virginia Law Review* 80: 1515–1651.

Oakeshott, Michael. 2004. *What Is History?: And Other Essays*. Luton: Andrews U.K. Ltd.

Obergefell v. Hodges. 576 U.S. 644 (2015).

Oncale v. Sundowner Offshore Services. 523 U.S. 75 (1998).

Opper, Thorsten. 2008. *Hadrian*. Cambridge, MA: Harvard University Press.

Palko v. Connecticut. 302 U.S. 319 (1937).

Richlin, Amy. 1992. *The Garden of Priapus: Sexuality and Aggression in Roman Humor*. Oxford: Oxford University Press.

———. 1993. "Not Before Homosexuality: The Materiality of the *Cinaedus* and the Roman Law against Love between Men." *Journal of the History of Sexuality* 3: 523–73.

Romer v. Evans. 517 U.S. 620 (1996).

Rosen, Jeffrey. 1993. "Sodom and Demurrer." https://newrepublic.com.

Sedgwick, Eve Kosofsky. 1990. *Epistemology of the Closet*. Berkeley: University of California Press.

Siegel, Reva. 1997. "Why Equal Protection No Longer Protects: The Evolving Forms of Status-Enforcing State Action." *Stanford Law Review* 49: 1111–48.

Skinner v. Oklahoma, *ex rel*. Williamson. 316 U.S. 535 (1942).

Solum, Lawrence B. 2010. "The Interpretation-Construction Distinction." *Constitutional Commentary* 27: 95–118.

———. 2015. "The Fixation Thesis: The Role of Historical Fact in Original Meaning." *Notre Dame Law Review* 91: 1–78.

Spivak, Gayatri Chakravorty. 2010 [1985]. "Can the Subaltern Speak?" In *Can the Subaltern Speak? Reflections on the History of an Idea*, edited by Rosalind C. Morris, 237–83. New York: Columbia University Press.

Stewart, Andrew F. 1997. *Art, Desire, and the Body in Ancient Greece*. Cambridge: Cambridge University Press.

Sullivan v. Finkelstein. 496 U.S. 617 (1990).

Sunstein, Cass R. 1988. "Sexual Orientation and the Constitution: A Note on the Relationship between Due Process and Equal Protection." *University of Chicago Law Review* 55: 1161–79.

Sussman, Lewis. 1994. "Antony as a *Miles Gloriosus* in Cicero's Second Philippic." *Scholia* 3: 53–83.

Taylor, Rabun. 1997. "Two Pathic Subcultures in Ancient Rome." *Journal of the History of Sexuality* 7: 319–71.

Thomas, Kendall. 1993. "The Eclipse of Reason: A Rhetorical Reading of *Bowers v. Hardwick*." *Virginia Law Review* 79: 1805–32.

Tribe, Laurence H. 2004. "*Lawrence v. Texas*: The 'Fundamental Right' that Dare Not Speak Its Name." *Harvard Law Review* 117: 1893–1955.

United States v. Windsor. 570 U.S. 744 (2013).

Valdes, Francisco. 1996. "Unpacking Hetero-Patriarchy: Tracing the Conflation of Sex, Gender & Sexual Orientation to Its Origins." *Yale Journal of Law & the Humanities* 8: 161–211.

Vout, Caroline. 2005. "Antinous, Archaeology and History." *Journal of Roman Studies* 95: 80–96.

Walters, Jonathan. 1997. "Invading the Roman Body: Manliness and Impenetrability in Roman Thought." In *Roman Sexualities*, edited by Judith P. Hallett and Marilyn B. Skinner, 29–43. Princeton, NJ: Princeton University Press.

Waters, Sarah. 1995. "'The Most Famous Fairy in History': Antinous and Homosexual Fantasy." *Journal of the History of Sexuality* 6: 194–230.

Williams, Craig. 1999. *Roman Homosexuality*. Oxford: Oxford University Press.

Wohl, Victoria. 2002. *Love Among the Ruins: The Erotics of Democracy in Classical Athens*. Princeton, NJ: Princeton University Press.

Zeitlin, Froma I. 1996. *Playing the Other: Gender and Society in Classical Greek Literature*. Chicago: University of Chicago Press.

2

The Sexual Subaltern and Law

Postcolonial Queer Imaginaries

RATNA KAPUR

In 1985, Gayatri Spivak, in her canonical text "Can the Subaltern Speak?," introduced the idea of epistemic violence. She argued that the introduction of a liberal imperial understanding of law in the colonial encounter constituted the most important example of epistemic violence (Spivak 1993, 77). In the late nineteenth century, during the period of British colonial rule, a polymorphous structure of law that was internally non-coherent and open-ended was displaced by British colonial law. The displacement resulted from the process of codifying and stabilizing law, partly through the education of colonial subjects and the alignment of their intentions with the racial and civilizing objectives of their imperial masters. These objectives were made explicit in Thomas Macaulay's infamous 1835 "Minute on Indian Education," which stated:

> We must at present do our best to form a class who may be interpreters
> between us and the millions whom we govern; a class of persons, Indian
> in blood and colour, but English in taste, in opinions, in morals, and in
> intellect. To that class we may leave it to refine the vernacular dialects of
> the country, to enrich those dialects with terms of science borrowed from
> the Western nomenclature, and to render them by degrees fit vehicles for
> conveying knowledge to the great mass of the population. (Spivak 1993,
> 77, quoting Thomas Babington Macaulay)

Spivak argues that the education of the colonial subject in the racial and civilizational project of the colonial power was complemented by "the epistemic violence of the legal project" (77). In light of this violence, Spivak questions whether the subaltern can ever speak or be heard.[1]

I discuss the significance of Spivak's notion of epistemic violence and the accompanying imperial formations of the subject for contemporary LGBT rights struggles and queer critique. Queer critique has exposed how rights struggles have secured recognition for marginalized communities, while also incorporating them into a heteronormative and reproductive framework and its assimilationist demands. At the same time, queer critique—or scholarship on the radical queer break with the sexed and gendered subject—remains embedded in the epistemic violence of the colonial encounter and its role in shaping the gender and sexuality of the native subject in law. The critiques continue to be partly produced through racist and colonial constructions of the "other" as homophobic, repressive, and primitive in its treatment of gender and sexuality. This chapter demonstrates how contemporary forms of sexual dissidence need to be understood alongside the epistemic violence of the colonial encounter in law.

* * *

In 2018, the Indian Supreme Court held that menstruating women must be allowed access to worship at Sabarimala, a popular temple in Kerala, a state in the southwestern part of India. The shrine is home to Ayyappa, a celibate deity. A lower court upheld a ban on women of menstruating age from worshipping at the shrine, stating that "young women should not offer worship in the temple so that even the slightest deviation from celibacy and austerity observed by the deity is not caused by the presence of such women" (S. Mahendran v. The Secretary, Tranvancore Devaswom Board, 1993). Reversing this decision in a majority ruling, the Supreme Court held that the prohibition violated the fundamental right to equality of women under the Indian Constitution. The Court stated that: "Any rule based on discrimination or segregation of women pertaining to biological characteristics is not only unfounded, indefensible and implausible but can also never pass the muster of constitutionality" (Indian Young Lawyers Association v. State of Kerala, 2019, hereinafter Ayyappa case).

The Court's decision was celebrated as a landmark case and as a victory for women's equality rights in India. However, a closer reading of the decision discloses that the story of Ayyappa runs contrary to this assessment. The legend of Ayyappa reveals that he was the son of the union between Siva and Vishnu, two male gods. During his life, Ayyappa's clos-est companion was Vavar, a Muslim. At the behest of Ayyappa, a mosque was built for Vavar in the town of Erumely, about 50 kilometers from Sabarimala. In addition, a shrine dedicated to Vavar adjoins the Sabari-mala shrine, with a visit to Vavar's sanctuary forming an integral part of the pilgrimage to Sabarimala (Vanita 2000). A significant aspect of the story is that Ayyappa wanted to do away with death as well as birth and reproduction, which were regarded as impediments to self-realization (Menon 2018a, 112–15). The case was hailed almost exclusively as a femi-nist victory (Jamal 2020; Kumari 2019). A central question addressed in this chapter is why would this case attract the attention of the LGBT community if it was about women's participation? More specifically, how does the Ayyappa legend invite queer intervention?

* * *

In this chapter, I discuss how the insurrectionary possibilities offered by a postcolonial queer reading of the Ayyappa case remain undetected. The explanation lies partly in LGBT rights interventions generally focusing on the universalizing and homogenizing dynamic of rights claims, accreting around specific constituencies/identities. Such interventions are directed at legal inclusion and the bestowal of rights on those subjects who have been disenfranchised, subordinated, stigmatized, criminalized, and regarded as less than human.[2] Based on faith in universal human rights, LGBT advo-cacy culminates in the globalization of a "global gay" identity: "[A] claim to 'gay and lesbian rights' as human rights depends on an understanding that the identities 'gay' and 'lesbian' are universal in the sense that they are present in all cultures, not just in the west" (Walker 2000, 62).

A second explanation lies in the limits of queer critique which fail to consider rival considerations of the relationship between gender, sexual-ity, culture, and knowledge systems that emerge from within the histories and epistemologies of the postcolony. Queer critique offers a significant break from a brand of feminism embedded in gender dualism and re-productive heteronormativity. However, these critiques have also repro-duced some of the racist and civilizational assumptions about the "other" that have been a notable feature of the liberal rights project (Ahmed 2011; Cossman 2012; Eng 2010, 2–3; Eng and Puar 2020, 5–6; Freccero 2007, 490–91; Kapur 2018; Puar 2007, 2; Rahman 2010). These assumptions include the integral role of the colonial encounter, antiblackness, and slavery in shaping understandings about gender and sexuality which continue to inform the postcolonial present. Alternative considerations of the productive relationship between gender, sexuality, and culture in the postcolony remain sidelined or marginalized in both contemporary LGBT rights interventions and the queer critical tradition.

While eschewing any nostalgia for a glorious, precolonial past of gender and sexuality, this chapter examines the ongoing epistemological erasures in the postcolonial present within the legal domain. Drawing attention to landmark rulings by the Indian Supreme Court on LGB and trans rights, I interrogate how these victories moved the political dial in the direction of queer normativity and reproduced an Anglo-American script on sexual freedom tethered to rights.[3] In the process, these "wins" obscure the transgressive possibilities that exist in nonliberal spaces and the alternative forms of subjectivity that flourish outside the realm of queer normativity. I conclude by revisiting the Ayyappa decision and demonstrating how a postcolonial queer reading draws attention to the flourishing and alternative lifeworlds that exist beyond the legal landscape. The analysis recuperates the transgressive possibilities that have been the hallmark of queer critique.

The chapter is divided into three parts. In the first part, I discuss the direction of LGBT politics within postcolonial India and its successes in securing rights and recognition. I then turn to discuss how a queer critique exposes the limits of these "victories" and identifies what is occluded by them. In the second part, I discuss the racial and civilizational conceits and epistemic violence that underpin prevalent queer critiques. These have been exposed by queer of color and postcolonial interventions. These interventions allow for the consideration of nonliberal epistemic possibilities that rest outside of Anglo-American experiences and histories. And last, I tentatively explore the prospect of recuperating queer radicality through an exploration of alternative expressions of sexual and gender subjectivity. I revisit the Ayyappa case as a postcolonial queer text.

Victories for LGBT Rights

In September 2018, the Constitutional Bench of the Indian Supreme Court declared that section 377 of the Indian Penal Code, 1860 (IPC)—a

colonial-era law on homosexuality that had criminalized sodomy—
was unconstitutional and held that discrimination based on sexuality
amounted to a violation of fundamental rights (Navtej Singh Johar v.
Union of India, 2018). The decision not only held that consensual carnal
intercourse among adults in the private sphere did not harm "the public
decency or morality," but also that "[r]espect for individual choice is the
very essence of liberty under law," and that the LGBT community pos-
sesses equal rights under the constitution (Johar 2018, 268.16, 255). The
decision categorically ruled that the Victorian (and implicitly Christian)
morality on which the provision was based could not withstand the test
of "constitutional morality" (349).[4] There was considerable emphasis on
the idea that India should not be left behind in the global march toward
progress (563). The Court set right an earlier verdict in 2013, delivered by
a smaller bench that upheld the provision, partly on the grounds that the
LGBT community constituted a "miniscule minority" and was therefore
presumably not a relevant constituency deserving of constitutional protection (643.5).[5] The decision declared that the majority cannot subsume
the rights of the minority and was hailed by the LGBT community in
India, and globally, as a landmark ruling and victory for human rights.

While the decision did not confer full legibility on LGBT subjects in
law or reduce the traumatic pressure of being homosexual in a homophobic environment, it removed a significant impediment to the full
pursuit of LGBT rights. Following the decision, many Indian gays and
lesbians participated in discussions about the possibility of same-sex
marriage (Bhogle 2019; Subramanyam and Samal 2019). Some couples
even married in the presence of temple deities, with traditional priests
conducting ceremonies, or through the formal exchange of garlands,
a ritual associated with some Indian marriages, and sought social and
legal recognition of these unions (Mishra 2019).[6] These sexual subjects,
who were previously cast as outsiders to "Indian culture," signaled their
intention to pursue the opening provided by the Navtej Singh Johar decision through a provocative and subversive appropriation of the institution of marriage.

In April 2014, the trans community in India was similarly ecstatic
over the Supreme Court's decision recognizing their human and fundamental rights to health and education, to be included in the category of "other" on government documents, and to marry (National

Legal Services Authority of India v. Union of India, 2014). The trans community—which had been a visible and valid social presence in "Indian culture" but was progressively disenfranchised and humiliated—hailed the decision as a victory, due to its official and formal recognition of the humanity of sexual minorities. Regardless of their sexual orientation, preference, or practice—which may or may not be same-sex—the Indian trans person is now allocated full selfhood through legal categorization as an entitled "third gender."[7]

These cases reflect the struggle of excluded bodies to realize their desire for recognition and humanity through human rights. It is undoubtedly important that illegible constituencies continue to pursue their political and personal desires through rights mechanisms. These landmark cases are a cause for celebration. They represent choices that are assimilationist, life-affirming, and redemptive for some.

The decisions are consistent with a trend, over the past few years, where the decriminalization of homosexuality and the increasing recognition of trans rights has been sweeping across the globe.[8] They indicate a sense of triumph and march toward ultimate freedom within the world's largest democracy—or at least that is how the story is told. There is no question that persecuted sexual minorities have suffered egregious forms of discrimination, harassment, and violence based on gender identity, sexual orientation, or preference—in addition to being considered less human and, at times, even nonhuman—whose lives, when lost, remain unworthy of being mourned, ungrieveable, and as a loss of no consequence (Butler 2006, xiv). LGBT rights claims have been based on the universalizing and homogenizing dynamic of rights claims, accreting around specific identities and directed at legal inclusion and the bestowal of rights upon subjects who have been disenfranchised, subordinated, and regarded as less than human (See *Yogyakarta Principles* 2007). Such efforts remain important in light of the continued resistance from a number of states toward additional rights and recognition, including Russia, Hungary, Poland, Uganda, and Kenya, among others (BBC 2021). It is thus important to recognize that when an entire community is conferred selfhood and humanity and is finally able to join the ranks of the entitled, rights-bearing citizenry, it represents a milestone and produces a catharsis born of decades of struggle, resistance, and hardship. The conferment of rights brings about a recognition of one's humanity and humanness (Williams 1992).

At the same time, the procurement of rights has not necessarily been liberating. In the various court proceedings discussed, LGBT rights claims were articulated and advanced within the existing dominant reproductive heteronormative order, an approach that has shaped the agenda of subsequent LGBT activism (Dave 2012; Dutta 2020; Jain and Kartik 2020; Jain et al. 2020). As has been argued in queer legal scholarship, this order is part of normalized commonsense thinking which disciplines and regulates the sexual subject into becoming acceptable, tolerable, and maybe even deserving of respect.[9] Yet, compliance does not protect sexual minorities from the possibility of being, once again, rendered precarious for failing to meet the dominant normative criteria.

For example, the influential framework of "coming out" narratives dominates how LGBT rights and visions are understood and taken up. These narratives tend to repudiate the varied genealogies and modalities of queer subjectivity, instead locating the issue of sexuality within the narrow dialectic of visibility and invisibility. It captures neither the very real and particular ambivalences, dangers, and dilemmas of homoerotic experience, nor the local imperatives and complexities negotiated by queers in non-urban or postcolonial contexts. Invisibility comes at a high emotional cost, but it may be a necessary form of self-protection—which may also mean the protection of others, both homosexual and heterosexual—in many parts of the world, especially where homosexuality is criminalized, and where being an "out queer" automatically means risking all modes of direct and indirect penalization. The assertion of queer selfhood through visibility may involve great losses, ranging from familial and social rejection and ostracism; to being deprived of home, livelihood, and services; to discrimination and humiliation; to violent assault; and sometimes even to death at the hands of the bigoted and/or the ignorant.

The rights claim of stigmatized and marginalized sexual subjects undoubtedly remains a compelling and important task for the queer political project, especially given that LGBT persons in great swathes of the world are reduced through state and social collusion to truncated, demeaned, and voiceless subjects, while rendered continually precarious through lack of legal recognition. The question is whether the degradation of LGBT persons can be largely alleviated by such interventions. The answer, in part, is that the liberating or transformative impact of such litigation will be limited, partly because of the failure of LGBT rights strategies to adequately interrogate and consider the implications of the normative and epistemological framework within which such pursuits are taken up.

The Queer Break and Its Limits

The term "queer" is an analytical tool intended to disrupt and subvert the dominant normative order and introduce a polymorphous understanding of gender, sex, and sexuality. In a range of disciplines, "queer" has functioned as a political metaphor with a broadened range of considerations that include political economy and neoliberalism, the geopolitics of the war on terror, and the national expressions of sexual, racial, and gendered hierarchies (Eng et al. 2005). Queer, in part, questions the way in which a range of genders and sexes have been marginalized by a heteronormative order. This order is based on a binarized and asymmetrical conception of sex and gender. Sex is asserted as being natural, immutable, and binary, from which male and female genders are biologically derived. All other expressions of sex and gender falling outside this heterosexual matrix are rendered illegible. The interrogation of this order reveals that sex and gender are not natural categories and that the heterosexual ideas about sex, gender, sexuality, and desire are also constructed. Despite the possibility that both sex and gender are open to a range of performances and expressions, heteronormativity continues to be privileged and to inform rights advocacy. Those subjects who are excluded or fail to conform experience physical, material, and political consequences.

Queer theory—as it initially emerged within the Anglo-American tradition—was intended to represent a profound break from feminist analysis on gender and sexuality that was overwhelmingly influenced by dominance or power feminism. The scholarship of Catharine MacKinnon, an American feminist scholar, embodied this position and focused on the eroticization of a domination vision of sexuality and gender (MacKinnon 1982, 1983, 1984, 1987). A fractious debate divided feminists. There were those who argued that this position only encouraged a conservative political and puritanical approach to sexuality. And there were others who sought to re-theorize sexuality through the lens of pleasure and danger in the context of the HIV/AIDS epidemic, which was decimating the gay community, together with the US Supreme Court's antigay stand, which upheld the criminalization of sodomy (Bowers v. Hardwick, 1986). Queer legal theorists, among others, developed a sophisticated critique against as well as alongside feminism. These included a rethinking of the categorization of "woman" as a universal and identity category but also of the gender essentialism and heteronormative impulse of dominance feminism, which was exclusionary by nature (Halley 2008). Some queer theorists offered ways in which to navigate a path between dominance feminism based on sexual subordination and sexuality studies cleansed of gender (Butler 1994; Huffer 2013).

Critiques of the heterosexual presumption that informed dominance feminism were directed at moving beyond it by re-theorizing dominant understandings of the subject. These challenges included putting the categories of sex, gender, and sexuality into crisis. For example, Butler argued that sexual dimorphism and the gender binary were the effects of the regulation of sexuality based on the heterosexual presumption. Gender was an illusion made to appear as reality through social performance and not the grounds upon which feminist politics must be conducted (Butler 1993a; Butler 1999, 173, 180). Similarly Eve Sedgwick interrogated the heterosexual presumption by moving sexuality outside the framework of gender as a category or identity and seeing the lush realm of possibilities arising from this move (Sedgwick 1990). The shift accommodates positions that argue for sexual orientation as both immutable and permanent, as well as floating and open. Sedgwick refused to choose, having concerns about the categorical violence that would occur in preferring either one or the other. To privilege constructivist over essentialist, or universalizing over minoritizing, gender-transitive over gender-separatist understandings of sexual choice, would have serious political costs.[10]

Queer theory has come a long way since the classic critiques on the heterosexual presumption were presented. It continues to offer a profound break from the dominion of feminism over gender and sexuality (Elliot 2010; Fineman et al. 2016). Its anti-normative critical capacities distinguish it from "LGBT" advocacy and scholarship. Queer critique has been invaluable in unmasking essentialist claims to subjectivity. Queer challenges to gender, sex, and sexuality have sought to create space for more polymorphous and pluralistic genders, sexes, and sexualities and dislodge the naturalized and universalized hegemonies in which this binary has been and continues to be embedded.

However, the purported redeployment of "queer" for transgressive political purposes in the domestic and transnational space has also produced its own set of normative impulses as well as racial, cultural, and epistemological exclusions. First, in the context of human rights, even though "queer" is understood as providing a critical intellectual impulse that questions normativity and drives the political agenda, it has frequently been collapsed with "LGBT," which, as discussed, has ended up reinforcing the dominant normative order of gender and sexuality, rather than producing freedom from it (Gross 2017; Kapur 2017; Langlois 2018; Otto 2015). The distinction between "queer" and "LGBT" has become increasingly blurred, with "Q" at times being added as part of the LGBT acronym, and with LGBT advocacy on occasion designated as a modality of "queer" work.[11] All too frequently the use of the term queer in both the scholarship and rights interventions ultimately cashes out at the same place—as identitarian, minoritarian, rights, and recognition based (Cohen 1997; Halperin 2003; Ruti 2017).

Second, queer of color critiques (QOCC) have pointed out how the focus on sexuality in both queer theory and LGBT rights advocacy remains embedded in Anglo-American experiences and histories structured around white sovereign embodiment and antiblackness.[12] Transnationally, these sustain the racial and cultural binaries that have been shaped by the legacies of the slave trade and colonial encounter (Arondekar 2009; Chiang and Wong 2017; Nyanzi 2014, 65–68; Rao 2020, 2). The divide remains between societies that are viewed as secular, tolerant, evolved, or "progressive" and those that continue to be perceived as being in a state of transition, deeply mired in religion, primitive, and un-modern, until the human rights of LGBT persons are secured.[13] For example, Jasbir Puar has traced the ways in which racism, Islamophobia, and nationalism were used to mobilize white queers to advance the US imperial and military agenda in Afghanistan after the 9/11 attacks. In her specific discussion of the Abu Ghraib torture of Iraqi prisoners by US soldiers in 2003, she highlights how the racial, cultural, and gendered dimensions of the scandal were almost entirely excluded from purview by queer scholars and rights advocates in their exclusive focus on sexuality (Massad 2002; Puar 2007, 79–114). She argues that being gay and racist is neither an anomaly nor exceptional, and that anti-Muslim racism is partly constitutive of liberal citizenry (Puar 2010; Sircar 2021). Other examples include the response of LGBT rights advocates to the targeting of homosexuals in Iran and Syria, which continues to reproduce racial and cultural divides in the name of freedom and serves to justify oppressive economic sanctions and violent military interventions (Kapur 2018, 65–67; Rao 2020). The scholarship and advocacy continue to exceptionalize sexuality while undertheorizing or overstating racialized otherness that is invariably displaced onto a Global North/Global South or us/them divide.

The trenchant critique by QOCC of prevalent queer theory has compelled consideration of a host of new questions for queer scholars and rights advocates. These include: "What does queer studies have to say about empire, globalization, neoliberalism, sovereignty, and terrorism? What does queer studies tell us about immigration, citizenship, prisons, welfare, mourning, and human rights?" (Eng et al. 2005, 2). While QOCC theory still remains largely rooted in an Anglo-American context and tied to particular narratives of racism, in its transnational modality it gestures toward a more postcolonial critique.

What remains outside the purview of much of queer legal scholarship is the serious consideration of other choices, lifeworlds, and ways of being that may be available in nonliberal, alternative registers, and its implications. The erasure or marginalization of such choices can in part be explained by queer theory's inability to interrogate its own epistemological framework that not only sets up a false binary between us and them, but also forecloses the possibility of epistemological critique and search for alternatives. Such considerations of alternative registers are partly made possible by postcolonial queer critique.

Postcolonial Queer Critique

Postcolonial (and decolonial) studies have consciously foregrounded knowledge from the global south and nonliberal spaces. They take seriously marginalized or alternative ways of thinking, knowing, knowledge, and lifeworlds from "elsewhere."[14] Postcolonial critiques, while diverse and at times contradictory, have at least three features in common. First, they question the narratives of progress and linear time that are central to rights claims. Second, they unpack the relationship between knowledge and power that constructs the non–European/Western subject as "other," and the racial, sexual, cultural, and epistemological exclusions that this has enabled (Cohn 1997; Ludden 1993; Majeed 1992; Mehta 1999). This relationship informs law and rights discourse. Finally, in foregrounding excluded knowledge, they open space for the reconceptualization of the subject and consideration of alternative epistemic possibilities that involve other ways of being, living, and flourishing in the world. Postcolonial queer imaginaries are located within this space.

Postcolonial queer critique illustrates how constructions of gender and sexuality do not operate around simplistic binaries and asymmetries of power between men and women, heterosexual and homosexual. And much like QOCC, it illuminates how the opposition to, or exclusion of, non-normative sexual groups cannot be understood exclusively through the lens of homophobia and/or primitiveness (Puri 2016; Vanita 2002). It challenges the temporal logics that have featured in the LGBT struggles for rights accumulation coupled with its promise of futurity. It also attends to the racial and civilizing narratives that have governed formations of gender and sexuality within the colonial context and remain pertinent today. While refusing to exonerate the native legacies that shaped the sexual subject in law and continue to inform the postcolonial present, postcolonial queer interventions illuminate the messiness of sexual subaltern historical narratives and subjectivity (Chatterjee 2018; Kapur 2005; Roy 2015; Turner 2014; Vanita 2002). The stories of the sexual subaltern emerge as encounters, rather than as perspicuous, fixed identities (Waites 2009).

The heterosexual presumption and gender categories that featured during the anticolonial struggles were tethered to culture and religion. This relationship was formative in shaping understandings of the family, sex, gender, and culture in the post-independence period (Currier and Gogul 2020; Hunt and Holmes 2015; McClintock 1995, 5–6; Moore-Gilbert 1996). An imperial heteronormalizing gender order continued to structure the sexual and moral codes of the native subject. Through mimicry, native elites co-produced this agenda as a marker of colonial modernity, striving to "become like" the white man—although never quite succeeding (Bhabha, 1994, 86, 89; Najmabadi 2005, 32–53). The legacies of this past inform the current conjuncture and LGBT rights advocacy. The conferment of rights on LGBT persons becomes the hallmark of modernity, where once again "the West" emerges as the standard-bearer (Puar 2007). Drawing on the critical devices of subaltern historiography, a postcolonial inquiry redeploys "queer" as an analytical tool for tracing the work that it does in postcolonial spaces.[15] This tracing includes identifying sexual dissidence not only within normative gender and sexual arrangements but also in politically conservative spaces. In the process, it makes explicit the limits of relying upon LGBT advocacy directed at rights accumulation and assimilation and rescues "queer" from its gradual slide into queer liberalism and colonial modernity. It further disengages queer theory from its Anglo-American moorings; continues the work of expanding the remit of queer beyond sex and desire; and calls for a reimagining of politics and subjectivity (Chatterjee 2018; Das Gupta 2011; Freeman 2010; Rao 2020, 1–2). The response must rest in taking advantage of the ambivalence of agency and learning to hear the subaltern voice, including those that emanate from within a nonliberal, alternative episteme.

In complicating the temporality of queer politics, the postcolonial critique guards against the hegemonic imposition of modern sexual identities as complete and fixed, or a queer critique that does not attend to the relevance of the colonial archives. It offers a detailed and nuanced reading of the archives, reflecting the complex ways in which race, gender, and culture interact to construct the sexual subaltern in law, as well as outside of legal spaces. There is no doubt that, much like the queer, the sexual subaltern is also vulnerable to being co-opted within the liberal worldview (Kapur 2010). Tracing the transformative thread of the subaltern remains an important, although delicate, theoretical task. It involves more consciously foregrounding the alternative epistemes through which the radicality of the sexual subaltern can be explored. This position complements queer of color scholarship and its search for "different paths to queerness" (Ferguson 2004; Muñoz 1999, 15).

At the same time, postcolonial queer critique remains distinct and historically specific. It illuminates the sexual subaltern struggles with national belonging, cultural authenticity, the influence of the neoliberal market, and the liberal episteme that structures law and rights. It further comprehends law as a terrain of power rather than of freedom or liberation, and it identifies the epistemic violence that is done in and through engagements with this terrain. This violence includes marginalizing or expunging other knowledge systems, lifeworlds, and understandings of the subject.

Claims for formal equal rights are brought into tension with a conscious challenge to dominant normative and epistemic assumptions about the subject on which law and rights claims are based. Here, location and performance in a postcolonial space lay bare the terms on which inclusion and exclusion operate in law that remain inscribed within liberal imperialism and colonial modernity. A postcolonial queer optics repudiates the claim of "homosexual sameness" while also eschewing nostalgia for a glorious precolonial past that seeks validation through cultural authenticity. This optics is linked to alternative registers of knowledge, which consciously seeks out spaces that can recuperate and unleash the transformative potential of queer in the legal arena.

Revisiting Ayyappa

I return to the Ayyappa decision, bringing the insights of postcolonial critique to unearth the queer radical possibilities that lay nestled in its subterranean passages. First, as discussed at the outset, the Supreme Court's reasoning in the Ayyappa case is treated as an issue confined to "Hindus" and remains embedded within gender dualism and reproductive heteronormativity that continue to structure sex discrimination cases and equal rights claims. Yet the story of Ayyappa runs contrary to this assessment, as reflected in the closer reading of the legend provided in the introduction to this chapter. The colorful legend of Ayyappa cannot be regarded exclusively as a place of worship for Hindus or understood within gender dualisms and a reproductive heteronormative framework. Its eclectic history speaks to the fluidity of gender, sexuality, and attraction for persons of all faiths, creeds, sexual minorities, and castes from across the country.

Second, revisiting the story of Ayyappa through a postcolonial queer lens builds on QOCC and postcolonial critiques that fundamentally challenge the temporal logics of rights as unilinear, teleological, and progressive. Within these logics the non-white, native "other" is viewed as Europe's regressive past, while Europe's present is positioned as the "other's" desirable future. Instead, the analysis offers a pushback against such an account by framing engagements with the other as encounters rather than rescue operations or progressive endeavors by the liberal white savior. The encounter exposes the parochialism of predominant queer pursuits in law together with the generative myth of law as progress (Fitzpatrick 1992). The argument is not a call to escape, avoid, or abandon the law, but to understand law's flattened, unidimensional portrayal of the world of desirable queer life as limited to the liberal episteme. It is about understanding the transnational or global effects of a legal project driven by this set of provincialized histories and logics. A postcolonial queer reading animates the other, transforming them from objects into subjects, while also marking the limit of what has been cast as progressive or liberatory politics.

Third, a postcolonial queer reading specifically brings the knowledge of the other and alternative epistemes, especially from the global south, into the conversation. The Ayyappa legend is based on an alternative epistemological universe and philosophical space that challenges all dualisms, including the temporal logics of birth and death to which these are confined, as false. The story moves away from a preoccupation with biological procreation as a natural desire. Ayyappa actively resists procreative heterosexuality and remains utterly uninterested in gendered reproduction (Menon 2018a, 126, 130–38). Being born of two male gods, Ayyappa's story brings the radical challenge of queer to the surface—that gender dualisms and reproductive sex are dispensable. Freedom from both is possible and not a necessity for a fulfilling life.[16] This epistemic challenge breaks free from the material, normative, and liberal constraints within which LGBT rights advocacy has functioned, while also offering an alternative space for resuscitation of queer radicality. In other words, in breaking away from reproductive heteronormativity and gender dualisms, Ayyappa opens a path for exploring queer life, subjectivity, and beingness in and through an alternative register (Kapur 2018, 214–35). At a deeper philosophical level, this path includes comprehending the implications of Ayyappa's intent to do away with life and death. This intent entails a move away from embodiment and relocating subjectivity beyond the confinements of the liberal individualism and the corporeal subject to "elsewhere." The space of elsewhere lies in the resolution of all dualities in the non-dual self, where the subject is equated with non-corporeal awareness or consciousness.[17]

Drawing attention to alternative epistemes is neither an adversarial position nor irrelevant to rights struggles and interventions, even though their inscriptions of selfhood and of the processes of being and becoming may seem incommensurable with the parameters of subjectivity as enunciated and affirmed within the existing liberal rights structure. The option appears incommensurable given the inability of rights advocates and critical scholarship, including predominant queer scholarship, to be open to or engage with or learn from the other coupled with the continuous assimilation of the other within a liberal fishbowl. The space of the other as devoid of thinking, theory, and knowledge production persists. But incommensurability or impossibility are not inevitable or unproductive. A postcolonial queer reading of the case highlights the fact that Ayyappa is a celibate god who "enjoys the company of other men," rather than selectively focusing on a tradition that is attempting to oppress or subordinate women. As Menon has pointed out, in the age of #MeToo, to have a god who is simply not interested in women can be liberating. Menon poses the question: "Ayyappa is interested in men. So why is he being dragged into a battle about women?" (2018b). In addition, such an intervention recuperates the dissident possibilities of queer through an exploration of alternative epistemes. This effort seeks to advance a more extensive or politically ambitious agenda through legal mechanisms and equality claims, while also remaining attentive to and pushing back against the epistemic violence that these mechanisms inflict. What remains problematic is that no LGBT groups chose to intervene in this case and instead relinquished an opportune moment to perform a postcolonial queer turn on the legal proceedings.

The story of Ayyappa transcends gender binaries and normative sexuality, providing an example of far-reaching possibilities of queer, once it transcends the limited horizons of the Eurocentric/Anglo-American universe and its epistemic limits. Rather than being absorbed into the problematic terrain of LGBT rights advocacy, the Ayyappa case can instead be deployed as an analytical tool to further problematize the existential bind in which such advocacy is enmeshed and offer productive exits.

Conclusion

"Queer" remains an important tool for political and self-emancipation. It is a tool that can be effectively regenerated in the turn toward nonliberal alternatives and philosophical spaces where different lifeworlds and ways of being flourish. This turn affords possibilities for those forms of life that remain unliveable or unrecognizable within the limits of liberal rights and reform, and unthinkable through confinement to myopic understandings of sex, gender, and beingness. It is an effort to return queer to the spirit of radicality that once infused it. The turn expands the queer legal project beyond the zone of sexuality, sexual and gender identities, and norms—where sex and sexuality are the primary signifiers and affirmers of embodied existence. It pushes in a direction that is about the transformation in subjectivity—what may be termed as internal revolution. Internal revolution locates the possibility of freedom from internal introspection and reflection—an internal Self that is free from the normative and liberal epistemological incarcerations through which LGBT rights claims are pursued. More important, it recuperates a space in law for the expression of queer radicality. This space brings back the possibility of imagining what we might become in the world, including through epistemic alignment with nonliberal articulations of subjectivity and freedom and the futurity of rights in such an alignment. Such alignment potentially encourages engagement with alternative inscriptions of human flourishing.

NOTES

1 Subaltern Studies emerged in the 1980s to inaugurate a field of historiography that focused on the implications of the colonial encounter: Guha 1994b. The subaltern was initially categorized as an empirical person or member of the peasant class, who had been excluded from the history of the colonial encounter, and the colonial or nationalist historical narratives that were invariably scripted by elite bourgeoisie groups. However, a more subversive understanding of the subaltern subsequently emerged that challenged the central pillars of Enlightenment ideals and contested Eurocentric, metropolitan, and bureaucratic systems of knowledge: Chakrabarty 1995; Guha 1983; Guha 1994a, vol. 1; Kapur, 2005, 26–29. See generally Chakrabarty 2000. Spivak (1993) was a critical intervention in this debate.

2 These efforts have culminated, for example, in adoption of the Yogyakarta Principles, which identify areas of discrimination faced by LGBT persons and include measures to alleviate such discrimination. *Yogyakarta Principles* 2007.

3 For a background on the litigation in this area in India and postcolonial tensions generated by judicial rulings see Kapur 2005, 2015, 2016; Naik 2017; Sheikh 2013.

4 Macaulay also drafted the provisions of the Indian Penal Code, 1860 (IPC). The anti-sodomy provisions included in the IPC were informed by a Christian theological orthodoxy that viewed homosexuality as abominable, detestable, and sinful.

5 In December 2013, the Supreme Court of India reversed a lower court's 2009 decision, which had decriminalized gay sex, by reading down section 377 of the Indian Penal Code: Suresh Kumar Koushal v. Naz Foundation, (2014) 1 SCC 1, reversing Naz Foundation v. Government of NCT of Delhi, 2009 (111) DRJ 1 (DB). See also Justice K.S. Puttaswamy (Retd) v. Union of India, (2017) 10 SCC 1, where the Court observed that sexual orientation is an essential attribute of privacy and that the *Koushal* decision was unsustainable: see, e.g., discussion on the essential nature of privacy at [297]–[299] (Chandrachud J).

6 See also Nikesh v. Union of India, Writ Petition (Civil), No. 4294/2020 (High Court of Kerala), challenging the lack of recognition of a marriage between two men who sought to have it registered under the provisions of the Special Marriage Act, 1956.

7 For an analysis of the equivocal reasoning in the case, where the Court oscillates between an essentialist and a socially constructed understanding of trans subjectivity, and the possible exclusionary impact that this could have on diverse gender-variant people, see Dutta 2014.

8 Regarding the decriminalization of homosexuality, Angola's new penal code, which decriminalizes same-sex relationships and prohibits discrimination based on sexual orientation, came into force on February 10, 2021. In 2019, Angola effectively decriminalized homosexuality when Parliament voted to overhaul the criminal statutes: Martina Schwikowski, "As Angola Decriminalizes Homosexuality, Where Does the African Continent Stand?" *DW*, February 10, 2019, www.dw.com; Sophia Purdy-Moore, "Angola Has Decriminalised Same-Sex Relationships. Will the Rest of Africa Follow?," *The Canary*, February 11, 2021, www.thecanary.co. On June 29, 2020, in Gabon, Parliament voted to remove the provision criminalizing homosexuality from its penal code: "Gabon: Decriminalisation of Same-Sex Relations a Welcome Step Says UN Expert," *Office of the High Commissioner for Human Rights*, July 1, 2020, www.ohchr.org. Botswana's High Court handed down a decision in favor of homosexuality being decriminalized in June 2019: "Botswana Decriminalises Homosexuality in Landmark Ruling," *BBC News*, June 11, 2019, www.bbc.com. At the same time there are also moves in the opposite direction: see "Homosexuality: The Countries Where It Is Illegal to Be Gay," *BBC News*, May 12, 2021, www.bbc.com. Regarding recognition of trans rights—Iceland introduced a Gender Autonomy Act in 2019: Jelena Ćirić, "Iceland's Gender Autonomy Act Is a Step Forward for Trans and Intersex Rights," *Iceland Review*, June 19, 2019, www.icelandreview.com; Pakistan Passed the Transgender Persons (Protection of Rights) Act in 2018: Sasha Ingber, "Pakistan Passes Historic Transgender Right

Bill," *NPR*, May 9, 2018, www.npr.org; Uruguay adopted a Comprehensive Law for Transgender Persons in 2018, which survived an attempted rollback in 2019: "Uruguay: Congress Adopts New Law on Transgender Rights," *Global Legal Monitor*, October 31, 2018, www.loc.gov; Oscar Lopez, "Effort to Roll Back Transgender Rights Fails in Uruguay," *Reuters*, August 6, 2019, www.reuters.com.

9   There is a large amount of queer legal literature that makes a similar point about the assimilationist problem with LGBT rights strategies. See for example, Bader and Baker 2019, 97–121; Bernstein 2018; Cossman 2007; Joshi 2012; Kapur 2018, 60–75; Richardson 2005; Stychin 1995; Waites 2009; Warner 2000.

10 At the same time, Sedgwick argued that the space that has been opened up owes "everything to the wealth of essentialist, minoritizing, and separatist gay thought and struggle": Sedgwick 1990, 13.

11 In fact there have been many pronouncements over the years regarding the demise of queer theory through the normativization of "queer," and that it is time for a requiem. Eng et al. 2005; Halberstam 1997; Halperin 2003.

12 Barnard 1999; Dhairyan 1991; Ferguson 2004; Gopinath 2005; Hoad 2007; Muñoz 1999; Nyanzi 2014; Nyongo 2018. This scholarship should be considered alongside the extensive literature on the exploitation and regulation of the black body under the conditions of slavery and heteronormative white supremacist ideologies: See, e.g., Cohen 1997, 453–57; Hartman 1997; Pinto 2020.

13 The persistence of this binary can in part be explained by queer theory's inability to interrogate its own normative commitments to secularism and its theological dimensions. This commitment not only sets up a false divide between us and them, it forecloses the possibility of epistemological critique. See, e.g., Grosfoguel 2007; Khan 2020. These foreclosures are addressed by postcolonial critiques discussed later in this chapter.

14 See, e.g., De Souza 2014; Grosfoguel 2007; Mahmood 2004; Medina 2012; Mignolo 2011; Tamale 2014. Canonical texts in postcolonial studies include: Bhabha 1994; Césaire 1972; Fanon 1961; Gandhi 1998; Said 1978, 1993.

15 See, e.g., Maryam Mulk-ara's story as a women-presenting male in Iran during the rule of Ayatollah Khomeini: Najmabadi 2005, 158–68.

16 This challenge must be distinguished from Lee Eldeman's association of queerness outside of kinship and reproduction with the death drive that rejects any futurity. Postcolonial critique is productive and offers the possibility of returning queer to revolution and radicality rather than the logic of annihilation. Edelman 2004. For an extensive critique of Edelman's position, see also Cornell and Seely 2016.

17 The turn toward alternative framings in critical and queer scholarship is not new: Ramberg 2014, Kapur 2021 (discussing the work of Frantz Fanon and Ali Shari'ati, two critical postcolonial thinkers who argued that revolution requires an alternative or nonliberal conception of the subject). See also the intellectual turn of Eve Sedgwick (2003) toward Tibetan Mahayan Buddhism; Michel Foucault's turn to "political spirituality" in his later work (2005, 14–19); Ghamari-Tabrizi 2016, 173–80; McWhorter 2003.

BIBLIOGRAPHY
Cases
Bowers v. Hardwick, 478 US 186 (1986)
Indian Young Lawyers Association v. State of Kerala (2019), 11 SCC 1
Justice K. S. Puttaswamy (Retd) v. Union of India (2017), 10 SCC 1
National Legal Services Authority of India v. Union of India (2014), 5 SCC 438
Navtej Singh Johar v. Union of India (2018), 10 SCC 1
Naz Foundation v. Government of NCT of Delhi, 2009 (111) DRJ 1 (DB)
Nikesh v. Union of India, Writ Petition (Civil), No. 4294/2020 (High Court of Kerala)
S. Mahendran v. The Secretary, Tranvancore Devaswom Board, AIR 1993 Ker 42
    (Kerala High Court)
Suresh Kumar Koushal v. Naz Foundation (2014), 1 SCC 1

Sources
Ahmed, Sara. 2011. "Problematic Proximities: Or Why Critiques of Gay Imperialism
    Matter." *Feminist Legal Studies* 19: 119–32.
Arondekar, Anjali. 2009. *For the Record: On Sexuality and the Colonial Archives.* Dur-
    ham, NC: Duke University Press.
Bader, Christopher D. and Joseph O. Baker. 2019. "Sexuality and Gender Identity: As-
    similation vs. Liberation." *Deviance Management: Insiders, Outsiders, Hiders, and
    Drifters*, 97–121. Berkeley: University of California Press.
Barnard, Ian. 1999. *Queer Race: Cultural Interventions in the Racial Politics of Queer.*
    New York: Taylor & Francis.
BBC. 2021. "Homosexuality: The Countries Where It Is Illegal to Be Gay." *BBC News*,
    May 12. www.bbc.com.
Bernstein, Mary. 2018. "Same-sex Marriage and the Assimilationist Dilemma: A Re-
    search Agenda on Marriage Equality and the Future of LGBTQ Activism, Politics,
    Communities, and Identities." *Journal of Homosexuality* 65(14): 1941–56.
Bhabha, Homi K. 1994. *The Location of Culture.* London: Routledge.
Bhogle, Satchit. 2019. "The Momentum of History: Realising Marriage Equality in
    India." *National University of Judicial Science Law Review* 12(3–4): 1–22.
Butler, Judith. 1993a. *Bodies that Matter: On the Discursive Limits of "Sex."* New York:
    Routledge.
———. 1993b. "Critically Queer." *GLQ: A Journal of Lesbian and Gay Studies* 1(1):
    17–32.
———. 1994. "Against Proper Objects." *Differences: A Journal of Feminist Cultural Stud-
    ies* 37(2–3): 1–26.
———. 1999 [1990]. *Gender Trouble: Feminism and the Subversion of Identity.* New
    York: Routledge.
———. 2006. *Precarious Life: Power of Mourning and Violence.* New York: Verso.
Césaire, Aimé. 1972. *Discourse on Colonialism.* Translated by Joan Pinkham. New York:
    Monthly Review Press. [*Discourse sur le colonialism.* Paris: Réclame, 1950.]

Chakrabarty, Dipesh. 1995. "Radical Histories and Question of Enlightenment Rationalism: Some Recent Critiques of *Subaltern Studies.*" *Economic and Political Weekly* 30(14): 751–59.

———. 2000. *Provincializing Europe: Postcolonial Thought and Historical Difference.* Princeton, NJ: Princeton University Press.

Chang, Steward. 2014. "The Postcolonial Problem for Global Gay Rights." *Boston University International Law Journal* 32: 309–54.

Chatterjee, Shraddha. 2018. *Queer Politics in India: Towards Sexual Subaltern Subjects.* London: Routledge.

Chiang, Howard and Alvin K. Wong. 2017. "Asia Is Burning: Queer Asia as Critique." *Culture, Theory and Critique* 58(2): 121–26.

Cohen, Cathy. 1997. "Punk, Bulldaggers, and Welfare Queens: The Radical Potential of Queer Politics." *GLQ: Journal of Lesbian and Gay Studies* 3: 437–65.

Cohn, Bernard S. 1997. *Colonialism and Its Forms of Knowledge: The British in India.* Princeton, NJ: Princeton University Press.

Cornell, Drucilla and Stephen D. Seely. 2016. *The Spirit of Revolution: Beyond the Dead Ends of Man.* Cambridge: Polity.

Cossman, Brenda. 2007. *Sexual Citizens: The Legal and Cultural Regulation of Sex and Belonging.* Stanford, CA: Stanford University Press.

———. 2012. "Continental Drift: Queer, Feminism, Postcolonial." *Jindal Global Law Review* 4(1): 17–35.

Currier, Ashley and Keeley B. Gogul. 2020. "African Antisodomy Laws as Unwanted Colonial Inheritances." *WSQ: Women's Studies Quarterly* 48(1–2): 103–21.

Das Gupta, Rohit K. 2011. "Queer Sexuality: A Cultural Narrative of India's Historical Archive." *Rupkatha Journal on Interdisciplinary Studies in Humanities* 3(4): 651–70.

Dave, Naisargi N. 2012. *Queer Activism in India: A Story in the Anthropology of Ethics.* Durham, NC: Duke University Press.

De Sousa, Santos. 2014. *Epistemologies of the South: Justice Against Epistemicide.* London: Routledge.

Dhairyan, Sagri. 1991. "Racing the Lesbian, Dodging White Critics." In *The Lesbian Postmodern*, edited by Laura Doan, 25–46. New York: Columbia University Press.

Dutta, Aniruddha. 2014. "Contradictory Tendencies: The Supreme Court's *NALSA* Judgment on Transgender Recognition and Rights." *Journal of Indian Law and Society* 5(2): 225–36.

———. 2020. "The End of Criminality? The Synecdochic Symbolism of Section 377." *National University of Juridical Science Law Review* 13(3): 1–19.

Edelman, Lee. 2004. *No Future: Queer Theory and the Death Drive.* Durham, NC: Duke University Press.

Elliot, Patricia. 2010. *Debates in Transgender, Queer, and Feminist Theory: Contested Sites.* Farnham: Ashgate.

Eng, David L. 2010. *The Feeling of Kinship: Queer Liberalism and the Racialization of Intimacy.* Durham, NC: Duke University Press.

Eng, David L., Judith Halberstam, and José Esteban Muñoz. 2005. "What's Queer about Queer Studies Now?" *Social Text* 23(3–4): 1–17.

Eng, David L. and Jaspir K. Puar. 2020. "Introduction: Left of Queer." *Social Text* 38(4): 1–23.

Fanon, Frantz. 1961. *The Wretched of the Earth*. Translated by Constance Farrington. New York: Grove Press.

Ferguson, Roderick A. 2004. *Aberrations in Black: Toward a Queer of Color Critique*. Minneapolis: University of Minnesota Press.

Fineman, Martha A., Jack E. Jackson, and Adam P. Romero (eds.). 2016. *Feminist and Queer Legal Theory: Intimate Encounters, Uncomfortable Conversations*. London: Routledge.

Fitzpatrick, Peter. 1992. *The Mythology of Modern Law*. London: Routledge.

Foucault, Michel. 2005. *The Hermeneutics of the Subject: Lectures at the Collège de France, 1981–1982*. Edited by Frédéric Gros. Translated by Graham Burchell. New York: Palgrave Macmillan.

Freccero, Carla. 2007. "Queer Times." *South Atlantic Quarterly* 106(3): 485–94.

Freeman, Elizabeth. 2010. *Time Binds: Queer Temporalities, Queer Histories*. Durham, NC: Duke University Press.

Gandhi, Leela. 1998. *Postcolonial Theory: A Critical Introduction*. New York: Columbia University Press.

Ghamari-Tabrizi, Behrooz. 2016. *Foucault in Iran: Islamic Revolution after the Enlightenment*. Minneapolis: University of Minnesota Press.

Gopinath, Gayatri. 2005. *Impossible Desires: Queer Diasporas and South Asian Cultures*. Durham, NC: Duke University Press.

Grosfoguel, Ramón. 2007. "The Epistemic Decolonial Turn: Beyond Political-economy Paradigms." *Cultural Studies* 21: 211–23.

Gross, Aeyal. 2017. "Homoglobalism: The Emergence of Global Gay Governance." In *Queering International Law: Possibilities, Alliances, Complicities*, edited by Dianne Otto, 148–70. London: Routledge.

Guha, Ranajit. 1983. *Elementary Aspects of Peasant Insurgency in Colonial India*. Delhi: Oxford University Press.

———. 1994a. *Subaltern Studies: Writings on South Asian History and Society*. Delhi: Oxford University Press.

———. 1994b. "Dominance without Hegemony and Its Historiography." In *Subaltern Studies: Writing on South Asian History and Society*, Vol. 6, edited by Ranajit Guha, 210–309. Delhi: Oxford University Press.

Halberstam, Judith. 1997. "Who's Afraid of Queer Theory?" In *Class Issues: Pedagogy, Cultural Studies, and the Public Sphere*, edited by Amitava Kumar, 256–75. New York: New York University Press.

Halley, Janet. 2008. *Split Decisions: How and Why to Take a Break from Feminism*. Princeton, NJ: Princeton University Press.

Halperin, David M. 2003. "The Normalization of Queer Theory." *Journal of Homosexuality* 45(2–4): 339–43.

Hartman, Saidiya. 1997. *Scenes of Subjection: Terror, Slavery, and Self-Making in Nineteenth-Century America.* New York: Oxford University Press.

Hoad, Neville Wallace. 2007. *African Intimacies: Race, Homosexuality, and Globalization.* Minneapolis: University of Minnesota Press.

Huffer, Lynne. 2013. *Are the Lips a Grave? A Queer Feminist on the Ethics of Sex.* New York: Columbia University Press.

Hunt, Sarah and Cindy Holmes. 2015. "Everyday Decolonization: Living a Decolonizing Queer Politics." *Journal of Lesbian Studies* 19(2): 154–72.

Jain, Dipika. 2017. "Shifting Subjects of State Legibility: Gender Minorities and the Law in India." *Berkeley Journal of Gender, Law & Justice* 32(1): 39–72.

Jain, Dipika, Abhina Aher, Simran Shaikh, Amrita Sarkar, and Brian Tronic. 2020. "Negotiating Violence: Everyday Queer Experiences of the Law." *Violence and Gender* 7(4): 141–49.

Jain, Dipika and Kavya Kartik. 2020. "Unjust Citizenship: The Law that Isn't." *NUJS Law Review* 13(2): 159–211.

Jamal, Ayesha. 2020. "Sabarimala Verdict: A Watershed Moment in the History of Affirmative Action." *The Leaflet,* October 30. www.theleaflet.in.

Jones, Spence. 2017. "Towards a Universal Construction of Transgender Rights: Harmonizing Doctrinal and Dialogic Strategies in Indian Jurisprudence." *Indonesian Journal of International & Comparative Law* 4(1): 91–124.

Joshi, Yuvraj. 2012. "Respectable Queerness." *Columbia Human Rights Law Review* 43(2): 415–67.

Kapur, Ratna. 2005. *Erotic Justice: Law and the New Politics of Postcolonialism.* London: GlassHouse.

———. 2010. "De-radicalising the Rights Claims of Sexual Subalterns through 'Tolerance.'" In *Queer Theory: Law, Culture, Empire,* edited by Robert Leckey and Kim Brooks, 37–52. New York: Routledge.

———. 2015. "Unruly Desires: Gay Governance and the Makeover of Sexuality in Postcolonial India." In *Global Justice and Desire: Queering Economy,* edited by Nikita Dhawan, Antke Engel, Christophe F. E. Holzhey, and Volker Woltersdorff, 115–32. London: Taylor & Francis.

———. 2016. "De-Criminalizing Queer Lives: Viewing Through a Postcolonial Feminist Optic." In *Routledge International Handbook of Criminology and Human Rights,* edited by Leanne Weber, Elaine Fishwick, and Marinella Marmo, 301–8. London: Routledge.

———. 2017. "The (Im)-Possibility of Queering International Human Rights Law." In *Queering International Law: Possibilities, Alliances, Complicities,* edited by Dianne Otto, 131–47. London: Routledge.

———. 2018. *Gender, Alterity and Human Rights: Freedom in a Fishbowl.* Cheltenham: Edward Elgar.

———. 2021. "On Violence, Revolution and the Self." *Postcolonial Studies* 24(2): 251–69.

Khan, Abeera. 2020. "Queer Secularity." *Lambda Nordica* 25(1): 133–39.

Kumari, Rashmi. 2019. "Menstruating Women and Celibate Gods: A Discourse Analysis of Women's Entry into Sabarimala Temple in Kerala, India." *Third World Thematics* 4(4–5): 288–305.

Langlois, Anthony. 2018. "Review Article: Curiosity, Paradox, and Dissatisfaction: Queer Analyses of Human Rights." *Millennium Journal of International Studies* 47(1): 153–65.

Ludden, David. 1993. "Orientalist Empiricism: Transformations of Colonial Knowledge." In *Orientalism and the Postcolonial Predicament: Perspectives on South Asia*, edited by Carol A. Breckenridge and Peter van der Veer, 250–78. Philadelphia: University of Pennsylvania Press.

MacKinnon, Catharine A. 1982. "Feminism, Marxism, Method, and the State: An Agenda for Theory." *Signs* 7(3): 515–44.

———. 1983. "Feminism, Marxism, Method, and the State: Toward Feminist Jurisprudence." *Signs* 8(4): 635–58.

———. 1984. "Reply to Miller, Acker and Barry, Johnson, West, and Gardiner." *Signs* 10(1): 184–88.

———. 1987. *Feminism Unmodified: Discourses of Life and Law*. Cambridge, MA: Harvard University Press.

Mahmood, Saba. 2004. *The Politics of Piety: Islamic Revival and the Feminist Subject*. Princeton, NJ: Princeton University Press.

Majeed, Javed. 1992. *Ungoverned Imaginings: James Mill's The History of British India and Orientalism*. Oxford: Oxford University Press.

Massad, Joseph. 2002. "Re-orienting Desire: The Gay International and the Arab World." *Public Culture* 10: 361–85.

McClintock, Anne. 1995. "Introduction: Postcolonialism and the Angel of Progress." In *Imperial Leather: Race, Gender, and Sexuality in the Colonial Contest*, 1–17. New York: Routledge.

McWhorter, Ladelle. 2003. "Foucault's Political Spirituality." *Philosophy Today* 47: 39–44.

Medina, José. 2012. *The Epistemology of Resistance: Gender and Racial Oppression, Epistemic Injustice and Resistant Imaginations*. Oxford: Oxford University Press.

Mehta, Uday Singh. 1999. *Liberalism and Empire: A Study in Nineteenth-Century British Liberal Thought*. Chicago: University of Chicago Press.

Menon, Madhavi. 2018a. *Infinite Variety: A History of Desire in India*. New Delhi: Speaking Tiger.

———. 2018b. "His God, Her's Too: Ayyappa Legends Showcase Him as Pro-Men, Not Anti-Women." *Indian Express*, October 30. https://indianexpress.com.

Mignolo, Walter. 2011. "Geopolitics of Sensing and Knowing: On (De)coloniality, Border Thinking and Epistemic Disobedience." *Postcolonial Studies* 14(3): 273–83.

Mishra, Samiratmaj. 2019. "Lesbian Marriage Raises Eyebrows in Indian Town." *Deutche Welle*, January 8. www.dw.com.

Moore-Gilbert, Bart. 1996. "Frantz Fanon: En-gendering Nationalist Discourses." *Women: A Cultural Review* 7(2): 125–35.

Muñoz, José Esteban. 1999. *Disidentifications: Queers of Color and the Performance of Politics*. Minneapolis: Minnesota University Press.

———. 2009. *Cruising Utopias: The Then and There of Queer Futurity*. New York: New York University Press.

Naik, Yeshwant. 2017. *Homosexuality in the Jurisprudence of the Supreme Court of India*. Cham: Springer International.

Najmabadi, Afsaneh. 2005. *Women with Mustaches and Men with Beards: Gender and Sexual Anxieties of Iranian Modernity*. Berkeley: University of California Press.

Nyanzi, Stella. 2014. "Queering Queer Africa." In *Reclaiming Afrikan: Queer Perspectives on Sexual and Gender Identities*, edited by Zethu Matebeni, 61–66. Athlone: Modaji Books.

Nyong'o, Tavia. 2018. *Afro-Fabulations: The Queer Drama of Black Life*. New York: New York University Press.

Otto, Dianne. 2015. "Queering Gender [Identity] in International Law." *Nordic Journal of Human Rights* 33: 299–318.

Pinto, Samantha. 2020. *Infamous Bodies: Early Black Women's Celebrity and the Afterlives of Rights*. Durham, NC: Duke University Press.

Puar, Jasbir K. 2007. *Terrorist Assemblages: Homonationalism in Queer Times*. Durham, NC: Duke University Press.

———. 2010. "To Be Gay and Racist Is No Anomaly." *Guardian*, June 2. www .theguardian.com.

Puri, Jyoti. 2016. *Sexual States: Governance and the Struggle over the Anti-sodomy Law in India*. Durham, NC: Duke University Press.

Rahman, Momin. 2010. "Queer as Intersectionality: Theorizing Gay Muslim Identities." *Sociology* 44(5): 944–61.

Ramberg, Lucinda. 2014. *Given to the Goddess: South Indian Devadasis and the Sexuality of Religion*. Durham, NC: Duke University Press.

Rao, Rahul. 2015. "Echoes of Imperialism in LGBT Activism." In *Echoes of Empire: Memory, Identity and Colonial Legacies*, edited by Kalypso A. Nicolaïdis, Berny Sèbe, and Gabrielle Maas, 353–70. London: I.B. Tauris.

———. 2020. *Out of Time: The Queer Politics of Postcoloniality*. New York: Oxford University Press.

Richardson, Diane. 2005. "Desiring Sameness? The Rise of a Neoliberal Politics of Normalisation." *Antipode* 37: 515–35.

Roy, Srila. 2015. "Affective Politics and the Sexual Subaltern: Lesbian Activism in Eastern India." In *New Subaltern Politics: Reconceptualizing Hegemony and Resistance in Contemporary India*, edited by Alf Gunvald Nilsen and Srila Roy, 149–73. New Delhi: Oxford University Press.

Ruti, Mari. 2017. *The Ethics of Opting Out: Queer Theory's Defiant Subjects*. New York: Columbia University Press.

Said, Edward. 1978. *Orientalism*. New York: Pantheon Books.

———. 1993. *Culture and Imperialism*. New York: Vintage Books.

Sedgwick, Eve Kosofsky. 1990. *Epistemology of the Closet.* Berkeley: University of California Press.

———. 2003. "Pedagogy of Buddhism." *Touching Feeling: Affect, Pedagogy, Performativity*, 153–81. Durham, NC: Duke University Press.

Sheikh, Danish. 2013. "The Road to Decriminalization: Litigating India's Anti-Sodomy Law." *Yale Human Rights and Development Law* 16: 104–32.

Sircar, Oishik. 2021. "A Deep and Ongoing Dive into the Brutal Humanism that Undergirds Liberal Humanism: An Interview with Jasbir Puar." *Humanity Journal* 11(3): 332–51.

Sircar, Oishik, and Dipika Jain. 2012. "New Intimacies, Old Desires: Law, Culture and Queer Politics in Neoliberal Times." *Jindal Global Law Review* 4(1): 1–16.

Spivak, Gayatri Chakravorty. 1993. "Can the Subaltern Speak?" In *Colonial Discourse and Post-Colonial Theory: A Reader*, edited by Patrick Williams and Laura Chrisman, 66–111. New York: Harvester Wheatsheaf.

Stychin, Carl. 1995. *Law's Desire: Sexuality and the Limits of Justice.* London: Routledge.

Subramanyam, Sughosh and Samal, Sanskruit. 2019. "Section 377: In Pursuit of Marriage Equality." *The Statesman*, March 7. www.thestatesman.com.

Tamale, Sylvia. 2014. "Exploring the Contours of African Sexualities: Religion, Law and Power." *African Human Rights Law Journal* 14: 150–77.

Turner, Ellen. 2014. "Indian Feminist Publishing and the Sexual Subaltern." *Rupkatha Journal of Interdisciplinary Studies in Humanities* 6(1): 131–41.

Valocchi, Stephen. 2005. "Not Yet Queer Enough: The Lessons of Queer Theory for the Sociology of Gender and Sexuality." *Gender & Society* 19(6): 750–70.

Vanita, Ruth. 2000. "Ayyappa and Vavar: Celibate Friends." In *Same-Sex Love in India: Readings from Literature and History*, edited by Saleem Kidwai and Ruth Vanita, 94–100. New York and Basingstoke: Palgrave.

———. 2002. *Queering India: Same-Sex Love and Eroticism in Indian Culture and Society*, edited by Ruth Vanita. New York; London: Routledge, Taylor & Francis.

Waites, Mathew. 2009. "Critique of 'Sexual Orientation' and 'Gender Identity' in Human Rights Discourse: Global Queer Politics Beyond the Yogyakarta Principles." *Contemporary Politics* 15: 137–56.

Walker, Kristen L. 2000. "Capitalism, Gay Identity and International Human Rights Law." *Australasian Gay and Lesbian Law Journal* 9: 58–73.

Warner, Michael. 2000. *The Trouble with Normal: Sex, Politics, and the Ethics of Queer Life.* Cambridge, MA: Harvard University Press.

Williams, Patricia. 1992. *The Alchemy of Race and Rights: Diary of a Law Professor.* Cambridge, MA: Harvard University Press.

The Yogyakarta Principles: Principles on the Application of International Human Rights Law in Relation to Sexual Orientation and Gender Identity. March 2007.

3

Contesting Colonial Criminalization

Customary Law's Significance for Decolonizing Queer Analysis

MATTHEW WAITES

The criminalization of same-sex sexual acts between consenting adults is an extensive form of oppression globally and a major critical concern for our times. Such criminalization applying to sexual acts between males, and less frequently also between females, continues in laws of 67 among the United Nations' 193 Member States (ILGA World 2020). These criminalizing states include thirty-five of the fifty-four states in the Commonwealth that emerged from the British Empire, suggesting that the British imperial legacy remains a significant factor in more than half of the countries where state criminalization persists (The Commonwealth Equality Network 2021; Lennox et al. 2021, 34–35). This chapter provides a discussion of how queer legal studies is contributing to, and might better contribute to, analysis of such criminalization and its contestation in light of decolonizing analyses. The original contribution is to address analysis of queer criminalization through attention to the neglected issue of customary law.

In international legal literatures customary law is a widely used and discussed concept. European colonialisms, imposing their own legal systems, formed a relationship with the legal systems of colonized peoples; and where such systems were recognized, customary law became a general concept in the English language used for description across many contexts. The concept of customary law has been widely adopted by colonized peoples (such as in Africa) seeking to re-assert their legal traditions in relation to states where colonial legal systems remain. Law literatures discuss customary law as a specific issue in the context of the wider discipline. Often legal scholars from the Global North who provide general accounts of customary law approach it with a tone of skepticism (Schauer 2007). Yet this approach differs markedly from that of recent law scholars in the Global South who integrate consideration of colonial power relations; for example, Sylvia Tamale, who discusses customary law in relation to legal pluralism and decolonial feminism (2020, 83–117).

The form of law known as customary law was generally recognized under British colonial governance, with an increasingly defined form from the early twentieth century, though with variation across time and territories. Most of the literature on customary law defines it as the law of particular peoples: for example, "a normative order observed by a population, having been formed by regular social behavior and the development of an accompanying sense of obligation" (Woodman 2012, 10). However, for critical analysis customary law is better conceived as discourse produced in the colonial encounter, through unequal and hierarchical exchanges between colonizers and colonized. Hence customary law is best thought of as a concept subtly different from indigenous law, where the latter is understood as the legal discourse of indigenous peoples. As will be demonstrated, customary law's place within colonial law and governance has been overlooked in international research literature on the criminalization of same-sex sexual acts, an omission that this chapter begins to investigate and address.

For queer legal studies, the starting point has to be an honest acknowledgment of how its configuration of academic research took form initially in Anglo-American contexts and that legal scholarship on sexualities and genders was slow to address Global South concerns, including colonial criminalization. With hindsight informed by postcolonial and decolonizing studies (e.g., Lugones 2008), it is explicable yet remarkable that gay liberation's foundational social histories of the regulation of homosexuality did not mention the British Empire's global criminalization of same-sex sexual acts prior to 2000 (Altman 1971; Weeks 1989). Yet it is also notable that the specifically queer legal studies initiated by scholars like Stychin focused on Western contexts (Stychin 1995), although he subsequently considered a wider global context problematizing Eurocentrism (Stychin 1998). A queer legal studies actively engaged with postcolonial studies began to emerge from the late 1990s (e.g., Spruill 2000), with scholars from formerly colonized contexts contesting the field (e.g., Kapur 2005); but sustained engagement with the criminalization of same-sex sexual acts in previously colonized states took longer. While there has been a rapid growth of research on criminalization in mainstream legal studies of homosexuality or sexual orientation (discussed below), there is much for queer legal studies to investigate in dialog with postcolonial and decolonial studies. This chapter seeks to make an innovative contribution through focusing on customary law.

Queer in the present context can be understood as a concept originating in the Anglophone West but actively taken up in preference against acronyms like "LGBT" (lesbian, gay, bisexual, and trans) by some Global South activists and scholars. Such usage of *queer* was notable, for example, in foundational documents of India's Voices Against 377 coalition that challenged criminalization of "Unnatural Offences" by Section 377 of the Indian Penal Code (Waites 2010). Such deployments have affirmed the flexibility and breadth of *queer* to encompass a variety of contextually specific identifications, such as kothi or hijra in Indian society. However, as the Queer Asia collective has argued, the concept may carry associations of privilege within activist or scholarly networks outside the West—for example in relation to class, caste, or racialization (Luther 2017; Luther and Ung Loh 2019). Hence the conception of a queer legal studies in this chapter is attentive to the potentially unfair privileging of queer studies within circuits of global knowledge-production. It is also important to note that the use of "same-sex sexual acts" rather than "same-gender sexual acts" as a conceptual framing is a methodological decision for exposition, corresponding to the focus of colonial legal statutes on bodily acts with an assumed sex dichotomy (such as "Indecent practices between males," discussed below); it certainly does not imply a normative, political, or analytical preference for sex over gender. The complex social negotiation of sex and gender remains.

From these starting points, the chapter will proceed in three main sections. The first section will provide an overview of the emergence of international literature addressing the criminalization of same-sex sexual activity, especially in relation to colonialisms. The next section turns to customary law, showing that this has been neglected in legal studies concerning criminalization of same-sex sexualities and gender-transgressive behaviors. The final main section then offers an original analysis of customary law in Kenya. A comparative analysis is undertaken, drawing on colonial surveys regarding customary law among different ethnic groups. It is argued that queer legal studies, suitably combined with insights from postcolonial and decolonizing studies, can contribute to better analysis of customary law and to revising global analyses of criminalization and decriminalization struggles. Thinking about customary law requires us to recognize when and where colonized peoples were *not* subject to colonial criminalizations, which in turn implies rethinking the meaning of decriminalization. Who is the subject of decriminalization?

Analyses of Colonial Criminalization in Queer Lives and Decriminalization Struggles

It was Indian queer activists and associated scholars such as Alok Gupta and Arvind Narrain who put the British Empire's criminal legacies on the global agenda for sexuality and gender politics, and for legal studies (Narrain and Bhan 2005; Narrain and Gupta 2011). A ground-breaking legal case was initiated by the Naz Foundation in 2001, seeking a "reading down" of the Indian Penal Code's Section 377 with respect to adult consensual sexual acts. The Naz Foundation commenced a new era of international contestations. The case came to be supported in court and externally by the Voices Against 377 coalition, a broad-based coalition of groups including sexual and gender minorities, and women's rights organizations (Waites 2010).

Gupta's report, *This Alien Legacy: The Origins of 'Sodomy' Laws in British Colonialism*, was published by Human Rights Watch with contributions from Scott Long and definitively put British colonial criminalization of same-sex sexual acts on the global agenda for critical analysis (Human Rights Watch 2008). The substantial and rigorous research producing *This Alien Legacy* originated from an NGO rather than an academic source, and the innovative work reflected the insight of Gupta and Long that an anticolonial framing could be valuable in supporting human rights claims and LGBT or queer movements. As various actors internationally began to make interventions from 2001, it was *This Alien Legacy* that emerged as the key synthetic text combining legal detail on criminalization with anticolonial analysis. *This Alien Legacy* differed from mainstream approaches to colonial sodomy laws, notably that of

Justice Michael Kirby from Australia, who lobbied the Commonwealth on LGBT human rights (for example, in the Commonwealth Eminent Persons Group, 2009–2011). Kirby's early publications advocated interventions in Commonwealth states using the same conceptual basis as the UK Wolfenden Report of 1957 (Committee on Homosexual Offences and Prostitution 1957; Kirby 2008). Kirby suggested that formerly colonized states learn from the British model of decriminalization; a model that focused on the public/private distinction without engaging postcolonial analysis (cf. Waites 2013).

The volume *Human Rights Sexual Orientation and Gender Identity in the Commonwealth: Struggles for Decriminalisation and Change*, co-edited by Lennox and Waites (2013a) represented the different approaches of Kirby and Gupta in distinct chapters, but drew especially on *This Alien Legacy*'s emphasis on strategies that addressed colonial contexts. In addition to data analysis of laws across all Commonwealth states, the volume detailed regulation and resistance struggles in sixteen states, while offering a comparative analysis of strategies adopted by movements (Lennox and Waites 2013b). This work has been updated in subsequent publications to document recent decriminalizations and contestations in Commonwealth states; for example, decriminalizations in India during 2018 and Botswana from 2019 (Lennox et al. 2021; Waites 2019a). While the British Empire criminalized same-sex acts most extensively, other European empires such as the Portuguese also criminalized such acts. Further analyses intriguingly suggest a tendency to decriminalization in states such as Mozambique (2015) and Angola (2019) (Gomes da Costa Santos and Waites 2019; Tabengwa and Waites 2019). Growing literatures center the transnational politics of LGBT rights and homophobia (e.g., Bosia and Weiss 2013; Farmer 2020), many with a particular focus on decriminalization contestations (Castéra and Tognon 2020; Gerber and Lindner 2021; Han and O'Mahoney 2018; Novak 2020; Waites 2019b).

While many analyses of colonial criminalization have focused on same-sex sexual acts, criminalization also occurred in relation to genders outside the colonial gender binary. Guyana criminalized certain gendered acts as "cross-dressing" until 2018, as Deroy and Baynes Henry (2018) discussed in an important contribution. Hijra people in India were subject to forms of colonial legal regulation that may be interpreted as criminalization in a broad sense. The main focus of the present chapter is on the criminalization of same-sex sexual acts, given the extensive existence of such laws and in order to challenge current analyses. However, implications for gendered regulations should also be kept in mind, especially with reference to Lugones's argument concerning "the coloniality of gender"—whereby European colonialisms exported a gender system of biological sex dimorphism associated with heterosexuality (Lugones 2008).

To frame an issue of legal regulation in terms of criminalization and decriminalization potentially raises some analytical challenges. From the perspective of critical legal studies, law may be considered only one of the social practices defining crime in societies. For example, advocates of replacing a focus on "crime" in criminology with a focus on "social harm" argue that social harm may be defined by criteria other than law, such as normative conceptions of human rights (Hillyard and Tombs 2007). Hence, to limit the definition of crime to within the scope of law would restrict parameters of inquiry. However, this chapter's purpose is to further investigate the forms of different types of law. Therefore, while the definition of crime and its relation to law are contested, for the specific purpose of this chapter criminalization refers to processes of law that prohibit, restrict, or impede actions that are understood as crimes because they are believed to involve a particular kind of public wrong that requires punishment (cf. Lacey 2020, 307–309). This conception of criminalization facilitates a focus on an under-researched critical issue in the criminalization and decriminalization literatures, highly relevant for decolonizing analyses: the issue of customary law.

The Absence of Customary Law in Analyses of Queer Criminalization

Customary law is a remarkable absence in almost all of the academic literature and political debates on colonial criminalization of same-sex sexual acts. Once noticed, this absence is so glaring that it seems to need explanation not only by the general neglect of customary law in legal studies but also by the discursive formations and ideological investments of actors producing research and knowledge claims—whether invested in decriminalizing by extending international human rights into states or by decolonizing—as surveyed in the following review. It is therefore necessary to document where and how attention to customary law has been omitted in existing literatures, before examining examples of primary sources on customary law. This process may enable methodological and theoretical adjustments for future queer legal studies to address criminalization through engagement with decolonizing perspectives.

* * *

Following the scramble for Africa, including the Berlin conference of 1884–1885 that assigned territories among European powers, customary law emerged as a central feature of British governance and criminal justice. Customary law was conceived in the British Empire as representing the traditional forms of collective legal practice among colonized peoples. The emergence of distinct legal practices was closely related to the conception of "indirect rule," the theory of which was promulgated by Frederick Lugard, High Commissioner of the Protectorate of Northern Nigeria at the beginning of the twentieth century (although some practices of indirect rule predate such conceptualization; Ikime 1968). The colonial legal system imposed divisions between higher level courts and so-called Native Tribunals where customary law was the central framework, although Native Tribunals were typically administered with imperial officials, and were thus characterized in a broad sense by "hybridity" (Bhabha 1994). Foucault's conception of "governmentality" is helpful for describing various colonial practices used to influence the conduct of subjects, including law (as previously advocated; Waites 2013, 170–75). British colonialism developed a mode of governmentality that institutionalized different practices of regulation for those colonizing and for the colonized.

One rare example of literature on decriminalization where the customary law issue has been broached is Scott Long's appendix in the Human Rights Watch (2003) report *More than a Name: State-Sponsored Homophobia and its Consequences in Southern Africa*, discussing South Africa, Namibia, Zimbabwe, Botswana, and Zambia. Following substantial discussion of the criminalizing effects of colonial laws, Long turns to customary law only in the final section, "The Realm of the Customary." Long rightly points out that customary law under colonialism "was contingent on white supervision, revision and veto," yet is rather dismissive, characterizing it as "less a system of law than a playbook for a spectator sport" (Human Rights Watch 2003, 291). Such characterization tends to downplay the real practice and implications of customary law. For Long, "The fact that custom in all African societies was complex, sometimes contradictory and almost always unwritten gave whites the privilege of writing it" (Human Rights Watch 2003, 291). Such overstatement loses sight of the ways some indigenous practices found representation in customary law for areas of communal affairs relatively ungoverned by the British. Long argued that customary law was concerned with assigning property in relation to marriage and kinship; yet colonial influences reshaped conceptions of marriage so "any residual place for sexual or gender nonconformity which customary practice might once have accorded was inevitably, in the new enactments, expunged" (Human Rights Watch 2003, 292). Long cites only one example of contemporary customary law addressing same-sex acts, via a newspaper report from Botswana. The report is of punishments of same-sex offenses with "lashes" and jail terms, yet without historical evidence Long implies that such attitudes from customary courts reflect homophobia. This provisional discussion suggests a need for further investigation.

Turning to consider more recent literature that has opened international debate over colonial criminalization of same-sex sexual acts, it is evident that attention to customary law is almost entirely lacking. The agenda-setting report *This Alien Legacy* from Human Rights Watch (2008) is a problematic text in this respect (Gomes da Costa Santos and Waites 2019, 312–13); and it seems to forget rather than pursue Long's earlier discussion. The report initiated a discourse that has since become internationally popularized, emphasizing a critical perspective on British colonial criminalization together with a strong argument that the colonial law was directed at all colonized peoples.

> Colonial legislators and jurists introduced such laws [Section 377 of the Indian Penal Code and similar], with no debates or "cultural consultations," to support colonial control. They believed laws could inculcate European morality into resistant masses. They brought in the legislation, in fact, because they thought "native" cultures did not punish "perverse" sex enough. The colonized needed compulsory re-education in sexual mores.

Imperial rulers held that, as long as they sweltered through the promiscuous proximities of settler societies, "native" viciousness and "white" virtue
had to be segregated: the latter praised and protected, the former policed
and kept subjected. (Human Rights Watch 2008, 5)

The report is explicit in claiming that Section 377 and similar laws were
devised to encompass both colonizers and colonized: "It was a colonial
attempt to set standards of behavior, both to reform the colonized and
to protect the colonizers against moral lapses" (Human Rights Watch
2008, 5).

Customary law is missing from this narrative; indirect rule is not considered. The text notably invokes "fact," and its publication by a human
rights organization would lead many audiences to assume its veracity. A
more realistic interpretation, however, is that the authors' anticolonial orientation seems to have led them to infer assumptions about the intentions
of colonial governance based on data from penal codes. Instead, there is
a need to hold open questions about the intentions of colonial authorities
and the scope of application of penal codes in relation to customary law.
Yet *This Alien Legacy* does not discuss customary law at all—it is mentioned only once (Human Rights Watch 2008, 25)—and does not consider
that its scope might delimit the relevance of colonial laws.

Undoubtedly, colonial authorities sought to regulate some sexuality
and gender practices; yet historical literatures show resistances, such as
fierce opposition to clitoridectomy prohibitions in Kenya frustrating intervention (Hyam 1990). Regarding same-sex sexual acts, a key dynamic
was the replication of English law on buggery in the colonies, as when
Macauley drafted the Indian Penal Code of 1860 to include Section 377.
Yet it is important to inquire if laws on same-sex sexual acts were intended to regulate colonizing populations, or the colonized, or both.
These complexities were not explored in *This Alien Legacy*.

The mainstream legal literature on decriminalization of homosexuality and LGBT human rights also fails to address customary law. Hence
the publications of Justice Michael Kirby proceed with a straightforward
narrative describing colonial criminalization across colonized territories,
taking this as requiring to be mirrored by decriminalization also applying
to all populations, without attention to the relatively obvious legal fact
of customary law that challenges the premise (e.g., Kirby 2008). Novak's

survey of recent legal rulings on decriminalization acknowledges that "most African subjects fell under the jurisdiction of a separate customary law system," yet he offers no further comment on the implications for conceptualizing the scope of criminalization, or his support of transnational human rights litigation and a "Commonwealth human rights strategy" (Novak 2020, 119). As such Novak's work embodies the problematic mainstream legal studies in which positive emphasis on global legal connections emerges partly through analytical neglect of customary law. Similarly, customary law is absent from indexes of the three-volume collection *Worldwide Perspectives on Lesbians, Gays and Bisexuals*, edited by a specialist on legal regulation in the Commonwealth (Gerber 2021a, 2021b, 2021c; Gerber and Lindner 2021). In sum, mainstream Western legal scholarship has omitted discussion of customary law due to some combination of unconscious or conscious bias and ignorance.

The absence of customary law is also clear in the global survey *State-Sponsored Homophobia*, published annually by the International Lesbian, Gay, Bisexual, Trans and Intersex Association (ILGA World 2020)—a foundational source for much research on criminalization (Human Rights Watch 2008; Lennox and Waites 2013a). The report's methodology takes states as the focus for defining law, with the effect of privileging law at the country level while implicitly lacking appreciation of legal pluralist perspectives that can acknowledge subnational systems. The report comments:

> When it concerns criminalisation, the main sources that we look at to ascertain whether the country indeed decriminalised are the criminal codes. For that reason we do not systematically cover other types of regulations that might be used to criminalise same-sex sexual activity. (ILGA World 2020, 15)

However, the report does mention a few specific incidents related to customary law such as in Peru and El Salvador "when it has come to our attention" (ILGA World 2020, 15). The section "Gaps and transitions from colonial laws" acknowledges that in locations like the French colonies, "a dual regime was identified, with an asymmetry between the law applied to natives and to those considered French citizens" (ILGA World 2020, 16). However: "In view of this and considering the difficulty of ascertaining when and how the law applied to natives because of the legal uncertainty associated with it, we decided to indicate as the date of decriminalisation the year in which French laws became valid, although noting reservations" (ILGA World 2020, 16). Hence the most globally influential survey of legal discrimination in relation to sexual orientation has been ignoring customary law over many years; even in the most recent version, its methodology systematically privileges European forms of criminal law. Rare references to specific cases do not shift the overall conceptual framework defining criminalization.

Meanwhile recent postcolonial and decolonial queer research is focused on past and present contexts and struggles, examining colonial histories and enduring colonialities. However, decolonizing sexualities research (Bakshi et al. 2016) has not yet yielded legal history studies of the regulation of same-sex sexual acts or gender beyond the binary with due attention to customary law. The focus of many decolonial sexualities researchers tends to be on critiquing colonial regulation or highlighting positive aspects of precolonial societies, with perhaps insufficient investigation of possible forms of precolonial regulation.

A queer legal theoretic approach to customary law could be especially generative, given queer theory's exploratory methodologies, its attention to sexuality and gender experiences outside social norms, and its willingness to break with rigid orthodoxies of both Eurocentric and decolonial approaches. The way forward surely includes attending to examples of how customary laws regulated sexuality and gender in particular contexts. The next section turns to examples from Kenya. Recent Kenyan legal scholarship on non-heterosexual sexuality, in accordance with decolonizing sexualities scholarship, has emphasized that "there were no laws criminalizing homosexual conduct between consenting adults in private before colonialism" because "such conduct was not [...] deemed worthy of formal legal sanction" (Wekesa 2017, 80); yet the following historical research offers evidence to the contrary.

Customary Law and the Regulation of Sexuality and Gender in Kenya

For a methodology to investigate customary law, analysis of colonial reports documenting such law in a particular colonial territory was selected. Kenya was chosen as an important territory in Africa, of regional significance and influence politically; this selection was made initially in the context of a comparative study in relation to Mozambique, since published (Gomes da Costa Santos and Waites 2019). The Kenya case has some obvious advantages for a study of customary law: Kenya includes a large number of different ethnic groups, suggesting the potential to compare interesting differences among populations. Kenya is a relatively large African state in terms of population.

Colonial reports on customary law for specific ethnic groups were selected as a form of primary source for data collection and analysis, especially in light of the lack of attention to these reports in existing legal research on colonial regulation of same-sex sexualities and genders. Such reports typically were produced by an individual with legal expertise appointed by British colonial authorities, who engaged in dialog with leaders of a specific ethnic group to ascertain practices—typically via one or more translators. The reports thus present systematic, structured accounts of customary law, produced with the objective of accurately documenting the understandings of societal leaders.

A substantial search of London libraries was used to identify relevant reports. The search began in the British Library, using guides to official publications for Kenya to identify relevant texts on customary law (Howell 1978; Thurston 1991). Searches then extended to identify reports in the Institute of Advanced Legal Studies library and the British Library of Political and Economic Science, also through checking the library catalog of SOAS (formerly School of Oriental and African Studies). Several relevant reports for specific peoples were found in print form, all reported here. Using a thematic analysis, each was systematically searched for relevant sections specifying any customary law that related to same-sex sexual acts or gender beyond the colonial gender binary.

Colonial reports on customary law have some obvious methodological disadvantages when considered in relation to decolonial politics and decolonizing methodologies (Smith 2012). Most obviously, such reports are colonial texts, written by the colonizers. Where reporting voices of the colonized, they did so largely through translation with the assistance of interpreters, with consequent scope for inaccuracies or mistakes. Reporting practices usually did not involve precise use of quotation within quotation marks; what is reportedly said was typically expressed within the narrative of the report author. Yet on closer consideration, and in light of the difficulties with other conceivable methods, the customary law reports also have some key advantages. In African contexts where oral traditions were important and written texts scarce, they provide a written record of law from the past that attempts to be synthetic. Most important, the overall objective of those producing the reports was to document as accurately as possible the beliefs and practices defining law and crime among colonized peoples, though this aim might have varied in relation to specific sensitive topics. From reading these documents, it seems clear that they were produced through systematic processes, with precise attention to detail. In contrast to many other kinds of text, there was an aspiration to objectivity which—although objectivity could not be achieved—makes the findings documented a unique and significant record, even while the uses of the information through colonial governance were highly problematic. Thus, the reports merit attention from postcolonial or decolonial scholars wishing to find out about precolonial practices defining criminality, even while other research methodologies such as oral history could clearly also contribute. As will be shown, it would be too simple to think that no colonial legal texts could provide valuable sources evidencing discourses of the colonized.

A useful introduction to Kenya's customary law is provided in works by Eugene Cotran, a UK judge and legal scholar who became a High Court Judge in Kenya in the late 1970s. Leading up to independence in 1963, Cotran was commissioned by the Colony of Kenya's authorities during 1961–62 to research and record "customary criminal offences." He produced an overall *Report on Customary Criminal Offences in Kenya* (1963a), and also published an article discussing customary law in different ethnic groups within Kenya, noting for example the existence of "woman-to-woman marriage" (1963b). In a later article, Cotran provides a particularly helpful overview of legal institutions and the developing relationships between so-called native courts implementing customary law, and the higher courts implementing English law in a "typically dual" system (1983, 42).

Most important, Cotran notes that the East Africa Order in Council of 1897 stated that new statutes would apply in a circumscribed context:

> Provided always that the said common law doctrines of equity and the statutes of general application shall be in force in the colony so far only as

the circumstances of the colony and its inhabitants permit and subject to such qualifications as local circumstances render necessary. (East Africa Order in Council 1897, quoted in Cotran 1983, 42)

A Native Tribunals Ordinance had specified in section 13a that "Native Tribunals" formed by a Council of Elders (but supervised by colonial administrative officials) were to implement "the native law and custom prevailing in the area," "so far as it is not repugnant to justice or morality" or inconsistent with other laws (Article 4(2), Kenya Colony Order in Council 1921, quoted in Cotran 1983, 43). Hence customary law could be overruled, effectively defined as inferior. However, customary law nevertheless had a defined legal status and scope applying to many practices of the colonized peoples.

Cotran outlines how the Indian Penal Code initially was applied to Kenya from 1897 and in 1930 was replaced by the Kenyan Penal Code (1983). These specified offenses applied in the main courts, above the so-called native courts. The Kenyan Penal Code included—and still includes—Section 162 prohibiting "Unnatural Offences," Section 163, "Attempt to commit unnatural offences," and Section 165, "Indecent practices between males," which together prohibit all sexual activity between males and some between females. The clear context of colonial criminalization thus forms the context for the comparative discussion of customary law. Previous analysis of how Sections 162, 163, and 165 were prosecuted in the higher courts, examining statistics from colonial "Blue Books" reporting data to the British government, has found that from 1901 to 1946, only nine convictions were recorded; and occasional instances of racialized reporting show prosecutions focused on "European" (white) and "Asiatic" (coastal) populations, but not "Natives" (indigenous groups) (Gomes da Costa Santos and Waites 2019, 315). This evidence suggests very little prosecution of indigenous people for "Unnatural Offences" under the Penal Code in the main courts.

With a broader understanding of the overall legal framework, higher court practices and how customary law was institutionalized, it is then possible to examine specific reports representing customary law for particular ethnic groups. Some of the data that follow have previously been presented (Gomes da Costa Santos and Waites 2019), but the discussion here allows for an improved methodological reflection and comparative analysis. Moreover, this is the first occasion for a focus centrally on customary law. Three reports on customary law in specific ethnic groups are examined, all produced after World War II; the analysis then turns to a comparison with wider commentaries on the law across Kenya.

In 1951, Penwill produced a study of Kamba customary law, published in a series "Custom and Tradition in East Africa" (1951). Penwill states the study relates to the Ulu Kamba and "does not necessarily apply to the Kamba of Kitui" (vii). Regarding methods, "its basis is the records of appeals heard by District Officers [. . .] and the case files of the Native Appeal Tribunal over the last two years"; the "material was discussed and put into a logical form with two senior elders" and also discussed with "all the Presidents of the ten tribunals" (vii). Chapter 7 covers "Adultery, Fornication and Unnatural Behaviour," including a section "Unnatural Behaviour" which states:

> If a man commits an unnatural offence with a young boy he must pay over a goat and a bull. If two men commit the offence together, each must pay a goat. Such cases are rare among the Kamba. [. . .] Such cases should now be charged under Section 155 of the Penal Code, but they are normally settled quietly in the locations without ever coming to the Courts. (Penwill 1951, 76)

Mention of Section 155 here seems to be a mistake by Penwill, since 165 would be the relevant section addressing "Indecent practices between males" (and 155 addresses "Premises used for prostitution"). The text is accompanied by comment on sexual crimes involving animals and it is also noted that: "The Kamba regard it as unnatural to have coition with a woman from behind. If a man does this, even with his wife, he must slaughter a goat for purification. By this act he has levelled himself with the animals." The framing of the discussion perhaps suggests a European line of questioning about sodomy as related to animal behavior, and possibly a Eurocentric interpretation of responses.

Second, a study of Nandi customary law was published by Snell a few years later (1954). In relation to research methods Snell stated that they had received "ready co-operation" of chiefs and elders (vii). The report covered "Unnatural Offences," stating:

> An offender caught in the act could be killed [. . .] Otherwise he would be beaten by members of his age-grade, or in a serious case would be cursed by the kokwet elders and held in social ridicule. (Snell 1954, 33)

In this case there seem to be a wide range of possible punishments, which might beg questions about whether different conceptions of crimes would exist in relation to the ages of participants and their partners; a homogenization might be occurring through the translation process in relation to the European category of "Unnatural Offences."

Third, a study of the Luo people's customary law by Wilson was published shortly before Kenya's independence (1961). The Luo are described as 12 Nilotic tribes in central Nyanza. Part II of the report is titled "Marriage Law and Customs" and within this there is a section ominously titled "Failure of the Union" in which there is comment related to same-sex sexual acts:

> Acts which traditionally carried the sanction of banishment enforced by the elders were: incest, sodomy, bestiality, homosexuality, premeditated murder, continual troublemaking, . . . witchcraft. (Wilson 1961, paragraph 176)

In this instance it is clear that Wilson's narrative uses the Anglophone western concepts of "homosexuality" and "sodomy" to translate information about crimes relating to same-sex sexual acts. In this report, information on research methods is limited and there is no further information about concepts used in African languages prior to translation.

Recent African sociolegal research can help us understand the problematic process of translation involved in producing these three reports. Alan Msosa's doctoral thesis has explained that in contemporary Malawi, references to homosexuality in the English language are often translated as relating to local linguistic terms that relate to sexual acts between older men and young men or boys (2018). Language differences and consequent mistranslations thus have a somewhat similar effect to when people in the West have equated homosexuality with pedophilia, leading to negative responses. Therefore, it would not be possible to fully understand customary law in the Kenyan examples without further research and understanding of the local linguistic and cultural systems.

Nevertheless, the English language summaries in the reports do provide some useful evidence about understandings.

Comparing the data on customary law for the Kamba, the Nandi, and the Luo, it seems that punishments varied very significantly between ethnic groups. Punishments ranged from being killed at the most extreme for the Nandi, to banishment for the Luo, to Kamba's lesser sanction of the payment of a goat for sex between two adult males. This is a substantial disparity in approaches and suggests the need to attend to varying practices of different ethnic groups in this respect. It can also be noted, for example, that only men and boys (with male pronouns) are mentioned for the Kamba and the Nandi; and in relation to the Luo the mention of sodomy also implies a male actor; whereas there is no reference to sexual acts between females being criminalized.

The analysis here has reported the data for each of the reports surveying customary law for a specific ethnic group that it was possible to find from a search of London libraries mentioned. Overall, it is striking that the data for each of the ethnic groups where reports on customary law could be found show a form of criminalization of same-sex sexual acts between males, outside colonial regulation. These findings require questioning the prevailing narrative in much current literature that the criminalization of same-sex sexual acts arrived with British colonialism. For example, *This Alien Legacy* asserted that: "Sodomy laws throughout Asia and sub-Saharan Africa have consistently been colonial impositions" (Human Rights Watch 2008, 10), tending to imply that there were no similar laws previously. Scott Long's appendix in the earlier Human Rights Watch report *More than a Name* was unambiguous in asserting that criminal laws on same-sex sexual behavior did not exist prior to colonialism:

> There is no reason to suppose that white colonists brought same-sex sexual behaviour to Africa for the first time. What they did bring, though, was the criminal categorization of that behavior. The acts were indigenous. The name and crime were imported. (Human Rights Watch 2003, 256)

By contrast, the findings here suggest there may have been some similar laws in certain ethnic groups. Of course, further investigation is needed in Kenya and additional colonized contexts; but a preliminary analysis from examining the case of Kenya is that prevailing international narratives of the colonial criminalization of same-sex sexual acts in existing literatures need to be reconsidered, to attend to the mediating effects of customary law.

Wider colonial reviews of law across Kenya were also examined and compared to the reports about specific ethnic groups, but the wider reviews make no mention of offenses specific to same-sex sexual acts in customary law. A report relating to customary law across Kenya by Phillips (1945), *Report on Native Tribunals*, omitted any mention of crimes relating to same-sex sexual acts, or gender diversity. In the wider discussion of "Sexual Cases," there is discussion of the law of marriage, including multiple offenses for adultery (1945, 266, paragraphs 795–98). The general comment is made that "Sexual cases originating in a native reserve, and in which all parties concerned are of the same tribe, would often, I think, be more suitably dealt with by a native court than by a European judge or magistrate" (266).

Cotran's 1963 report on customary law across Kenya also differs from the discussed reports on specific ethnic groups. Cotran's report (1963a) specified a "method of investigation" involving a review of "all written materials on customary law" including unpublished material, together with some observation at courts (2). The report outlines various criminal offenses related to sexuality—such as for adultery with a married woman or circumcision without parental consent—yet noticeably omits any reference to offenses covering same-sex sexual acts. This omission is interesting since Cotran's stated method should have involved reading the previously discussed reports on specific groups. Cotran is now deceased and it is not possible to know the reason for the omission. One possibility is that references to same-sex acts could have been omitted due to British moral attitudes, but it seems more likely to have been due to the perceived unimportance of these acts for the report. The omission might suggest that customary law for other ethnic groups beyond the Kamba, Nandi, and Luo may not have mentioned same-sex sexual acts.

The omission of reference to crimes concerning same-sex sexual acts in reports across Kenya by both Phillips (1945) and Cotran (1963a) thus might suggest disregard for the issue or possibly a decision to leave it invisible in 1963. The neglect of attention to customary law on same-sex sexual acts in these colonial overviews is echoed in contemporary neglect of such aspects of customary law from prevailing activist, intel-lectual, and academic voices in the contemporary international move-ment for LGBT human rights and equality, and some queer decolonizing movements.

Conclusion

This chapter has argued that a queer legal studies engaged with post-colonial and decolonial studies has much potential to rethink analysis of colonial criminalizations of same-sex sexual acts and criminalization of transgressive gender practices. It has been demonstrated that con-temporary international literatures addressing such criminalizations and resistant decriminalization struggles have neglected the issue of customary law. Revealing the neglect of customary law in narratives of colonial criminalization poses important questions about how to revise narratives of decriminalization.

The research presented here has some clear implications for future studies. The rich data from colonial reports on customary law suggest that these are valuable potential sources for future studies. The reports shed light on the historical situation rather than relying on contempo-rary manifestations of customary law. Hence the investigation suggests a research agenda for exploring colonial reports on customary law in different countries, in the British Empire context, and perhaps in other empires.

Findings from Kenya clearly demonstrate that customary law held a defined legal status within the colonial legal system and that for several ethnic groups—though not others—there is evidence of specific laws applying to same-sex sexual acts. This demonstrates that we should not speak of colonial criminal codes determining criminalization across all populations. Rather it is demonstrated that colonial criminal codes were only applied to the colonized in specific contexts, especially where en-gaging in sexual acts with a member of the colonizing population (as suggested in Aldrich's research in territories such as Papua New Guinea: Aldrich 2003).

The findings clearly show criminalization of sexual acts between males for several ethnic groups, though there are no such examples for sexual acts between females. Whether criminalization of males related to only specific sexual acts such as anal intercourse is difficult to judge given problems of translation and interpretation. However, the evidence challenges narratives in international literatures that portray criminalization only arriving with colonialism.

Furthermore, if findings from Kenya are used to reflect back on international literatures concerning criminalization of same-sex acts, this points to a need for critical reappraisal and rethinking in queer legal studies and more widely. Since the Human Rights Watch (2008) report *This Alien Legacy*, the prevailing analysis informing international sexual politics has been of an emphasis on pervasive colonial criminalization by the British Empire. By contrast, the analysis here suggests a need to problematize how LGBT and queer actors in activism and research, from both North and South, have constructed and adhered to a discourse of comprehensive colonial criminalization that has systematically downplayed the existence of customary law. Therefore, a clear implication of taking seriously decolonial analyses must be to take customary law seriously. The extent of colonial statutory criminalization has been overstated, and there is an urgent need for researchers to investigate the current status and forms of customary law across many contexts.

NOTE

An early version of this chapter was presented at the conference Anti-69: Against the Mythologies of the 1969 Criminal Code Reform, organized by Gary Kinsman and colleagues, March 23–24, 2019 at Carleton University in Ottawa, Canada (https://anti-69 .ca/). Thanks to everyone who engaged with the paper there.

BIBLIOGRAPHY

Aldrich, Robert. 2003. *Colonialism and Homosexuality*. Abingdon: Routledge.
Altman, Dennis. 1971. *Homosexual: Oppression and Liberation*. New York: Outerbridge & Dienstfrey.
Bakshi, Sandeep, Suhraiya Jivraj, and Silvia Posocco (eds.). 2016. *Decolonizing Sexualities: Transnational Perspectives, Critical Interventions*. Oxford: Counterpress.
Bhabha, Homi K. 1994. *The Location of Culture*. London: Routledge.
Bosia, Michael J. and Meredith L. Weiss. 2013. "Political Homophobia in Comparative Perspective." In *Global Homophobia*, edited by Meredith L. Weiss and Michael J. Bosia, 1–29. Urbana: University of Illinois Press.
Castéra, Grégory and Giulia Tognon. 2020. "The Past and Present of Against Nature Laws." *The Against Nature Journal* 1: 126–28.

Committee on Homosexual Offences and Prostitution, Home Office and Scottish Home Department. 1957. *Report of the Committee of Homosexual Offences and Prostitution.* Cmnd 247. London: HMSO.

Cotran, Eugene. 1963a. *Report on Customary Criminal Offences in Kenya.* Nairobi: Kenya Government Printer.

———. 1963b. "The Unification of Laws in East Africa." *Journal of Modern African Studies* 1(2): 209–20.

———. 1983. "The Development and Reform of the Law in Kenya." *Journal of African Law* 27(1): 42–61.

Deroy, Pere and Namela Baynes Henry. 2018. "Violence and LGBT Human Rights in Guyana." In *Envisioning Global LGBT Human Rights: (Neo)colonialism, Neoliberalism, Resistance and Hope*, edited by Nancy Nicol, Adrian Jjuuko, Richard Lusimbo, Nick Mulé, Susan Ursel, Amar Wahab, and Phyllis Waugh, 157–75. London: School of Advanced Study.

Farmer, Matthew. 2020. *Transnational LGBT Activism and UK-Based NGOs: Colonialism and Power.* Cham: Palgrave Macmillan.

Gerber, Paula (ed.). 2021a. *Worldwide Perspectives on Lesbians, Gays and Bisexuals. Volume 1: Culture and History.* Santa Barbara, CA: Praeger Press.

———. 2021b. *Worldwide Perspectives on Lesbians, Gays and Bisexuals. Volume 2: Law.* Santa Barbara, CA: Praeger Press.

———. 2021c. *Worldwide Perspectives on Lesbians, Gays and Bisexuals. Volume 3: The Global Picture.* Santa Barbara, CA: Praeger Press.

Gerber, Paula and Phoebe Irving Lindner. 2021. "Pathways to Decriminalizing Homosexual Conduct." In *Worldwide Perspectives on Lesbians, Gays and Bisexuals. Volume 2: Law*, edited by Paula Gerber, 94–142. Santa Barbara, CA: Praeger Press.

Gomes da Costa Santos, Gustavo and Matthew Waites. 2019. "Comparative Colonialisms for Queer Analysis: Comparing British and Portuguese Colonial Legacies for Same-Sex Sexualities and Gender Diversity in Africa—Setting a Transnational Research Agenda." *International Review of Sociology: Revue Internationale de Sociologie* 29(2): 297–326.

Han, Enze and Joseph O'Mahoney. 2018. *British Colonialism and the Criminalization of Homosexuality: Queens, Crime and Empire.* London: Routledge.

Hillyard, Paddy and Steve Tombs. 2007. "From 'Crime' to Social Harm?" *Crime, Law and Social Change* 48: 9–25.

Howell, John Bruce. 1978. *Kenya Subject Guide to Official Publications.* Washington, DC: US Library of Congress.

Human Rights Watch. 2003. *More than a Name: State-Sponsored Homophobia and Its Consequences in Southern Africa.* New York: Human Rights Watch. www.hrw.org.

———. 2008. *This Alien Legacy: The Origins of "Sodomy" Laws in British Colonialism.* New York: Human Rights Watch. www.hrw.org.

Hyam, Ronald. 1990. *Empire and Sexuality: The British Experience.* Manchester: Manchester University Press.

Ikime, Obaro. 1968. "Reconsidering Indirect Rule: The Nigerian Example." *Journal of the Historical Society of Nigeria* 4(3): 421–38.

ILGA World: Lucas Ramon Mendos, Kellyn Botha, Rafael Carrano Lelis, Enrique López de la Peña, Ilia Savelev, and Daron Tan. 2020. *State-Sponsored Homophobia 2020: Global Legislation Overview Update*. Geneva: ILGA. https://ilga.org.

Kapur, Ratna. 2005. *Erotic Justice: Postcolonialism, Subjects and Rights*. London: Glass House Press.

Kirby, Michael. 2008. "Lessons from the Wolfenden Report." *Commonwealth Law Bulletin* 34(3): 551–59.

Lacey, Nicola. 2020. "Approaching or Re-thinking the Realm of Criminal Law?" *Criminal Law and Philosophy* 14(3): 307–18.

Lennox, Corinne and Matthew Waites (eds.). 2013a. *Human Rights, Sexual Orientation and Gender Identity in the Commonwealth: Struggles for Decriminalisation and Change*. London: School of Advanced Study.

———. 2013b. "Conclusion. Comparative Analysis of Decriminalisation and Change Across the Commonwealth: Understanding Contexts and Discerning Strategies." In *Human Rights, Sexual Orientation and Gender Identity in the Commonwealth: Struggles for Decriminalisation and Change*, edited by Corinne Lennox and Matthew Waites, 507–47. London: School of Advanced Study.

Lennox, Corinne, Monica Tabengwa, and Matthew Waites. 2021. "Contesting Lesbian, Gay and Bisexual Human Rights in the Commonwealth." In *Worldwide Perspectives on Lesbians, Gays and Bisexuals. Volume 3: The Global Picture*, edited by Paula Gerber, 31–54. Santa Barbara, CA: Praeger Press.

Lugones, Maria. 2008. "The Coloniality of Gender." *Worlds and Knowledges Otherwise.* (Spring): 1–17.

Luther, J. Daniel. 2017. "Queer Theory." *The Year's Work in Critical and Cultural Theory* 25(1): 231–51.

Luther, J. Daniel and Jennifer Ung Loh. 2019. "Introduction." In *'Queer' Asia: Decolonising and Reimagining Sexuality and Gender*, edited by J. Daniel Luther and Jennifer Ung Loh, 1–26. London: Zed Books.

Msosa, Alan. 2018. *Human Rights and Same-Sex Intimacies in Malawi*. PhD thesis, University of Essex.

Narrain, Arvind and Gautam Bhan (eds.). 2005. *Because I Have a Voice: Queer Politics in India*. New Delhi: Yoda Press.

———. 2011. *Law Like Love: Queer Perspectives on Law*. New Delhi: Yoda Press.

Novak, Andrew. 2020. *Transnational Human Rights Litigation: Challenging the Death Penalty and the Criminalization of Homosexuality in the Commonwealth*. Cham: Springer.

Penwill, D. J. 1951. *Kamba Customary Law: Notes Taken in the Machakos District of Kenya Colony*. London: Macmillan & Co.

Phillips, Arthur; Legal Department, Colony and Protectorate of Kenya. 1945. *Report on Native Tribunals*. Nairobi: Government Printer, Kenya Colony and Protectorate.

Schauer, F. 2007. "Pitfalls in the Interpretation of Customary Law." In *The Nature of Customary Law: Legal, Historical and Philosophical Perspectives*, edited by Amanda Perrau-Saussine and James Bernard Murphy, 13–34. Cambridge: Cambridge University Press.

Smith, Linda Tuhiwai. 2012. *Decolonizing Methodologies: Research and Indigenous Peoples*, 2nd edition. London: Zed Books.

Snell, Geoffrey S. 1954. *Nandi Customary Law*. London: Macmillan & Co.

Spruill, J. 2000. "A Post-with/out a Past? Sexual Orientation and the Post-colonial Moment in South Africa." In *Sexuality in the Legal Arena*, edited by Carl Stychin and Didi Herman, 3–16. London: Athlone Press.

Stychin, Carl. 1995. *Law's Desire: Sexuality and the Limits of Justice*. London: Routledge.

———. 1998. *A Nation by Rights: National Cultures, Sexual Identity Politics and the Discourse of Rights*. Philadelphia, PA: Temple University Press.

Tabengwa, Monica and Matthew Waites. 2019. "Africa and the Contestation of Sexual and Gender Diversity: Imperial and Contemporary Regulation." In *Oxford Handbook of Global LGBT and Sexual Diversity Politics*, edited by Michael J. Bosia, Sandra M. McEvoy, and Momin Rahman, 201–15. Oxford: Oxford University Press.

Tamale, S. 2020. *Decolonization and Afro-Feminism*. Wakefield: Daraja Press.

The Commonwealth Equality Network. 2021. *The Commonwealth Equality Network*. www.commonwealthequality.org/.

Thurston, Anne. 1991. *Guide to Archives and Manuscripts Relating to Kenya and East Africa in the United Kingdom. Volume 1: Official Records*. London: Hans Zell Publishers.

Waites, Matthew. 2010. "Human Rights, Sexual Orientation and the Generation of Childhoods: Analysing the Partial Decriminalisation of 'Unnatural Offences' in India." *International Journal of Human Rights* 14(6): 971–93.

———. 2013. "United Kingdom: Confronting Criminal Histories and Theorising Decriminalisation as Citizenship and Governmentality." In *Human Rights, Sexual Orientation and Gender Identity in the Commonwealth: Struggles for Decriminalisation and Change*, edited by Corinne Lennox and Matthew Waites, 145–81. London: School of Advanced Study.

———. 2019a. "LGBT and Queer Politics in the Commonwealth." In *Oxford Encyclopedia of LGBT Politics and Policy*, edited by Donald P. Haider-Markel. Oxford: Oxford University Press. doi:10.1093/acrefore/9780190228637.013.1257

———. 2019b. "Decolonizing the Boomerang Effect in Global Queer Politics: A New Critical Framework for Sociological Analysis of Human Rights Contestation." *International Sociology* 34(4): 382–401.

Weeks, Jeffrey. 1989. *Sex Politics and Society: The Regulation of Sexuality since 1800*, 2nd edition. London: Routledge & Kegan Paul.

Wekesa, Seth Muchuma. 2017. "Decriminalisation of Homosexuality in Kenya: The Prospects and Challenges." In *Protecting the Human Rights of Sexual Minorities in Contemporary Africa*, edited by Sylvie Namwase and Adrian Jjuuko, 79–108. Pretoria: Pretoria University Law Press.

Wilson, Gordon. 1961. *Luo Customary Law and Marriage Laws*. Nairobi: Government Printer.

Woodman, Gordon R. 2012. "A Survey of Customary Laws in Africa in Search of Lessons for the Future." In *The Future of African Customary Law*, edited by Jeanmarie Fenrich, Paolo Galizzi, and Tracy E. Higgins, 9–30. Cambridge: Cambridge University Press.

4

Contamination to Congratulation

The Discursive and Legal Careers of the Homosexual in the United States and Cuba

LIBBY ADLER

In the United States, the 1950s was a time not only of the Red Scare, but also of the anti-homosexual witch hunts known as the "Lavender Scare." The two were entwined: Homosexuals threatened communist infiltration in the frightened American mind. During the same decade, pre-revolutionary Cuba was under the dictatorship of Fulgencio Batista. While US corporate interests exploited Caribbean labor and expropriated Cuban natural resources, Batista permitted the American mafia to run Havana. Cuban women and men provided sexual services to American corporate executives, military personnel, and tourists. Once Fidel Castro's forces took control of the island in 1959, the national indignities of prostitution and homosexual defilement demanded to be expunged. Homosexuality's close association with imperialist capitalist exploitation rendered it especially toxic in the revolutionary imagination.

Events of the second half of the twentieth century would alter the conception of homosexuality in these two countries, enabling in each case a limited range of legal reforms. This chapter revolves around the before and after of just one among many impactful historical phenomena: the dissolution of the Soviet Union. The analysis is comparative in a critical sense: It is not meant to establish unified understandings of either legal system, but rather to challenge the exclusivity of liberal legal rights as the route to homosexual advancement, to discern the influence of political economic circumstances and nationalist discourse on the range of available legal reforms, and to observe the distributive consequences of those reforms (Mattei 2019, 819–31).

For the United States, victory in the Cold War diminished national anxiety about communism while permitting a surge in gay advancement. States began adopting anti-discrimination measures, courts began protecting gay parents, and localities began registering domestic partners for a limited array of rights.[1] These advances did little for the most marginalized along axes of race, class, and region while rewarding those whose lives mimicked the bourgeois family ideal.

Cuba developed itself into a socialist state during the time of the Soviet Empire, effectuating property redistribution, raising its literacy rate, and developing an enviable healthcare system. The first few decades of the Revolution were difficult ones to be identified as homosexual,[2] but by the mid-1970s, the conditions for homosexuals began to improve, largely through proliferation of progressive sex education curricula. Progress came despite the absence of liberal legal rights such as privacy, expression, or assembly, and without the benefit of grassroots organizing, civil rights litigation, or private sector initiative. The collapse of the Eastern Bloc as the 1980s drew to a close, however, inaugurated Cuba's "Special Period." As Cuba lost its principal trading partner and economic support, the US embargo tightened on the tiny surviving communist outpost. Faced with shortages of food, medicine, building supplies, and other commodities, Cuba opened itself to international tourism, an aperture through which the forces of global capitalism would gush. Cuba's fateful decision, combined with desperation among its people, meant a resurgence of sexual commerce. That resurgence in turn surfaced racial and other hierarchical fissures within Cuba, stratifying in particular the homosexual population.

Once regarded in the United States as a threat of communist infiltration and in Cuba as a symbol of the indignities wrought by American capitalist imperialism, homosexuality—as a discursive artifact—evolved. The post-Soviet period inaugurated new forms of progress in both countries. Each nation, initially anxious to expel the contaminant of homosexuality and project it into its enemy, made legal reforms that were assimilable to its own global economic circumstances while subpopulations based on race, gender presentation, and related hierarchies of privilege remained unequally positioned to benefit. Eventually both countries would narrate homosexual advancement as a triumph of their own political economic systems.

The trajectories of these two entwined nations illustrate the malleability of homosexuality as a discursive artifact, capable of serving seemingly contradictory nationalist narratives deployed by global rivals. Moreover, the two contrasting paths to homosexual emancipation contain both optimistic and pessimistic suggestions. Optimistically, proponents of homosexual emancipation have more arrows in their quiver than they might have imagined; liberal rights are not their only option. Pessimistically, homosexual advancement, even outside of a capitalist state, harbors the potential to misallocate its benefits, intensifying racial and other intransigent hierarchies.

United States: The Lavender Scare

Homophobia in the United States did not begin with Senator Joe McCarthy (R-WI); changes in American life in the decades preceding his rise would prime the pump. In the 1930s and 1940s, a swirl of anxieties attached to the proto-socialistic features of the New Deal. Conservatives reviled the new social insurance programs, which they deemed at odds with American "self-reliance" (Johnson 2004, 95). In their view, federal aid functioned like an overbearing mother, widely believed to cause male homosexuality (Johnson 2004, 95). Literary critic Lee Edelman explains,

> gay men were assumed . . . to be overly fond of and close to their mothers, even as they were assumed . . . to hate women. . . . It was . . . the too loving mother that heterosexual culture loved to hate, the smothering mother who destroyed her son through overprotection and overindulgence. . . . [T]he mother stands accused . . . of effeminizing her son, of preventing his "natural" development into heterosexual manhood. (Edelman 1992, 276)

Conservatives charged that the New Deal analogously robbed Americans of their virility and self-reliance, producing dependency in its stead. "To many critics, bureaucracy was guilty of smothering the individual will of American citizens. . . . Accomplishing on a societal level what . . . mothers . . . were feared to be doing on a familial level" (Johnson 2004, 95).

Critics further suspected that men in government evidenced a lack of masculine independence (Johnson 2004, 92). Worst among them were the intellectuals, whose social science expertise was viewed as professorial and effete (93).

A profusion of new federal jobs during the New Deal prompted thousands to move to Washington, DC (Johnson 2004, 42). While racial discrimination persisted, white job applicants could often rely on their merits and exam performance (43). Some positions were reserved for men, yet a fresh set of work opportunities did exist for white single women (44). Growth in population alone meant more homosexuality in the District (43). Increasing urbanization, the Great Migration of Black southerners to northern cities, and European immigration all contributed to the emergence of gay and lesbian social and political community.

These population changes combined with fluctuations in family life heightened anxiety, for which homophobia was a perfect expression. As historian John D'Emilio explains, "the Great Depression and World War II seriously disrupted family life, traditional gender arrangements, and patterns of sexual behavior" (1992a, 65). The hardships of the 1930s led to delayed marriage and falling birth rates, both of which were partially reversed with wartime prosperity. Still, the war brought increased rates of divorce and abandonment, as well as an influx of women into jobs formerly reserved for men. At the same time, single-sex military environments and women's organizations gave rise to fresh gay and lesbian opportunities and subcultures (D'Emilio 1992a, 65). Historian Margot Canaday points to an obsessive focus by the military on lesbianism within its ranks in the years following the war (2009, 175, 180). While it had been regarded as a heroic sacrifice for women to forgo family life in favor of service to the nation in wartime, by the 1950s, women who chose to continue their military careers and avoid marriage raised suspicions (177–78).

The insecurities wrought by these decades teed up the anti-homosexual crusade of Joe McCarthy. In February 1950, McCarthy famously inaugurated the second Red Scare, declaring in a speech delivered from Wheeling, West Virginia that there were two hundred and five "card carrying" communists working in President Harry Truman's State Department (Johnson 2004, 15). As the details of McCarthy's initial pronouncement emerged, it turned out that some of the alleged communists were actually homosexuals, but McCarthy saw a connection: "[h]omosexuality . . . was the psychological maladjustment that led people toward communism" (Johnson 2004, 16). Secretary of State Dean Acheson and Deputy Undersecretary John Peurifoy went before a congressional committee to respond to McCarthy's charge. They conceded that the State Department had discharged a number of "security risks" (16). Pushed to specify, Peurifoy testified that ninety-one "people of moral weakness" had been forced to resign, mainly, he reluctantly admitted, for homosexuality (17).

Peurifoy's admission prompted an investigation into the State Department (D'Emilio 1992a, 59) and an intense period of scouring for homosexuals throughout the federal government, ending careers and destroying lives. McCarthy's House Un-American Activities Committee (HUAC) hearings ostensibly ferreted out communist and homosexual infiltrators. Those unlucky enough to be so identified lost their jobs and were often blacklisted from their professions. The presence of homosexuals in government also helped to prove the general "depravity of the Roosevelt-Truman bureaucracy" (Johnson 2004, 18).

Lafayette Park, one block from the White House, emerged as a postwar gay cruising spot (Johnson 2004, 47). Starting in 1947, the Park and other known cruising areas were ruthlessly policed under the auspices of the "Pervert Elimination Campaign" (59). "[H]undreds of men were arrested and charged with disorderly conduct, loitering, [and] indecency. . . . [T]hose against whom the evidence was insufficient were simply fingerprinted and added to the 'pervert file'" (59). All of this was justified as being preservative of national security (62).

As Johnson has demonstrated, these dual scares, Red and Lavender, did more than coincide temporally. Their entanglement was deeply ideological. "Security principles" governing State Department personnel excluded anyone "known for 'habitual drunkenness, sexual perversion, moral turpitude, financial irresponsibility or criminal record'" (Johnson 2004, 21). Excluding such persons was premised on the idea that "'a person who has such basic weakness of character' . . . might be led into an association with a subversive individual or group" (21). Homosexuals were conclusively presumed deficient in character and "emotional stability," as well as vulnerable to blackmail by Soviet spies, presenting the constant threat of betrayal (D'Emilio 1992a, 59–60). Meanwhile, the relentless rhetorical "pairing of 'Communists and queers' led many [Americans] to see them as indistinguishable threats" (Johnson 2004, 31).

McCarthy had asserted in his Wheeling speech that communism was atheistic and anti-family, citing "collective child-care as evidence of communism's antipathy toward the patriarchal family" (Johnson 2004, 36). Homosexuals, presumptively hostile toward the patriarchal family, his logic suggested, would gravitate toward such an ideology. Another congressman contended that China had a history of embracing homosexuality that dated back "long before the time of Confucius," and that the Soviets also supported homosexuality[3] (36). Conservatives urged that homosexuality was a "Communist plot," designed "to make us 'physically weak'"—that it was "Stalin's Atom Bomb" (37). Senator Kenneth Wherry (R-NE) asserted:

> The Russians had acquired a list of homosexuals throughout the world that had been compiled by Hitler as an espionage tool. Using this list, Russians were prying secrets out of government employees. Even worse, Soviet agents were targeting heterosexual female civil servants . . . "enticing them into a life of Lesbianism." (Johnson 2004, 80)

Politicians were also anxious to avoid a return to prewar economic conditions (D'Emilio 1992a, 67). A stable economy in which women were restored to domesticity while men earned a household income was tightly bound with containment of the communist threat.

> When placed in [historical] context, the Cold War era's preoccupation with the homosexual menace appears less like a bizarre, irrational expression of McCarthyism and emerges, instead, as an integral component of postwar American society and politics. The anti-homosexual campaigns of the 1950s represented but one front in a widespread effort to reconstruct patterns of sexuality and gender relations shaken by depression and war. (D'Emilio 1992a, 68)

Further, the new geopolitical threat of mutual annihilation increased social-psychic strain.

Pressures upon the nationalistic self-image of postwar America found articulation through the portrayal of homosexual activity as the proximate
cause of perceived danger to the nation at a time of unprecedented concern about the possibility of national—and global—destruction. (Edelman 1992, 277)

In the 1950s, postwar anxiety fostered American fear of homosexuality as a communist contaminant that had to be rooted out in the name
of national security.[4] Threats to traditional gender roles combined with
presumed homosexual moral weakness, contempt for family, and vulnerability to blackmail, all on the heels of the New Deal, positioned
the homosexual threat in the heart of the national body politic. The
discursive entwinement of homosexuality with communism drove a
compulsion to hunt and to expel—literally from government jobs and
figuratively from the US system into its communist enemy.

Cuba: Becoming Socialist

Centuries of colonialism, slavery, economic imperialism, and rebellion
have combined to shape Cuban attitudes about gender and sexuality. We
pick up the story, however, with the early years of the Cold War and the
presidency of Fulgencio Batista, who governed the island from 1952 until
the end of 1958. Batista let the US mafia run Cuba's capital city. Booze,
drugs, gambling, and sexual adventure attracted US travelers and put
millions into mob coffers (Hamilton 2012, 27). While rural Cubans and
migratory workers from around the Caribbean labored under slave-like
conditions in service of US sugar, tobacco, and nickel interests, Havana's
Cuban men and women staffed casinos and resort hotels and catered
to the sexual appetites of US military personnel, corporate employees,
and tourists. Male homosexuals actually benefitted from "[p]referential
hiring" in tourist venues to accommodate sexual demand (Kirk 2017).
It was a period of gross inequality, as the wealthiest Cubans enjoyed the
rewards of partnering with foreign capitalists, while the majority suffered extreme poverty and exploitation.

Rebel forces took the capital on January 1, 1959. Fidel Castro's revolutionary government promptly began nationalizing foreign assets,
destroying any likelihood of friendly relations with its neighbor to the

north. US President Dwight Eisenhower instituted a partial trade embargo in 1960, which President John F. Kennedy would soon make total. Hoping to thwart a communist foothold off the shores of Miami, Kennedy launched the disastrous Bay of Pigs invasion in 1961. Castro officially declared Marxism-Leninism to be Cuban state policy the same year. The Soviet Union quickly became Cuba's most important ally and economic partner (Suchlicki 2002, 142–49).

In 1962, Castro declared racism to be officially vanquished by the equality of all under socialism, and formally speaking, race discrimination was (and continues to be) prohibited (Allen 2011, 63).[5] Cuba's embrace of women's equality evolved to accommodate a specific political-economic agenda. During the early years of the Revolution, while Cubans still imagined that their standard of living would "Americanize" (Chase 2015, 137), Castro encouraged women to purchase domestically produced goods (139). As souring trade relations with the United States imposed food shortages and rising discontent, however, the government called on women to suffer nobly and to rebuke American consumerism by exercising "self-restraint for the greater good of the collective" (147).

An array of early women's organizations merged into the Federacíon de Mujeres Cubanas (Federation of Cuban Women, FMC) in 1960. The FMC was founded by Vilma Espín, wife of Raúl Castro (Fidel's brother). Espín staunchly resisted identification with feminism, which she deemed American and bourgeois. Rather than advancing women's interests, the FMC sought to maximize women's contribution to the Revolution. It did so initially by focusing on women as consumers, even suggesting that "food lines [were] potential sites of female solidarity" (Chase 2015, 165).

Espín's FMC made eradication of prostitution a top priority. Prostitution was, according to political scientist Megan Daigle, "elevated past a mere social problem to a powerful symbol of Cuba's subordination to foreign powers" (Daigle 2015, 50). Recalcitrant women were sent to re-education centers to learn honorable skills such as sewing (Daigle 2015, 51–52; Hamilton 2012, 27). The FMC worked as well on access to contraception and abortion, the latter of which Cuba decriminalized in 1965 (Kirk 2017).

Among Cuba's most significant achievements in the arena of sex equity was its Family Code of 1975. It set forth rules for marriage, divorce, custody, and child support, but most famously, it established the requirement of equal participation between husbands and wives in household duties, including childcare (Hamilton 2012, 33). While generally unenforced, this powerful symbol marked a significant departure from previously held assumptions about the respective roles of men and women, shaped in part by the legacy of *machismo*, a culturally specific ideal of Latin American masculinity, further particularized in Cuba by the iconic bearded "New Man" of the Cuban Revolution (Daigle 2015, 54).

Cuba's "New Man," epitomized by Argentine rebel doctor Ernesto "Che" Guevara, was courageous, inexhaustible by physical labor, and sexually passionate yet disciplined. Male effeminacy was entirely inconsistent with this vision in part because it evoked the indignities of the Batista period (Bejel 2001, 99). Prostitution, urban decay, and imperialism discursively melded in the figure of the male homosexual (100).

Cuban vocabulary historically has reflected an idealized taxonomy of men who engage in same-sex sexual practices that is not uncommon in Latin America: *burragónes* are masculine, exclusively insertive, and carry an uncompromised heterosexual identity (Allen 2011, 75; Stout 2014, 27); while *maricónes* (*fags*) are effeminate, anally receptive, and regarded as homosexual (Leiner 1994, 22). Only the latter retained their association with the profligacy and humiliation of the Batista period (Lumsden 1996, 58). The maricón was understood to be "an artifact of capitalist bourgeois decadence. . . . a coward and untrustworthy" (Allen 2011, 68; Kirk 2017).

The young regime determined that "anti-social" figures such as the maricónes were in need of rehabilitation through agricultural labor (Bejel 2001, 100). In 1965, Cuba established the internationally reviled work camps known as *Unidades Militares para Ayudar Producción* (Military Units to Aid Production, UMAPs) to reverse the consequences of capitalist corruption and instill the socialist value of physical labor (101–2).[6]

Cuba also established "Yellow Brigades" to masculinize effeminate boys (Leiner 1994, 33–34). Raids and entrapment were commonplace. Universities, the arts, and many workplaces were purged of both male and female homosexuals. "Although the UMAP camps were reserved for men, there were also reports of women in same-sex relationships being purged from universities, mistreated in prisons, and expelled from boarding schools" (Hamilton 2012, 41). Neighborhood-based *Comités para la Defensa de la Revolución* (Committees for the Defense of the Revolution, CDRs) "reported 'suspected homosexuals' to the authorities" (Hamilton 2012, 39). A state newspaper explained, "No homosexual represents the Revolution, which is a matter of men, of fists and not feathers, of courage and not trembling, of certainty and not intrigue, of creative valor and not of sweet surprises" (39).

Cuba's anti-homosexual legal offensive culminated in 1971, when its First National Congress on Education and Culture formally declared homosexuality to be "against socialist morality" (Kirk 2017). The Congress resolved to exclude homosexuals from government and positions in which they might influence youth (Lumsden 1996, 73). Purges followed.

From the early 1960s through the first half of the 1970s, homosexuality—defined largely by male effeminacy and penetrability—represented a grave threat in the Cuban revolutionary imagination. Compounding the ideological residue of Spanish Colonialism was the painful indignity of Havana as "a playground for American gangsters and tourists" (Lumsden 1996, 57). If the battle against prostitution waged by the FMC served as "an 'allegory' for the fight against capitalist exploitation" (Daigle 2015, 146), how much more critical to make men out of the maricónes who subjected themselves to sexual exploitation by American capitalists? Homosexuality was imagined as irredeemably incompatible with the Revolution—an intolerable, decadent, bourgeois contaminant to be extirpated by law and labor.

United States: The Gay Rights Decades

The 1970s in the United States witnessed the flourishing of second-wave feminism, the sexual revolution, expanding access to contraception and abortion, no-fault divorce, and the ecstasy of post-Stonewall gay liberation. These phenomena combined to alter dramatically the sexual landscape. That landscape transformed again in the following decade, which introduced the savage destruction of the AIDS epidemic as well as the activism that AIDS spurred. As "family only" hospital visitation and intestate death brought about new appreciation for the benefits of partnership recognition, gay *liberation* gave way to gay *equality*. The wish for legally respected relationships, along with related phenomena such as the lesbian baby boom, increasingly girded by a rhetoric of love and financial interdependence, turned the key in the ignition that would eventually take us to same-sex marriage.

During these same decades, feminists clashed over the politics of pornography, sex work, butch-femme aesthetics, and sadomasochism, as moralists berated their libertine sisters during the "Sex Wars" (Khan 2014, 57–64). Believing sex to be principally a domain of male domination and danger rather than female agency and pleasure, radical feminists and later cultural feminists valorized non-hierarchical forms of lesbian sexuality, consistent with an ethic of care (Echols 1989, 244, 256). Lesbians who embraced this brand of feminism never identified with gay male sexual adventurism of the 1970s, dismissing it as reflective of masculine values (Echols 1989, 244; Khan 2014, 66–67). Lesbian solidarity with gay men through the staggering losses of the 1980s followed by the political shift toward same-sex marriage, however, fostered an invigorated gay/lesbian affinity.

At the same time that these dramas were unfolding, a broader set of national forces were at work. The election of Ronald Reagan to the presidency in 1980 represented the ascendance of neoliberal, racist "family values" espoused by political voices eager to bludgeon low-income, single mothers with moralistic condemnations of sexual licentiousness and welfare dependency (Cohen 1997, 456). Family values rhetoric justified diminution of the social safety net and privatization of responsibility for poverty. Even after the return of the White House to Democratic control in 1993, President Bill Clinton signed the 1994 crime bill (now widely blamed, along with Reagan's "war on drugs," for the scourge of mass incarceration) as well as the 1996 "welfare reform" law. Congressional findings in the welfare law declared "Marriage is the foundation of a successful society" and tied marriage to responsible parenting (Pub. L. 104–193, title I, §101, Aug. 22, 1996, 110 Stat. 2110). Among the Act's stated purposes is "end[ing] the dependence of needy parents on government benefits by promoting job preparation, work, and marriage" (42 U.S.C. §601 (a) (2)).

Directing financial responsibility away from the public sector and toward the marital dyad set the stage for the (so far) thirty-year period beginning in the early 1990s during which gay rights have been on the move. The federal constitutional right to engage in private, consensual, same-sex sodomy materialized in 2003 (*Lawrence v. Texas*, 539 U.S. 558 (2003)), although it was preceded by years of state-level advocacy. Anti-discrimination provisions started accruing at all governmental levels, shielding gay people in employment, housing, and public accommodations. The first real victory for the same-sex marriage campaign was won in the highest court in Massachusetts,[7] also in 2003, but that too was built atop a mountain of local domestic partnership ordinances, voluntary corporate provision of domestic partner benefits (Ball 2019, 95–125), judicial recognition of contractual arrangements between same-sex partners, and judicial conferment of parenting rights on equitable bases (NeJaime 2016, 1199).

The specific legal advances that gay rights advocates made should be understood as constrained by their political context. It is no accident that gay legal advocacy emphasized sexual privacy, hate crimes, employment anti-discrimination, and marriage. The national setting in which the reform agenda was set is powerfully conditioned both by neoliberalism's characteristic aversion to public sector responsibility for Americans' health, housing, and nutrition and its tendency toward criminalization. Legal victories have consequently rewarded privileged sectors of the lgbt constituency while leaving racial, regional, and economic inequalities intact.

As American Studies scholar Lisa Duggan observes, the ascent in the 1980s of identity politics was epiphenomenal to the rise of neoliberalism, neglecting distributive concerns that would pose a more serious challenge to the economic order (2003, 42). It is less disruptive to permit same-sex couples to share employer-based health insurance than to provide universal coverage, to grant privacy to gay homeowners while policing homeless lgbt youth than to make housing available to all, and to add protected categories to anti-discrimination law than to confront the deeper inequality wrought by employment at will.[8]

Legal scholar Derrick Bell famously argued that the Black civil rights victories of the 1950s and 1960s were enabled by the convergence of the justice imperative with US foreign policy interests (2004, 59–69). Bell's *convergence thesis* was supported by the historical study of Mary L. Dudziak, who showed that, from the announcement of the Truman Doctrine in 1947, foreign policy experts believed that the United States had to represent itself as a beacon of freedom and equality to win over former colonial countries that might otherwise come under Soviet influence. The harsh—and increasingly televised—reality of white supremacist rule exposed what China and the Soviet Union charged was American hypocrisy, thereby hampering US geopolitical objectives. To counter the communist narrative, therefore, the United States

> revealed, rather than concealed, the nation's past failings, and it did so for the purpose of presenting American history as a story of redemption. In this story, democracy as a system of government was the vehicle for national reconciliation . . . Democracy, not totalitarian forms of government . . . provided a context that made . . . redemption possible. (Dudziak 2000, 49)

Civil rights advocates pushed the United States to live up to its promise (Dudziak 2000, 67–77). Starting with *Shelley v. Kraemer* (334 US 1 (1948)), the US Department of Justice submitted *amicus curiae* briefs in civil rights cases arguing that racial inequality was impeding foreign policy objectives (Dudziak 2000, 91). This rationale played a continuing role all the way through passage of the Civil Rights Act of 1964 and Voting Rights Act of 1965 (203–40).

US foreign policy objectives have proven significant in the context of homosexual identity as well. In 1980, thousands of Cubans sought refuge on US shores, many having departed Cuba to escape anti-homosexual persecution. The United States faced a contest between its policy prohibiting entry to homosexuals and its anti-communist ideology. The latter prevailed and the prohibition was suspended (Argulles and Rich 1985, 128). The following decade, the Bureau of Immigration Appeals (BIA) granted a petition to withhold deportation of a homosexual Cuban named Armando Toboso-Alfonso (20 I&N Dec. 819 (BIA 1994)).[9] The decision required a finding that Toboso-Alfonso was a "member of a particular social group" in Cuba and that his "life or freedom would be threatened" there (Immigration & Nationality Act of 1952, § 243(h) (1990)). In what became a landmark BIA precedent, the opinion carefully highlights that it was Toboso-Alfonso's *identity* as a homosexual, rather than any *acts* he committed, that subjected him to persecution in Cuba. At the time, sodomy remained a criminal offense in about half of US states.

Years after the Cold War receded and the War on Terror succeeded to its position in the American mind, gender studies scholar Jasbir Puar introduced "homonationalism" as "a deep critique of [how] lesbian and gay liberal rights discourses . . . produce narratives of progress and modernity" (Puar 2013, 337). US gays now serve as objects of liberal toleration, putting into relief intolerance exhibited by unenlightened Muslim others (Puar 2007, xxiii). While gays of the Cold War represented peril to national security and the American way of life, gays of the War on Terror are super-patriots, exemplars of the virtues of American liberalism—a new "convergence" for a new era.

Coastal, urban, and predominantly white gays and lesbians in the United States have begun in earnest to enjoy broad social acceptance, legally respected domesticity, and educational and professional inclusion. Trans populations, lgbt people of color, lgbt youth, and other vulnerable subpopulations, however, continue to suffer disproportionately high rates of poverty, hunger, homelessness, and criminalization. The march to same-sex marriage, hate crimes inclusion, privacy, and anti-discrimination has neglected the wealth gap between gay haves and have-nots, leaving that gap more severe than in the US population at large (Adler 2020).

The US gay rights story is one of astonishing progress, but not for everyone. For those already pushed to the margins by the tendencies of capitalism, a gay rights path forged under conditions of neoliberalism was likely to leave its most vulnerable behind, vindicating those rights that were most easily absorbed into the economic order. How might the trajectory differ under Cuban socialism?

Cuba: Socialist Forms of Progress

The second half of the 1970s showed some improvement for homosexuals in Cuba. Purges came to an end as the government took formal steps to end discrimination based on sexual orientation. In 1975, Cuba's National Assembly invalidated the exclusion of "homosexuals from obtaining positions of power" (Stout 2014, 40), and in 1978 it repealed Cuba's ban on homosexual teachers (Hamilton 2012, 43).

Penologically, the last year of the decade was a mixed bag. Cuba decriminalized private homosexual acts but left the prohibition against public displays of homosexuality intact and enacted a prohibition against *peligrosidad* (*dangerousness*):

> A dangerous state is considered the special proclivity in which a person is found to commit crimes, demonstrated by their conduct which is seen to be in manifest contradiction with the norms of socialist morality. (Daigle 2015, 119, translating the relevant language from Article 72 of the Cuban Penal Code)

This nebulous provision allocated broad discretion to arrest, jail, and/or reeducate persons violating expectations of public demeanor; such violations included same-sex affection, male effeminacy, and "transgender performance" (Allen 2011, 72).

Still, the conceptualization of homosexuality gradually (if incompletely) evolved from a criminal concern to a "medical and psychological" one (Leiner 1994, 43). Espín and a Cuban physician established the Grupo Nacional de Trabajo de Educación Sexual (National Group for Work on Sexual Education, GNTES) under the auspices of the FMC in 1972 (Kirk 2017). GNTES worked closely with East German consultants over the course of the 1970s to develop a progressive sexual education program targeted to every age level and for use in medical training. This program pushed Cuba toward normalization of homosexuality.

East German experts authored many of the key texts, notably Siegfried Schnabl's best-selling *Man and Woman in Intimacy* (first published in 1978, published in Spanish in 1979), which "discuss[ed] homosexuality in a respectful and empathetic way" (Bejel 2001, 107; Kirk 2017). The final chapter addressed male and female homosexuality and characterized each as simply "a variant" that should not be "classified as an illness" (Kirk 2017). The work of Schnabl and others would emphasize health, call for respect, and depict "sexuality as an important component of the national expression of socialist ideology" (Kirk 2017). Marx and Engels, Schnabl stressed, viewed sexuality as important to human happiness (2017). This compared favorably, he argued, with "repressive capitalist societies, which viewed homosexuality as a perversion"[10] (2017). GNTES also created a "multidisciplinary team" in 1979 to specialize in the care of transgender[11] Cubans, eventually undertaking gender-affirming surgeries under its national healthcare system (Kirk 2017).

The next decade was off to a difficult start with the Mariel boatlift—an exodus of about 125,000 Cubans whom Fidel Castro grudgingly permitted to leave in 1980. Such "scum," Castro made clear, were not wanted in Cuba anyway. Convicts and homosexuals were actively encouraged to emigrate, prompting some who were departing for economic reasons or in pursuit of liberal freedoms to feign homosexual affect (Peña 2013, 30).

The 1980s proceeded with steps forward and back. The 1985 departure of an especially homophobic Minister of the Interior (who oversees the police) marked one positive development. Sex ed was seeping into Cuban consciousness and the law slowly followed its sympathetic lead. In 1987, Cuba's revised penal code ceased to prohibit "public ostentation" of homosexuality (Kirk 2017). The vague "dangerousness" law, however, continued to leave an opening for differential treatment based on sexuality, gender presentation, and race (Daigle 2015, 124; Lumsden 1996, 87). Evidence of progress could also be observed in the arts, in which "homoerotic themes" were increasingly tolerated and even rewarded (Bejel 2001, 110).

Castro blamed the United States for the arrival of AIDS, reinvigorating discursive associations among imperialism, moral decay, and homosexuality. The absence of rights to expression and assembly precluded the organizing that the epidemic prompted in the United States. In 1986, Cuba established a quarantine system to control the spread of HIV (Leiner 1994, 117–57). Mandatory and demonstrably illiberal, the quarantine drew international criticism. Contemporaneous accounts, however, indicate that conditions were not inhumane. Persons in one among several regional sanitoriums received free, first-rate care and lived with partners (including same-sex partners) who were also HIV-positive in decent conditions (118–19). They visited with family and enjoyed outings to the beach or movies. Those who demonstrated "responsibility" were returned to their communities (120).

Near the end of the decade, GNTES reestablished itself as the *Centro Nacional de Educación Sexual* (Cuban National Center for Sex Education, CENESEX). At the helm is Mariela Castro Espín—daughter of Raúl Castro and Vilma Espín. Castro Espín is a psychologist and member of the National Assembly. Under her leadership, CENESEX has become a strong voice for homosexual and transgender equality. The internationally respected center publishes an academic journal, administers anti-homophobic and anti-transphobic sex education across the island, advances legislative reform (including pushing for same-sex marriage and lesbian access to assisted reproductive technologies), and sponsors cultural events (Kirk 2011, 151–57). "Let's make Cuba more revolutionary!" cheers Castro Espín ("Mariela Castro's March: Cuba's LGBT Revolution," HBO 2016, directed by Jon Alpert).

Under Cuban socialism, progress for homosexual populations has not been driven by impact litigation, grassroots organizing, or corporate sector initiative. Legal reform has not relied on rights to assembly, free speech, or privacy, or occurred under an equality-seeking identity banner. Most advances have "been *granted* by the benevolent state—rather than *won* . . . and only on the Revolution's terms" (Daigle 2015, 66). As Fidel famously proclaimed in 1961, "Dentro de la Revolución, todo; contra de la Revolución, nada" ("Within the Revolution, everything; against the Revolution, nothing") (Allen 2011, 146).

In some respects, advances on Revolutionary terms have been broadly distributed. Cubans of all sexualities and races benefit from improvements in literacy and health (Stout 2014, 38). Cuba's achievements across the 1970s and '80s in education and medicine—notwithstanding vestigial racial biases and homo- and transphobia—reduced discrimination and criminalization to the benefit of the many, not just the few.

In the 1990s, however, inequalities surfaced in the general Cuban population and the homosexual population specifically. When the Soviet Union collapsed, so did Cuba's economy, which had been heavily reliant on trade with the Eastern Bloc. Cuba entered its *Período Especial en Tiempos de Paz* (Special Period in Peacetime, or just Special Period). Imports, exports, and GDP all plummeted. Income and production fell precipitously, electrical outages became frequent, and severe shortages of food, soap, and other basic consumer goods imposed immense hardship on the Cuban people, spurring an escalation of black market activity (Cabezas 2009, 61–62). The government was forced to "integrate [Cuba] into capitalist markets" by allowing foreign investment, introducing the dollar, and legalizing limited self-employment (62–64). In addition, Cuba had little choice but to pry itself open to international tourism (Hamilton 2012, 45).

Dual currencies and the establishment of "dollar stores" providing access to foreign commodities generated new levels of inequality and gave

rise to racial fissures that had been less prominent (by no means eliminated) in previous decades. Light-skinned[12] Cubans were more likely to
have relatives in the United States sending them goods and remittances
(Allen 2011, 120). Moreover, employment in the tourist sector was the
highest paying, which meant an "inver[sion of] the social pyramid" as
"doctors, lawyers, economists, and engineers" left state employment to
work as "taxi drivers, hotel housekeeping staff, waiters, and bartend-
ers" (Cabezas 2009, 65–66). Hotel jobs were given to workers with a
buena presencia (good presence—a euphemism for light skin) (Cabezas
2009, 80).

Desperation for goods and currency, combined with an influx of
tourists from Canada and Western Europe, meant a resurgence of sexual
commerce, both hetero- and homosexual. When anthropologist Noelle
Stout went to Cuba at the start of the new century to

> investigate how state-sponsored initiatives to promote gay tolerance . . .
> had had an impact on the lives of gays and lesbians. . . . people redirected
> the conversation to . . . rising inequalities and the sex trade. [Increased]
> gay tolerance [was] often overshadowed by the rise of poverty and the re-
> turn of socioeconomic disparities. . . . [as] sexual labor in Havana [again
> became] a defining factor of queer social life. (Stout 2014, 7)

After interviewing people across a range of homosexual subpopulations, Stout reports, "the introduction of foreign tourism split Havana's
queer social worlds between "respectable" gays involved with the arts
and those tied to [hustling] and the sex trade" (2014, 10). Homosexual
Cubans inhabiting the privileged end of the spectrum regarded homosexuals in the sex trade[13] as untrustworthy and consumerist, echoing
stereotypes from the early years of the Revolution (15).

Within the sex trade, there is additional stratification (Allen 2011,
175). Resort hotels, where some commercial sex is initiated, engage in
discriminatory hiring based on skin tone because "hotel managers believe that European and Canadian visitors expected fair-skinned service
staff" (Hamilton 2012, 77). Sex workers barred from hotel employment
are limited to meeting tourists on the street, where police harassment
is a fact of life. No one is technically arrested for prostitution or homosexuality, but as historian Carrie Hamilton explains,

the legal excuse . . . is the general ban on Cubans frequenting tourist areas, a prohibition designed in part to curb hustling. But although in theory any Cuban can be subject to arrest for being caught in the company of tourists, men who have sex with men are particularly likely to be targeted because public spaces are their main location for socializing. . . . [In addition,] the police always have recourse to the "danger" law. (Hamilton 2012, 197)

Cuba was pushed by the breakup of the Soviet Union to make ideological compromises, opening up to capitalist markets and international tourism. These compromises fortified the impulse to crack down on the sex trade. If sex work were left unaddressed, observed one young Cuban, "our beautiful little Cuba would go back to being called the great brothel of America . . . because there was no whore or fag in the world more prized than the whores and fags of this country" (Daigle 2015, 177). Consequently, even as Mariela Castro Espín leads state-approved congas chanting *Socialism yes, homophobia no!*[14] and as foreign investors take comfort in Cuba's official policy of tolerance, economic hardship and police surveillance eclipse these positive steps for those who find themselves once again condemned as anathema to socialist values.

Conclusion

The United States and Cuba both experienced anxiety related to their global positions in the mid-twentieth century. They managed that anxiety with a shared compulsion to expel the homosexual contaminant and project it into a despised political-economic other. Global stimuli changed, however, revising discourses and shaping legal reform.

For the United States, lgbt law reform was enabled in part by the end of the Cold War and took specific forms that were amenable to the civil rights paradigm and neoliberal privatization trends. The undeniable expansion of civil rights, however, left unaddressed the racial, economic, and gendered inequalities within the US lgbt population. Still, for purposes of geopolitics, visible progress culminating in a constitutional right to same-sex marriage evidences the triumph of American liberalism compared with rival systems (Russian still, but also Islamic).

Rights assertion had little to do with advances for homosexuals in Cuba, which lacks a liberal rights consciousness, eschews identity-based claims, and virtually precludes grassroots organizing.[15] Progress has occurred on socialist terms, focusing on education and health and resulting in limited forms of inclusion, decriminalization, and de-pathologization. Official messaging across the island casts homosexual tolerance as tied to the socialist value of human fulfillment. "Inside Cuba . . . the Revolution is typically perceived not as a single moment or epoch, but as an ongoing process" (Hamilton 2012, 13). Homosexual advancement is accordingly a triumph of the Revolution. The hardships of the Special Period, however, revived inequalities that had somewhat abated during the early decades of Cuban socialism, as international tourism brought sexual commerce back into the foreground of homo-sexual existence.

Homosexuality in these two stories reveals itself to be not merely a cluster of desires, sex acts, relationships, and gender expressions, but a malleable discursive artifact. The question of whether homosexual emancipation can be realized by either of the two competing political-economic systems, therefore, must be further specified: First, can homosexuality be deployed in service of both capitalist and socialist nationalist projects? For purposes of this question, the specific content of the term "homosexual" is only marginally of interest. What matters is its array of discursive associations, from traitor to patriot, from counter-revolutionary to exemplar of the ongoing Revolution, from feared infil-trator to proof of systemic superiority. Taking in this range, the answer to the first question is surely *yes*. American and Cuban systems have both proven capable of deploying homosexuality as a feared enemy within *and* as a symbol of emancipatory progress (and consequently grounds upon which to castigate an ideological foe). Following political scientist Michael J. Bosia, perhaps neither Cuba nor the United States is intrinsi-cally homophobic or homophilic, but rather "indifferent to questions of sexuality outside their effect on state building" (2015, 39). Indeed, the homosexual of nationalist discourse need not bear much relationship to those bodies deemed homosexual in the streets of Havana or Greenwich Village; the homosexual is no more than an artifactual representation of nationalist anxiety, or, alternatively, national progress and systemic self-justification.

Second, is homosexuality a distributive formation that can be absorbed—via law reform—into capitalist and socialist societies? For purposes of this question, homosexuality as a category remains malleable and refers to a range, but it also comes closer to the ground, becoming a referent for an amalgamation of desires, sex acts, and gender expressions that are not unlimited. Specific acts occurring between or among specific bodies and specific gendered performances draw legal treatment, even as law helps to shape the contours of these acts and performances. The answer to the second question, then, also appears to be *yes* but with the crucial caveat that different legal possibilities and changing global conditions can generate inconsistent outcomes across racial and other hierarchies of privilege. For purposes of law reform, homosexuality—even confined to its rough ambit of sexual and gendered meanings—exists in a moment, in a legal culture, and enmeshed in cross-cutting identity conditions.

NOTES

1 Progress was accompanied by setbacks all along, including government indifference in the early years of the HIV/AIDS epidemic, scapegoating of gays and lesbians in electoral campaigns, and legal backlash against same-sex partnership recognition in the form of "Defense of Marriage" laws.

2 I mostly use *lgbt*, *gay*, or *lesbian* when referring to US populations, but *homosexual* when referring to Cubans. With apologies to those who chafe against this terminology, identities have not formed identically in every national context. In Cuba, *homosexual* is not synonymous with *gay* in US usage.

3 The Bolsheviks decriminalized sodomy in 1918, but Stalin reversed that move in 1934 (Hirshman 2012, 29).

4 The 1950s also saw the first documented "homophile" organizations, including the Mattachine Society and the Daughters of Bilitis (D'Emilio 1992a, 17–56; Faderman 1991, 148–49). Mattachine was famously launched by a gay communist, Harry Hay, along with a few like-minded men. As it grew, new leadership succumbed to the pressures of the McCarthy era, eventually dissolving the national organization (D'Emilio 1992a, 37–52). In the 1960s, however, Frank Kameny launched an independent chapter in the District of Columbia to combat federal government witch hunts (Johnson 2004, 179–84). The movement's first *legal* victories were achieved in the late 1950s and early 1960s, largely—as legal scholar Carlos Ball has chronicled—under the First Amendment. Gay litigants prevailed after being targeted by obscenity law enforcement and denied their right to associate (Ball 2017, 36–45, 58–69). Constitutional victories under the right to privacy or equal protection clause of the Fourteenth Amendment were

not yet conceivable, nor were gay family law reforms possible at a time when *gay* and *family* were considered antipodal.

5 The history of slavery and the Jim Crow employment norms brought to Cuba by US corporations have left a residue, but a distinct "silence" regarding continuing racial inequity governs (Allen 2011, 66).

6 Religious dissidents and other nonconformists were also sent to the UMAPs, which closed in 1968 under domestic pressure as well as international criticism from such celebrities as Graham Greene, Jean-Paul Sartre, and Allen Ginsberg (Bejel 2001, 101; Hamilton 2012, 40).

7 There were a couple of *almosts* before the Massachusetts case. See Baehr v. Lewin, 74 Haw. 530 (Haw. 1993) and Baker v. Vermont, 744 A.2d 864 (Vt. 1999).

8 Thanks to Karen Engle for this insight.

9 Thanks to Rachel Rosenbloom for direction here.

10 Lgbt identities have been medicalized in the United States, too. The American Psychiatric Association recognized homosexuality as a benign variant rather than a pathology in 1973, soon introducing Gender Identity Disorder. Both changes are evident in American Psychiatric Association, *Diagnostic and Statistical Manual of Mental Disorders*, 3rd edition (Washington, DC: American Psychiatric Association, 1980), 265–66.

11 I use this term with trepidation. Cuba's taxonomy of gender variance does not map perfectly onto US usage.

12 I eschew US racial categories in favor of reference to skin tone because Cuba's taxonomy does not match US usage.

13 Ethnologists have teased out an array of conduct and identities involving sexual exchange. This rich variation goes unaddressed here for reasons of space and is collected under the terms *sexual commerce* and *sex trade*.

14 See www.vice.com.

15 Since this chapter was drafted, Cuba recognized same-sex marriage with the passage of its 2022 Family Code. Along with marriage, gay identity and gay rights as global phenomena have definitively arrived in Cuba, transforming the country's gendered and sexual norms, vocabularies, and laws surveyed in this chapter.

BIBLIOGRAPHY

Adler, Libby. 2020. "Distributive Justice for LGBTQ People." In *Oxford Encyclopedia of LGBT Politics and Policy*, edited by Bruno Perreau, x–x. Available online: Oxford University Press. doi:10.1093/acrefore/9780190228637.013.1235.

Allen, Jafari S. 2011. *Venceremos? The Erotics of Black Self-Making in Cuba*. Durham, NC: Duke University Press.

Argulles, Lourdes and B. R. Rich. 1985. "Homosexuality, Homophobia, and Revolution: Notes toward an Understanding of the Cuban Lesbian and Gay Male Experience, Part II." *Signs: Journal of Women in Culture and Society* 11(1): 120–36.

Ball, Carlos A. 2017. *The First Amendment and LGBT Equality: A Contentious History*. Cambridge, MA: Harvard University Press.

———. 2019. *The Queering of Corporate America: How Big Business Went from LGBTQ Adversary to Ally*. Boston: Beacon Press.

Bejel, Emilio. 2001. *Gay Cuban Nation*. Chicago: University of Chicago Press.

Bell, Derrick. 2004. *Silent Covenants: Brown v. Board and the Unfulfilled Hopes for Racial Reform*. New York: Oxford University Press.

Bosia, Michael J. 2015. "To Love or to Loathe: Modernity, Homophobia, and LGBT Rights." In *Sexualities in World Politics: How LGBTQ Claims Shape International Relations*, edited by M. Lavinas Picq and M. Thiel, 38–53. Abingdon: Routledge.

Cabezas, Amalia L. 2009. *Economies of Desire: Sex and Tourism in Cuba and the Dominican Republic*. Philadelphia, PA: Temple University Press.

Canaday, Margot. 2009. *The Straight State: Sexuality and Citizenship in Twentieth-Century America*. Princeton, NJ: Princeton University Press.

Chase, Michelle. 2015. *Revolution Within the Revolution: Women and Gender Politics in Cuba, 1952–1962*. Chapel Hill: University of North Carolina Press.

Cohen, Cathy J. 1997. "Punks, Bulldaggers, and Welfare Queens: The Radical Potential of Queer Politics?" *GLQ* 3: 437–65.

Daigle, Megan. 2015. *From Cuba with Love: Sex and Money in the Twenty-First Century*. Oakland: University of California Press.

D'Emilio, John. 1992a. "Dreams Deferred." In *Making Trouble: Essays on Gay History, Politics, and the University*, 17–56. London: Routledge.

———. 1992b. "The Homosexual Menace." In *Making Trouble: Essays on Gay History, Politics, and the University*, 57–73. London: Routledge.

Dudziak, Mary L. 2000. *Cold War Civil Rights: Race and the Image of American Democracy*. Princeton, NJ: Princeton University Press.

Duggan, Lisa. 2003. *Twilight of Equality? Neoliberalism, Cultural Politics and the Attack on Democracy*. Boston: Beacon Press.

Echols, Alice. 1989. *Daring to Be Bad: Radical Feminism in America 1967–1975*. Minneapolis: University of Minnesota Press.

Edelman, Lee. 1992. "Tearooms and Sympathy, or, The Epistemology of the Water Closet." In *Nationalisms and Sexualities*, edited by A. Parker, M. Russo, D. Sommer, and P. Yaeger, 263–83. New York: Routledge.

Faderman, Lillian. 1991. *Odd Girls and Twilight Lovers: A History of Lesbian Life in Twentieth Century America*. New York: Penguin Books.

Hamilton, Carrie. 2012. *Sexual Revolutions in Cuba: Passion, Politics, and Memory*. Chapel Hill: University of North Carolina Press.

Hirshman, Linda. 2012. *Victory: The Triumphant Gay Revolution*. New York: Harper Perennial.

Johnson, David K. 2004. *The Lavender Scare: The Cold War Persecution of Gays and Lesbians in the Federal Government*. Chicago: University of Chicago Press.

Khan, Ummni. 2014. *Vicarious Kinks: S/M in the Socio-Legal Imaginary*. Toronto: University of Toronto Press.

Kirk, Emily J. 2011. "Setting the Agenda for Cuban Sexuality: The Role of Cuba's CENESEX." *Canadian Journal of Latin American and Caribbean Studies* 36(72): 143–63.

———. 2017. *Cuba's Gay Revolution: Normalizing Sexual Diversity Through a Health-Based Approach*. Lexington Studies on Cuba. Lanham, MD: Lexington Books. EBSCOhost.

Leiner, Marvin. 1994. *Sexual Politics in Cuba: Machismo, Homosexuality, and AIDS*. Boulder, CO: Westview Press.

Lumsden, Ian. 1996. *Machos, Maricones, and Gays: Cuba and Homosexuality*. Philadelphia, PA: Temple University Press.

Mattei, Ugo. 2019. "Comparative Law and Critical Legal Studies." In *The Oxford Handbook of Comparative Law*, 2nd edition, edited by Mathias Reimann and Reinhard Zimmerman, 815–36. Oxford: Oxford University Press.

NeJaime, Douglas. 2016. "Marriage Equality and the New Parenthood." *Harvard Law Review* 129(5): 1185–1266.

Peña, Susana. 2013. *¡Oye Loca! From the Mariel Boatlift to Gay Cuban Miami*. Minneapolis: University of Minnesota Press.

Puar, Jasbir. 2007. *Terrorist Assemblages: Homonationalism in Queer Times*. Durham, NC: Duke University Press.

———. 2013. "Rethinking Homonationalism." *International Journal of Middle East Studies* 45(2): 336–39.

Stout, Noelle M. 2014. *After Love: Queer Intimacy and Erotic Economies in Post-Soviet Cuba*. Durham, NC: Duke University Press.

Suchlicki, Jaime. 2002. *Cuba: from Columbus to Castro and Beyond*. Washington, DC: Brassey's.

PART II

Queer Figures

5

The Kinky Brat

Speak Pleasure to Power

UMMNI KHAN

In 2017, Hulu produced a television series (Miller 2017) based on Margaret Atwood's acclaimed 1985 dystopian novel, *The Handmaid's Tale* (Atwood 1985). In the story, our heroine, June, struggles against a totalitarian regime that subjects her and other "handmaids" to ritual rape and forced surrogacy. In 2018, critics called out two lingerie companies for selling handmaid-inspired outfits that were said to eroticize misogyny and sexual slavery. First, Lunya christened the red version of its camisole "Offred," the name imposed on June, to convey her status as property *of Fred*, the man with whom she is forced to have sex (Ahsan 2018). A few months later, Yandy produced the "Brave Red Maiden" Halloween costume, which updated the handmaids' uniform with leg-revealing and bodice-hugging details (Mercado 2018).

Feminist media accused the companies of "missing the point" and "equating women's lingerie with rape and subjugation" (Elderkin 2018; Kane 2018). Natalie Bronfman, a costume designer who worked on *The Handmaid's Tale*, stated that by creating such an outfit, "in theory, you are promoting the abuse of women" (Trzcinski 2021). *Huffington Post* sarcastically quipped: "[b]ecause nothing gets someone all hot and bothered quite like an 'Offred' camisole" (Wanshel 2018). More prescriptively, Ariel Sobel opined in her *Advocate* article that, "[h]er character [Offred] is not one that will turn you on; she's a sex slave forced to bear children by a brutal patriarchy that treats women as subhuman" (Sobel 2018).

I beg to differ. Offred turned me on. Indeed, it was the scheduled rapes perpetrated by Fred and his wife, and not the consensual love making with her secret beau Nick, that got me sincerely "hot and bothered." Unfortunately, I learned about the controversy too late to purchase a sexy handmaid outfit. The critical backlash forced the two companies to immediately withdraw their products and issue apologies. These opposing reactions to the handmaid lingerie—feminist disgust and my delight—exemplify something I want to stage in this chapter: a face-off between the feminist killjoy and the kinky brat.

While the "feminist killjoy" has historically operated as a misogynist epithet within mainstream society, Sara Ahmed has recently reclaimed the figure as one of resistance and world-making. As an identity or an analytic lens, this empowering use of the term has now proliferated across the academic, activist, and social media landscapes. In her monograph on the topic, Ahmed concretizes feminism through autobiographical narratives that feature her embodying the killjoy, thus showing that, "the personal is theoretical" (Ahmed 2017, 10). Just as Ahmed has been accused of being a killjoy, I have been called a brat all my life. Using the killjoy as my foil, this chapter presents the kinky brat—a personality and role that I argue holds both ontological and epistemological significance outside of standard BDSM (bondage, dominance sadomasochism) practice. In other words, like the killjoy, the kinky brat is a way of being in the world, and a way of accessing unique knowledge. But while the killjoy's mission is to expose and challenge oppressive or offensive phenomena (speaking truth to power), the kinky brat is interested in playful interventions and teasing out joy (speaking pleasure to power). As will be elaborated below, I support and embody both tendencies. However, the killjoy polemic seems to foreclose divergent feminist becomings.

In conceiving of the kinky brat, I begin by providing an overview of kink and its status within law and society. I continue by explaining brat identity and play within the kink context. Extrapolating from this, as well as common definitions, I sketch the kinky brat as a personification of an epistemological and methodological approach. I further consider how the killjoy/brat dyad maps onto other theoretical tensions and sexuality debates within the history of feminism. Finally, I apply the theory to the handmaid's sexy attire scandals, where I launch a bratty defense of these cultural artifacts by teasing out the kinkiness of the show and of Halloween costumes in general. However, I complicate this kinky redemption with a killjoy analysis of how *The Handmaid's Tale* television series positions a white woman as a feminist savior who embodies histories of racialized violence. In this way, I demonstrate how brat and killjoy perspectives can be complementary as well as conflicting. Throughout the chapter, I invoke Ahmed's feminist killjoy as a foil to flesh out the kinky brat's contrasting sensibility and insights. The main goal is to sketch out this attention-seeking figure, who refuses to apologize for positive or ambivalent reactions to certain phenomena considered inherently undesirable or beyond the pale—whether by feminists, mainstream society, or both.

Kink and BDSM—A Quick Overview

Kink operates as an affirming umbrella term for a wide variety of practices, identities, and desires. Often referred to as SM (sadomasochism) or BDSM (bondage, dominance, sadomasochism), it signifies pleasure, satisfaction, or fulfillment derived from some form of consensual power play. BDSM practices can include constraints with ropes or other devices; dominant and submissive dynamics (whether temporary or through the adoption of a 24/7 Dom/sub lifestyle); role-playing; and the experience of pain as a positive or wanted experience. It can also include fetishism, which conveys attraction toward, or arousal from, objects not conventionally associated with sexuality. For some, kink is an exotic diversion used to add variety to one's sexual repertoire. For others, it is a central component of their self-understanding, a crucial part of their relationality, or an exclusive way of forging intimate connection. While most people consider kink an erotic practice, for others it is experienced as art or performance, immutable orientation, recreation, athleticism, spirituality, or therapy. However, according to some detractors, kinky desires, identities, or practices are symptoms of an underlying problem.

In mainstream society—including law, medicine, pop culture, and everyday "common sense"—kink is disparaged. Some forms are criminalized, some pathologized, and fictional representations often portray it as abusive, harmful, or laughable. Kinksters must also contend with radical feminism, which portrays kink as fundamentally patriarchal, harming both the practitioners and society as a whole. But the status of BDSM has evolved in the last few decades. Alongside pejorative representations, there are also positive portrayals. There is some feminist tolerance for mild kinky practices, so long as it conforms to what I see as normative politics. Acceptable BDSM is practiced privately or at an

official kink event between people who are "safe, sane, and consensual."
Consensual in this context means the relevant activities have been labeled BDSM, limits and safe words are determined beforehand, and
the substance and sequencing of the activities are clear, scripted, and
predictable. Kinky activities that deviate from these parameters can
sometimes be seen as irresponsible. There is also progressive disdain for
the "mainstreaming" of kink. For example, when the *Fifty Shades of Grey*
movie came out, not only did conservative commentators condemn the
love story based on an anti-kink ideology, but there were also BDSM
practitioners, allies, and sex-positive or sex-critical scholars who saw it
as a dangerous distortion of genuine BDSM (Green 2015). The story was
derided as "mommy porn," and its fans as heteronormative wannabes
who would naively believe that the portrayal of BDSM in the film was
a blueprint for a kinky relationship in real life. This progressive policing, in my view, is another form of misogyny and sexual stratification,
and reflects a strain of elitism in some BDSM politics. I parse the idea
of BDSM normativity and elitism toward the end of this chapter, when
considering the objections to the handmaid sexy outfits.

The Kinky Brat

In common parlance, a brat refers to a badly behaving child who delights
in her disobedience. She'll throw a tantrum when you lay down the law.
The term is often collocated with spoiled, suggesting that her naughti-
ness is due to a lack of discipline. Her caregivers indulged her, and she
got away with mischief. And now look. She's spoiled. While the term is
generally pejorative, the kink world—as it does with many putdowns—
reclaims the figure for empowerment and pleasure.

A kinky brat within BDSM play is a bit of a chimeric figure, adopting attributes associated with both top and bottom roles. Some oft-cited
definitions of the brat are "a submissive who enjoys rebelling in a childlike way against their dominant" (Wiseman 2011, 369), or a kinkster who
presents as "resistant and bratty" (Easton and Hardy 2001, 20). Jessica
M. W. Kratzer describes the brat as a submissive who "seems to want
to defy or wrest control" (Kratzer 2020, 42). A brat will wriggle out of
her restraints. A brat will talk back. After being ordered to get on her
knees, she'll goad, "make me." After being spanked, she'll taunt, "is that

all you got?" Not all kinksters appreciate the brat or want to engage in brat play. Some Doms will condemn her as a badly behaved—that is, a substandard—submissive. But what they don't understand is that she's not a *submissive* submissive. In some ways, she's topping from the bottom. She's exerting a type of power that is coded and indirect. It is not the power of endurance to withstand intense pain, or to transmute degradation into masochistic pride. It's the power—and the pleasure—of resistance to authority. Like a skilled screenwriter, the brat knows every good scene must be grounded in conflict.

In the following section, I take the kinky brat out of explicit BDSM contexts to see what she might be able to show us through her defiance and odd pleasure-seeking.

The Kinky Brat and the Feminist Killjoy as Rival Siblings

Although I juxtapose Sara Ahmed's work to my project, the brat shares some commonality with two figures Ahmed has described in extended analyses: the willful subject and the feminist killjoy (2014; 2017). In both cases, Ahmed reclaims attributes that others have branded as defects. The willful subject defies authority and swerves away from conventional pathways. Ahmed identifies the willful subject as "kin" to the feminist killjoy, who refuses to go along with happiness scripts that oppress, silence, and erase herself or others. In her book, *Living a Feminist Life*, Ahmed pays homage to the killjoy as the quintessential feminist figure, ending the book with a "Killjoy Manifesto" that outlines an anti-oppression praxis (2017). Comprised of ten principles (like the Ten Commandments), the manifesto calls for personal commitments that range from broad attitudinal stances ("I am not willing to get over histories that are not over," 261) to micro practices ("I am not willing to laugh at jokes designed to cause offense," 262). Most of the principles rest on a rejection of happiness (refusing happiness as one's cause; being willing to cause unhappiness; supporting others causing unhappiness; living a life others deem unhappy, 257–68).

The kinky brat is similarly willful and has—at times—an oppositional relationship to conventional happiness narratives. As a self-proclaimed brat, I believe my own philosophy of life aligns with nearly all of Ahmed's principles. I'm willing to cause unhappiness in exactly the way she contemplates, naming what I perceive to be an oppressive practice, pattern, or attitude, even if it disrupts the harmony of a group. I am also prepared to cause unhappiness through brattiness. My outspoken defense of risky BDSM, catcalling, and purchasing sexual services from a pleasure-positive perspective has caused unhappiness for feminists who fundamentally oppose these practices. Causing unhappiness is an unavoidable part of doing critical scholarship (or for that matter, going against the mainstream from any direction, including from the far right). But I would never center my politics on killing joy. I am instead preoccupied with happiness and searching out ways to recognize and cultivate joy. The killjoy is motivated—it seems to me—mostly by negative affect, or, in the words of Elizabeth Stephens, "bad feelings." As Stephens elaborates, Ahmed's work is part of a broader feminist and queer turn toward negativity. This trend could include Ann Cvetkovich's work on depression, Jack Halberstam's on failure, Judith Butler's on mourning, and Lauren Berlant's on "cruel optimism" (Stephens 2015, 274). But Ahmed is not just making space for the killjoy. I would applaud that, since I've been one myself—these days less as a feminist, and more as a vegetarian, often being the downer when the veal gets ordered (although even here, happiness is still my root motivation, just centered on that of the calves rather than the carnivores). What bugs me is Ahmed's personification of feminism into this figure. She conflates killing joy with doing feminism. The book is called *Living a Feminist Life*, as if one can exhaustively define what a "feminist" life would be. This title is reminiscent of MacKinnon's book, *Feminism Unmodified* (1987). Both books assume an authority to pronounce what constitutes genuine feminism, even though it would be more accurate to specify which branch of feminism is being promoted in their books, that is, "radical" or "anti-porn" (in the case of MacKinnon), or killjoy (in the case of Ahmed).

Ahmed and I have notable similarities and differences in our identities and backgrounds that I believe may be relevant for this discussion. We are both South Asian Muslims who grew up in white-dominated settler states. We are about the same age and we both reap the benefits of light-skin privilege. There are also some notable differences. She's biracial with one white parent, and I'm South Asian on both sides. She's a lesbian while I'm married to a guy, and no matter how much I insist I'm queer (*I really am!*), I still access hetero privilege much of the time. But given our similar backgrounds, I harbor a touch of Brown girl rivalry with Ahmed (obviously unrequited since she almost certainly does not know who I am, and probably never will). We can take this further by positioning this one-sided rivalry within a sibling context. While not as analyzed as parental complexes (such as Jung's Imago, or Freud's Oedipal and Electra paradigms), sibling and birth order theories can provide insight into the feminist killjoy/kinky brat dyad. As Daniel Hayes suggests, we can "think of psychoanalysis as a sort of useful and pleasurable fiction about the self and its possibilities" (2008, 288).

From this perspective, I would like to creatively explore how the sibling rivalry may be at play. On the most micro level, Ahmed and I can be cast as professional siblings because of our shared identity as scholars, the overlapping themes of our writing, our similar backgrounds, and our closeness in age. Within this dynamic, I draw on birth order theory—not because she is slightly older than I am, but because her success, fame, and influence set her up as a rival, as well as someone for me to rebel against. For example, I resent how she presents her experiences of dealing with misogyny, racism, Islamophobia, and heterosexism, as if they necessarily inculcated a killjoy attitude, opinion, or tendency. This erases those of us with similar experiences who turned out differently. As the symbolic "baby of the family" (as well as the literal one in my own nuclear family), I am driven to stake out an alternative to her brand of feminism. Moreover, as a spoiled brat, I want a theory and methodology that accord with my pleasure-seeking personality.

The complex dynamic between the brat and the killjoy can be traced to many different theories, tensions, and contrasting positions. While the two share feminist and queer roots, the killjoy draws more heavily from lesbian feminism than the brat. Consider that in Ahmed's killjoy treatise, *Living a Feminist Life*, she dedicates a full chapter to celebrating the lesbian feminist figure as a quintessential killjoy. While queerness is referenced throughout this book, there is no chapter on the queer figure as a killjoy, although significantly, there is criticism of queer perspectives that Ahmed believes are demeaning or unfair toward lesbian feminism. In terms of kink, lesbian feminism is a part of our history. For example, Samois, a late-'70s high-profile support group for kinky women, defined its membership as "feminist lesbians who share a positive interest in sadomasochism" (1979). But as time went on, kinksters increasingly seemed to find more resonance in other identities and theories, such as leatherdyke, sex-positive feminism, sex-radical feminism, and queer (Khan 2014, 111). In my view, kink is queer, particularly if we position queer in relation to Eve Sedgwick's "universalizing" perspective on same-sex desire (1990, 1). In Sedgwick's view, homosexuality holds symbolic and material relevance to people of all sexual orientations. Similarly, I understand kink to be of relevance across the vanilla/kinky and normative/non-normative spectrums. And just as Sedgwick destabilized the homo/hetero binary, I am untethering kink from a fixed identity, sexual subculture, set of desires, or concrete practices, and arguing for its conceptual capaciousness.

The brat/killjoy dyad could also be aligned with Sedgwick's theory on paranoid and reparative positions. Taking paranoia outside of clinical contexts and into reading positions, Sedgewick argued that the paranoid theorist operates through a "hermeneutic of suspicion" (2003, 124). The killjoy clearly privileges a paranoid perspective in her suspicion of mainstream practices and her pursuit to uncover the hidden violence lurking, for example, in lingerie or a Halloween costume. On the other hand, the reparative position allows the possibility that one can find surprise, joy, and sustenance even in cultural practices that appear to undermine one's interests. If we consider that much of kink is about reworking hegemonic, violent, and oppressive relations for both pleasure and subversion, one might say that reparative is the theory and kink is the practice. Thus, the kinky brat offers perspectives that could potentially recuperate, or at least complicate, some maligned, policed, or criminalized activity.

Extending this framework to the macro level, the killjoy/brat tensions can inform a number of feminist divides. Take the 1980s feminist sex wars. At the time (and still to this day arguably), radical feminism posited sexuality as the lynchpin to female subordination. Carol Vance's 1982 Barnard conference is often touted as the event that launched the first high-profile attack on this narrow view (Vance and Scholar and the Feminist Conference 1984). Vance's audacity in creating a platform to theorize pleasure alongside danger in relation to female sexuality was arguably a bratty move. This defiance of feminist orthodoxy spawned vehement and heavy-handed responses from *big sister*, including petitions, protests, and appeals to university officials to cancel the event, with allegations it was being run by "sexual perverts" (Vance 1993, 294). The radical feminist critics could be understood as killjoys, who took the position that enjoyment of kink, pornography, or identities like butch and femme, reinforced patriarchal ideology. But the brats insisted on their right to explore the complexity of female sexuality, which included making conceptual room for props and personas plucked from patriarchal culture. This response is not just defiance, but a refusal of the terms of radical feminism, as exemplified by Gayle Rubin's iconic contribution to the conference and its edited book collection, *Thinking Sex* (1984). In this nascently queer essay, Rubin challenged feminism's exclusive authority to theorize sexuality through the lens of gender hierarchy. She contended that many forms of erotic injustice—like the persecution of kinky people—do not fit neatly, or at all, within the male dominance-female subordination master narrative.

If Rubin's essay can be classified as epistemologically bratty, other artifacts from the time exemplify a brat sensibility even more directly, performing the playfulness and pleasure that Rubin defended. For example, the lesbian magazine, *On Our Backs* (1984–2006), flouted radical feminist strictures, creating positive and sexy space for lesbian pornography, kinky practices, and controversial identities such as butch, femme, or leatherdyke. The title itself is a rhetorically bratty move as it satirizes *Off Our Backs* (1970–2008), a radical feminist magazine that dedicated substantial content to critiquing such practices. Furthermore, the sex-positive title is a rejection of feminist essentialism, reclaiming pleasures branded as patriarchal, such as the submissive pleasure of being *on our backs*.

Another example worth mentioning is the 1990s DIY publication, *Brat Attack: The Zine for Leatherdykes and Other Bad Girrrlz.* The title uses the brat as a synecdoche for lesbian kink, and the contents reject radical feminist dogma through the use of dark humor, hyperbole, and self-reflection. As Dana Collins explains, *Brat Attack* did not displace radical feminist ideology with counter-truths, but rather sought to "blur key binaries—of fantasy and 'real life,' positive and negative imagery, liberated and contained sexualities, aesthetics, and politics—while calling attention to the mediated nature of all representations" (1999, 67). Following Rubin's lead, this next generation of lesbian kinksters was interested in destabilizing binaries and de-exceptionalizing pornographic imagery, rather than advancing a new sexual hierarchy.

The final text I want to review, *Bad Attitude/s on Trial: Pornography, Feminism, and the Butler Decision* (Cossman et al. 1997), shows the killjoy/brat distinction is not a stable binary, but rather a conceptual vehicle to illustrate contrasting political priorities and identifications within particular historical moments. The book can be contextualized as a salvo in the Canadian sex wars, with two targets. First, the book critiques the Supreme Court of Canada's decision in *R v. Butler*, which justified the criminalization of pornography using feminist, rather than moralizing, rhetoric (*R. v. Butler*, [1992] 1 S.C.R. 452). Second, the book challenges anti-porn feminist engagement with the case, which included a legal intervention to support porn censorship in the name of protecting women, as well as lauding the eventual judgment as a "feminist victory." With this in mind, *Bad Attitude/s on Trial* can be seen from one point of view to reflect the killjoy perspective. The authors killed (or at least maimed) feminist joy by exposing how the precedent came to be used against queer erotica, for example through justification of homophobic book seizures at the border, withdrawal of funding for queer performances, and police raids of feminist and queer bookstores. From another perspective, the book is a kinky brat text. For example, the title references the lesbian erotic magazine, *Bad Attitude*, which a trial judge deemed obscene under a *Butler* analysis based primarily on its inclusion of a lesbian BDSM short story. Thus, on a literal level, the book is bratty because of its defense of kinky erotica. But, more broadly, it's bratty because of its destabilization of essentialist claims on the meaning of sexual texts and its insistence on sexual pleasure as an epistemological resource. For example, this is expressed in Shannon Bell's chapter, which dissolves the distinction between philosophy and pornography. Bell's provocation deploys poetic-critical text alongside hard-core photographs, arousing both sexual feelings and philosophical thoughts on the nature of truth and representation.

In the same vein as *Brat Attack* and *Bad Attitude/s on Trial*, my issue with Ahmed's Killjoy is not the act of being a killjoy itself, but rather the privileging of such acts as quintessentially feminist and implicitly morally superior to happiness-seeking. Ahmed's normative take on humor will illustrate this point. In the first part of her conclusion in *Living a Feminist Life*, she outlines a "killjoy toolkit" which includes humor as a way to "lighten the load" when dealing with the "heavy history" of the world. Killjoy humor provides "resources to bear witness, to expose things, to bring things to the surface, so they can be laughed at" (2017, 246). Acceptable humor, then, is a feminist coping method, a way of bonding between fellow killjoys, and a way of articulating oppressive power relations that generally go unsaid. Conversely, her manifesto outlines unacceptable humor with the fourth principle, stating: "I am not willing to laugh at jokes designed to cause offence" (261). In her 600+ word gloss on the topic, she instructs the reader that when hearing an "offensive" joke, "[d]o not be tempted to laugh. If the situation is humorless, we need not to add humor to it. If the situation is unfunny, we need not to make light of it; we need not to make it fun" (261). I reject this principle. First, it reminds me of earlier divisions between feminist "erotica" and patriarchal "pornography," an essentialist distinction built on respectability politics and the imperative to suppress one's desires to fit a feminist persona. Second, how does one determine for certain what a joke is designed to do? Have we not all made a joke with the intention of creating shared merriment, only to find we missed the mark? Third, and most important, genuine laughter, like crying or arousal, is an involuntary response, and as such, often escapes the discipline of our conscience. On some level, Ahmed seems to understand this corporeal connection by choosing the word "tempted." In common parlance, temptations often refer to carnal enticements related to sex, sleep, food, or drink. Her decree tacitly acknowledges that the body may have its own anarchic reaction to comical stimuli, even when our intellect labels the joke offensive. Ahmed's comments about humor are thus—at least in part—about policing a wayward body. If a joke is perceived as one "designed to cause offence," the killjoy will either not find it funny in the first place or smother any laughter that would otherwise erupt.

As a kinky brat, I assess the situation differently. It turns out that some "offensive" jokes make me genuinely—and involuntarily—laugh, just as sexual violence in fictional media can turn me on. But instead of suppressing the feeling or succumbing to shame, I cherish the moment, taking pleasure where I find it. Alongside this hedonistic impulse, I also investigate what embodied meanings it might hold, instead of (or in addition to) the initial Pavlovian response instilled by patriarchy. In a broad sense, I believe my not-infrequent attraction to "rape culture" texts is based on my temperament; there is a fundamental playfulness to my personality. Like play-based learning, play-based outlooks are not prescriptive or goal-oriented, they are process-oriented. I thus understand role-playing, fantasy, music, or narratives as sites of intensity and mystery, where I can process the human condition, including our shared vulnerability to violence, sexual or otherwise. And I have this understanding, despite my identity as a queer South Asian Muslim woman who has had negative personal experiences with discrimination and patriarchy. From this, I extrapolate that whether one is more a killjoy or a brat is not necessarily contingent on whether one has been subject to discrimination or sexual violence. As a result, I object to privileging the killjoy as the face of feminism, which erases alternative play-based epistemologies.

In the next section, I will apply this theory to the concrete example of the aforementioned *The Handmaid's Tale* scandal and show what a kinky brat perspective might bring to the conversation.

The Handmaid's Tale

As stated in the introduction, in 2018, two companies were forced to discontinue the sale of sexy clothing items inspired by *The Handmaid's Tale* television series. Feminist activists had publicly called out this merchandise for trivializing sexual violence. If we assess the situation in Ahmed's terms, killjoys disrupted the happiness of the companies selling the products. Importantly, killjoys also negated the happiness of their naive sisters who would have blithely worn the items without realizing their complicity with rape culture. Conversely, the kinky brat likes to play dress-up. She might happily have donned a sexy handmaid outfit and pretended an icy upper-crust wife was holding her down while the patriarch enjoyed his *droit du seigneur*. Moreover, the kinky brat delights in shocking her killjoy counterparts by confessing her pleasure in the very sexual violence that is being placed off-limits for erotic play. As Foucault has pointed out, the confession itself can become a source of erotic discourse (1990). In this way, killjoying can enhance kinky pleasure by creating more furtive desires to reveal, taboos to flout, and authority figures to defy. As Julia Creet has argued, anti-SM feminism has created narratives and proscriptions that are ripe for erotic appropriation by kinksters (1991). Taking it even further in relation to MacKinnon's writings, Samia Vasa states, "[t]he S/M textuality of MacKinnon undoes its own radical feminist critique of sexuality by amplifying and aggravating pleasure in the name of ending it" (2019, 111). In other words, killjoy critique can itself become an SM scene.

I want to build on these insights to consider *The Handmaid's Tale* as an SM narrative dressed in the justificatory cloak of the feminist dystopian genre. On the most patent level, the story provides ideal building blocks for perverse pleasures. In the new state of Gilead, we have a highly authoritarian society, unique costumes for each social stratum, rigid rules covering everyday minutiae, slut-shaming, emotional humiliation, corporeal punishment, and of course, rape as a sexual ritual. All these narrative aspects can easily be reimagined as erotic role play. But beyond its susceptibility as derivative kink, I see the story itself as a form of vicarious kink. In other words, despite or perhaps even because of its didactic elements, its consumption offers many erotic pleasures.

On a broad level, feminist film theory can elucidate the SM pleasures harboring within *The Handmaid's Tale* series. An ongoing dialog within this field is whether films provide the spectator with a fundamentally sadistic or masochistic experience. On the sadistic side we have Laura Mulvey's classic 1975 text, *Visual Pleasure, and Narrative Cinema*, which appropriates psychoanalytic theory as a "political weapon" to expose the patriarchal underpinning of mainstream film (1989). In this text, Mulvey coined and theorized the "male gaze," arguing a director's cinematic choices encourage audience members, regardless of their gender, to experience Hollywood film from the perspective of the sadistic, voyeuristic, and objectifying heterosexual male. Particularly interesting to note for our purposes is the killjoy agenda in the piece. In both the introduction and the conclusion, Mulvey explicitly states that her aim is to attack and destroy the erotic pleasure of narrative cinema.

On the masochism side, Gaylyn Studlar's work argues for a more expansive and heterogenous understanding of the multiple pleasures encoded in film spectatorship (1984). While Studlar's work also draws on psychoanalysis, instead of focusing on the phallic stage and castration anxiety (as Mulvey did), she considers the pre-genital oral phase, where the mother figure dominates. Taking her cue from Deleuze rather than Freud, she argues audience members can and do identify with and across gender identities, that narrative suspense reflects masochistic ambivalence in both wanting and fearing loss of self in the mother, and that spectatorship necessitates submission to the story. I side with Studlar, whom I will claim as a fellow kinky brat, as she sets out to articulate unrecognized pleasure and agency. While she does not deny that sadism or the male gaze can form part of the pleasure of looking, she insists that this pleasure exists alongside masochistic pleasures, including identification with female characters. Building on this insight, it seems to me that narrative fiction in film—or television in the case of *The Handmaid's Tale*—may involve spectator fluidity between top and bottom roles.

In *The Handmaid's Tale*, the cinematography of the mandatory sex scenes invites the spectator to assume multiple positions of pleasure. In episode one, the viewer witnesses "the Ceremony" for the first time. This "sacred ritual" involves Offred lying on her back between the legs of Serena Joy, the "barren" wife, who holds the handmaid's wrists down to symbolically unite their bodies. Offred's knees are extended, her dress hitched up, while the head of the household, Fred Waterford, proceeds to copulate with her. The scene provides close-ups of all the characters, point-of-view reverse-shots from Offred's and Fred's perspectives, and a long shot—peeping Tom style—that takes in the whole scene from above Fred's shoulder. All their faces are impassive and detached, despite the physical and supposedly spiritual connection of the sexual-surrogate triad. It is clear this feminist show is not intended to cater to the male gaze, as defined by Mulvey. Much of the scene either invites identification with Offred through medium close-up shots or shows the world through her eyes as the rape takes place. But we also look down at Offred at other times, witnessing what Fred would see as he thrusts in and out of her. While the sex is not depicted as "sexy" in a conventional way, the spectator is provided multiple gazes. Scopophilia—the pleasure derived from looking associated with spectatorship—is cultivated from the vantage point of dominance, submission, as well as omniscient voyeurism.

I found the scene arousing as well as upsetting. A subsequent scene dramatizes this affective inner conflict. Four episodes later, "the Ceremony" takes place again, but this time Fred breaks the rules by looking lustily at Offred during the sexual intercourse and caressing her thighs. Offred shakes her head at Fred, and through voiceover we hear her silently begging Fred to stop his intimate transgression, for which *she* could be blamed and punished. He ignores her mute entreaty and as he continues, Offred's face flushes and her breathing quickens, indicating heightened emotion. We know she is scared and angry, but unwanted sexual arousal is also suggested. This is confirmed when in the subsequent scene, Offred confronts Fred about his breach of Gilead law, and he replies, "I didn't mind it. I don't think you did either." This scene is emblematic of the ambivalent thrills of the show in general. Like Offred, the spectator may be horrified by what's happening, but there is also pleasure in the scene—for some of us anyway—even if we feel violated by it. Throughout the show, we witness Offred and others being humiliated and brutalized. This indulges sadistic voyeurism, while fostering masochism through identification and more broadly by narrative surrender, even as sadness, anger, and disgust are also elicited. As Weber suggests, "*The Handmaid's Tale* participates in a spectacle of violent rupture that could well be called torture porn. By this I mean that the formal and ideological components of the series conspire to create a scopophilic and anticipatory pleasure in waiting for and watching characters be hurt" (Weber 2018, 193). However, I argue that spectator pleasure in *The Handmaid's Tale* should not be characterized as gratifying sadism and masochism as separate elements, or during separate moments of the film, but rather that these pleasures are ultimately indivisible. In Deleuzian terms, they are a series of orchestrated sensations that produce a flow of intensities (Bertetto 2017).

Importantly, SM pleasure in fictional texts like *The Handmaid's Tale* can easily go unacknowledged for two reasons. First, as Mulvey and Studlar point out, effective narrative fiction allows the spectator to "lose" themselves in the story and remain unaware of psychic satisfactions they may be experiencing. Second, because the show's dystopian genre and feminist branding clearly position its moral stance as being *against* the depicted patriarchal order, the spectator can gorge on intensely violent and graphic "torture porn" (Weber 2018), while still maintaining feminist integrity. The show, after all, is ostensibly about using dystopian allegory to confront patriarchal brutality from the past, present, and potential future. The consciousness-raising agenda of the show may spare viewers (or at least its fans) from considering their own erotic complicity in the spectacle of violence.

As a kinky brat, I embrace the affective chaos that marks the SM experience offered by *The Handmaid's Tale*, understanding that extracting pleasure from representations of sexual violence does not mean endorsing or enjoying such acts in real life. However, as a woman of color, the show's privileging of whiteness brings out my inner killjoy. In the novel, Atwood characterizes Gilead as a white supremacist society, with Black people forcibly resettled elsewhere. On the other hand, the worldmaking of the TV show portrays a low birth rate crisis that has magically removed race as a marker of difference or hierarchy. While this far-fetched conceit allows for a multiracial cast, the narrative choice is nonetheless troubling.

Excellent scholarship and cultural commentary have been dedicated to analyzing the show's white-centeredness, and its inclusion of racialized characters alongside its erasure of historical slavery and ongoing anti-Black racism (Bastién 2017; Priya 2017). For purposes of this chapter, I want to point out some interlocking whiteness-related fantasies relevant to the Halloween/lingerie controversy. As many critics have argued, both the television show and the novel feature the experiences and trauma of enslaved Black people in general, and Black women in particular, but cast white womanhood in the starring, suffering role (Crawley 2018).

The show centers on June, a middle-class white woman who undergoes devastating experiences, including violent separation from her child, assignment as property and reproductive vessel for an elite family, sexual assault, corporeal punishment to "correct" misbehavior, and torture to compel disclosure of rebel intelligence. As Crawley explains, the spectator is drawn into her experiences: "[t]he show's exploration of female bodies in pain is focalised through the body of Offred, who we are invited to identify with intimately through cinematic techniques and affect" (2018, 337). In this way, the show allows the audience to play and eroticize terrorizing episodes from the past and the present, without having to consider white women's complicity with structural and quotidian racial violence. But we also see June finding her strength and emerging as a folk hero of the resistance movement. Importantly, much of her heroism derives from her status as mother to a Black child (from her life before the coup) and a white baby (conceived during an illicit consensual affair while she is a Handmaid). The show can thus be cast as both a "white slavery" and a neoliberal "white savior" fantasy, as June not only personifies both sides of the Madonna/(trafficked) whore binary but is also portrayed as a key liberator of Gilead's mixed-race victims.

Ahmed's work on the phenomenology of whiteness provides further insight into June's racial significance (2007). June is presented as "worldly" (to use Ahmed's term), while the narrative displaces racialized histories, specificities, and subjectivities. The white viewer can easily delve into this fantasy because, as Ahmed states, "[t]o be comfortable is to be so at ease with one's environment that it is hard to distinguish where one's body ends and the world begins" (2007, 158). June's white body becomes the blank screen upon which racial violence is simultaneously projected and whitewashed, allowing white viewers to vicariously access these experiences without considering racial contexts. The non-white viewer, on the other hand, must first erase their racialization in order to identify with a white protagonist. Paradoxically, it is through June's whiteness that the non-white viewer then arrives back to their embodied knowledge of racial violence. This is an *uncomfortable* spectator experience. Indeed, it is a form of racial alienation, but given the standard casting of white actors as central characters and heroic figures, many of us are used to this circuitous identificatory process, even if we continue to resent it.

In my analysis of *The Handmaid's Tale* so far, I've drawn on kinky brattiness to discern SM pleasures in its consumption, and killjoyness to interrogate the show's investment in white mythologies of saviorhood and worldliness. What can account for these divergent reactions when both involve a disavowed fantasy? I am not opposed to race play within BDSM contexts, including when white people are involved, but in this instance, I do not see it as kinky "play" as much as pandering to white supremacy. On a pragmatic level, I am critical of the casting choice of a white heroine, as this marginalizes racialized actors who are consistently cast as "friend" or "love interest" to the central white character. On a symbolic level, the casting further contributes to the reification of whiteness as neutral and universal both within the narrative, and (I'm guessing) for many white spectators. There is obvious pleasure for many white people to have white supremacy naturalized. As Anthony Paul Farley states, "[whiteness is not a color; it is a way of feeling pleasure in and about one's body. The [B]lack body is needed to fulfill this desire for race-pleasure" (Farley 1997, 458). Thus, I am taking a normative stance, seeking not only to expose, but also to extinguish, white pleasure in simultaneously appropriating and erasing racial histories of violence and dehumanization. To me, white fantasies in *The Handmaid's Tale* series are not kinky, but rather a reinforcement of real-world racial stratification.

Halloween

Revisiting the costume controversy, sexy Halloween costumes have long been a target for feminist killjoy organizations, academics, and commentators. Each year, bloggers bemoan revealing costumes they believe lead to a host of social ills (Orozco 2018; Tergesen 2018). In academic scholarship, a 2016 social science article addressing "women's revealing Halloween costumes" argued that this trend leads to the "problem" of sexualization and objectification (Lennon et al. 2016). The article does not consider sexual desire as a potentially empowering site for women, nor does it address the pleasure and agency in choosing a costume or eliciting erotic attention. Instead, women who dress sexy are seen as "self-objectifying," which interferes with "task performance" (creativity and self-expression in adornment is precluded, it seems, from constituting a "task"). A 2011 article on the topic considers Halloween costumes as performances of gender (Macmillan et al. 2011). This article at least considers the pleasures women may derive from dressing up in feminine and sexy ways, even if it then proceeds to demean such pleasure as "narcissism" and "superficial." Moreover, the article cites numerous authors who declare there is no agency in such practices.

As a high-femme whose boobs are often bursting out of my top, I must say these killjoys make me want to stick my tongue out at them. Consider in the film *Mean Girls* when the protagonist says, "[i]n girl world, Halloween is the one night of the year when a girl can dress like a total slut, and no other girls can say anything about it" (Waters 2004). Unfortunately, feminist moral entrepreneurs actually have a lot to say about it, given their preoccupation with sexualization. Feminist scholarship on the harms of sexy Halloween costumes exemplifies femmephobia, "a type of prejudice, discrimination or antagonism that is directed at someone who is perceived to identify, embody or express femininely and towards people or objects gendered femininely" (Blair and Hoskin 2015, 232). While the articles condemn the negative attributes that some interviewees associated with women in sexy feminine costumes, they themselves conveyed what femme theorist Rhea Ashley Hoskin calls "pious femmephobia." This form of gender regulation engages in "[s]haming the feminine person or enactment through positioning the femmephobic offender as morally superior or intellectually enlightened " (Hoskin 2013, 36). I would elaborate that there is a particular form of feminist femmephobia through which femmes are belittled as unthinking dupes of the patriarchy who uphold hegemonic femininity. Thus, despite good intentions, as Lara Karaian argues, the discourse of sexualization paradoxically erases agency and responsibilizes females who are purportedly "self-objectifying" (Karaian 2015).

As women's revealing, tight, and slinky Halloween costumes are a standard cite of femmephobic moralizing, it is no surprise that a sexy handmaid outfit attracted such feminist ire. What is interesting to note from a killjoy perspective is that handmaid costumes are not censured in general but only if they are donned for the purpose of pleasure and playfulness. After the show came out, activists en masse slipped on handmaid outfits during demonstrations against misogynist people, policies, laws, and state decisions. As one *Guardian* article observed, the outfit "has emerged as one of the most powerful current feminist symbols of protest, in a subversive inversion of its association with the oppression of women" (Beaumont and Holpuch 2018).

In the case of political protest, then, the handmaid outfit is able to translate its fictional meaning into empowerment, despite, for example, the problematic trope of white saviorhood in the show. But in the case of erotic enjoyment and role play, the killjoys insist that the symbol reproduces female subordination. Tellingly, millennial /Gen Z women's magazine, *Bustle* (which includes femme-positive beauty tips and celeb gossip), wrote about the two uses of the handmaid costume, stating:

> If you want to be sexy for Halloween, by all means dress sexy. There are plenty of sexy Halloween costumes that don't reference a show about rape and misogyny. You can even join Halloween goers and protestors alike and dress up as a handmaid. Make a statement in your red cloak. Just maybe don't make it "sexy" if you don't want to be counterproductive to the cause. (Mercado 2018)

This killjoy conclusion masquerades as sex-positive advice. The reader is given license to *either* "dress sexy" *or* wear the handmaid costume. The article thus perpetuates the broader ideology of sexual exceptionalism, where sexy artifacts and representations are read as more literal, risky, and prescriptive than their non-sexual equivalents.

Furthermore, consider that *Bustle* includes many articles that encourage people to explore their kinky interests (Chatel 2018; McGowan 2020). However, because these sexy Handmaid outfits are not marketed for BDSM practitioners, and instead target a mainstream audience interested in looking sexy, even ostensibly kink-positive commentators condemn them as rape culture. But kink is not exclusively practiced by members who identify as kinky or form part of the BDSM community. The desire to eroticize or play with signifiers of violence is part of everyday life, including in relation to Halloween dress-up rituals. I have explored other examples of this phenomenon in previous publications, including "rapey" music, which I interpret as a type of aural kink in which lyrics that appear to celebrate sexual coercion are enjoyed as role play and fetish (Khan 2017). I have also co-authored a kink-centered defense of a video game where the player's main goal is to commit sexual assault and get away with it (Khan and Ketterling 2019). Finally, I have argued that anti-SM discourse, whether by legal actors or radical feminists, is itself a form of vicarious kink, where the condemner can revel in deviant desires with impunity because of their moral agenda (Khan 2014). As I have suggested throughout, kink is about, in part, eroticizing artifacts, activities, and power differentials that are not generally recognized as sexual—whether in relation to music, gaming, moralizing, or donning an outfit culturally associated with rape.

Conclusion—I'm Sorry, Aunt Lydia

In *The Handmaid's Tale* television series, a climactic scene at the end of season one occurs when June is ordered to stone an insubordinate handmaid to death. Instead of launching the rock at her condemned peer, June drops it to the ground and says to her matronly supervisor, "I'm sorry, Aunt Lydia." Emboldened by this act of defiance, all the other handmaids who were meant to join in the execution follow suit. It is an ironically powerful line, as earlier in her handmaid training, June had been forced to utter an insincere apology for a minor transgression. In this moment, the handmaids' repeated line, "I'm sorry," inverts its literal meaning from one of remorse to one of unapologetic refusal. Killjoys rejoice in these kinds of dramatic performances and inversions, whether in the show or transported to the streets in real life. However, the elasticity of signification is not recognized when it comes to kinksters reformulating the muck of patriarchy, violence, and social stratification into role play, fantasy, and dress-up. Sexified inversions are interpreted as patriarchal replications, and if women participate, their actions are deemed false consciousness, self-objectification, or narcissism—or at the very least, counterproductive. While this perpetuates stigma or erasure, for kinky brats, these condemnations can sometimes enhance the thrill of transgression.

* * *

In this chapter, I've introduced the kinky brat as a pleasure-positive figure, an interpretive lens, and a way of being in the world that extends BDSM phenomenology and epistemology into broader contexts. Although I have used Ahmed's feminist killjoy as a foil, as I've demonstrated, the kinky brat is not opposed to killjoyness. There is overlap between these two willful subjects, and the same analysis can draw insight from both perspectives. To vivify the overlaps and distinctions between the killjoy and the brat, I imagine their relationship as siblings in a queer family who offer rival interpretations. However, I object to feminist killjoys negating alternative pleasure-centered ways of knowing or implicitly telling us brats to grow up. *I'm sorry, killjoys.* The kinky brat—who is indelibly spoiled—feels the world differently.

BIBLIOGRAPHY

Ahmed, Sara. 2007. "A Phenomenology of Whiteness." *Feminist Theory* 8(2): 149–68. https://doi.org/10.1177/1464700107078139.

———. 2014. *Willful Subjects*. Durham, NC: Duke University Press.

———. 2017. *Living a Feminist Life*. Durham, NC: Duke University Press.

Ahsan, Sadaf. 2018. "Nope. Not Everything Needs to Be Made Sexy. We're Looking at You, Lingerie 'Inspired by The Handmaid's Tale.'" *National Post*, April 18. https://nationalpost.com.

Atwood, Margaret. 1985. *The Handmaid's Tale*. London: Virago.

Bastién, Angelica Jade. 2017. "In Its First Season, *The Handmaid's Tale* Greatest Failing Is How It Handles Race." *Vulture*, June 14. www.vulture.com.

Beaumont, Peter and Amanda Holpuch. 2018. "How *The Handmaid's Tale* Dressed Protests across the World." *The Guardian*, August 3. www.theguardian.com.

Bertetto, Paolo. 2017. "Concept, Sensation, Intensity: Deleuze's Theory of Art and Cinema." *Sociology and Anthropology* 5(9): 792–97.

Blair, Karen L. and Rhea Ashley Hoskin. 2015. "Experiences of Femme Identity: Coming Out, Invisibility and Femmephobia." *Psychology & Sexuality* 6(3): 229–44. https://doi.org/10.1080/19419899.2014.921860.

Chatel, Amanda. 2018. "Top 5 Sexual Fetishes & Kinks, According to a New Survey." *Bustle*, September 14. www.bustle.com.

Collins, Dana. 1999. "'No Experts: Guaranteed!': Do-It-Yourself Sex Radicalism and the Production of the Lesbian Sex Zine 'Brat Attack.'" *Signs* 25(1): 65–89.

Cossman, Brenda, Shannon Bell, Lisa Gotell, and Becky Ross. 1997. *Bad Attitude/s on Trial: Pornography, Feminism, and the Butler Decision*. Toronto: University of Toronto Press. https://doi.org/10.3138/9781442671157.

Crawley, Karen. 2018. "Reproducing Whiteness: Feminist Genres, Legal Subjectivity and the Post-Racial Dystopia of *The Handmaid's Tale* (2017–)." *Law and Critique* 29(3): 333–58.

Creet, Julia. 1991. "Daughter of the Movement: The Psychodynamics of Lesbian S/M Fantasy." *Differences* 3(2): 135–59.

Easton, Dossie and Janet W. Hardy. 2001. *The New Bottoming Book*. San Francisco, CA; London: Greenery; Turnaround.

Elderkin, Beth. 2018. "Someone's Making Handmaid's Tale–Inspired Lingerie which Seems Like a Very Bad Idea Indeed." *Gizmodo*, April 16. https://gizmodo.com.

Farley, Anthony Paul. 1997. "The Black Body as Fetish Object." *Oregon Law Review* 76: 457–536.

Foucault, Michel. 1990. *The History of Sexuality: An Introduction*. New York: Vintage.

Green, Emma. 2015. "Consent Isn't Enough: The Troubling Sex of *Fifty Shades*." *The Atlantic*, February 10. www.theatlantic.com.

Hayes, Daniel. 2008. "Sibling Rivalry." *Contemporary Psychoanalysis* 44(2): 280–88.

Hoskin, Rhea Ashley. 2013. "Femme Theory: Femininity's Challenge to Western Feminist Pedagogies." PhD diss., Queen's University. ProQuest Dissertations Publishing.

Kane, Vivian. 2018. "Who Asked for This Line of Sexy Handmaid's Tale Sleepwear?" *The Mary Sue*, April 18. www.themarysue.com.

Karaian, Lara. 2015. "What Is Self-Exploitation? Rethinking the Relationship between Sexualization and 'Sexting' in Law and Order Times." In *Children, Sexuality and Sexualization*, edited by Emma Renold, Jessica Ringrose, and R. Danielle Egan, 337–51. London: Palgrave Macmillan.

Khan, Ummni. 2014. *Vicarious Kinks: S/M in the Socio-Legal Imaginary*. Toronto: University of Toronto Press.

———. 2017. "Fetishizing Music as Rape Culture." *Studies in Gender and Sexuality* 18(1). https://doi.org/10.1080/15240657.2017.1276782.

Khan, Ummni and Jean Ketterling. 2019. "Rape as Play: Yellow Peril Panic and a Defence of Fantasy." In *The Asian Yearbook of Human Rights and Humanitarian Law*, edited by Javaid Rehman, Ayesha Shahid, and Steve Foster, 357–95. Boston: Brill.

Kratzer, Jessica M. (ed.). 2020. *Communication in Kink: Understanding the Influence of the Fifty Shades of Grey Phenomenon*. Lanham, MD: Lexington Books.

Lennon, Sharron J., Zhiying Zheng, and Aziz Fatnassi. 2016. "Women's Revealing Halloween Costumes: Other-Objectification and Sexualization." *Fashion and Textiles* 3(1): 21. https://doi.org/10.1186/s40691-016-0073-x.

MacKinnon, Catharine A. 1987. *Feminism Unmodified: Discourses on Life and Law*. Cambridge, MA: Harvard University Press.

Macmillan, Craig, Annette Lynch, and Linda Bradley. 2011. "Agonic and Hedonic Power: The Performance of Gender by Young Adults on Halloween." *Paideusis* 5 (January): 1–30.

McGowan, Emma. 2020. "Where Do Kinks Come From? It's Complicated." *Bustle*, May 15. www.bustle.com.

Mercado, Mia. 2018. "Sexy 'Handmaid's Tale' Costumes Just Hit the Internet." *Bustle*, September 19. www.bustle.com.

Miller, Bruce. 2017. "The Handmaid's Tale." Hulu.

Mulvey, Laura. 1989. "Visual Pleasure and Narrative Cinema." In *Visual and Other Pleasures*, edited by Laura Mulvey, 14–26. London: Palgrave Macmillan. https://doi .org/10.1007/978-1-349-19798-9_3.

Orozco, Isabelle. 2018. "Why Sexualized Halloween Costumes Are Scarier than You Think." *Psychology Benefits Society* (blog). October 31X. https://psychologybenefits.org.

Priya. 2017. "Get Out of Gilead: Anti-Blackness in 'The Handmaid's Tale.'" *Bitch Media*, April 14. https://www.bitchmedia.org.

Rubin, Gayle. 1984. "Thinking Sex: Notes for a Radical Theory of the Politics of Sexuality." In *Pleasure and Danger: Exploring Female Sexuality*, edited by Carole S. Vance, 267–319. Boston: Routledge and K. Paul.

Samois. 1979. *What Color Is Your Handerchief: A Lesbian S/M Sexuality Reader*. Berkeley, CA: Samois.

Sedgwick, Eve Kosofsky. 1990. *Epistemology of the Closet*. Berkeley: University of California Press.

———. 2003. "Paranoid Reading and Reparative Reading, or, You're So Paranoid, You Probably Think This Essay Is About You." In *Touching Feeling: Affect, Pedagogy, Performativity*, 123–52. Durham, NC: Duke University Press. https://doi.org/10.1515 /9780822384786-007.

Sobel, Ariel. 2018. "'Handmaid's Tale'-Inspired Lingerie Sparks Outrage." *Advocate*, April 17. www.advocate.com.

Stephens, Elizabeth. 2015. "Bad Feelings." *Australian Feminist Studies* 30(85): 273–82. https://doi.org/10.1080/08164649.2015.1113907.

Studlar, Gaylyn. 1984. "Masochism and the Perverse Pleasures of the Cinema." *Quarterly Review of Film Studies* 9(4): 267–82. https://doi.org/10.1080 /10509208409361219.

Tergesen, Maren. 2018. "Feeling Sexy or Feeling Sexualized? Negotiating Halloween Costumes and Their Social Costs." *The UBC AMS Sexual Assault Support Center (SASC)* (blog). October 24. www.amssasc.ca/blog/feeling-sexy-or-feeling-sexualized -negotiating-halloween-costumes-and-their-social-costs/.

Trzcinski, Matthew. 2021. "'The Handmaid's Tale' Halloween Outfits 'Offended' Some of the Show's Makers." *Showbiz Cheat Sheet*, May 10. www.cheatsheet.com.

Vance, Carole S. 1993. "More Danger, More Pleasure: A Decade after the Barnard Sexuality Conference Symposium: Women, Censorship, and Pornography." *New York Law School Law Review* 38: 289–318.

Vance, Carole S. and Scholar and the Feminist Conference (eds.). 1984. *Pleasure and Danger: Exploring Female Sexuality*. Boston: Routledge & K. Paul.

Vasa, Samia. 2019. "Toward an S/M Theory of MacKinnon." *Differences* 30(1): 100–118. https://doi.org/10.1215/10407391-7481274.

Wanshel, Elyse. 2018. "Now a Company Is Using 'The Handmaid's Tale' to Sell Lingerie." *HuffPost Canada*, April 17, 2018. www.huffpost.com.

Waters, Mark, dir. 2004. *Mean Girls*. Paramount Pictures.

Weber, Brenda R. 2018. "Torture Porn in Dystopic Feminism." *Communication, Culture and Critique* 11(1): 192–94. https://doi.org/10.1093/ccc/tcx011.

Wiseman, Jay. 2011. *SM 101: A Realistic Introduction*. SCB Distributors.

6

Oversexed, Undersexed, "No Sex"

*Queer Subjects and the Anti-Chinese Movement
in the Age of Capital*

EVELYN KESSLER

In the winter of 1878, Denis Kearney called for nothing short of a political takeover. Founder of the newly formed Workingmen's Party of California, Kearney addressed his appeal to "fellow workingmen," laboring in all corners of the United States in the wake of a devastating economic depression. "We have petitioned congress in vain," he declared. "Our moneyed men have ruled for the past thirty years," their "unbridled wealth" and "unprincipled greed" left to fester. Now, the country was hurling into "a crisis of unparalleled distress." Wages were low and work hard to come by. People were struggling to feed their families. The only solution, as Kearney saw it, was for ordinary workers to wrest political power from the hands of propertied elites and install their own at every level of government—from city halls and statehouses, to the judiciary and the presidency. In his condemnation of capitalist power, Kearney reserved his most scathing rebuke for a particular group of workers: Chinese immigrants. "These cheap slaves fill every place," he exclaimed. "Our employers are being so trained that only slave labor can please them" ("California Workingmen's Party Address" 1878).

Kearney was not the first to suggest that Chinese men arrived on America's shores unfree, bound to long contracts that rendered them chattel. Western observers had long accused Chinese emigrant laborers of being "slave-like." It was an accusation that took on particular virulence in the American West in the 1850s and 1860s, as news of California gold and construction of the transcontinental railroads brought thousands across the Pacific (Jung 2006; Lowe 2015, 101–33; Ngai 2015;

Smith 2013). Kearney's demand was a familiar one—that Chinese immigrants be expelled and permanently excluded from the United States on grounds of unfair competition for white workers. "Chinamen must leave us," he resolved. But the labor leader offered an addendum. The Chinese, he wrote, "seem to have no sex" ("California Workingmen's Party Address" 1878).

Here Kearney articulated the stakes of the anti-Chinese labor movement in terms both gendered and material. He accused Chinese immigrants of undercutting the subsistence of an American household by accepting below-market wages. Their dress was "scant and cheap," their living quarters cramped and dingy ("twenty in a room ten by ten"), their bodies subsistent on rice alone. These conditions were possible, Kearney claimed, because Chinese workers had "no wives, children, or dependents." He suggested their domestic arrangements were a matter of intractable racial difference, and it was precisely those arrangements that enabled them to strike otherwise untenable wage bargains. He warned, however, that such would be the fate of the American working man, his wife and daughter driven to prostitution—unless the state intervened. Indeed, Kearney and other labor leaders were demanding a state that positively affirmed white men's roles as providers and protectors and their concomitant rights to rest, comfort, and familial intimacy ("California Workingmen's Party Address" 1878; Leong 2001; Lowe, 2015; Shah 2011). For them, Chinese immigrants embodied unfettered capitalism taken to its logical conclusion.

The anti-Chinese labor movement of the late nineteenth century sought to reconcile perceived tensions between the liberal democratic order and the lived realities of industrial wage work. Wage labor had long been regarded as a mark of hierarchy and dependency, inimical to self-possessive individualism and republican virtue. Its ascendance with the Industrial Revolution thus gave urgency to ideological justification. Although many believed contract labor to be a mere way station to independent production, wages would become newly conceived as the province of independent men who—unlike wives or enslaved peoples—bought and sold labor at will, on equal footing (Boydston 1990; Cott 1977; Foner 1970; Stanley 1996). Later, with the abolition of chattel slavery, all men were putatively free, their rights as enfranchised citizens constitutive of their independence in the market and their dominion as heads of household. But gone were the days when most working men could hope to run their own shops or till their own soil (Currarino 2011; Stanley 1998).

Emancipation had promised to resolve the contradictions of a society that was half free and half slave. Yet an impersonal market increasingly muddled the lines between consent and coercion, independence and dependence, male and female. Certainly, there were people who fell outside the bounds of such distinctions since the earliest days of the market revolution; working women, especially Black women, did not conform to ideologies of separate sexual spheres as they struggled to eke out a living in the wage system (Hartman 2019; Rockman 2009; Stansell 1986). But for many white men, the growth of corporate capitalism after the American Civil War—fueled by the consolidation and accumulation of wealth, at the expense of virtually all else—drove unprecedented levels of precarity (Currarino 2011; Levy 2012; Stanley 1998). The anti-Chinese labor movement responded to this new economic crisis by assailing the power of capital, and in so doing argued that capitalism without legal restraint would render all working Americans like the Chinese—in a word, queer.

This chapter takes queer to mean a subject position defined through and against gendered and sexualized norms. Here I draw from scholars who have marshaled queer analysis not to examine a self-referential identity—not always, at least—but to interrogate the discursive construction of gender and sexual formations (Butler 1990; Cossman 2019; Halperin 1995). I try to heed warnings against a prescriptive approach to queer theory, so as not to suggest it entails any one method in particular or that a predictable set of insights can be gleaned from its use (Berlant and Warner 1995).

Still, as an analytic, queer theory is especially helpful in thinking about alterity. The queer and the normative were mutually constitutive in the history of the anti-Chinese labor movement, as its members declared what they were not and what they refused to become. In the barest of terms, they declared themselves not Chinese—and so here too, queer theory proves instructive. The queer "other" was deeply embedded in notions of the racial "other." Just as historian Moon-Ho Jung defines the unfree "coolie" as a "conglomeration of racial imaginings," the queer Chinese figure was an imagined subject—a composite of contradictions that reveals more about the people who created it than the people it allegedly described. Moreover, for histories tied to problems of migration and labor, queer theory offers insight into discourses of the body: the physical body that occupies space and becomes inscribed with a variety of social meanings, as well as the body politic, tied to sexual and social reproduction in ways both real and imagined (Butler 1993; Cohen 1999; Jung 2006; Puar 2005; Ruskola 2010).[1]

Of course, people in the nineteenth century did not use the term "queer" when railing against Chinese immigrants and their supposed conspiracy with capital. Nor did Chinese immigrants describe themselves as such. In fact, they frequently asserted themselves as normative legal subjects, invoking principles of equal protection and due process recently enshrined in the Fourteenth Amendment (Atkinson 2020; McClain 1994). There was little intellectual consistency in attempts to cast the market as a queering force, the Chinese its queer pawns and conspirators. That inconsistency is precisely what makes this history ripe for queer analysis.

Placing this history within queer studies sheds light on the unique nature of the anti-Chinese campaign and the terms of federal exclusion that would come to pass in 1882. No other immigrant group in the United States had experienced such totalizing disqualification for entry—not the Irish nor the Slavs, the Italians nor the Jews. Irish immigrants on the East Coast drew the ire of nativists and labor unions, both for their Catholicism and for their undercutting labor's price in a competitive market. After the American Civil War, an influx of immigrants from Southern and Eastern Europe reignited nativist hostility. These new immigrant populations endured substandard housing, dangerous working conditions, and episodic violence. Yet complete legal exclusion was reserved for just one group (Daniels 2002; Jacobson 1998; Salyer 1995).

Historians have long documented exclusionist discourse, along with the constellation of discriminatory laws that policed Chinese people within the United States and at its borders. Scholars have argued that anti-Chinese rhetoric cultivated a shared racial identity among European immigrants and Anglo-Americans, and spurred violent attacks that robbed Chinese people of their livelihoods, or sometimes of their very lives (Almaguer 1994; Lew-Williams 2018; Saxton 1971). More recent work has suggested that the anti-Chinese movement gained widespread support at the national level as western states grew more politically powerful, or because of changing diplomatic and trade objectives (Chang 2012; Zhu 2013). Scholars have also situated this history in terms of the federal government's plenary power and a growing state bureaucracy (Harota 2013; Salyer 1995).

This inquiry works from a different vantage point: the vast terrain of gendered and sexual arguments in the anti-Chinese labor movement. The chapter interrogates why discursive constructions of Chinese immigrants contained "dissonances and resonances, lapses and excesses of meaning"—why those constructions were so, well, queer (Sedgwick 1993, 8). At stake, I argue, was the viability of America's popular politics and the legitimacy of its gender relations and political economy.

The chapter weaves together two strands of existing scholarship. The first has traced an emergent labor politics and the consolidation of white identity within the anti-Chinese campaign, from the docks of San Francisco to the bayous of Louisiana. This literature has focused principally on Chinese male labor in the context of slave emancipation and free labor ideology (Almaguer 1994; Jung 2006; Saxton 1971; Smith 2013). The second body of scholarship to which I am indebted has analyzed the sexualization of Chinese people during the first waves of migration to the United States. These studies have paid particular attention to constructions of Chinese men as lacking in manhood and Chinese women as lacking in female virtue (Leong 2001; Luibhéid 2002; Sears 2008; Shah 2001). By bringing together these two bodies of literature, this chapter is in critical dialog with histories of capitalism and theories of social reproduction that place gender and sex at the heart of capitalist development and class formation (Boydston 1990; Chitty 2020; Glenn 2004).

Denis Kearney's attack on an exploitative labor system, undertaken within a racist movement, queered Chinese men and women alike. Indeed, Chinese women played an outsized role in anti-Chinese discourse, given that they constituted such a small minority of the immigrant population in the United States. The figure of the Chinese female prostitute captured the imagination of anti-Chinese leaders, who described her as both a mirror image and counterpoint to the Chinese male laborer. Scholars have estimated that anywhere from 20 to 90 percent of Chinese women who resided in the American West in the late nineteenth century did, in fact, work as prostitutes. How many did so willingly remains an open question (Cheng Hirata 1979; Tong 1994; Yung 1999). This chapter does not attempt to offer or dispute numbers, nor does it seek to enter a debate about the relative freedom or unfreedom of Chinese sex workers. Irrespective of race, at the time prostitution was regarded as inherently coercive; sex as work laid bare the cruelties of a market driven to excess (Stanley 1998, 218–63).[2]

Chinese women were presumed to be prostitutes as a matter of course. In speeches, written campaign materials, and ultimately the law itself, the Chinese woman was portrayed as a helpless victim ripped from her homeland, her chastity auctioned to the highest bidder. But she was also often depicted as a seductress without chastity. Gendered and sexualized constructions of Chinese women eluded any one signifier.

The same proved true for Chinese men. In Kearney's formulation, male Chinese laborers were sexless cogs, devoid of personal desires or intimate attachments. But other anti-Chinese thinkers and activists depicted Chinese men as licentious aggressors who preyed on women and then disposed of them.[3]

Oversexed, undersexed, "no sex"—the internal incoherence of these representations nevertheless cohered into a single queer figure. Bound in unfree labor and unmoored from the bonds of marriage, Chinese immigrants came to define by negation the meaning of freedom in a liberal, capitalist society.

The campaign against Chinese male laborers began nearly as soon as they first arrived. With news of gold in 1848, thousands of white Americans flocked to the West Coast. Others in search of opportunity came from Europe and Latin America, especially Mexico and Chile. And a significant number hailed from China's Guangdong Province, where most financed their journey using credit tickets, to be repaid with first earnings (Johnson 2000, 57–98; Mei 1979; Takaki 1989, 35–6). In spring 1852, California Governor John Bigler convened a special session of the state legislature, celebrating most of these newcomers as welcome recipients of American largesse. But when it came to Chinese immigrants, the governor struck a different tone. He warned that California, less than two years into its statehood, faced an existential crisis from a "tide of Asiatic immigration" that bore "the iron rigor of despotism" (Bigler 1852).

The despotism Bigler spoke of was a kind of indentured servitude. As he explained, Chinese men worked "under contracts to labor for a term of years in our mines, at merely nominal wages" (Bigler 1852). Some in fact arrived as independent prospectors or as members of egalitarian cooperatives. But credit tickets reeked of debt peonage, and those who did labor under contract were said to accept wages lower than men of Anglo, French, and German descent—who, in turn, agitated for restrictions on Chinese participation in the labor market (Ngai 2015; Saxton 1971, 67–91).

These early anti-Chinese groups declared themselves counterweights to monied interests. By the early 1850s, investors and landowners were lobbying for greater legal enforcement of low-wage, long-term contracts. In the first few months of 1852 alone, two bills came before the state legislature that would have compelled foreign-born workers to stay at their jobs for five, even ten years' time, under threat of fines and criminal prosecution. Those particular efforts failed, but seemed to portend the undue influence of money in California politics (Smith 2013). "Our laborers wish to keep up the value of their toil to a fair standard of competition among themselves," entreated members of the state assembly, "but you [Mr. Speaker] allow capitalists to import Chinese labor upon them, and the equilibrium is destroyed, capital is triumphant, and the laboring poor of America must submit to the unholy sacrifice" (Assembly Proceedings 1855, 485).

Theirs was a two-pronged argument. The exploited Chinese worker and the rapacious capitalist together undermined the bargaining power of the white working class. Only the law could ensure equal footing between labor and capital. Whether Bigler himself aligned with this view or acceded to political pressure, he called on the legislature to void agreements between employers and Chinese workers that proved "exceptions to the rule . . . [of] the universal validity of contracts." He cautioned that, without intervention, cheap labor would inundate the market to such a degree that free men could no longer make an honest living for their families (Bigler 1852).

But the governor did not claim that Chinese men lacked families of their own. "Most of them are married," he said of these immigrant laborers, "and while absent, $1.50 to $2 per month is paid to their families for subsistence, and the amount deducted from their wages" (Bigler 1852).

166 I EVELYN KESSLER

That the survival of Chinese households hinged on unfair labor agreements provided further proof of the corrosive effects of an unregulated wage economy. Workers could be compelled to suffer through the most exploitative of conditions for the sake of their families, whether Chinese or American.

Soon enough, though, observers began to suggest there was something a bit queer about the Chinese, something that made not just their labor but their very beings incompatible with an American way of life. "You would be puzzled to distinguish the women from the men, so inconsiderable are the differences in dress and figure," the anti-slavery writer Hinton Helper argued in 1855. Providing readers with a taxonomy of gross racial caricature, Helper detailed the "garb, features, physical proportions and deportment" of Chinese immigrants, all of which looked "very unlike any body else." Of particular interest to Helper was the queue, the long and braided hairstyle customary for Chinese men of the time. If the queue resembled anything in American culture, Helper wrote, it was the ribboned plaits of young girls (Helper 1855, 86–96).

Although he declared their gender expression strange, Helper insisted that the threat Chinese immigrants posed to the country was a familiar one. Born into a slaveholding family in North Carolina, Helper had become a critic of chattel slavery on economic rather than moral grounds; it was not the inhumanity of enslavement that moved Helper, but the promise of an industrial, free market South. He warned that Chinese immigrants would degrade white labor and stymie economic development in the West, just as he believed slave labor did in the South. "I should not wonder at all," he wrote, "if the copper of the Pacific yet becomes as great a subject of discord and dissension as the ebony of the Atlantic" (Helper 1855, 96).

When civil war erupted six years later, some anti-Chinese agitators seized the opportunity to nationalize their cause. Like Helper, they declared every Chinese immigrant a slave, irrevocably so, and therefore claimed Chinese exclusion to be part and parcel of the abolitionist project. In early 1862, President Abraham Lincoln signed the Coolie Trade Prohibition Act into law. US consuls would now require Chinese immigrants to verify that they freely sought entry into the country. Lawmakers celebrated the legislation as the end of yet another slave trade and as a moral victory for the Union cause (Act of February 19, 1862 (Coolie

Trade Prohibition Act), Ch. 27, 12 Stat. 340 (repealed 1974); Jung 2006, 33–38; Smith 2013, 194–95).

But for the anti-Chinese movement, the law fell short—its language did not presume that all Chinese labored under coercive agreements. In fact, the legislation endorsed the "free and voluntary emigration of any Chinese subject." After the war, analogies of abolition and exclusion proved even more tenuous. The federal government signed the Burlingame Treaty in 1868, ensuring Chinese nationals free entry into the country and equal protection under the law. Worse still for opponents of Chinese immigration, a revolution in civil rights extended new privileges and protections to citizens and non-citizens alike. To some observers, those protections seemed to exclude the rights of white workingmen; in the 1873 *Slaughterhouse* cases, for example, the Supreme Court adopted a narrow interpretation of the Thirteenth and Fourteenth Amendments, to effectively deny white men's claims to work of their own choosing (Jung 2006, 33–38; Labbé and Lurie 2003; Schrecker 2010; Smith 2013, 194–95).

Immigration from China to the western United States increased through the next decade. Employers recruited thousands of Chinese men to work in mines and factories, on farms and urban construction sites, and to lay railroad track that would span the continent. By 1870, there were more than 60,000 people of Chinese descent in the United States; in California, they accounted for a quarter of the entire labor force (Chan 1989; Chang 2019; Takaki 1989, 79–99). "No system similar to slavery, serfdom or peonage prevails among these laborers," railroad executive Leland Stanford assured federal officials in 1865. "Without them it would be impossible to complete the western portion of this great national enterprise, within the time required by the Acts of Congress"—impossible, Stanford claimed, because white men simply would refuse to do the work required. Of the Chinese he said, "More prudent and economical, they are contented with less wages" (Stanford 1865, 890).

Even in his defense of hiring Chinese laborers, Stanford perpetuated the idea that there was something peculiar about them. They were supposedly very unlike the American worker—willing to do work Americans would not, accepting as pay a pittance that Americans would not. Yet it was Stanford's own company that would, just one year after his testimony, violently suppress thousands of Chinese railroad workers striking for better wages and shorter hours. Stanford belonged to a small cohort of monied men who wielded political influence and starvation wages like cudgels, further enriching themselves through bribery, insider trading, and the dispossession of industrial laborers, farmers, and indigenous peoples. For many working Americans, the state-subsidized transcontinental railroads came to represent a corrupt partnership between government and corporations (Beckert 2001; Takaki 1989, 86; White 2012).

The grift and maleficence of the railroads were of a piece, yet another example of capitalist overreach and illiberal accumulation. A national labor movement reinvigorated after the war would seize upon such examples in their fight to affirm the dignity of workers. "What is the advantage of 'cheap labor' to a country?" asked journalist and trade unionist John Swinton in 1870. "Is it that it enables capitalists to pile up more capital, millionaires to double their millions, or manufacturers to enlarge their profits?" A prominent writer for the *New York Times* and *New York Tribune*, Swinton did not challenge the material or ideological foundations of capitalism itself. Rather, he demanded a capitalism that gave "the workingman such returns as will enable him to live a free and manly life." Earlier in the century, many decades before Swinton took to writing, Americans had feared the market revolution would encroach upon the home and fundamentally alter family life. Now, Swinton argued, the market threatened to destroy the home altogether (Swinton 1870, 10).

At fault, of course, were employers, for whom Swinton made little effort to hide his contempt: "'Cheap labor!' cry the capitalists, 'We must have cheap labor!'" But just as dangerous were those workers who answered their call—and like a growing number of labor activists, Swinton believed Chinese immigrants uniquely and inherently pliant. Indeed, he wrote, "Chinamen are the cheapest laborers in the world." He warned that they endangered all white workingmen, not just those in the West. He told the story of a Massachusetts shoe manufacturer who reduced his employees' wages and responded to their protests by importing Chinese laborers to cross the picket line (Swinton 1870, 3–4). "I doubt, on many accounts, if the American would succeed as a competitor with the Chinaman on any terms," Swinton remarked, "but he could certainly have no chance whatever on any other terms than by the abolition of the household, and by denying himself the appliances of personal civilization" (9).

More was at stake than the male breadwinner. Swinton warned of sexual degeneracy and gender perversion in myriad forms. Tapping into fears of sexual danger salient to his nineteenth-century readers, he invoked the threat of interracial sex and marriage. "Chinese immigration is almost wholly of the male sex . . . which will result," he predicted, "in the growth of a half-breed Chinese-American type" (Lui 2004; Pascoe 2009; Swinton 1870, 7–8). His solution was not to acquiesce to "schemes for equalizing the number of the sexes," for he suggested that Chinese immigrants could not be incorporated into a normative family structure—their labor and gender performance marked them as queer, irreversibly so, and they bore it on their bodies. The "most loathsome and destructive diseases are terribly prevalent among them," he wrote, "prevalent to such an extent that the blood and physical organism, as well as the moral and mental qualities of the Chinese race, are profoundly affected by them" (Swinton 1870, 14).

The source of their degeneracy mattered little. Was it that their "foul and mortifying vices" bred disease, or that the disease bred vice? Either way, he declared Chinese people a pestilence that would infect and eventually consume the American body. He reminded his readers that they "themselves constitute the sovereign power," and thus had every right to insist upon an American standard of living, free of compulsion or contagion. The first step was to reject the "incestuous and Sodomite Chinese men" arriving at the San Francisco harbor each day. The suggestion that Chinese men preferred to have sex with each other seemingly belied Swinton's concerns of "a half-breed Chinese-American type." But the Chinese laborer occupied a capacious category of perversion. His deviance could take the form of both interracial and homosexual sex—this in addition to the sex he was presumably having with the "ship-loads of lewd Chinese women," as Swinton described them (Swinton 1870, 14).

Chinese women loomed large in the popular imagination of the time. For although Swinton acknowledged that women accounted for a small fraction of the Chinese people migrating to the United States, he joined a growing number captivated by the figure of the Chinese prostitute. As early as the 1850s and 1860s, anti-Chinese leaders in the West declared

Chinese sex workers as dangerous a threat as those men who worked in mines and factories.

Indeed, the language of contamination that came to pervade the anti-Chinese campaign found some of its first expression in attacks on Chinese women. Consider an 1868 petition to California's state senate from the Anti-Coolie Association, a group formed for "the protection of white labor from annihilation by the millions of Asia." The petition began with a familiar argument: "That whatever present benefit may be derived from the employment of Chinese, as a cheap system of labor, is chiefly confined to a few capitalists." Not least of the harms to working people were the "large numbers of Chinawomen [who] infest our cities for the vilest purposes, and are a source of pollution to the large rising generation of young men" ("Anti-Coolie Memorial" 1868, 3–4).[4] The Chinese prostitute was said to be a sexual aggressor and vector of disease; she lured white men and weakened their bodies, debilitating their competition with Chinese laborers. Retellings of white men's sexual encounters with Chinese prostitutes cast the women alone as deviant, absolving white men of their participation in the commercial sex market.

Chinese men, on the other hand, were often cast as perverse by dint of their association with Chinese women. "Can he be pure whose sister is the vilest strumpet on earth?" asked the Workingmen's Party of California in an 1879 pamphlet entitled *"The Chinese Must Go": The Labor Agitators; or, The Battle for Bread*. The pamphlet derided wealthy Americans who hired Chinese men as domestic servants. It warned that Chinese men would literally pollute the American home, as they prepared meals, bathed children, and tended to living quarters. *The Battle for Bread* encouraged readers to visit San Francisco's Chinatown and observe for themselves a neighborhood of filth and disease. But it also warned that "the luxury and debauchery of the Orient are brought into the houses of the rich." White society women were said to be especially susceptible to the charms of Chinese men, who showed them "how the great ladies of China are waited upon by the eunuchs" (Workingmen's Party of California 1879, 25–26). Even in the absence of sexuality, and even in squalor, the Chinese worker could embody the dangers of abundance.

The argument was not about the right of an American elite to exist, so much as it was about an American elite that had been corrupted. In *The Battle for Bread*, the Workingmen's Party did not call for the eradication of economic inequality or class difference. It instead resolved to "lift the poor and unfortunate out of the gutter of wretchedness and despair, and confine the rich to a rational and virtuous life in strict obedience to a righteous law." The party described its vision for the future as one within reach. "There is room in California for ten millions of happy people if the land and the means of cultivating it were more equally distributed," it insisted. "Under the land-grabber, the monopolist and cheap Chinese labor, there is not one million, and a third of them are in poverty and despair." But under the leadership of the Workingmen's Party, "Poverty will be without privation and wealth without vice and ostentation" (Workingmen's Party of California 1879, 11). Standing in the way of that future was the Chinese immigrant, who represented a deviance flexible in meaning—poor and extravagant, repulsive and seductive, all at once and all in excess.

As easily as one could encounter stories of lascivious Chinese women, one could find stories of helpless victims, representing a kind of excess in vulnerability and exploitation. Sometimes these warring narratives resided within a single account. According to one local newspaper in 1861, "The cities and towns of California swarm with these miserable, wretched harlot-serfs—putrid, festering, moral sores in every community where they exist." The category "harlot-serf" lacked coherence, suggesting both agency and servility. Still, the newspaper claimed with certainty that these women were "bought and sold among the male Chinamen as any other property" ("Chinese Slavery in California" 1861).[5] For its part, The Battle for Bread derided the Chinese woman as a "strumpet"—indeed, the vilest on earth—but not before expressing sympathy for her plight. "She comes here a slave," it read. "She is taught to lie that she may get here . . . Thus bound she has no will of her own" (Workingmen's Party of California 1879, 24).

The coerced lie was less instrumental to this sex traffic than the employers who demanded it and the immigration officials who enabled it. As the pamphlet explained, "Our Consul pretends to believe her when he really does no such thing. But capital has told him he must. All the subtlety of law is brought into play to hold her in bonds" (Workingmen's Party of California 1879, 24). That corporations ensured women's enslavement through legal means implied a conspiracy, one that demanded more than either incremental legal reform or humanitarian rescue (as some Christian groups had endeavored). Whether under the auspices of a political party or local periodical or guild, the anti-Chinese campaign maintained that only the strictest of immigration laws would rid the country of the Chinese problem and rein in the power of capital.

Unfettered capitalism was thus understood to facilitate and benefit from a commercialized sex economy. Anti-Chinese activists argued that American employers worked in concert with Chinese men—wealthy Chinese merchants and creditors, along with those very laborers they were accused of exploiting. Driving down wages went hand in hand with pushing sex into the realm of commodity exchange. "Each China steamer now brings consignments of women destined to be placed in the market," exclaimed the *San Francisco Chronicle* in 1869. With a "keen eye for speculation," both American and Chinese capitalists "saw that a traffic in women would be productive of enormous profits." The *Chronicle* went on to paint a ghastly scene of diseased women left to die alone in back alleys (*"Horrors of a Great City"* 1869).[6]

The materiality of the critique—of bodies stolen, plagued, discarded—spoke to material concerns over the postbellum capitalist order. The popular press had taken to depicting corporations as ravenous monsters. Periodicals frequently included illustrations of a "Standard Oil" or "Railroad Monopoly" octopus, looming over America's towns and cities, extending its tentacles to constrict and consume everything in its grasp. Descriptions of Chinese prostitution drew on similar themes of insatiability. But the *Chronicle* also invoked an older image, one of an auction block, a site of that recently abolished traffic in souls (*"Horrors of a Great City"* 1869).[7]

Similar claims of enslavement were made in the US Congress during debates over the Thirteenth Amendment. "Sir, they do not propagate in this country," cried out a congressman from California who opposed Chinese immigration. "They buy and sell their women like cattle, and the trade is mostly for the purposes of prostitution. That is their character. You cannot make citizens of them" (*Congressional Globe* 1866, 1056). When the congressman proclaimed Chinese people ineligible for citizenship, he drew upon centuries of legal and cultural tradition, alleging they did not practice an ideal form of heterosexual monogamy. Their supposed failure to enter a voluntary and permanent union undermined the spirit of national union (Cott 2000).

Free or unfree, oversexed or undersexed, Chinese men and women together served as negative referents for an idealized American sexual regime—one organized by legible and consistent markers of sex differ- ence; infused with sentiment and obligation; and removed from the bas- est of market logics. It was a regime that found its purest expression in the nuclear family. The anti-Chinese movement invoked the family as the primary site of both socialization and intimate feeling. Its economic argument tied sustenance to emotional nourishment and gendered well- being. Higher wages not only allowed the male head of household to fulfill his duty to provide, but also strengthened intimate ties between man and wife, father and child (Cott 2000; Shah 2011).

A California state legislative report in 1877 made explicit the link be- tween Chinese exclusion and a sexual division of labor, with an essay entitled "Caucasian vs. Mongolian." Authored by H. R. Clement, identi- fied only as a "Member of the San Francisco Bar," the essay described Chinese people as suited for capitalist exploitation—indeed, their bod- ies and sexual arrangements seemed designed for it. Clement wrote that Chinese laborers could "live upon the least possible amount of air and food." In contrast, white laborers had to feed their families "meat, vegetables, and wheat bread" and ensure "separate rooms for [their] grown up children of different sexes" (Clement 1878, 267–68). Clem- ent insisted that Chinese labor interfered with a man's responsibility to uphold normative relations of gender and sex—not just for the sake of his own family, but for the sake of the republic. "The nation is a collec- tion of families," he argued. "Society has been organized with reference to it. Commerce, laws, trades, and values are created and *adjusted* with reference to the 'family relation.' *Wages are regulated with reference to it.* The assumption that every man among us is to have a family and a home enters into all our calculations" (267, 274; italics in original). Clement described a nation in perfect balance: There was an economic system and a cultural one, the two working in harmony to ensure comfort and prosperity for working-class families.

But of course, it was a nation off-kilter. "Chinese Cheap Labor—Will the Question Regulate Itself?" asked Clement. The trajectory of indus- trial capitalism had proved it would not. Left to its own devices, the "cold, calculating commercial spirit of political economy" would ex- ploit workers without consideration of "human sympathy." Clement

continued, describing the "'law of competition' and 'demand and supply'" as a "frigid philosophy," endorsed by "statesmen, judges, scholars,
and *literati*" from their "'elevated plateau.'" On the ground were working
families, suffering. The market would not self-regulate for their benefit
(Clement 1878, 269–72; italics in original).

Yet his was not an outright challenge to capitalist accumulation outright. Clement advocated for an industrial system designed "without
disaster to our capitalists." He endorsed the economic theories of Adam
Smith. What vexed Clement was *unbridled* capitalist accumulation, devoid of feeling and without reference to "the wants of the people." As he
asserted, "The prosperity of a country does not so much depend upon
concentrating capital as distributing it." Clement articulated a vision of
state and market in which the government ensured such distribution. If
wages rendered labor an impersonal market commodity, it nonetheless
had to enable and sustain the intimacy and comforts of the domestic
sphere. "Any enterprise that depends for its existence upon procuring
cheap labor must necessarily exist upon the *privations* and *sufferings of
the laborer*," Clement argued, "unless he *is a laborer belonging to an inferior race*" (Clement 1878, 269–72).

A rhetoric of queer, racial difference gave new meaning and explanation to the unrelenting, dizzying growth of capitalist society. As those
corporate tentacles took hold of ever more Americans, they threatened
to reach across the boundaries of market and home, male and female—
categories of difference the Chinese were said to neither honor nor understand. Clement warned that Chinese labor would soon force wives
out of the home for the sake of family survival. But of course, family
survival had always depended on the labor of women, whether or not
they stayed within the sacred confines of the home. The wage system
simply could not exist without women's scrimping and saving, cooking
and mending. Such work had supplemented family income and created
surplus value since the earliest days of industrialization. Clement thus
joined a long cultural and economic tradition when he rendered housework invisible, as if it were wholly apart from the political economy
(Boydston 1990).

In the postbellum era, however, white women—daughters, but also
some wives—increasingly worked for wages. Although industrial capitalism had not effaced men's legal rights over women, the incorporation

of women into wage work—even just the threat of it—chipped away at male authority. Economic necessity lay bare the sheer impossibility of the male breadwinner model for many working people. Yet under these destabilizing conditions, there still remained a dividing line between men's work and women's work (Boydston 1990; Kessler-Harris 1982; Stanley 1996; Stansell 1986).

It was a line that Chinese men allegedly crossed. By taking jobs in the garment industry or in the homes of the well-to-do, Chinese men seemed to presage a labor market without gender difference. According to anti-Chinese activists, accepting such work also had more immediate material consequences: Chinese men supposedly took jobs from white women, leaving them no choice but to sell their bodies. Chants of "Give Our Boys and Girls Employment" broke out at an anti-Chinese rally in 1876, drawing a crowd of 25,000 people to San Francisco's Union Hall. One speaker declared that Chinese immigration "has taken labor from women" and therefore "driven too many of them to resort to practices of shame and guilt" ("Anti-Chinese" 1876).

It was a charge repeated again and again by anti-Chinese leaders. Consider once more *The Battle for Bread*, the 1879 pamphlet published by the Workingmen's Party of California. "You cannot discern that he is a man," the pamphlet said of the Chinese domestic worker. "All his passions have been whipped into servile obedience." So devoid of sex was the Chinese man that he would be "called into the bedroom, or the bathroom without a thought." In contrast to the libidinal figure who trafficked in sex slaves, this particular queer construction lacked sexual drive altogether. "He can lace Madam's corsets, or arrange the girls' petticoats, smooth their pillows, or tuck in their feet," exclaimed the pamphlet. "Why, bless you, he is not a man!" The presence of this queer figure, capable of any and all work, meant "the poor are denied service because they are no slaves; because they have sex, and shame, and sense of propriety" (Workingmen's Party of California 1879, 24–25).

Chinese immigrants had come to embody the ravages of industrial capitalism—ravaging white wages, white virtue, white bodies, the white body politic. Certainly, there were labor leaders who refused to blame immigrants for the devastation wrought by this brave new world. National Labor Union co-founder William H. Sylvis, for example, declared in 1867 that "the interests of labor are identical throughout the world"

(Sylvis 1872, 181). Others too came to the defense of Chinese people. No less eminent a cultural figure than Mark Twain would offer the image of a productive and resourceful immigrant, though he infused his critique with classist disdain. "No Californian *gentleman or lady* ever abuses or oppresses a Chinaman, under any circumstances, an explanation that seems to be much needed in the East," wrote Twain. "Only the scum of the population do it" (Twain 1871, 111–12, italics in original).

But the political tides were shifting. An economic depression in 1873 engulfed the nation and led to the mass dissolution of jobs, life savings, and families. In the 1874 midterm election, Democrats at the federal level seized control of the House and made substantial gains in the Senate; their victory was in part credited to an anti-monopolist, anti-Chinese platform, and to the growing contingent of voters out West (White 2017, 253–86; Zhu 2013, 40–43). When California held a constitutional convention in 1878, the Workingmen's Party accounted for a third of all delegates. Denis Kearney himself did not participate in the convention, as he had recently been arrested for inciting a riot in the affluent San Francisco neighborhood of Nob Hill, "within the sacred precincts of the magnates of the railroad corporation" (*Debates and Proceedings of the Constitutional Convention of the State of California* 1880, 312).

The anti-Chinese movement had effectively constructed a queer symbol of freedom's antithesis. In harnessing a language of gender and sexual normativity, the movement affirmed the place of white wage workers within the liberal, capitalist order—differentiating them from a people decidedly outside its bounds. The federal government passed its first significant anti-Chinese legislation with the Page Act of 1875 (Act of March 3, 1875 (Page Act), Ch. 141, 18 Stat. 477, repealed 1974). The law explicitly forbade "the importation into the United States of women for the purposes of prostitution," and granted immigration officials almost total discretionary power. In effect, it rendered immigration nearly impossible for Chinese women—substantiating their cultural image as sexually deviant, and emboldening anti-Chinese agitators to pursue total exclusion (Abrams 2005; Luibhéid 2002; Peffer 1986).

During debates over the Chinese Exclusion Act in 1882, a congressman declared that total exclusion would once and for all extinguish from American soil the "twin relic[s] of the barbarism of slavery." Here he referred to the traffic of labor and sex, two queer unfreedoms inextricably linked (*Congressional Record* 1882b, 1932). Such characterizations of Chinese immigrants did not go wholly unchallenged. One notable objection came from Senator George Hoar of Massachusetts. "[I]t is not the slave, or the apprentice, or the prostitute, or the leper, or the thief, but the laborer at whom this legislation strikes its blow," Hoar argued on the Senate floor. Indeed, the law exempted Chinese merchants and diplomats. As the senator explained, such provisions would deny "the right of every man who desires to improve his condition by honest labor—his labor being no man's property but his own—to go anywhere on the face of the earth that he pleases" (*Congressional Record* 1882a, 1517). Hoar struggled to find support among his colleagues, and would himself become a target of the anti-Chinese movement, even after exclusion had been put into effect. *The Wasp*, a popular satirical magazine known for its colorful lithographs, devoted an entire illustrated page to Hoar in 1889 (see figure 6.1). A Chinese man was depicted greeting Hoar with a wide embrace and a kiss on the cheek—a sort of conscription into sexual aberrance. "Together at last," read the caption.

"These cheap slaves fill every place" had been a prophetic warning, though not as Denis Kearney had intended. The labor leader proclaimed an invasion of physical bodies, in mines and lumber yards, in city streets and homes. In reality, these queer figures took space in newspapers and journals and party platforms. They occupied the pulpits of public lectures and echoed through the halls of Congress. At once durable and elastic, the queer Chinese subject persisted well beyond the Chinese Exclusion Act of 1882 and found purchase with a remarkably diverse range of Americans. No matter the size of the local Chinese population, anti-Chinese rhetoric seemed to resonate in "every place." A language of exclusion operated within and through contradictory sexual norms, and so it could contort to be almost anything and live almost anywhere. Now, as they did then, contradictions abound in discursive representations of marginalized people. This history serves to show that those contradictions cannot be dismissed as merely unintelligible, or as necessarily destabilizing to prevailing power structures.

In a system predicated on infinite growth—with seemingly infinite capacities to extract and exploit—Americans sought to carve out finite boundaries of nation, gender, and sex. Yet the underlying economic conditions that had inspired animus against Chinese immigrants remained.

Figure 6.1. "Together at Last," *The Wasp* (San Francisco, 1889)

With many of those same conditions persisting into our own time, more queer approaches to historical study are needed to untangle the alluring power of exclusionist politics and their capacity to entrench rather than challenge relations of unequal power.

NOTES

1 A queer lens is certainly not the only means of interrogating the discursive figuring of bodies and belonging. See, for example, Roberts 1997.

2 Marx described sex work as inherent to capitalist exploitation, "only a specific expression of the general prostitution of the laborer." See Marx 1964, 133.

3 The sex worker as both abject and woefully unlucky have been long-standing tropes in the United States and Europe, marshaled for a number of policy ends. See, for example, Walkowitz 1982. Scholars have drawn similar attention to the social construction of disabled subjects as simultaneously hypersexual and sexless, predatory and pitiful. See Perlin and Lynch 2014.

4 For a history of Chinese immigrants and public health, see Shah 2001.

5 For further discussion of the "harlot-serf," see Smith 2013, 164–68.

6 For legal analogies between corporations and Chinese immigrants, see Atkinson 2020.

7 For corporations as octopuses in political commentary, see, for example, "The Curse of California" 1882; "The Menace of the Hour" 1889; Norris 1901.

BIBLIOGRAPHY

Abrams, Kerry. 2005. "Polygamy, Prostitution, and the Federalization of Immigration Law." *Columbia Law Review* 105(3): 641–716.

Almaguer, Tomás. 1994. *Racial Fault Lines: The Historical Origins of White Supremacy in California*. Berkeley: University of California Press.

"Anti-Chinese: Immense Anti-Chinese Demonstration at Union Hall." 1876. *Daily Alta California*, April 6.

"Anti-Coolie Memorial." 1869. *Appendix to Journals of Senate and Assembly of the Seventeenth Session of the Legislature of the State of California, Volume 2*. Sacramentio, CA: D.W. Gelwicks, State Printer.

Assembly Proceedings. 1855. *Journal of the Sixth Session of the Assembly of California*. Sacramento, CA: B. B. Redding, State Printer.

Atkinson, Evelyn. 2020. "Slaves, Coolies, and Shareholders: Corporations Claim the Fourteenth Amendment." *Journal of the Civil War Era* 10(1): 54–80.

Beckert, Sven. 2001. *The Monied Metropolis: New York City and the Consolidation of the American Bourgeoisie, 1850–1896*. Cambridge: Cambridge University Press.

Berlant, Lauren and Michael Warner. 1995. "What Does Queer Theory Teach Us About X?" *PMLA* 110(3): 343–49.

Bigler, John. 1852. "Governor's Special Message." *Daily Alta California*, April 25.

Boydston, Jeanne. 1990. *Home and Work: Housework, Wages, and the Ideology of Labor in the Early Republic*. New York: Oxford University Press.

Butler, Judith. 1990. *Gender Trouble: Feminism and the Subversion of Identity*. New York: Routledge.

———. 1993. *Bodies that Matter: On the Discursive Limits of "Sex."* New York: Routledge.

"California Workingmen's Party Address." 1878. *The Daily Argus*, January 7.

Chan, Sucheng. 1989. *This Bittersweet Soil: The Chinese in California Agriculture, 1860–1910*. Berkeley: University of California Press.

Chang, Gordon H. 2012. "China and the Pursuit of America's Destiny: Nineteenth-Century Imagining and Why Immigration Restriction Took So Long." *Journal of Asian American Studies* 15(2): 145–69.

———. 2019. *Ghosts on Gold Mountain: The Epic Story of the Chinese Who Built the Transcontinental Railroad*. Boston: Mariner Books.

Cheng Hirata, Lucie. 1979. "Free, Indentured, Enslaved: Chinese Prostitutes in Nineteenth-Century America." *Signs* 5(1): 3–29.

"Chinese Slavery in California." 1861. *Trinity Journal*, March 2.

Chitty, Christopher. 2020. *Sexual Hegemony: Statecraft, Sodomy, and Capital in the Rise of the World System*. Durham, NC: Duke University Press.

Clement, H. R. 1878. "Caucasian vs. Mongolian" in "Report of Special Committee on Chinese Immigration." *Appendix to Journals of the Senate and Assembly of the Twenty-Second Session of the Legislature of the State of California*, Vol. 3, 267–68.

Cohen, Cathy. 1999. *The Boundaries of Blackness: AIDS and the Breakdown of Black Politics*. Chicago: University of Chicago Press.

Congressional Globe. 1866. 39th Congress, 1st Session, February 27.

Congressional Record. 1882a. 47th Congress, 1st Session, March 1.

Congressional Record. 1882b. 47th Congress, 1st Session, March 15.

Cossman, Brenda. 2019. "Queering Queer Legal Studies: An Unreconstructed Ode to Eve Sedgwick (and Others)." *Queer Legal Studies* 6(1): 23–38.

Cott, Nancy. 1977. *The Bonds of Womanhood: "Woman's Sphere" in New England, 1780–1835*. New Haven, CT: Yale University Press.

———. 2000. *Public Vows: A History of Marriage and the Nation*. Cambridge, MA: Harvard University Press.

Currarino, Rosanne. 2011. *The Labor Question in America: Economic Democracy in the Gilded Age*. Champaign: University of Illinois Press.

"The Curse of California." 1882. *The Wasp*, August 19.

Daniels, Roger. 2002. *Coming to America: A History of Immigration and Ethnicity in American Life*. New York: Harper.

Debates and Proceedings of the Constitutional Convention of the State of California. 1880. Sacramento: State Office.

Foner, Eric. 1970. *Free Soil, Free Labor, Free Men: The Ideology of the Republican Party before the Civil War*. New York: Oxford University Press.

Frye, Matthew Jacobson. 1998. *Whiteness of a Different Color: European Immigrants and the Alchemy of Race*. Cambridge, MA: Harvard University Press.

Glenn, Evelyn Nakano. 2004. *Unequal Freedom: How Race and Gender Shaped American Citizenship and Labor*. Cambridge, MA: Harvard University Press.

Halperin, David M. 1995. *Saint Foucault: Towards a Gay Hagiography*. New York: Oxford University Press.

Harota, Hidetaka. 2013. "The Moment of Transition: State Officials, the Federal Government, and the Formation of American Immigration Policy." *Journal of American History* 99(4): 1092–1108.

Hartman, Saidiya. 2019. *Wayward Lives, Beautiful Experiments: Intimate Histories of Social Upheaval*. New York: W.W. Norton.

Helper, Hinton R. 1855. *The Land of Gold: Reality Versus Fiction*. Baltimore, MD: H. Taylor.

———. 1857. *The Impending Crisis of the South: How to Meet It*. New York: Burdick Brothers.

"Horrors of a Great City: Chinadom by Day and by Night." 1869. *San Francisco Chronicle*, December 5.

Johnson, Susan Lee. 2000. *Roaring Camp: The Social World of the California Gold Rush*. New York: W.W. Norton.

Jung, Moon-Ho. 2006. *Coolies and Cane: Race, Labor, and Sugar in the Age of Emancipation*. Baltimore, MD: Johns Hopkins University Press.

Kessler-Harris, Alice. 1982. *Out to Work: A History of Wage-Earning in the United States*. New York: Oxford University Press.

Labbé, Ronald M. and Jonathan Lurie. 2003. *The Slaughterhouse Cases: Regulation, Reconstruction, and the Fourteenth Amendment*. Lawrence: University Press of Kansas.

Leong, Karen. L. 2001. "'A Distinct and Antagonistic Race': Constructions of Chinese Manhood in the Exclusionist Debates." In *Across the Great Divide: Cultures of Manhood in the American West*, edited by Matthew Basso, Laura McCall, and Dee Garceau. New York: Routledge.

Levy, Jonathan. 2012. *Freaks of Fortune: The Emerging World of Capitalism and Risk in America*. Cambridge, MA: Harvard University Press.

Lew-Williams, Beth. 2018. *The Chinese Must Go: Violence, Exclusion, and the Making of the Alien in America*. Cambridge, MA: Harvard University Press.

Lowe, Lisa. 2015. *The Intimacy of Four Continents*. Durham, NC: Duke University Press.

Lui, Mary Ting Yi. 2004. *The Chinatown Trunk Mystery: Murder, Miscegenation, and Other Dangerous Encounters in Turn-of-the-Century New York City*. Princeton, NJ: Princeton University Press.

Luibhéid, Eithne. 2002. *Entry Denied: Controlling Sexuality at the Border*. Minneapolis: University of Minnesota Press.

Marx, Karl. 1964. *Economic and Philosophical Manuscripts of 1844*. Translated by Martin Milligan. New York: International Publishers.

McClain Jr., Charles J. 1994. *In Search of Equality: The Chinese Struggle against Discrimination in Nineteenth-Century America*. Berkeley: University of California Press.

Mei, June. 1979. "Socioeconomic Origins of Emigration: Guangdong to California, 1850–1882." *Modern China* 5(4): 463–501.

"The Menace of the Hour." 1889. *The Verdict*, January 30.

Ngai, Mae M. 2015. "Chinese Gold Miners and the 'Chinese Question' in Nineteenth-Century California and Victoria." *Journal of American History* 10(4): 1082–1105.

Norris, Frank. 1901. *The Octopus: A Story of California*. New York: Doubleday.

Pascoe, Peggy. 2009. *What Comes Naturally: Miscegenation Law and the Making of Race in America*. New York: Oxford University Press.

Peffer, George Anthony. 1986. "Forbidden Families: Emigration Experiences of Chinese Women Under the Page Law, 1875–1882." *Journal of American Ethnic History* 6(1): 28–46.

Perlin, Michael L. and Alison Lynch. 2014. "All His Sexless Patients: Persons with Mental Disabilities and the Competence to Have Sex." *Washington Law Review* 89: 257–300.

Puar, Jasbir K. 2005. "Queer Times, Queer Assemblages." *Social Text* 23(3–4): 121–39.

Roberts, Dorothy. 1997. *Killing the Black Body: Race. Reproduction, and the Meaning of Liberty*. New York: Vintage Books.

Rockman, Seth. 2009. *Scraping By: Wage Labor, Slavery, and Survival in Early Baltimore*. Baltimore, MD: Johns Hopkins University Press.

Ruskola, Teemu. 2010. "Raping Like a State." *UCLA Law Review* 57: 1478–1536.

Salyer, Lucy. 1995. *Laws Harsh as Tigers: Chinese Immigrants and the Shaping of Modern Immigration Law*. Chapel Hill: University of North Carolina Press.

Saxton, Alexander. 1971. *The Indispensable Enemy: Labor and the Anti-Chinese Movement in California*. Berkeley: University of California Press.

Schrecker, John. 2010. "'For the Equality of Men—For the Equality of Nations': Anson Burlingame and China's First Embassy to the United States, 1868." *Journal of American-East Asian Relations* 17(1): 9–34.

Sears, Clare. 2008. "All That Glitters: Trans-ing California's Gold Rush Migrations." *GLQ: A Journal of Lesbian and Gay Studies* 14(2–3): 383–412.

Sedgwick, Eve Kosofsky. 1993. *Tendencies*. Durham, NC: Duke University Press.

Shah, Nayan. 2001. *Contagious Divides: Epidemics and Race in San Francisco's Chinatown*. Berkeley: University of California Press.

———. 2011. *Stranger Intimacy: Contesting Race, Sexuality, and the Law in the North American West*. Berkeley: University of California Press.

Smith, Stacey L. 2013. *Freedom's Frontier: California and the Struggle Over Unfree Labor, Emancipation, and Reconstruction*. Chapel Hill: University of North Carolina Press.

Stanford, Leland. 1865. "Chinese Labor." *Annual Report of the Department of the Interior*. Washigngton, DC: US Government Printing Office.

Stanley, Amy Dru. 1996. "Home Life and the Morality of the Market." In *The Market Revolution in America: Social, Political, and Religious Expressions, 1800–1880*, edited by Melvyn Stokes and Stephen Conway. Charlottesville: University of Virginia Press.

———. 1998. *From Bondage to Contract: Wage Labor, Marriage, and the Market in the Age of Slave Emancipation*. New York: Cambridge University Press.

Stansell, Christine. 1986. *City of Women: Sex and Class in New York, 1789–1860*. Urbana: University of Illinois Press.

Swinton, John. 1870. *The New Chinese-American Question*. New York: American News Company.

Sylvis, James C. (ed.). 1872. *The Life, Speeches, Labors and Essays of William H. Sylvis*. Philadelphia: Claxton, Remsen & Haffelfinger.

Takaki, Ronald. 1989. *Strangers from a Different Shore: A History of Asian Americans*. Boston: Little Brown.

Tong, Benson. 1994. *Unsubmissive Women: Chinese Prostitutes in Nineteenth-Century San Francisco*. Norman: University of Oklahoma Press.

Twain, Mark. 1871. *Roughing It*. New York: Harper and Brothers.

Walkowitz, Judith R. 1982. *Prostitution and Victorian Society: Women, Class, and the State*. New York: Cambridge University Press.

White, Richard. 2012. *Railroaded: The Transcontinentals and the Making of Modern America*. New York: W.W. Norton.

———. 2017. *The Republic for Which It Stands: The United States During Reconstruction and the Gilded Age, 1865–1896*. New York: Oxford University Press.

Workingmen's Party of California. 1879. *"The Chinese Must Go": The Labor Agitators; or, The Battle for Bread*. San Francisco: G.W. Greene.

Yung, Judy. 1999. Unbound Voices: A Documentary History of Chinese Women in San Francisco. Berkeley: University of California Press.

Zhu, Liping. 2013. *The Road to Chinese Exclusion: The Denver Riot, 1880 Election, and Rise of the West*. Lawrence: University Press of Kansas.

7

Donorsexuality after *Dobbs*

MARY ANNE CASE

For the better part of a century, the US Supreme Court has issued a series of decisions "the underlying premise of [which is] that the Constitution protects 'the right of the individual . . . to be free from unwarranted governmental intrusion into . . . the decision whether to bear or beget a child'" (Carey v. Population Services International 1977). The most controversial line of such decisions, protecting from "unwarranted governmental intrusion" an individual's right to choose to terminate a pregnancy through abortion (Roe v. Wade 1973; Planned Parenthood of Southeastern Pa. v. Casey 1992; June Med. Servs. L.L.C. v. Russo 2020), has been decisively overruled (Dobbs v. Jackson Women's Health Organization 2022). The same conservative justices who have eliminated abortion rights have for the entirety of their legal careers expressed skepticism of or downright hostility to the entire line of cases in which their predecessors on the Court have protected sexual and reproductive rights (Greene 2010, 717).

Now might therefore be a particularly opportune time to examine with lawyerly precision exactly what this line of cases can be read actually to protect, as well as to begin to consider how much of these protections may be vulnerable in the aftermath of the successful attack on abortion rights. This chapter will undertake such an examination from an unusual angle. It will focus on the motivations and behaviors, the resulting legal problems and possible rights claims, of men who make an atypical set of decisions to beget children: They offer their own fresh sperm on a non-commercial basis directly to significant numbers of women, often not personally well known to them, for purposes of DIY artificial insemination. Among the legal risks these high-volume non-anonymous sperm donors run is the prospect that the Food and Drug Administration, as well as state regulatory authorities, can threaten them with fines and imprisonment if they continue to provide their sperm without either complying with the restrictive and expensive rules for commercial sperm banks or demonstrating that they are exempt from these rules because, notably, the person to whom they will transfer their fresh sperm for insemination purposes is "a sexually intimate partner" of the donor.[1]

The FDA regulations leave the term "sexual intimacy" undefined, which itself raises interesting questions in light of the variety of sexual practices and attitudes manifested in connection with sperm donation. But even more remarkable from the perspective of doctrinal constitutional law is that the regulations, which a lower court has upheld, explicitly privilege *sexual* intimacy. This, as will be discussed below, seems a poor fit with the regulations' goal of protecting health and safety, but is a much better fit with the actual holdings in the line of modern substantive due process cases covering sexual and reproductive rights, which, if carefully analyzed, can be seen to more clearly, frequently, and unequivocally protect a right to sexual intimacy in the absence of procreative intent (or even procreative possibility) than they protect a right to procreate.

As I delve into the doctrine, I will also provide a more concrete sense of what is at stake by describing in some detail the situations of three actual high-volume providers of fresh sperm, each broadly representative of a type of donor that raises distinct legal issues with broader implications. The first is Trent Arsenault, the original, self-described donorsexual, whose reproductive activities are tightly connected to sexual practices he himself sees as amounting to a sexual orientation. The second is Ari Nagel, best known by the sobriquet the Sperminator bestowed on him by the *New York Post*, but who calls himself, as I will call him here, Super Dad, because of a commitment to be as much as possible an involved father in the lives of his more than 100 donor offspring (Lewak 2016a). The third, who calls himself Joe Donor to conceal his identity, I shall note in passing as an example of those men whose announced goal is to maximize the number of their donor offspring in explicit quest of a world record, and who prefer to provide their sperm donation in the form, not of transfer in a sterile receptacle for artificial insemination (A.I.) by the recipient, but of so-called natural insemination (N.I.), i.e., unprotected vaginal intercourse for the purpose of impregnation

(Schneider et al. 2014). I have selected these three for purposes of illustrating the landscape of the law, not because I see them as in any way representative of the by now quite large and varied pool of free sperm donors who offer their services on a variety of Internet sites and other venues (Acker 2013; Bergen and Delacroix 2019; Russell 2021). Although free sperm donation is not only a worldwide but also a cross-border phenomenon, and although two of the men I discuss, Ari Nagel and Joe Donor, travel the world over to provide their sperm to persons of many nationalities in many foreign venues, my focus is on American law and the activities of the donors within the United States.

The doctrinal conclusion of my reflections on where the law with respect to these donors may stand after *Dobbs* will not be any of the now familiar modern substantive due process cases, but instead an older equal protection case, *Skinner v. Oklahoma*. In 1942, *Skinner* vindicated more directly than any other case before or since the right to procreate. The Court held it to be a violation of convicted chicken thief Jack Skinner's fundamental right to procreate for the state of Oklahoma to order him to be sterilized when those convicted of equally serious crimes like embezzlement were not eligible for sterilization. Although its age and the legal basis on which it rests shelter *Skinner*'s holding from the full force of the destructive tornado unleashed by the *Dobbs* majority on other Supreme Court sexual and reproductive rights decisions, new questions inevitably will arise in a post-*Dobbs* world when applying strict scrutiny, as *Skinner* requires, to laws restricting for some and not for others what the opening sentences of the *Skinner* majority opinion called "a sensitive and important area of human rights . . .—the right to have offspring" (Skinner v. Oklahoma 1942, 536).

The Donorsexual and the Right to Fuck

When Trent Arsenault first came to the attention of the FDA and the national media a decade ago, he was in his mid-thirties, a computer engineer for Hewlett Packard in Silicon Valley, and the biological father of more than a dozen offspring conceived over a five-year period with sperm he had delivered fresh in a cup to couples who contacted him on his website or on other websites matching would-be donors of free sperm with potential recipients seeking it for purposes of impregnation.

Arsenault was, he said, a virgin, and, more than that, a "donorsexual" who did not have and never expected to have any other sexual outlet than filling hundreds of cups with semen for immediate delivery to ovulating would-be parents. He had "committed 100 percent of [his] sexual energy for producing sperm for childless couples to have babies" (Huffington Post 2012). He claims to have known that "donorsexual" was his identity when he was ten years old but said he "really doesn't know why" any more than others know "why they were born straight or gay" (Donohue 2012).

His religious background clearly played a role in Arsenault's sexual identity formation, however. He was raised in the Assemblies of God, the world's largest Pentecostal church, of which his father, the Reverend Charles Arsenault, is a leading minister. His parents tried long and unsuccessfully to help him meet a nice young woman to settle down with, but, at age sixteen, "he and his best friend made a pact to devote their lives to science and never to marry."[2] Arsenault turns to a scripture verse, Matthew 19:11–12, to sum up his commitment to reproducing while avoiding partnered sex: "Jesus said, 'Some people were born differently to be celibate, so accept the fact and use it to further God's kingdom'" (Donohue 2012).

He remembers hearing prayers offered throughout his youth for women struggling with infertility. He had "instilled in [him] to be a servant to others," and, having begun with "the normal volunteer things (soup kitchens, missionary trips, building playgrounds)," he then sought a way to put his unusual sexuality to use helping others. The Assemblies of God doctrine Arsenault was raised with was that even infertile heterosexual married couples should limit themselves to adoption and avoid donor insemination; the church also discriminated against gays and lesbians. But Arsenault realized that this view "shuts out quite a large group of people wanting to have children" and asked, "What do you think Jesus would do?" (Wallace 2012). Thinking it "wrong to discriminate," he held onto the basic teachings of Christianity even as he "parted with the church's ideas and hung up the hat on religion" (Donohue 2012). He vowed to begin "helping the very group that my church discriminated against, which was gays and lesbians." The first recipients of his sperm donations were lesbian couples. He saw what he was doing as "an applied version of the part of Christianity that he likes best—compassion achieved through an ascetic, personalized life-hack of the Silicon Valley variety" (Wallace 2012). His parents, however, saw him as a "servant to sinners," perhaps all the more so once they learned that he had posted on porn sites many videos of himself masturbating into a donation cup, videos that have earned millions of views and an appreciative, mostly gay male fan base.

The FDA saw Arsenault as an "establishment" or "firm" illegally engaged in the manufacture and distribution of semen without complying with all the applicable rules on registration, testing, recordkeeping, and storage. The rules, designed for commercial sperm banks, required, among other things, testing for STDs (something Arsenault did do, but not as frequently as the rules required) and cryogenically quarantining the semen for six months before thawing for use (something both Arsenault and his recipients, who wanted to use fresh sperm because of evidence that it was more likely to be effective in producing pregnancy, wished to avoid). The rules allowed an exemption for donor screening and testing for "[r]eproductive cells or tissue donated by a sexually intimate partner of the recipient for reproductive use."[3] Through his lawyer, Arsenault offered to prove that he and his intended recipients did qualify as sexually intimate partners, but the FDA refused even to consider his evidence, finding that Arsenault could at most qualify as a "'directed donor' . . . who knows and is known by the recipient before donation" but still had to comply with stringent requirements (Abbasi 2013, 32). One of his would-be recipients, a lesbian who had miscarried an earlier pregnancy achieved with Arsenault's sperm and wanted to try again, then filed suit in federal court, represented by Arsenault's lawyer, claiming, inter alia, that the FDAs regulations were "unconstitutional to the extent that they operate to regulate noncommercial, sexually intimate choices and activity protected by the rights to privacy, bodily integrity and autonomy, liberty, life, due process, and equal protection guaranteed by the First, Fifth, Ninth, and Tenth Amendments to the United States Constitution" (Complaint: Doe v. Hamburg 2013). Her suit was dismissed on prudential standing grounds, with the district court finding that because she was not the direct target of the FDA's enforcement action, only Arsenault's constitutional rights, not hers, were directly at stake and he should have been the one to sue (Doe v. Hamburg 2013).

Doe alleged in her complaint that she was in a long-term monogamous lesbian relationship and "does not engage in heterosexual intercourse." Had she and Arsenault both been willing to let her masturbate him to orgasm rather than taking delivery of his sperm in a cup, she might more credibly have been able to allege that their relationship was sexual,[4] but such a sex act, violating both participants' commitments and sense of self, not only seems a bizarre price to have to pay for the opportunity to reproduce with the person of one's choice but also might not qualify as intimate to the FDA (Case 1993, 1655). And while the relationship between private, non-anonymous semen donors and their recipients might indeed be "an intimate exchange and an expression of personal trust," as claimed by Arsenault's lawyer in her law review article about the case (Abbasi 2013, 39), it would not therefore qualify as sexual. The FDA insisted it "cannot accept an expanded definition of the term 'sexually intimate partner.'"[5]

Among the questions the FDA's classification scheme raises is not only what counts as "a sexually intimate partner[ship]," but also why it has the privilege of exemption. The most mundane explanation may be that the FDA's rules dealt only with concern about communicable, not heritable, diseases. The FDA may simply have assumed that the bodies and bodily fluids of those in a sexually intimate relationship were likely already to be in close enough contact to have spread any communicable diseases from one partner to the other, such that the precautions of further testing and quarantining would be superfluous. This, of course, creates perverse incentives for those providing and using donated sperm. As Beth Gardner, founder of the Known Donor Registry, a site that connects people interested in private donation, puts it, the regulations force donations underground, "putting desperate women at a greater risk of being coerced into sex or obtaining sperm from unscrupulous donors who have foregone screening. . . . It's not the realm of government to decide who I'm allowed to have a baby with and how I'm going to make that happen. That's my business" (Vogel 2012). Although a directed donor and especially the intended recipient may have preferred A.I. precisely because of its comparative safety, they can avoid trouble with the FDA by reverting instead to N.I., that is to say to unprotected penile vaginal sexual intercourse, which is far more risky from a number of perspectives not limited to that of potentially communicable diseases. A regulatory scheme that leaves Arsenault at greater risk for fines and jail than the likes of Joe Donor, who makes clear his strong preference for N.I., and, by preserving his anonymity, blocks other, non-bodily forms of intimate connection with his recipients, seems far from desirable. It has some of the same flaws judges a hundred years ago found in laws preventing couples from marrying in the absence of a health certification that the would-be husband was free of venereal disease, which also may have encouraged far more dangerous and undesirable activity than they prevented (Peterson v. Vidule 1914).

Considerations of constitutional law as well as epidemiology might have prompted the FDA to give special accommodations to sexually intimate partners, however. Even the *Dobbs* majority acknowledged "rights recognized in past decisions involving matters such as intimate sexual relations," from which it sought to distinguish the abortion right it was extinguishing (Dobbs 2022). The Supreme Court had long acknowledged "that sexual intimacy is 'a sensitive, key relationship of human existence, central to family life, community welfare, and the development of human personality'" (Bowers v. Hardwick 1986, 205; Paris Adult Theatre I v. Slaton 1973, 63) and had granted an increasingly broader swath of sexual intimacy constitutional protection, especially from criminal prosecution, in the progression of cases from *Griswold v. Connecticut* through *Lawrence v. Texas*. What these cases protected was the sexual relations themselves, divorced from any necessary connection to procreation or family.

From my earliest days as a legal scholar, long before the Court extended constitutional protection to "private, consensual sexual intimacy between two adult persons of the same sex" (US v. Windsor 2013, 769) by overruling *Bowers* in *Lawrence v. Texas*, I have been arguing that the best (in the sense of most lawyerly) way to understand *Griswold* and its progeny was as a "progression of . . . requests for the same legal right to couple" (Case 1993, 1653). At the time I meant to encompass both "pair bonding and copulating" (1644) under the term "coupling," but in the context of this chapter I will focus even more narrowly on the court's recognition of a right to fuck (privately, consensually, non-commercially, but not necessarily particularly intimately in other respects). The method I use to extract this right from the case law is one familiar in analysis of the development of the common law, which is thought to yield principles (whether to the judge, the scholar, or the lawyer) when one lines up a series of related cases and abstracts from them a rule of decision that accounts for them apart from their more particular facts, something one generally needs a line of cases to discern.[6]

In the specific context of sexual and reproductive constitutional rights, one thing I am trying to get at with this method is the possibility that there is a midpoint between the extremes Justice Harlan posits in his famous *Poe v. Ullman* dissent (later incorporated in full as his concurrence in *Griswold*). Harlan wrote:

> The full scope of the liberty guaranteed by the Due Process Clause cannot be found in or limited by the precise terms of the specific guarantees elsewhere provided in the Constitution. This "liberty" is not a series of isolated points pricked out in terms of the taking of property; the freedom of speech, press, and religion; the right to keep and bear arms; the freedom from unreasonable searches and seizures; and so on. It is a rational continuum which, broadly speaking, includes a freedom from all substantial arbitrary impositions and purposeless restraints. (*Poe v. Ullman* 1961, 1777)

The contrast here is between mere incorporation of the bill of rights and a much broader scope for substantive due process under the Fourteenth Amendment (the former warmly embraced and the latter harshly repudiated by the right on the present Supreme Court) (Case 2019).[7] I want to suggest that one can in addition take the rights "pricked out" in the at first seemingly isolated holdings of the various cases in the area of sexual and reproductive rights and connect them, to see what shape of more general guarantee reveals itself when the more specific ones are lined up together. This is what Justice Scalia himself did in a series of dissents from Justice Kennedy's various gay rights opinions, in each case connecting the dots and seeing what for him was a nightmare vision of what was to come (albeit a dream for queer theorists like me, who saw the same figure as Scalia when we, too, connected the dots).[8]

Even though the term "common law constitutionalism" (Strauss 1996, 879) was developed by those on the left, justices on the right of the Court have both applied and described a common law method of analyzing constitutional cases (Case 2000, 1462; Case 2019). It fits particularly well with the argument by some conservative scholars that only the judgment (that is to say narrowly the result) and not the opinion in a Supreme Court case is actually the law (Hartnett 1999). While far from identical to the present Court majority's emphasis on history and tradition, it more closely tracks an earlier version of emphasis on history and tradition, Scalia's insistence on looking for the narrowest possible specification of a right previously recognized by the Court to see whether it was available to a claimant in a case before the Court.

Famously, in a lengthy footnote that attracted much attention but not a Court majority, Justice Scalia declared that the correct level of generality at which to pose the question whether Michael H., who wanted to maintain contact with the daughter he had conceived in an adulterous relationship with another man's wife, was entitled to a hearing on his parentage was not "whether parenthood is an interest that historically has received our attention and protection," as Justice Brennan had argued, but instead whether the "natural father of a child adulterously conceived" had received such protection. Scalia asked:

> Why should the relevant category not be even more general [than parenthood]—perhaps "family relationships"; or "personal relationships"; or even "emotional attachments in general"? Though the dissent has no basis for the level of generality it would select, we do: We refer to the most specific level at which a relevant tradition protecting, or denying protection to, the asserted right can be identified. (*Michael H. v. Gerald D.* 1989, 128 n.6)

At the "most specific level at which a relevant tradition protecting . . . [an] asserted right [in the *Griswold* line of cases] can be identified," what emerges is the right to fuck, as generations of distinguished scholars, using much politer language, have been arguing almost from the start. Let me cite just a few examples here. Richard Posner categorized as "the sexual freedom cases" the line of contraception and abortion cases beginning with *Griswold* together with *Stanley v. Georgia*, a case protecting the right to possess obscene materials in the home (1979).[9] (As Posner noted, *Eisenstadt v. Baird* cited *Stanley* as support for the extension of the right to obtain contraceptives to the unmarried.) In 1986, the year *Bowers* was decided, Richard Mohr—unlike Posner an enthusiast for cases protecting sexual freedom—insisted that "though the Court has failed to acknowledge the logical conclusion to its privacy decisions, the privacy decisions protect the right to have sex. . . . The rationale for the right to purchase contraceptives and own pornography must be derived from the right to use them—to guide one's sex life by one's own lights compatible with a like ability on the part of others" (1986, 80). A few years later, Nan Hunter stressed that the "same aim of the law [that underlay the New England Puritans' antisodomy laws]—discouragement of nonprocreative sex—underlay the statutes prohibiting the use of birth control devices which were stricken as unconstitutional by the Supreme Court in the 1960s" (1992, 536). Hunter pointed out the *Bowers*' majority's error in asserting "that a privacy claim on behalf of 'homosexual sodomy' bore no relationship to the claims" in the *Griswold* line: "Michael Hardwick, as a person engaged in sodomy, had the same relationship to procreation as persons using birth control during heterosexual intercourse: none, which was precisely the point. The issue in *Hardwick* should have been controlled by *Griswold* and *Eisenstadt*" (1992, 536). The Massachusetts law struck down in *Eisenstadt* provided support for Hunter's argument in that it prohibited alike the distribution of any "article intended to be used for self-abuse, . . . the prevention of conception or for causing unlawful abortion" (Eisenstadt v. Baird 1972, 441 n.2).[10] The Massachusetts legislature thus demonstrated that it viewed non-procreative masturbation, contraception, and abortion as equivalent evils.

When *Bowers* gave way to *Lawrence*, Hunter noted that the *Lawrence* Court "modified the meaning" of *Griswold*, *Eisenstadt*, *Carey*, and *Roe* to focus less on "procreation and procreative decision making" and "more on sexual conduct . . . with a greater acknowledgment that what had been before the Court was sexual activity, not simply decisions about whether to become a parent" (Hunter 2004, 1110).

Mohr and Hunter, as gay rights activists, welcomed *Lawrence*'s extension of protections to more forms of non-procreative sex. But, more recently, Kim Mutcherson, an advocate for reproductive justice, observed:

> From a strictly legal standpoint, after *Skinner v. Oklahoma*, in which the Court articulated a fundamental right to procreate, courts have reinforced a liberty interest in sexual activity. . . . However, the Court's endorsement

of a right to sexual activity, especially as articulated based on the facts of *Lawrence*, has no connection to procreative liberty. In fact, it is much easier to find Supreme Court jurisprudence supporting the constitutional right to nonprocreative sex than to procreative sex. (2015, 35)

As I have suggested above and will explain further below, Mutcherson's quite correct observation has completely different implications in the aftermath of *Dobbs*, because *Skinner*, a World War II–era equal protection case, has a much better chance of surviving as a precedent than the sexual rights cases from the era of the Warren Court to the present, even though the author of the *Skinner* majority opinion, Justice Douglas, also wrote the majority opinion in *Griswold*.

Super Dad and the Right to Procreate

Stanley v. Georgia, involving protection for obscene films used in the home as masturbatory aids, is an appropriate precedent in support of Donorsexual Trent Arsenault, whose exercise of his right to beget children takes the form of acts of masturbation he records in pornographic videos he makes freely available for consumption by others, just as he makes his sperm available. For Super Dad Ari Nagel, however, a more appropriate precedent may be *Stanley v. Illinois*, the 1972 Supreme Court case in which an unmarried father who had lived with his three biological children and their mother for decades before her death was held entitled not to be deprived upon her death of custody of the children absent evidence that he was unfit as a parent (Stanley v. Illinois 1972). This is because, despite being called the Sperminator by the press, despite also using as his principal procreative technique masturbation, with increasingly rare forays into ordinary non-reproductively motivated sexual intercourse (which led to the conception of his oldest child and Nagel's marriage to the mother) and N.I. (which produced about a dozen of his more than 100 donor conceived children), Nagel's activities, and his potential legal problems, are far more focused on the creation of unconventional families than on the expression of an unconventional sexuality.

It is worth noting that the majority in *Roe* cites only *Stanley v. Georgia* while in *Casey* both *Stanley* cases are cited (*Illinois* by the plurality, the Stevens concurrence, and the Rehnquist dissent; *Georgia* only by Stevens). In *Dobbs*, only *Stanley v. Illinois* makes an appearance, and only in the dissent, where it is cited as "offering constitutional protection to untraditional 'family unit[s]'" as part of a string cite illustrating the proposition that "*Roe* and *Casey* fit neatly into a long line of decisions protecting from government intrusion a wealth of private choices about family matters, child rearing, intimate relationships, and procreation." These choices, the dissent insists, the Court has "repeatedly said" that "liberty requires" be made by "the individual and not the government" even "when those living in 1868 would not have recognized the claim—because they would not have seen the person making it as a full-fledged member of the community."[11]

Although the *Dobbs* dissenters directly mention "whom to have sex with" as among the "particular choices . . . cases safeguard," the other choices on their list are all familial: "whom to marry; . . . what family members to live with; how to raise children—and crucially, whether and when to have children." In the decade between the time the FDA first ordered Arsenault to cease and desist his sperm donations in 2009 and the Supreme Court of Israel ordered Ari Nagel to do likewise in 2019, the attention of the US Supreme Court shifted away from sexual intimacy and toward family formation. There is a similar contrast between the FDA's concern with Arsenault's potentially spreading communicable diseases through too frequent donation and the state of Israel's concern that Ari Nagel was spreading his capacity to serve as a father too thin by too frequent donation.

Although six women preparing for IVF already had frozen sperm from Nagel in readiness at Israeli storage facilities, and others wanted him to provide them with fresh sperm on his next trip to the country, the Israeli Supreme Court, invoking "Israeli law requiring complete anonymity in gamete donation, except where two people plan to co-parent the resulting child," voiced "real and serious concern about the ability of the petitioner to actually serve as the father to over 38 children, both financially and in the essence of what a father's rule [*sic*][12] is within the family" (Willows 2019).[13] Nagel thought the decision made no sense and "felt terrible for the women denied his sperm [who] ended up purchasing frozen anonymous sperm. How are *they* going to be a father? But *that's* completely allowed and acceptable" (Klein 2020).[14]

Importantly, the clear lesson of the US Supreme Court's relevant constitutional rights cases in both substantive due process and equal protection frameworks for more than half a century is that there is no "essence" to a father's role in the family. While it is essential that children not be abused or neglected, the division of labor between parents and the role each assumes in parenting is for the parents to shape for themselves. This was the paramount lesson not only of Ruth Bader Ginsburg's life,[15] but also of the revolution she as advocate brought about in constitutional sex discrimination law, exemplified by *Weinberger v. Wiesenfeld* (1975). In that case, upon the death of a breadwinner mother in childbirth, the father, represented in the Supreme Court by Ginsburg, successfully sued for social security survivor's benefits so he could stay home to care for his child.[16] This is also what lay behind the emphasis on the need to protect and validate a same-sex couple's parenting in Kennedy's same-sex marriage opinions. Moreover, so long as a father is not willfully failing to provide for his existing children, the state may not curtail his ability to form new family bonds because he is too poor adequately to support his family members (Zablocki v. Redhail 1978). In a series of cases involving fathers not married to the mothers of their children, the Court did hold that such fathers had to "grasp the opportunity" biological paternity offered to them "to develop a relationship with the child" if they wanted to be recognized as fathers and not risk losing their rights, especially to another man willing to care for, provide for, and adopt the child, such as the mother's new husband, but it pointed to a variety of options under state law for so doing (Lehr v. Robertson 1983, 262). If the cases best supporting Arsenault's rights are *Stanley v. Georgia* and the line from *Griswold* to *Lawrence*, those best supporting Nagel's rights, in addition to the above-mentioned cases involving the role of a father, are *Moore v. City of East Cleveland* (1977), giving the multi-generational household of a matriarch the right to continue to reside together in a neighborhood zoned for single-family occupancy despite an ordinance more restrictively defining "family" for zoning purposes, and *Obergefell*. Nagel is creating an alternative family structure, but one not without long historical precedent. The precedents include extended families such as the one in *Moore* and the polygamists that the dissenters in *Obergefell* correctly say can use Kennedy's majority opinion to ground a claim to legal recognition (or at least an end to legal prosecution) with far more support in millennia of history and tradition than the same-sex couples to whom Kennedy extends recognition. Indeed, some critics have suggested men like Nagel are "estranged patriarchs" (Bergen and Delacroix 2019),[17] that they are reinforcing heterosexist traditions rather than breaking with them or improving on them.

That Mrs. Moore and her descendants are in the line of claimants whose victories support Nagel's right to continue to beget children suggests a different, more progressive way structurally to analyze Nagel's familial choices than as patriarchal. In her scholarship, including *The Neutered Mother, the Sexual Family, and Other Twentieth Century Tragedies*, feminist legal theorist Martha Fineman has long argued that for American law to see the sexual couple rather than a mother[18] and child as the foundation of the family was a mistake that would help entrench patriarchy (1995). She argued that state recognition of marriage should be abolished and sexual partners' relationships governed by ordinary criminal and civil laws, including contract. The result would be that fathers would get such access to their children as they were able to contract with mothers to obtain, on such terms as the mother was prepared to agree to. In response to the objection that fathers might then well not contribute, especially financially, to raising their children to the extent they are obligated to under current law, Fineman made clear her approach was premised on robust state support for parenting and other forms of caring for those inevitably or derivatively dependent.

Fineman may not see Nagel as her paradigmatic father of the future, but I will argue that he comes fascinatingly close to fulfilling her conditions concerning fathers contracting with the mothers of their children. He will give his sperm free of charge to literally anyone who asks for it, seeking only that he be reimbursed for travel expenses (Lewak 2019). He will do so in the recipient's preferred manner, fresh in a cup in an informal setting, in a clinic, through a medical intermediary, or, at least in the early days, through sexual intercourse. (TheMauryShowOfficial 2017; Rashty 2021). His first two successful donations, were, he says, to a partnered lesbian with whom he had penetrative sex and to a straight single woman for IVF in a clinic.

Nagel does not discriminate and he asks few questions of those who approach him for donations. Many of those he impregnates seem to be poor; one of those he impregnated was an eighteen-year-old living in a homeless shelter, in a lesbian relationship with a partner living in another shelter (Lewak 2019). He feels his faith in this decision was vindicated: She had spent much of her young life acting as a de facto parent for a sister half her age, seemed mature, and is now a high school graduate, employed, married, and the mother of a second child with Nagel (Doctor Oz May 2021). In another case, however, psychological problems he might have learned about before insemination had he inquired or investigated caused such a crisis after the birth of the child that Nagel had to step up to assume temporary full-time custody until an alternative permanent placement could be found. But step up he did (Ingber 2022). He is also paying a sizeable chunk of his limited income as a math professor in child support to five of the mothers of nine of his donor-conceived children, who sued him despite their having agreed not to in agreements he knew in advance would be legally unenforceable. He appears to pay the child support cheerfully and it has not deterred him from continuing to donate (Monroe 2021).

If Arsenault's claims sound in reproductive rights, Nagel's sound more in reproductive justice. "I have 77 children, that's true, but then you look at the three women that we just saw on the screen and they don't have 77 children," Nagel told Dr. Oz on Fox News in 2021. "For them, it's about them having their first child or their second child. So it's not so much don't focus on me, [as] more focus on them, . . . who just want to have a family" (Moore 2021). Most of his recipients appear to be women of color, and many name the prohibitive cost of paying for sperm as one of the reasons to turn to him.[19] The many dozens of children he has helped women of color conceive and give birth to makes Super Dad's version of reproductive justice a possible counterpoint to the claim, long propounded by Justice Thomas and discussed in the *Dobbs* majority opinion, that some "proponents of liberal access to abortion . . . have been motivated by a desire to suppress the size of the African-American population" (Dobbs 2022).

Nagel's relationship with any resulting child is as much in the mother's control as all the other aspects of his process. He will be present at the birth if asked or never have contact again after the handover of his sperm if not desired. Some mothers list him on a birth certificate or give the child his last name; others give the child his first name or a variant thereof (Monroe 2021). Nagel says he married a small number of the religiously observant single women to whom he has donated, so the children would not be born bastards, soon followed by an agreed upon divorce (Rashty 2021). Some of the mothers list their partner or spouse as the second parent and others list no second parent. He explains that some of the children call him dad, some donor dad, some Ari, and "some never call" (Doctor Oz September 2021). He is willing to be made known to and to have contact with the children if, when, and to the extent the mother wishes. Nagel says that he keeps in touch with his offspring as much as the moms allow (Klein 2020). A disproportionate amount of the contact appears to be at celebratory occasions like birthday parties and gatherings of groups of his offspring and their mothers; he clearly experiences the joys of parenting more than the hard work, as he freely acknowledges (Lewak 2016b). But he is also so public about his many other children and his interactions with them and their mothers that recent mothers (unlike the mother of his first, unplanned child, who was reportedly not pleased to learn he was donating sperm; Lewak 2016b) can know exactly what they themselves can expect, including the unavoidable constraints on his time, geographic mobility,[20] and financial resources. This knowledge may give mothers a degree of predictability and control which mothers who conceive in marriage or a heterosexual relationship can never be sure of having, while offering advantages anonymous sperm from a clinic does not, among them a lower risk of accidental incest between his offspring, who can know of each other's existence more readily than those conceived with sperm from an anonymous donor. The openly available knowledge about so many other mothers and children also affords those who choose it the opportunity to connect with one another, whether for rare events and distanced contacts or frequently and intimately enough to think of each other as family. They can even bring would-be parents among their existing circle of friends and family into the fold of recipients for Nagel's sperm.

These are in large part families existing apart from the law—like polyamorous (although perhaps not like polygamous) relationships, the relationships between and among Ari Nagel, his children, and those who on occasion call themselves his baby mamas (Monroe 2021) can be productive without being legally recognized or enforced. What they are asking of the law is in large part "to be let alone," to "be free from all substantial arbitrary impositions and purposeless restraints" (*Poe v. Ullman* 1961) in forming and maintaining their families, whether of a single mother and her child conceived with Nagel's sperm or of a broad network of mothers whose children know one another, know Nagel, and know the biological ties that connect them.

By and large up to now, in the shadow of constitutional rights at least as much as in the shadow of other law, Nagel and those who have chosen his sperm in the United States have indeed managed to be left alone. Nagel claims even the New York Department of Health, which served him with a cease and desist order similar to the one Trent Arsenault received from the FDA, backed down. "In the end," he said, "I think when I clarified what I'm actually doing, it's ultimately an infringement on every man's right, I think, to have a child. . . . [T]hey said they reserve the right to pursue legal action in the future, but for now, I can continue doing what I'm doing, because of course, I'm not operating a licensed sperm bank" (NZ Herald 2021). To the extent being left alone depends for donors like Nagel on the norms of modern constitutional law in the area of sexual, reproductive, and familial rights largely grounded in substantive due process precedents, their continued ability to be free of substantial legal impositions may well not survive *Dobbs*.

Skinner's Equal Protection Holding and the Post-*Dobbs* Quest for Sexual and Reproductive Comparators

Like all other scholars of US constitutional law, whatever their normative views, I am coming to terms with the prospect that the very near future could see the complete undoing of all of what had been the settled constitutional case law of sexual and reproductive rights stretching back from the beginning of this decade to the early 1970s, a decade after Justice Harlan first outlined the rights-protective terrain to come in his *Poe v. Ullman* (1961) opinion. It is literally difficult to imagine what will become of so many expectations far more settled than those of the likes of high-volume non-commercial donors of fresh sperm and those eager to receive their sperm for insemination if *Griswold* and all its progeny, along with all the cases that depended more indirectly on *Griswold*, disappear as good law. Let me end this chapter by suggesting that there is a precedent directly on point for reproductive, as well as sexual and familial rights, that has several advantages in the imminent fight for survival as law that *Griswold* and its progeny lack: Its result was unanimous; its holding is grounded in the equal protection clause, not substantive due process; and it dates from 1942, well before the era of the Warren Court so disliked by conservatives and the early Burger Court, with its perhaps surprisingly rights-friendly case law in matters of sex and reproduction.

Skinner v. Oklahoma is an equal protection case and, whatever the current conservative majority may think of any particular equal protection case, the conservatives do not view equal protection as a per se illegitimate or suspect basis for a holding, in the way they seem to view substantive due process. In fact, the current court has been moving in the direction of an almost obsessive focus on equality in many areas of constitutional law, including free exercise and free speech.

It is true that *Skinner*'s author is Justice Douglas, who also authored the majority opinion in *Griswold*. But *Griswold*'s result was not unanimous, as *Skinner*'s was.[21] It is also true that *Skinner* evidences the same lack of concern for doctrinal niceties that scholars have long seen as the hallmark of Douglas's approach to judging. As Ted White cogently put it, "a significant feature of Douglas's opinions was their espousal of positions that were doctrinally novel without extensive justification of the doctrinal innovation or more than cursory recognition of its novelty" (White 1988, 66).[22] But, while the reasoning and language of *Griswold* (the idea that there are emanations from penumbras of the various Amendments in the Bill of Rights, for example) has consistently attracted scorn and has never been taken up in later cases, the reasoning and language of *Skinner* have become staples of US constitutional law. *Skinner* was the first case to introduce the term "strict scrutiny" to constitutional law.[23] Moreover, it applied this scrutiny to a right explicitly called "fundamental," the right of "marriage and procreation." By holding it an equal protection violation for the state of Oklahoma to sterilize those convicted of some crimes and not others, *Skinner* is not only the first, but also to date the only Supreme Court case explicitly and directly protecting an individual's right to procreate. Douglas pointed out that the power to decide who may not reproduce, in addition to depriving the individual "of one of the basic civil rights of man," also risked "invidious discriminations . . . against groups or types of individuals in violation of the constitutional guaranty of just and equal laws."[24]

Especially because the actual discrimination in *Skinner* (between chicken thieves like Skinner, who were eligible for sterilization and embezzlers, who, although equally felonious and not demonstrably less likely to produce criminal offspring,[25] were ineligible) was not a classically invidious one, applying *Skinner* in the context of sexual and procreative rights post- *Dobbs* opens up a host of possible comparators for both donorsexuals and super dads. Should any of these comparators be given more rights to procreate with insufficient justification for the difference in rights, donorsexuals and super dads could potentially make out an equal protection violation. In the case of Trent Arsenault, who has consistently articulated an underlying religious motivation for his choices of how and to whom to donate,[26] a claim under the free exercise clause or federal RFRA (Religious Freedom Restoration Act) could also potentially be made out, as equality has become increasingly central to the Court's conservative majority's free exercise jurisprudence (Fulton v. City of Philadelphia 2021; Roman Catholic Diocese of Brooklyn v. Cuomo 2021, Carson v. Makin 2022). To even begin to consider in any detail the potential comparators that could ground an equal protection claim for high-volume non-commercial donors of fresh sperm would require a chapter several times the length of this one.[27] A small sample of the many possible comparators includes sperm banks and those who donate through them, fertile promiscuous men who have unprotected sex with many women, and perhaps most intriguing of all, those motivated to procreate to the maximum biological extent possible within marriage, such as television's infamous Duggar family or participants in the Quiverful movement.

Let me end with an observation that might frighten even those eager to see substantive due process sexual and reproductive rights taken away from those such as the gays, lesbians, bisexuals, and unmarried heterosexuals who currently enjoy them: A significant feature of equal protection violations is that they can generally be cured by ratcheting either up or down, either by expanding the rights of those unequally deprived or contracting the rights of those unequally privileged. Without existing substantive due process sexual and reproductive rights as a backstop, an application of *Skinner* just as much within the power of a court as extending the privileges to reproduce now granted by law to married heterosexuals to donorsexuals and super dads is the possibility that even married heterosexuals can have their affirmative reproductive freedom curtailed. Little more than incest prohibitions on marriage now seems to remain from the notion that we should prevent the unfit from reproducing. But, as defenders of *Roe v. Wade* often reminded opponents, if there is no constitutional protection for decisions on whether to bear or beget a child, that can cut both ways. There are no longer the barriers that were in place pre-*Dobbs* to a democratic decision to adopt a one child policy, ban all access to reproductive technologies, or require that those seeking to reproduce biologically—even with no technological intervention and even when married—undergo the same rigorous scrutiny of their qualifications as those seeking to adopt now do. At least as much as with respect to fetal life, views on who should be licensed to reproduce are likely to vary drastically between states, just as they now do with respect to which books and concepts should be banned from the school curriculum. While Texas might refuse a license to any prospective parents who would allow their minor child to begin gender transition, other states might see parents who would categorically refuse to allow their child to come out as gay or gender non-conforming as unfit and deny them a parenting license. The post-*Dobbs* world is potentially one of less reproductive freedom for everyone.

NOTES

1 21 C.F.R. § 1271.15(e) (2012). For further discussion, see, e.g., Abbasi 2013 (law review article by attorney who unsuccessfully challenged the application of these regulations).

2 Those inclined to suspect that but for his religious upbringing, Arsenault might have happily settled down in a relationship with another man should consider that among the articles linked to on his Facebook page are accounts by self-identified asexuals who express aversion to a physical sexual relationship with another human being and that he also identifies as a germophobe (Benjamin 2012).

3 21 C.F.R. § 1271.3(I) (2012); see also 69 F.R. § 29786, 29793 (2004) (making clear there are three categories of reproductive donors: anonymous, directed, and sexually intimate).

4 Masturbating another to orgasm to achieve purely reproductive aims rather than any sexual gratification does not necessarily qualify as a sex act in the law, as witness the exemptions in statutes criminalizing bestiality for farmers

manually stimulating their male farm animals so as to use the resulting ejaculate to artificially inseminate female animals. Whether or not a donor's deliberately producing ejaculate is necessarily sexual, clearly Arsenault eroticizes it. And, just as some who offer N.I. sometimes claim to approach the act clinically so, for example, lesbian couples can eroticize the act of insemination (and not just because an orgasm is thought to improve the odds of conception by helping move the sperm). There seems to be no available information on how many gay male couples producing ejaculate to fertilize a donor egg or provide to the surrogate who will bear their child masturbate one another to orgasm. In my contribution to the collective work "Pregnant Man," I criticized Darren Rosenblum, who invited a group of legal scholars and his surrogate to reflect on the process by which he and his husband conceived a child, for erroneously assuming that for "bioparents" conception is necessarily a pleasurable, sexual, mutual process even as he unnecessarily shaped his own process to be more isolated and competitive than a "sexually intimate" act of partnership, given that he and his husband "each masturbated [alone] in a clinical room" filled with straight porn. See Rosenblum et al. 2010.

5 CBER's Mem. Supp. Mot. To Deny Hearing Req. & Summ. J. 8, Feb. 7, 2011.

6 What the French call jurisprudence constant and the Germans, staendige Rechtsprechung.

7 Given that the right on the current Court has set its collective face against substantive due process but embraced incorporation with a vengeance, extending it to an unprecedented level in their recent cases protecting religion and guns under the incorporated First and Second Amendments, it is extraordinarily important to remind them and ourselves that, as Harlan and Scalia (two justices with generally recognized extraordinary legal skills) clearly recognized, all incorporation of the enumerated rights in the Bill of Rights is nothing more or less than substantive due process (Case 2019, 13–17).

8 Thus, Scalia correctly predicted in his dissents that the result in *Romer v. Evans* entailed the overruling of *Bowers*; that *Lawrence*, which did indeed overrule *Bowers*, entailed constitutional protection for same-sex marriage; and that *Windsor*, which struck down the federal Defense of Marriage Act, entailed that the states also had to recognize same-sex marriages (Case 2019, 10–13). Cf. Mary Anne Case, *After Gender the Destruction of Man*, 31 *Pace Law Review* 802, 809 (2011).

9 Posner did not then approve of these cases. He wrote, "Nothing in the language, legislative history, or background of the Constitution, the Bill of Rights, or the Fourteenth Amendment shows any evidence of an intent to limit state regulation of the family, save perhaps when the regulation is along racial or otherwise invidious lines. . . . Neither in the Fourth Amendment nor elsewhere in the Constitution is there reference to a policy of allowing people to engage in sexual activity without fear of giving birth." The argument Posner made in 1979 is of course precisely the one the *Dobbs* majority, egged on by Clarence Thomas in his *Dobbs* concurrence, may soon use to overrule the whole line of sexual freedom cases.

But so long as the cases remain good law, they also remain guarantors of sexual freedom.

10 Such legislation descended from the infamous "anti-vice" crusades of Anthony Comstock, which led to the passage of the federal Comstock laws and similar criminal statutes in many states.

11 Among those not "recognized as full-fledged members of the community" in 1868 were not only women and unmarried fathers but members of the Church of Jesus Christ of Latter-day Saints, who were seen to be literally and figuratively at war with the United States. A decade after 1868, in *Reynolds v. US*, the Supreme Court held that members of the LDS church had no federal constitutional right to engage in polygamy, even though the taking of multiple wives was required of LDS men by the tenets of their faith. A century and a quarter later, Chief Justice Roberts, dissenting with his conservative colleagues from the holding in *Obergefell*, correctly noted that the "majority's reasoning [in support of a federal constitutional right to same-sex marriage] would apply with equal force to the claim of a fundamental right to plural marriage." *Obergefell* at 2622. It remains to be seen whether, so long as *Obergefell* remains good law, the new conservative majority would respond affirmatively to an equal protection and religious freedom demand by religiously motivated polygamists that they be granted the marriage rights *Obergefell* extended to same-sex couples.

12 But need to check the Hebrew opinion to see if the court really said "role" not "rule."

13 The Israeli Department of Health told one of the women, "Considering the number of women whom Mr Nagel impregnated with his sperm . . . it is our position that the claim of an intention to perform true joint parenthood with Mr Nagel is not sincere or reasonable" (Klein 2020).

14 Compare Nagel's argument here with Beth Gardner's above—each has a cogent argument that the legal restrictions on sperm donation put those in need of sperm to conceive to a worse set of choices.

15 Not only did her husband Marty do all the cooking for the household, Ruth also insisted that the school her son attended call the boy's father at least as often as his mother when there was an issue concerning the boy.

16 Even Justice Rehnquist, who had previously inveighed against the likely effect of the Equal Rights Amendment on family roles, voted for Wiesenfeld, saying that it was the child's right to the care of a parent that mattered, not the sex of the parent. For a discussion of Rehnquist's dramatic evolution on constitutional sex discrimination law, see Case 2009. Though Rehnquist may have signed on to the current constitutional law of sex discrimination, in part from a genuine change of heart and in part because he is the consummate common-law justice, there is no reason to be confident any member of the *Dobbs* majority has signed on. See, e.g., Case 2014 (demonstrating that the current constitutional law of sex equality has no originalist warrant).

17 The term comes from the work of Nicole Bergen, who describes the six informal online sperm donors she interviewed as all altruistic but also "rarely in fulfilling

relationships themselves" and sometimes "attracted to the idea of having as many biological offspring as possible, to create a kind of clan amongst the various families" (Russell 2021) (describing the research in Bergen and Delacroix 2019).

18 "Mother" for Fineman is a capacious category, covering any person of any sex who cares for the inevitably dependent and is as a result likely to become derivatively dependent.

19 If the women of color have reasons to turn to him specifically because of the color of his skin, for example from desires concerning their child's skin color or aversive reactions to men of color based on experience or stereotyping, such reasons have not often been reported. But poor women, whether of color or not, may see a donor like Nagel as a good way out of the dilemma sociologist Kathryn Edin reports many poor women face—they do not want to tie themselves to men who would drag them down financially and be inclined to behave more patriarchally the closer the tie. See, e.g., Edin 2000, 11–26.

20 For example, Nagel seems willing to do some babysitting for his offspring, but that is usually only possible in the New York area where he is based, or in places like Florida where he spends substantial time. His offspring, meanwhile, span the globe.

21 Justice Stone concurred only in the result, opining that due process, not equal protection, was the correct doctrinal framework for the case.

22 As White observed: "Two paradigmatic Douglas majority opinions can be found in *Skinner v. Oklahoma* and *Griswold v. Connecticut*, decided twenty-three years apart. The *Skinner* and *Griswold* cases, not often linked by constitutional commentators, are remarkably similar in several respects. Both were doctrinally audacious opinions whose innovativeness was cryptically, even assertively presented; both involved end runs around apparently insurmountable analytical barriers; and both touched upon a theme—the decision to procreate and thus to pass on one's legacy of individuality to one's progeny and hence to posterity—that touched deep currents in Douglas' life."

23 Korematsu, the Japanese internment case generally credited with establishing strict scrutiny as the test for racial classifications, came two years later and in any event never used the term, speaking instead of "most exacting scrutiny."

24 When Douglas held in *Skinner* that to select with insufficient justification those convicted of some crimes and not others for sterilization was to commit "as invidious a discrimination as . . . selec[ting] a particular race or nationality for oppressive treatment," he was not only writing against the background of Nazi oppression of Jews and Roma, but most likely with the knowledge that the discrimination on the face of the Oklahoma statute, which called for thieves to be sterilized but exempted from sterilization those convicted "of violation of the prohibitory laws, revenue acts, embezzlement, or political offenses," was a discrimination that would have a disparate negative impact on persons of color, and was likely intended to do so.

25 Steven Siegel has argued that the level of scrutiny applied in *Skinner* is not actually strict, but only rationality with bite, because the state acknowledged having

no basis for its assumption that chicken thievery was likely to be more heritable than embezzlement (perhaps especially since the legislatively chosen category was crimes of moral turpitude rather than of, for example, crimes of violence; Siegel 2006).

26 Ari Nagel, like Arsenault, was brought up in a devoutly religious household, in Nagel's case as an orthodox Jew in the famously ultra-orthodox community of Monsey, New Jersey. Though both have moved away from the particulars of the faith in which they were brought up, Nagel, like Arsenault, has referenced his religious upbringing in describing his felt need to "increase and multiply" as his parents, siblings, and former neighbors had done.

27 I will be exploring some of the potential comparators in a forthcoming article in the University of Chicago Legal Forum's Symposium issue on The Body.

BIBLIOGRAPHY

Abbasi, Amber D. 2013. "The Curious Case of Trent Arsenault: Questioning FDA Regulatory Authority Over Private Sperm Donation." *Annals of Health Law* 22: 1–42.

Acker, Jacqueline. 2013. "The Case for an Unregulated Private Sperm Donation Market." *UCLA Women's Law Journal* 20: 1–38.

Bergen, Nicole and Celine Delacroix. 2019. "Bypassing the Sperm Bank: Documenting the Experiences of Online Informal Sperm Donors." *Critical Public Health* 29: 1–12.

Case, Mary Anne. 1993. "Couples and Coupling in the Public Sphere: A Comment on the Legal History of Litigating for Lesbian and Gay Rights." *Virginia Law Review* 79: 1643–94.

———. 2000. "The Very Stereotype the Law Condemns." *Cornell Law Review* 85: 1447–91.

———. 2009. "Feminist Fundamentalism on the Frontier Between Government and Family Responsibility for Children." *Utah Law Review* 2009: 381–406.

———. 2014. "The Ladies? Forget About Them. A Feminist Perspective on the Limits of Originalism." *Constitutional Commentary* 29: 431–56.

———. 2019. "Scalia as Procrustes for the Majority, Scalia as Cassandra in Dissent." In *Justice Scalia: Rhetoric and the Rule of Law*, edited by Brian G. Slocum and Francis J. Mootz III. Chicago: University of Chicago Press.

Doctor Oz. 2021, May 5. "Meet the Controversial Donor Giving It Away—77 Babies and Counting!." https://www.youtube.com/watch?v=129KjFHpgtM.

———. 2021, September 30. "100 Kids and Counting from One Controversial Sperm Donor." https://www.youtube.com/watch?v=vUhgYsmiFwo.

Donohue, Caitlin. 2012. "Donorsexual: One Main Explains Why He Spreads His Sperm Around." *48 Hills*. August 3. https://sfbgarchive.48hills.org.

Edin, Kathryn. 2000. "A Few Good Men: Why Poor Mothers Don't Marry or Remarry." *American Prospect*. January 3.

Fineman, Martha. 1995. *The Neutered Mother, the Sexual Family, and Other Twentieth Century Tragedies*. New York: Routledge.

Greene, Jamal. 2010. "The So-Called Right to Privacy." *UC Davis Law Review* 43(February): 715–45.

Hartnett, Edward. 1999. "A Matter of Judgment, Not a Matter of Opinion." *N.Y.U. Law Review* 74: 123–60.

Huffington Post. 2012. "Trent Arsenault, Donorsexual Virgin Father of 14 Kids, Answers Your Questions." February 3. www.huffpost.com.

Hunter, Nan D. 1992. "Life After Hardwick." *Harvard Civil Rights-Civil Liberties Law Review* 27: 531–54.

———. 2004. "Living with *Lawrence*." *Minnesota Law Review* 88: 1103–39.

Ingber, Jason. 2022. "Most Prolific Sperm Donor in the USA." April 10. https://www
.youtube.com/watch?v=-FvwyBsU1MY.

Klein, Amy. 2020. "Whose Sperm Is This?." *The Tel Aviv Review of Books*. Autumn.
www.tarb.co.il.

Lewak, Doree. 2016a. "Professor Who Donates Sperm in City Bathrooms Has Sired 22 Kids." *New York Post*. June 12. https://nypost.com.

———. 2016b. "Sperm Donor Who Sired 22 Kids Has a Wife—And She's Not Happy."
New York Post. June 19. https://nypost.com.

———. 2019. "The Sperminator's 50th Baby Mama Is a Homeless 18-Year-Old from Harlem." *New York Post*. June 15. https://nypost.com.

Mohr, Richard D. 1986. "Mr. Justice Douglas at Sodom: Gays and Privacy." *Columbia Human Rights Review* 18: 43–110.

Monroe, Rachel. 2021. "Have Sperm, Will Travel." *Esquire*. October 20. www.esquire
.com.

Moore, Cortney. 2021. "'Sperminator' Who's Close to Fathering 100 Children Says 'Don't Focus on Me.'" Fox News. May 4. www.foxnews.com.

Mutcherson, Kimberly. 2015. "Procreative Pluralism." *Berkeley Journal of Gender, Law & Justice* 30(2015): 22–75.

NZ Herald. 2021. "'Sperminator': Prolific Sperm Donor Ari Nagel Speaks Out." *NZ Herald*. May 5. www.nzherald.co.nz.

Posner, Richard. 1979. "The Uncertain Protection of Privacy by the Supreme Court."
Supreme Court Review 1979: 173–216.

Rashty, Sandy. 2021. "Meet the American Jew with Almost as Many Children as Abraham." *Jewish News*. December 9. www.jewishnews.co.uk.

Rosenblum, Darren, Noa Ben-Asher, Mary Anne Case, Elizabeth F. Emens, Berta E. Hernandez-Truyol, Vivian M. Gutierrez, Lisas C. Ikemoto, Angela Onwuachi-Willig, Jacob Willig-Onwuachi, Kimberly Mutcherson, Peter Siegelman, and Beth Jones. 2010. "Pregnant Man?: A Conversation." *Yale Journal of Law and Feminism* 22: 207–77.

Russell, Tonya. 2021. "The Sperm Donation Is Free, but There's the Catch." *The Atlantic*. May 21. www.theatlantic.com.

Scalia, Antonin. 2000. "Common-Law Courts in a Civil Law System: The Role of United States Federal Courts in Interpreting the Constitution and Laws." In

Antonin Scalia, *Federal Courts and the Law*. Princeton, NJ: Princeton University Press.

Schneider, Jeff, Muriel Pearson, and Alexa Valiente. 2014. "Meet the Men Having Sex with Strangers to Help Them Have Babies." ABC News. November 13. https://abcnews.go.com.

Siegel, Stephen. 2006. "The Origin of the Compelling Interest Test and Strict Scrutiny." *American Journal of Legal History* 48: 355–407.

Strauss, David. 1996. "Common Law Constitutional Interpretation." *University of Chicago Law Review* 63: 877–935.

TheMauryShowOfficial. 2017. "Meet The Sperminator . . . He Has 29 Kids with 24 Women and Claims Them All!." October 24. https://www.youtube.com/watch?v=TJSXi_3qtWs.

Vogel, Lauren. 2012. "Age, Sex, Location . . . Sperm Count?." *Canadian Medical Association Journal* 184(7): E347–E348.

Wallace, Benjamin. 2012. "The Virgin Father." *New York Magazine*. February 3. https://nymag.com.

White, Edward. 1988. "The Anti-Judge: William O. Douglas and the Ambiguities of Individuality." *Virginia Law Review* 71: 17–86.

Willows, Jen. 2019. "Israel's High Court Rejects Prolific US Sperm Donor's Petition." PET. February 15. www.progress.org.uk.

COURT CASES CITED

Bowers v. Hardwick, 478 U.S. 186 (1986)

Carey v. Population Services International, 431 U.S. 678 (1977)

Carson v. Makin (2022)

Dobbs v. Jackson Women's Health Organization (2022)

Doe v. Hamburg N.D. Cal. C 12–03412 (EMC) (2013)

Eisenstadt v. Baird, 405 U.S. 438 (1972)

Fulton v. City of Philadelphia, 593 U.S. ___ (2021)

June Med. Servs. L.L.C. v. Russo, 591. U.S. 1101 (2020)

Korematsu v. United States, 323 U.S. 214 (1944)

Lehr v. Robertson, 463 U.S. 248 (1983)

Michael H. v. Gerald D., 491 U.S. 110 (1989)

Moore v. City of East Cleveland, 431 U.S. 494 (1977)

Obergefell v. Hodges, 576 U.S. 644 (2015)

Paris Adult Theatre I v. Slaton, 413 U.S. 49 (1973)

Peterson v. Vidule, 157 Wis. 641 (1914)

Planned Parenthood of Southeastern Pa. v. Casey, 505 U.S. 833 (1992)

Poe v. Ullman, 81 S. Ct. 1752 (1961)

Reynolds v. United States, 98 U.S. 145 (1879)

Roe v. Wade, 410 U.S. 113 (1973)

Roman Catholic Diocese of Brooklyn v. Cuomo, 2021

Romer v. Evans, 517 U.S. 620 (1996)
Skinner v. Oklahoma, 316 U.S. 535 (1942)
Stanley v. Illinois, 405 U.S. 645 (1972)
United States v. Windsor, 570 U.S. 744 (2013)
Weinberger v. Wiesenfeld, 420 U.S. 636 (1975)
Zablocki v. Redhail, 434 U.S. 374 (1978)

PART III

Policed Men

8

Queer Risk Knowledge

From HIV to COVID-19

KYLE KIRKUP

Flattening the curve has flattened our sex lives. As SARS-CoV-2 (COVID-19) began to spread rapidly across the globe beginning in early 2020, government leaders imposed a range of strict physical distancing measures (Borges do Nascimento et al. 2020; Guan et al. 2020). Officials hoped that the collective societal embrace of these restrictions until vaccines were widely distributed would allow societies to reduce new COVID-19 infections, avoid overburdening medical systems, and ultimately save lives (S. Roberts 2020). In many jurisdictions, government officials forbade people from gathering in groups outside their immediate households. They also instructed the public to wear masks where physical distancing was impossible (M. Roberts 2020), and ordered that schools and businesses be shuttered (Rocca 2020; Stewart et al. 2020). These physical distancing measures, typically enforced through legal prohibitions (The Health Protection [Coronavirus, Restrictions] [England] Regulations 2020; Luscombe and McClelland 2020a, 2020b), community condemnation (Gerster and Russell 2020), and neoliberal self-governance (Cossman 2007, 2013; Lupton 1999) constructed sex—at least with those outside one's immediate circle—as risky. Yet, not all actors took the same approach with regard to questions of risk and sex amid a global pandemic. For example, in the early days of lockdown measures, public health officials in the Canadian province of British Columbia suggested a variety of different sexual options, from masturbation to virtual sex to, perhaps most famously, glory holes (BC Centre for Disease Control 2020). In the age of COVID-19, the glory hole[1]— long a symbol of queer sexual risk strategies (Holmes et al. 2010)—had gone mainstream.

This chapter reads sex in the HIV/AIDS pandemic beside sex in the age of COVID-19 (Sedgwick 2003). Since the 1980s, the risk of contracting HIV, along with coming into conflict with a series of attendant criminal offenses, has loomed large. Communities have developed strategies to negotiate risk, without foregoing sex altogether (Hoppe 2018; Kirkup 2020; Shayo Buchanan 2014). In view of this history, this chapter asks: Forty years after the beginning of HIV/AIDS, how do we collectively negotiate risk and sexual contagion in the midst of a pandemic?

In drawing lines of inquiry between the plural and contested meanings of risk and sexual contagion across the two pandemics, there are important reasons to resist easy comparisons between HIV/AIDS and COVID-19. Shame, ongoing marginalization, government indifference, and open hostility directed at people living with HIV are but three reasons to avoid facile comparisons with COVID-19 (Moore 2020; Renfro 2020). There are also important reasons to foreground the stark reality that sexual risk surfaces in a variety of contexts beyond the scope of this chapter's account of sexual contagion. Many communities, including women (Katz et al. 2017), people of color (Ritchie 2017), sex workers (Slane and van der Meulen 2018), trans and non-binary communities (Sharpe 2019), and the various intersections between, are all negotiating risk in their everyday sexual lives.

This chapter argues that queer strategies developed since the 1980s have seeped into the ways we collectively describe and negotiate the risk of sexual contagion. Such an approach to risk is queer not only because it emerged out of the practices of minority sexual communities, particularly men who have sex with men. Instead, I argue that this approach is queer for three reasons. First, it refuses either/or dichotomies. Rather than seeing particular sexual activities as either dangerous or safe—and attempting to eliminate all risk through strict isolation measures—a queer account of risk recognizes the importance of sex. Second, the approach is queer because it foregrounds the pursuit of pleasure. Sex is a necessary and important part of life. Third, the approach is queer because it is fundamentally opposed to punishing rulebreakers through the legal apparatuses of the carceral state. Ultimately, the chapter argues that a queer approach to risk helps us collectively navigate the anxieties and pleasures of sex in the age of COVID-19.

The chapter proceeds in three parts. The first part surveys the critical criminology literature on legal risk, analyzing the hybrid forms of knowledge that people use to determine whether a practice is risky. The second part briefly recounts the history of how queer risk knowledge coalesced to help people negotiate sex in the early days of the HIV/AIDS pandemic. This section then proceeds to use the criminalization of HIV nondisclosure to reveal how people continue to use this store of knowledge as they negotiate contemporary sexual practices deemed physically and legally risky. The third part brings the analysis to the present moment, examining how the amalgam of queer risk knowledge created over four decades has seeped into the ways we collectively understand and negotiate sexual contagion in the age of COVID-19.

Theorizing Legal Risk

We live in a society where risk is all around us (Adams 1995; Beck 1992; Harcourt 2007). Risk is typically described using the language of assessment and prevention (Valverde et al. 2005). For example, when we tell others that we are avoiding sex because of COVID-19, or we make plans to have sex once we have the requisite number of COVID-19 vaccinations, we reveal that we have absorbed knowledge from a variety of sources circulating across our various social networks. We also intimate that we are drawing on these sources to help guide our own regimes of neoliberal self-governance (Cossman 2007, 2013; Lupton 1999).

It is important to avoid understanding risk in a static way—risk moves across an assemblage of historical, situational, geographical, and temporal contexts (Epstein 1996; Valverde et al. 2005). For example, we do not describe the risk of contracting or transmitting HIV today in precisely the same way that we might have in the early 1980s. Much has been learned about HIV/AIDS over the past four decades. The emergence of "undetectable viral loads" (Prevention Access Campaign 2020) and pre-exposure prophylaxis (PrEP), to provide just two examples, have fundamentally altered how we collectively understand the risk of sexual contagion in our everyday lives (McClelland 2019). Similarly, we know much more about the risk of COVID-19 today than we did in early 2020 (McKie 2020). At the same time, we cannot understand HIV-related risk without attending to pervasive social inequalities, which troublingly construct certain people as more "at risk" than others (Canadian Public Health Association 2014; Centers for Disease Control and Prevention 2020; Treatment Action Campaign 2017). Nor can we approach risk without thinking through the complex constellation of factors that appear during a particular sexual encounter that render it more or less risky. Whether a condom was used, which sexual activities were performed, and the presence or absence of sexually transmitted infections (STIs) all shape the meanings we ascribe, both collectively and individually, to risk (Kirkup 2014–2015).

We decide whether particular sexual practices are risky by accessing a variety of sources of knowledge that circulate within our social networks. Some scholars prefer the term "risk knowledges" to foreground the plural, contested, and often contradictory sources we use to assess risk (Valverde et al. 2005). In some strands of the literature, risk is described in classically rational, scientific ways (Adams 1995). For example, the insurance broker who inputs a series of predetermined factors to assess the risk that a particular driver will get in a car accident—and therefore what their monthly insurance premium will be—is relying on classically rational data to predict future outcomes (Jain 2006; Valverde et al.). Yet, it would be a mistake to think that risk is a purely rational construct. Risk knowledge is always already emotionally laden. Following the work of Mary Douglas, cultural theories of risk emphasize the extent to which emotions such as fear, disgust, and arousal shape how we negotiate the prospect of uncertainty in our lives (Douglas 1992). For example, despite repeatedly being told by their doctor that the risk of contracting HIV while taking PrEP is negligible, a person may avoid having sex with people living with HIV (including those maintaining an undetectable viral load as a result of antiretrovirals). The fear is not rooted in scientific studies communicated by medical actors, but rather in a variety of other sites, including the stigma that has long been directed at people living with HIV and the psychology of risk.

In this chapter, I attend to hybrid forms of risk knowledge (Moore and Valverde 2010) in order to construct a queer account of risk. Even supposedly cold, calculated, risk assessments are always already shaped by emotions—we might talk about risk in ways that seem scientific, citing statistics and probabilities, only to quickly find ourselves slipping into emotionally-coded risk talk (Moore and Valverde 2010). An approach that refuses this rational-emotional dichotomy also has important methodological implications: It allows us to analyze classically rational materials (e.g., graphics setting out new COVID-19 infections) while also attending to how risk knowledge simultaneously circulates more emotionally across networked communities. Put differently, this chapter demonstrates how hybrid forms of risk knowledge about the transmission of HIV and COVID-19 are "circulating, changing, being taken apart, and reassembled in new shapes" (Valverde et al. 2005, 89). The next section examines how sex and safer sex practices during the HIV/AIDS pandemic helped set the template for how we negotiate the risk of sexual contagion in the age of COVID-19.

A Queer Account of Risk

Having theorized the hybrid sources of risk knowledge that circulate across our social networks in both rational and emotional terms, this section offers a queer account of risk. It unfolds in two parts. First, it provides an account of how discourses of risk coalesced to help people negotiate sex in the midst of the HIV/AIDS pandemic. A queer account of risk refuses to categorize sex as either dangerous or safe, better attends to the pursuit of pleasure, and is fundamentally opposed to doling out criminal punishment to those alleged to have broken the rules. Second, the section uses the criminalization of HIV nondisclosure to track how a queer account of risk might help us understand the ways in which communities negotiate contemporary sexual practices deemed risky. Ultimately, this section of the chapter argues that forty years of strategies designed to navigate the risk of HIV has fundamentally shaped the way questions of danger and uncertainty function in relation to sexual contagion.

Pre-HIV/AIDS Risk Navigation Strategies

The meanings we assign to the risk of sexual contagion did not begin with HIV/AIDS. During the late 1800s, for example, public health officials and lawmakers became progressively more concerned with increased rates of STIs in port towns with significant migration patterns (Backhouse 1985). In an effort to curb STI rates, officials proposed a mixture of abstinence-based sexual education and legal approaches that sought to criminalize the spread of sexual contagion (Meyer 1991). Early STI prevention efforts were typically directed at heterosexual activities between male soldiers and female sex workers. This dynamic, however, changed between the 1930s and the 1960s. Anxieties about commercial sex started to meld with concerns about the ascendance of homosexuality in public life, which led to an increase in public health interventions and state surveillance. Sex workers and homosexuals were often targeted by the same government responses because of "their disregard for conventional morality and gender norms, habitual lack of consideration for laws regulating sexuality, and cause of public nuisance" (McKay 2016, 444). In the face of this dynamic, sex workers and homosexuals began to develop sexual harm reduction strategies that would mitigate the spread of STIs. For example, the groups shared the technique of post-intercourse douching with antiseptic solutions to avoid contracting STIs (Patton 1996). These forms of risk knowledge, circulating across networked communities of sex workers and homosexuals, ultimately formed the basis for the proliferation of community-developed safer sex guidelines in the decades that followed.

Beginning in the 1960s, the number of Anglo-American gay rights organizations grew. In the face of increasing STI levels within the community, these organizations consolidated individual risk management techniques into community-produced literature (McKay 2016, 444). The first formal safer sex guidelines were created between 1979 and 1981 by the National Coalition of Gay Sexually Transmitted Disease Services and the Bay Area Physicians for Human Rights (BAPHR) (Blair 2017). Activists and researchers worked together to produce the guidelines (Escoffier 1998). The BAPHR guidelines, however, relied heavily on biomedical knowledge, which conveyed the idea that "risk reduction was highly complex and technical, a matter of percentages and mysterious fluid properties rather than familiarity with a condom and willingness to explore pleasures beyond intercourse" (Patton 1996, 102). Perhaps unsurprisingly, the guidelines failed to receive meaningful uptake at the community level (Blair 2017).

The history of BAPHR underscores the clear need to convey safer sex messaging in ways that tap into both the scientific and emotional dimensions of risk. This brings us to the colorful history of how drag queens became creators and disseminators of risk knowledge strategies. In the early 1980s, the Sisters of Perpetual Indulgence translated the lifeless, scientific BAPHR guidelines into *Play Fair!*, a humorous guide to safer sex. The differences between the approaches were stark. Take, for example, the BAPHR's scientific guidelines on the use of lubricant during anal sex. The guidelines note: "Scented lubricants may [cause] a chemically induced proctitis (rectal inflammation), the use of hand lotions and other scented products for these purposes are discouraged" (Blair 2017, 875). In comparison, the Sisters of Perpetual Indulgence's *Play Fair!* guidelines were far more effective in meeting community needs and understandings: "Buy lubricants free of fancy perfume [and] scents . . . The chemicals can inflame your ass" (Calisphere 1982; Escoffier 1998). As this truncated history reveals, in the pre–HIV/AIDS era, networked communities developed a series of strategies to avoid sexual contagion.

Risk Navigation Strategies in the Early Days of HIV/AIDS: Either/Or Dichotomies and the Pursuit of Pleasure

In June 1981, the US Centers for Disease Control and Prevention reported a cluster of cases of pneumocystis pneumonia targeting healthy gay men (Centers for Disease Control and Prevention 1981). In the early days of the HIV/AIDS pandemic, there existed significant internal division among the gay community about the appropriate sexual response to the risk of contagion. For example, there were internal divisions about safer sex itself. Some activists rejected the language of safer sex altogether, suggesting that it "implied a normalizing of what had been transgressive, and smothered an essential *frisson* of desire" (Escoffier 1998, 3). There was also significant disagreement about promiscuity within gay communities. In 1982, Richard Berkowitz and Michael Callen published the widely read "We Know Who We Are: Two Gay Men Declare War on Promiscuity," which called on gay men to curb their allegedly promiscuous behavior (Callen et al. 1982). The article provoked outrage in some circles, as it appeared to blame the hedonism of gay life for contributing to the spread of HIV (Epstein 1996). Around the same time, other activists adopted less polarizing accounts, suggesting that people would need to make their own decisions about sex, risk, and HIV (Crimp 1987; Robertson 2005). Such approaches understood sexual risk assessments as "pliable and negotiated," rather than being rigidly fixed as either safe or dangerous (Gastaldo et al. 2009, 400).

Public health officials adopted indifferent—if not actively hostile—attitudes to people living with HIV. Indeed, officials often invoked "public health" in ways that deliberately excluded a variety of communities, including men who have sex with men, people of color, sex workers, people who used drugs, and the myriad intersections between these constituencies (Kinsman 2006). Public health officials typically "carve[d] up the sexual act into an array of who-put-what-into-wheres, which [were] often distinguished in black and white terms as either safe or not" (Hoppe 2018, 191). This either/or approach was intimately connected with abstinence-only messaging—any risk, the story went, was too much risk (Marcus 2020).

By 1983, members of the gay community had reached enough of a consensus to reject the either/or, abstinence-based decrees promulgated by public health officials. That year, with the publication of *How to Have Sex in an Epidemic*, Berkowitz and Callen, with support from virologist Joseph Sonnabend, shifted away from a critique of promiscuity to a somewhat more sex-positive, harm reduction approach (Berkowitz and Callen 1983). The publication offered advice on everything from rimming to water sports to condom use to love to fist fucking. Rather than commanding gay men to stop having sex, the handbook underscored safer sex strategies that would allow them to treat sex as a necessary part of life (Marcus 2020).

As information about the threat of HIV circulated across networks, communities developed new techniques for what we might describe as actuarial self-governance. We can think of inventions such as the use of condoms and dental dams for oral sex as expressions of the types of risk knowledge circulating across networked communities. In a July 1989 issue of *Outweek: New York's Lesbian and Gay News Magazine*, the unnamed authors of a section entitled "Safer Sex Guidelines" provide instructions for sex during the HIV/AIDS pandemic: "USE A CONDOM DURING ORAL SEX. If you don't, avoid placing the head of your partner's cock in your mouth. HIV-infected cum or precum can enter your blood-stream through cuts, tears or ulcers in your mouth . . . USE DENTAL DAMS DURING ORAL-VAGINAL SEX. HIV is present in some amounts of vaginal secretions, urine, menstrual blood, and infection-related vaginal discharge" (Outweek Magazine 1989). The message then shifts its affective register from urgent medical instruction (signaled by the use of capital letters) to sex positivity, concluding: "Remember, sex is good, and gay sex is great. Don't avoid sex, just avoid the virus. Learn to eroticize safer sex and you can protect others, remain safe and have fun" (Outweek Magazine 1989, 66). The authors here were describing HIV self-governance strategies in emotional terms. They reminded readers that "gay sex is great," counseled against abstinence, and even endeavored to transform condom and dental dam use into a site of possibilities for arousal (Elizabeth 2019). Over time, these approaches started to seep into public health messaging. Especially in the early days of the epidemic, public health messaging had called for either/or, abstinence thinking rather than clear strategies designed to minimize HIV risk while still tapping into the pleasure of sex (Batza 2018).

Language used to describe the fluid nature of risk, along with attendant risk negotiation strategies such as condoms and dental dams, coalesced during the HIV/AIDS epidemic (Monahan 2020). Rather than classifying activities as either dangerous or safe, a queer approach to risk invites us to recognize the importance of sex, even in moments of profound uncertainty. A queer approach also foregrounds the pursuit of pleasure as part of the risk assessment process.

A Queer Anti-Carceralism

The criminalization of HIV nondisclosure, an issue that did not fully emerge until the late 1980s, reveals the extent to which communities have been forced to navigate additional risks caused not by sexual contagion itself, but rather by the construction of HIV nondisclosure and transmission as a serious criminal offense (Shayo Buchanan 2014). Beyond rejecting an either/or approach to risk and attending to the pursuit of pleasure, this chapter argues that a queer approach to risk is fundamentally opposed to using the criminal law to combat the spread of sexual contagion. In doing so, this account is necessarily rooted in the long history of queer anti-carceralism, decarceration, and abolitionist literatures (Spade 2011; Mogul et al. 2011).

While Anglo-American jurisdictions have taken a variety of approaches to the criminalization of HIV/AIDS (Blecher-Cohen 2021;

Hoppe 2018, 39, 216–20; Kirkup 2020), queer community organizations
have consistently opposed the use of the criminal law to effectively man-
age risk (Canadian Coalition to Reform HIV Criminalization 2017). Like
virtually every aspect of the criminal legal system, the burdens of HIV
criminalization have not been evenly distributed. Black heterosexual
men make up a disproportionate number of prosecutions in both the
United States (Shayo Buchanan 2014; Hoppe 2018) and Canada (Hastings et al. 2017). Indigenous women and gay men have also found themselves disproportionately targeted under regimes of HIV criminalization
(Kirkup 2020).

As a direct consequence of this criminalized landscape, people living with HIV are forced to negotiate the risk of criminalization in their
everyday sexual lives. Put differently, HIV criminalization has become
its own risk to be managed. In the face of the ongoing potential risk of
HIV-related charges, people living with HIV could elect to never have
sex again as a strategy to avoid coming into conflict with the criminal
legal system. Instead, people living with HIV have often elected to take
a series of harm reduction steps to help minimize the risk that they will
be wrongly accused of failing to disclose their status to sexual partners.
These strategies include publicly foregrounding their status in general
online dating profiles and searching for sex within online HIV-positive
communities (Davis et al. 2006). Yet, even this approach is not without risks. As Graig Cote, a proponent of HIV decriminalization in the
United States, explains: "Unless you have it written down, you have witnesses, it's recorded . . . Even if it's on the sites, like Grindr or all the sites,
you can't prove that somebody read that" (Pfleger 2019). Given that there
are no guiding standards about whether nonverbal consent is enough to
discharge an individual's duty to disclose their HIV-positive status (Mc-
Callum 2014, 688), this strategy may not be enough to avoid coming into
conflict with the criminal legal system.

In view of this dynamic, where laws criminalizing HIV nondisclosure
have themselves become a form of risk, a growing number of activists
and civil society organizations have called on state actors to move away
from our collective reliance on the criminal law to regulate sexual contagion. For example, the Canadian Coalition to Reform HIV Criminalization published a Community Consensus Statement on Ending Unjust
HIV Criminalization in November 2017. The statement, now endorsed

by more than 170 Canadian civil society organizations, called for criminal prosecutions to be limited to the intentional and actual transmission of HIV. Rather than resorting to the criminal law, the statement called for an approach that "[is] based on the best available evidence, [is] proportionate to an objectively reasonable assessment of risk, and [is] no more intrusive or restrictive than necessary" (Canadian Coalition to Reform HIV Criminalization 2017, 2). Writing about similar law reform dynamics in the United States, Trevor Hoppe explains, "Even as state lawmakers and appeals courts winnow their laws in ways that would seem to limit their scope, the basic notion that punishment is an appropriate tool for controlling the spread of disease remains unchallenged. Ultimately, if we are to resist the impulse to punish disease, we must find a way to move beyond blame" (Hoppe 2017, 203–4). As this brief recounting of the criminalization of HIV non-disclosure reveals, a queer account of risk is anti-carceral (Lamble 2013; Spade 2011).

In the next section, my argument is that the emergence of COVID-19 has helped usher in a new era, one where a queer account of risk developed out of the HIV/AIDS pandemic may be in a moment of finding more mainstream audiences.

Sexual Risk in the Age of COVID-19

Having brought theories of risk together with practices developed over the past forty years of the HIV/AIDS pandemic, this third and final part of the chapter moves us to the present moment, examining how the amalgam of queer risk knowledge has set the template for our approach to the risk of acquiring and transmitting COVID-19 while having sex. In short, this section argues that a queer account of risk might help us navigate the anxieties and pleasures of sex in the age of COVID-19.

As COVID-19 moved across the globe in early 2020, government officials developed a series of strict social distancing measures. These measures were typically enforced through a mixture of community condemnation (for example, people shaming rule breakers on social media platforms) and neoliberal self-governance (for example, people donning masks and avoiding risky activities). In some moments, state actors intervened to enforce rules using the criminal law. When they did, people of color, sex workers, and men who have sex with men, along with others located at multiple axes of oppression, found themselves ensnared by police and bylaw officers who seemed more invested in punishment than in promoting education to support people tasked with navigating the risks of COVID-19. In the relatively early days of the COVID-19 pandemic, for example, police conducted an undercover sting operation and arrested men who organized and attended a group sex party through the popular hookup app, Grindr (Marr 2020). After the arrests, the attendees' names, photos, and employers were printed in a local newspaper (Reynolds 2020). These dynamics underscored the myriad problems with attempting to use state-based legal punishments to flatten the COVID-19 curve, and police were rightly criticized for their approaches.

In response, a series of civil society actors such as the Canadian Civil Liberties Association argued that the use of punitive legal enforcements was unlikely to combat the spread of COVID-19 and threatened to ensnare already vulnerable communities in racist legal systems (Luscombe and McClelland 2020a, 2020b). After the Ontario government announced the creation of sweeping powers allowing police to stop people on the street to determine whether they were complying with COVID-19 measures, the executive director of the Canadian Civil Liberties Association bleakly predicted: "Racialized minorities, Indigenous, Black people, people of colour will be stopped and will be during this time, living in fear" (Andersen 2021).

By contrast, public health actors developed their own messaging, which tended to bear little resemblance to draconian carceral approaches. It is important to notice this shift away from criminal law, particularly given the hostile posture that public health officials have long adopted (and continue to adopt) in relation to marginalized communities (Kinsman 2006). Public health messages often drew on the stores of queer risk knowledge that had coalesced during the early days of the HIV/AIDS pandemic—rather than seeing activities as either dangerous or safe, this messaging relied on the language of scientific and emotional risk in an effort to encourage people to engage in regimes of actuarial self-governance in their own sexual lives. The messaging was careful to foreground the pleasure and intimacy of sex, even in the context of a global pandemic. It was also implicitly, and sometimes explicitly, anti-carceral. For example, in response to a troubling editorial about the need to criminalize COVID-19 nondisclosure using existing HIV case law (David 2020), three leading Canadian HIV nondisclosure experts urged caution: "One hallmark of the rush to criminalize HIV has been the adoption of laws, or the overly broad interpretation or application of pre-existing laws, driven by misinformation, fear and stigma rather than science. In the context of the current COVID-19 pandemic, the same concerns are glaringly obvious" (Elliott et al. 2020).

Public health actors used queer risk knowledge to underscore the dangers—and pleasures—of sex during COVID-19. For example, in the midst of lockdown measures, public health officials in the Canadian province of British Columbia offered a variety of different sexual options, from masturbation ("You are your safest sex partner. Masturbating by yourself (solo sex) will not spread COVID-19. If you masturbate with a partner(s), physical distancing will lower your chance of getting COVID-19"), to virtual sex ("Video dates, phone chats, sexting, online chat rooms and group cam rooms are ways to engage in sexual activity with no chance of spreading COVID-19. Be aware of the risks of sharing information or photos online, and web camming"). They also provided concrete strategies to reduce the risks associated with in-person sex, suggesting that people use "barriers, like walls (e.g., glory holes), that allow for sexual contact but prevent close face-to-face contact" (BC Centre for Disease Control 2020).

New York City Public Health's "Safer Sex and COVID-19" bulletin is similarly replete with instances of queer risk knowledge operating across rational and emotional registers. It explained:

> Sex is a normal part of life and should always be with the consent of all parties. This document offers strategies to reduce the risk of spreading COVID-19 during sex. Decisions about sex and sexuality need to be balanced with personal and public health. During this extended public health emergency, people will and should have sex. Consider using harm reduction strategies to reduce the risk to yourself, your partners, and our community. (NYC Health 2020)

Like the public health messaging from the province of British Columbia, the bulletin advises people to have sex outdoors ("Pick larger, more open, and well-ventilated space"), and encourages sexting and digital sex parties ("If you usually meet your sex partners online or make a living by having sex, consider taking a break from in-person dates. Video dates, sexting, subscription-based fan platforms, sexy 'Zoom parties' or chat rooms may be options for you" (NYC Health 2020). Of course, none of these strategies forestall risk, nor could they. Outdoor sex and digital sexting may replace the health risks of acquiring and transmitting COVID-19 with the legal risks of public indecency and the non-consensual distribution of intimate images.

A series of what we might call community "do-it yourself" responses borrowing from the HIV/AIDS queer risk playbook also emerged as a direct consequence of COVID-19. Sex columnist Bobby Box noted: "As the days grow longer, isolation, combined with a buzzing horniness has inspired alternatives, and many have taken to Skype, Zoom, and Face-Time to get off. If you're up for it, virtual orgies are available as well" (Box 2020). In a piece published in *Slate* in March 2020, writer Andrew Kahn announced: "I Went to a Sex Party on Zoom." Kahn described the "soothing tones" of the event organizer, who seemed to recognize the futility of abstinence messaging: "I just want to make sure everyone feels like they have an outlet." Describing the new world of online sex parties, however, Kahn seemed to appreciate that even safer, digital sex is not without risks ("Though I know my angles on FaceTime, Snap-chat, and Skype, I've never cammed, and I keep my face out of most of my nudes. I wasn't sure if I'd breach that policy tonight") (Kahn 2020). These technologies were, of course, not available in the height of the HIV/AIDS pandemic. There is likely a case that queer sex positivity helped create the technologies that are now being used widely during the COVID-19 pandemic. Kahn's reference to keeping his face out of his nudes appeared to reflect queer risk knowledge already circulating across networked communities—avoiding showing one's face and body in the same photo constitutes a harm reduction strategy designed to reduce the likelihood of later being identified if the recipient shares the images.

When people describe sexual activities in terms of subjectivized risk levels, when they rely on hybrid forms of knowledge that commingle rational assessment with emotional attachment, when they refuse to abandon the pursuit of pleasure, and when they are fundamentally opposed to using the criminal law to punish COVID-19 rule breakers, they are drawing on approaches that are at least four decades in the making. Queer risk has gone mainstream.

Conclusion

Like HIV/AIDS, COVID-19 is here for the foreseeable future. As of this writing there is tempered optimism that vaccines will be effectively distributed and that case counts will go down. However, sex will continue to carry with it COVID-19-related risks. This chapter has argued that queer risk strategies that coalesced over the course of the HIV/AIDS pandemic may serve as a useful guide to help us negotiate sex in our everyday lives during this moment.

What might this account, one that foregrounds four decades of risk navigation strategies developed to respond to the threat of sexual contagion, reveal about queer legal theory more generally? This chapter has argued that there are at least three insights. First, a queer account of risk opens up space to think beyond dualities such as safety and danger. It also reminds us that those categories are always and necessarily moralized (Halperin 1995; Jagose 1996). Second, a queer account of risk allows us to better attend to the pleasure (and, as Bersani reminds us, disappointment) of sex (Bersani 1987; Muñoz 2009). Third, criminal laws are particularly ill-suited to grappling with the complexity of sexual risk. Police, prisons, and other criminal law actors are unlikely to teach people how to engage in the regimes of self-governance required to combat the spread of COVID-19 (Ball 2016; Lamble et al. 2020).

Ultimately, this chapter invites us to recognize that, in our age of neoliberal self-governance, sex will always constitute a site where we navigate the risk of contagion. Drawing on a rich body of queer theory, I have sought to carry a brief for sex against the tides of erotophobia. I have argued that a queer approach to risk recognizes the importance of sex, even in moments of uncertainty. Since early 2020, people around the world have been experimenting with new forms of sex as they construct makeshift glory holes and find their best angles for digital sex. Some of the sex was probably terrific, and much of it was probably disappointing.

In both instances, however, the sex helped flatten the curve in the midst of a global pandemic.

NOTE

1 Designed to facilitate and eroticize anonymity between sexual partners, the glory hole is typically a wall or piece of fabric with a hole cut into it.

BIBLIOGRAPHY

Adams, John. 1995. *Risk*. London and New York: Routledge.

Andersen, Ross. 2021. "Revised Police Measures Still Dangerous to Ontarians of Colour, Advocates Say." www.ctvnews.ca.

Backhouse, Constance B. 1985. "Nineteenth-Century Canadian Prostitution Law Reflection of a Discriminatory Society." *Social History/Histoire Sociale* 18(36): 387.

Ball, Mathew. 2016. *Criminology and Queer Theory: Dangerous Bedfellows?* London: Palgrave Macmillan.

Batza, Katie. 2018. *Before AIDS: Gay Health Politics in the 1970s*. Philadelphia: University of Pennsylvania Press.

BC Centre for Disease Control. 2020. "Covid-19 and Sex." www.bccdc.ca.

Beck, Ulrich. 1992. *Risk Society: Towards a New Modernity*. London and New York: Sage.

Berkowitz, Richard and Michael Callen. 1983. *How to Have Sex in an Epidemic: One Approach*. New York: News From the Front Publications.

Bersani, Leo. 1987. "Is the Rectum a Grave?" *AIDS: Cultural Analysis/Cultural Activism* 43: 197–222.

Blair, Thomas R. 2017. "Safe Sex in the 1970s: Community Practitioners on the Eve of AIDS." *American Journal of Public Health* 107, no. 6 (June): 874. https://doi.org/10.2105/AJPH.2017.303704.

Blecher-Cohen, Joshua D. 2021. "Disability Law and HIV Criminalization." *Yale Law Journal* 130: 1560.

Borges do Nascimento, Israel Júnior et al. 2020. "Novel Coronavirus Infection (COVID-19) in Humans: A Scoping Review and Meta-Analysis." *Journal of Clinical Medicine* 9(4): 946. https://doi.org/10.3390/jcm9040941.

Box, Bobby. 2020. "Some Gays Refuse to Let COVID-19 Keep Them from Hooking Up." http://inmagazine.ca.

Calisphere. 1982. "Play Fair Pamphlet." https://calisphere.org.

Callen, Michael et al. 1982. "We Know Who We Are: Two Gay Men Declare War on Promiscuity." http://richardberkowitz.com.

Canadian Coalition to Reform HIV Criminalization. 2017. *Community Consensus Statement*. www.hivcriminalization.ca.

Canadian Public Health Association. 2014. "Factors Impacting Vulnerability to HIV and Other STBBIs." www.cpha.ca.

Centers for Disease Control and Prevention. 1981. "Pneumocystis Pneumonia—Los Angeles." *Morbidity and Mortality Weekly Report* 30.

———. 2010. "Establishing a Holistic Framework to Reduce Inequities in HIV, Viral Hepatitis, STDs, and Tuberculosis in the United States." *Atlanta: U.S. Department of Health and Human Services.* https://doi.org/10.1037/e584282012-001.

Cossman, Brenda. 2007. *Sexual Citizens: The Legal and Cultural Regulation of Sex and Belonging.* Stanford, CA: Stanford University Press.

———. 2013. "Anxiety Governance." *Law & Social Inquiry* 38(4): 892.

Crimp, Douglas. 1987. "How to Have Promiscuity in an Epidemic." *AIDS: Cultural Analysis/Cultural Activism* 43: 237.

Davari, M. et al. 2020. "Antiretroviral Therapy and the Risk of Sexual Transmission of HIV: A Systematic Review and Meta-Analysis." *HIV Medicine* 21(6): 349–57. https://doi.org/10.1111/hiv.12841.

David, Lawrence. 2020. "COVID-19 and Consent to Sexual Activity." www.thelawyersdaily.ca.

Davis, Mark et al. 2006. "E-dating, Identity and HIV Prevention: Theorising Sexualities, Risk and Network Society." *Social Health and Illness* 28: 457.

Douglas, Mary. 1992. *Risk and Blame: Essays in Cultural Theory.* London and New York: Routledge.

Elizabeth, Anna. 2019. "Nobody Uses Dental Dams." www.theatlantic.com.

Elliott, Richard, Ryan Peck, and Léa Pelletier-Marcotte. 2020. "Prosecuting COVID-19 Non-disclosure Misguided." www.thelawyersdaily.ca.

Epstein, Steven. 1996. "The Nature of a New Threat." In *Impure Science: AIDS, Activism, and the Politics of Knowledge*, 1st edition. Berkeley: University of California Press.

Escoffier, Jeffrey. 1998. "The Invention of Safer Sex: Vernacular Knowledge, Gay Politics and HIV Prevention." *Berkeley Journal of Sociology* 43(3): 1. www.jstor.org.

Gastaldo, Denise et al. 2009. "Unprotected Sex among Men Who Have Sex with Men in Canada: Exploring Rationales and Expanding HIV Prevention." *Critical Public Health* 19(3–4): 400. https://doi.org/10.1080/09581590802566453.

Gerster, Jane and Andrew Russell. 2020. "Fines, Snitch Lines: Crackdown on Coronavirus Rule Breakers Could Have Consequences." http://globalnews.ca.

Grant, Martha Shaffer and Alison Symington. 2013. "Focus: R v Mabior and R v DC: Sex, HIV, and Non-Disclosure, Take Two: Introduction." *University of Toronto Law Journal* 63(3): 462.

Guan, Wei-jie et al. 2020. "Clinical Characteristics of Coronavirus Disease 2019 in China." *New England Journal of Medicine* 3. https://doi.org/10.1056/NEJMoa2002032.

Halperin, David M. 1995. *Saint Foucault: Towards a Gay Hagiography.* New York; London: Oxford University Press.

Harcourt, Bernard E. 2007. *Against Prediction: Punishing and Policing in an Actuarial Age.* Chicago: University of Chicago Press.

Hastings, Colin, Cécile Kazatchkine, and Eric Mykhalovskiy. 2017. *HIV Criminalization in Canada: Key Trends and Patterns.* Toronto: Canadian HIV/AIDS Legal Network.

The Health Protection (Coronavirus, Restrictions) (England) Regulations 2020, SI 2020/350, reg. 6. www.legislation.gov.uk.

Holmes, Dave et al. 2010. "Faceless Sex: Glory Holes and Sexual Assemblages." *Nursing Philosophy* 11(4): 250.

Hoppe, Trevor. 2018. *Punishing Disease: HIV and the Criminalization of Sickness.* Oakland: University of California Press.

Jagose, Annamarie. 1996. *Queer Theory: An Introduction.* New York: New York University Press.

Jain, Lochlann. 2006. *Injury: The Politics of Product Design and Safety Law in the United States.* Princeton, NJ: Princeton University Press.

Kahn, Andrew. 2020. "Coronavirus Diaries: I Went to a Sex Party on Zoom." https://slate.com.

Katz, Jennifer et al. 2017. "White Female Bystanders' Responses to a Black Woman at Risk for Incapacitated Sexual Assault." *Psychology of Women Quarterly* 41(2): 273–85.

Kinsman, Gary. 2006. "'Responsibility' as a Strategy of Governance: Regulating People Living with AIDS and Lesbians and Gay Men in Ontario." *Economy and Society* 25(3): 393.

Kirkup, Kyle. 2014–2015. "Releasing Stigma: Police, Journalists, and Crimes of HIV Non-Disclosure." *Ottawa Law Review* 46(1): 127.

———. 2020. "The Gross Indecency of Criminalizing HIV Non-Disclosure." *University of Toronto Law Journal* 73(3): 263.

Lamble, Sarah. 2013. "Queer Necropolitics and the Expanding Carceral State: Interrogating Sexual Investments in Punishment." *Law and Critique* 24: 229.

Lamble, Sarah et al. 2020. "Guest Editorial: Queer Theory and Criminology." *Criminology & Criminal Justice* 20(5): 504.

LeMessurier, Jennifer et al. 2018. "Risk of Sexual Transmission of Human Immunodeficiency Virus with Antiretroviral Therapy, Suppressed Viral Load and Condom Use: A Systematic Review." *CMAJ* 190(46): E1350–60. https://doi.org/10.1503/cmaj.180311.

Lupton, Debra. 1999. *Risk.* London and New York: Routledge.

Luscombe, Alex and Alexander McClelland. 2020a. "Policing the Pandemic Enforcement Report, April 14 2020–May 1 2020." *Policing the Pandemic Mapping Project.* https://doi.org/10.31235/osf.io/9pn27.

———. 2020b. "Policing the Pandemic: Tracking the Policing of Covid-19 across Canada." *Policing the Pandemic Mapping Project.* https://doi.org/10.31235/osf.io/9pn27.

Marcus, Julia. 2020. "Quarantine Fatigue Is Real." www.theatlantic.com.

Marr, Rhuaridh. 2020. "Georgia Police Criticized after Arresting Nine Men in Grindr Sex Sting." www.metroweekly.com

McCallum, Alexandra. 2014. "Criminalizing the Transmission of HIV: Consent, Disclosure, and Online Dating." *Utah Law Review* 3(5): 677.

McClelland, Alexander. 2019. "Unprepared." http://maisonneuve.org.

McKay, Richard A. 2016. "Before HIV." In *The Routledge History of Disease*, 1st edition, edited by Mark Jackson, 439–57. London: Routledge.

McKie, Robin. 2020. "Coronavirus: What Do Scientists Know about Covid-19 So Far." www.theguardian.com.

Meyer, Gregg S. 1991. "Criminal Punishment for the Transmission of Sexually Trans-mitted Diseases: Lessons from Syphilis." *Bulletin of the History of Medicine* 65(4): 552. www.jstor.org.

Milton, Josh. 2020. "Police Arrest Nine Queer Men in Grindr Sex Sting Operation Dubbed 'Cataclysmic Failure' of Justice." www.pinknews.co.uk.

Mogul, Joel L., Andrea J. Ritchie, and Kay Whitlock. 2011. *Queen (In)Justice: The Crimi-nalization of LGBT People in the United States*. Boston: Beacon Press.

Monahan, Sean. 2020. "What Gay Men Can Teach Us about Surviving the Coronavi-rus." www.theguardian.com.

Moore, Dawn and Mariana Valverde. 2010. "Maidens at Risk: 'Date Rape Drugs' and the Formation of Hybrid Risk Knowledges." *Economy and Society* 29(4): 514.

Moore, Sam. 2020. "It's Time to Stop Comparing COVID-19 to HIV." www.dailyxtra .com.

Muñoz, José Esteban. 2009. *Cruising Utopia: The Then and There of Queer Futurity*. New York: New York University Press.

Mykhalovskiy, Eric and Glenn Betteridge. 2012. "Who? What? Where? When? And with What Consequences? An Analysis of Criminal Cases of HIV Non-Disclosure in Canada." *Canadian Journal of Law and Society* 27(1): 31.

NYC Health. 2020. "Safer Sex and COVID-19." www1.nyc.gov.

Outweek Magazine: New York's Lesbian and Gay News Magazine. 1989, July 31. www .outweek.net.

Patton, Cindy. 1996. *Fatal Advice: How Safe-Sex Education Went Wrong*. Durham, NC: Duke University Press.

Pfleger, Paige. 2019. "Keeping Your HIV Status Secret Can Be a Crime. Experts Say That Hurts Public Health." https://will.illinois.edu.

Prevention Access Campaign. 2020. "Undetectable = Untransmittable." www .preventionaccess.org.

Renfro, Paul M. 2020. "Coronavirus Is Different from AIDS." www.washingtonpost .com.

Reynolds, Daniel. 2020. "Georgia Police Arrest Nine Men in Grindr Sex Sting." www .advocate.com.

Ritchie, Andrea J. 2017. *Invisible No More: Police Violence Against Black Women and Women of Color*. Boston: Beacon Press.

Roberts, Michelle. 2020. "Where Do I Need to Wear a Face Covering?" www.bbc.com.

Roberts, Siobhan. 2020. "Flattening the Coronovirus Curve." www.nytimes.com.

Robertson, Mark L. 2005. "An Annotated Chronology of the History of AIDS in To-ronto: The First Five Years, 1981–1986." *Canadian Bulletin of Medical History* 22(2): 316. https://doi.org/10.3138/cbmh.22.2.313.

Rocca, Ryan. 2020. "Coronavirus: Closure of Ontario's Non-Essential Businesses Ex-tended to May 6." https://globalnews.ca.

R v. Cuerrier, [1998] 2 SCR 371.

R v. DC, 2012 SCC 48.

R v. Mabior, 2012 SCC 47.

Sedgwick, Eve Kosofsky. 2003. *Touching Feeling: Affect, Pedagogy, Performativity*. Durham, NC: Duke University Press.

Shaffer, Martha. 2013. "Sex, Lies, and HIV: Mabior and the Concept of Sexual Fraud." *University of Toronto Law Journal* 63(3): 466.

Sharpe, Alex. 2019. *Sexual Intimacy and Gender Identity 'Fraud': Reframing the Legal and Ethical Debate*. London and New York: Routledge.

Shayo Buchanan, Kim. 2014. "When Is HIV a Crime? Sexuality, Gender and Consent." *Minnesota Law Review* 99(4): 1231.

Slane, Andrea and Emily van der Meulen. 2018. "'We Are Not Criminals': Sex Work Clients in Canada and the Constitution of Risk Knowledge." *Canadian Journal of Law and Society* 33(3): 291.

Spade, Dean. 2011. *Normal Life: Administrative Violence: Critical Trans Politics, and the Limits of Law*. Durham, NC: Duke University Press.

Stewart, Heather, Rowena Mason, and Vikram Dodd. 2020. "Boris Johnson Orders UK Lockdown to Be Enforced by Police." www.theguardian.com.

Symington, Alison. 2013. "Injustice Amplified by HIV Non-Disclosure Ruling." *University of Toronto Law Journal* 63(3): 485.

Treatment Action Campaign. 2017. "Structural and Social Determinants of Health (SSDHs)." www.treatmentactiongroup.org.

Valverde, Mariana et al. 2005. "Legal Knowledges of Risks." In *Law and Risk*, edited by the Law Commission of Canada, 86–120. Vancouver: UBC Press.

Weait, Matthew. 2007. *Intimacy and Responsibility: The Criminalisation of HIV Transmission*. New York: Routledge-Cavendish.

9

Queer Intimacies and Criminal Law

Queer Legal Praxis and the UK Poppers Ban

CHRIS ASHFORD

The late artist Derek Jarman's "Queer Manifesto" proclaimed: "queer is not about gay or lesbian—it's about sex."[1] Applying queer theory to law arguably seeks to understand how the law regulates sex and in turn the sexual lived experience of people rather than a narrow understanding of law rooted in identity politics. To view law—at least in much of the Global North—through the prism of identity politics, we have seen a significant shift in the codification of rights, such as same-sex marriage. We can also point, I suggest, to moments of queer praxis when we see the limits of these normative advancements in ephemeral encounters with law and sex in which queer sexual existence remains limited. This chapter describes one moment of praxis.

In August 2020, Priti Patel—then the British Home Secretary[2]—wrote to the Advisory Council on the Misuse of Drugs (ACMD)[3] to set out their work program for 2020–23.[4] Toward the end of the letter, Patel noted that "alkyl nitrates, known as poppers, have been widely used recreationally since the 1970s and are used for their muscle-relaxing effects, especially by homosexual men as an aid to sex."

Why, the ACMD members could perhaps understandably be thinking, is the British Home Secretary sharing her insights into the long-documented benefits of poppers for anal sex? Patel went on: "In 2016 the ACMD advised that they did not fall within the scope of the definition of a psychoactive substance in the Psychoactive Substances Act 2016 because they did not have a direct effect on the central nervous system. However, a Court of Appeal judgment in 2018[5] confirmed that substances which have only an indirect psychoactive effect can still be captured by the 2016 Act. As a consequence the lawfulness of the supply of poppers is uncertain. Put simply, the British government has no idea whether supply (and, although not stated in the letter, possession) offenses apply to poppers. Patel added that she was "minded to remove the uncertainty by explicitly exempting poppers from the 2016 Act."

The origins of the confusion and uncertainty lie in the passing of the Psychoactive Substances Act 2016. This law—covering the whole of the UK—was designed to supplement existing drug laws to address so-called "legal highs" such as Spice that are not covered by existing legislation, but were seen as increasingly problematic for widespread public misuse.[6] Local media frequently ran features depicting "zombies" passed out in public spaces as a result of the drug (BBC 2016a).

The legislation was so far-reaching in framing the law around "psychoactive substances" that coffee also fell within the scope of the legislation and needed to be included in the appendix of exempted substances. Poppers were debated alongside these other legal substances, and Parliament made the decision not to add them to the exempted list.

The legislative journey of this law[7] and the surrounding parliamentary debates saw one Member of Parliament "outing" himself as a poppers user. He would later be described by one British tabloid newspaper as "pickled on poppers," while a former British Government Minister would be reported as using poppers at Cabinet meetings, highlighting poppers' use beyond sex (Ashford 2016). Zmith—in his comprehensive history of poppers—has suggested that after the Psychoactive Substances Act, "poppers were not controlled by legislation any more than they already were" (Zmith 2021, 117), yet if the Home Secretary is unclear whether the government has banned poppers or not, it is little surprise that many others are unclear as well. At the moment the legislation was passed, Parliament passed a law that included poppers as a criminalized substance, but bizarrely, the government's view (and arguably that of Parliament as they were informed of this during the passing) was that it wouldn't actually be applied to poppers in practical reality. Confusion has followed in the years since.

The UK is not alone in recently debating the legality of poppers. In the United States, there has been a complex legal landscape in which poppers were sold in many states as VHS head cleaner, leather cleaner, liquid incense, room freshener, or even fingernail polish (Archer 2013; Le et al. 2020), while in 2013, Health Canada initiated a crackdown on poppers products (Schwartz et al. 2020). In 2018, Australia's Therapeutic Goods Administration (TGA) proposed a ban on poppers, prompting a public debate and opposition from queer activists. Whereas in the UK, poppers are typically sold as "aromas," Australia would refer to them as leather or VHS cleaner (similar to head cleaner in the United States—preserving the notion of "VHS" in the queer lexicon long after anyone actually used VHS cassettes or possessed a player).

In 2019, the Australian TGA "down scheduled" amyl nitrate, meaning the classic poppers formula would be legal, but only with a prescription. Most poppers in Australia (and similarly in the UK and North America) are no longer made with amyl but instead feature alkyl nitrates, which would also require a prescription in Australia. This creates a landscape in which poppers cease to be legal for sale in adult stores and saunas, reducing the availability of poppers within queer venues and medicalizing an aspect of queer sex. As Badge has noted, this also increases the chance of gay venues being raided by police, noting a 2020 Queensland prosecution of an eighteen-year-old for "possessing a restricted substance" while carrying poppers (Badge 2019).

These legal interventions should be viewed in the context of ongoing and long-established documentation of poppers as a commonly used drug to enhance sex, particularly receptive anal intercourse (Vaccher et al. 2020). While there have also been periodic concerns and panics (Zmith 2021, 74) relating to the consumption of poppers, the 2016 UK legislation came at a time of apparent LGBTQ legal progress in both civil and criminal law. Yet when with regard to sex—and poppers as the provider of ephemeral pleasure and bliss, as an enabler particularly of anal sex between men—the law is coded once more as prohibitive of queerness. Poppers are instead presented as the ultimate "gateway drug" to law's imagined "worse," poppers opening the gateway of the arse to blissful fucking.

Law's treatment of poppers—a substance integral for many men who have sex with men, for sexual encounters and more broadly multipurposed as part of gay male culture—produces an ephemeral state, like the pleasure of poppers, and in this state we can arguably achieve what I term "queer legal praxis," an ephemeral encounter with the law's attitude toward queer existence. When we step outside the boundaries of normativity and provide a flash of sexualized queerness, we encounter an instance of queer praxis, and specifically in these legislative (or case law) moments, queer legal praxis. The chapter explores the history of sociolegal encounters with poppers and analyzes the 2016 legislation in the context of queer legal praxis.

The Poppers Phenomenon

Long established as the most used drug in gay male sexual encounters, and a fixture of many gay men's nightstands/bedside tables and freezers,[8] the term "poppers" stems from their earlier incarnation in glass vials that would be broken or "popped" to release fumes. Known by a range of brand names that echo through queer history, such as Jungle Juice,[9] Rush, and Liquid Gold, poppers produce a powerful vasodilating effect and mild psychoactive effects (Hall et al. 2015). Poppers—often alongside marijuana—were the more "in control," moderate drug of choice for those engaging in gay male encounters in the 1970s in contrast to acid, MDMA, and "angel dust" (Jack Fritscher, quoted in Hemry 2008, 480). Poppers were and remain a key aspect of gay male sexuality operating in a sociable and sometimes sexual space that facilitated the expression of queer desire. Poppers lubricate desire but also, and nearly literally, act as lubricant, opening up orifices for penetration (see Coxon 1996, 101; Elaime et al. 2008). The giddy high of poppers is a pleasure in its own right, which likely explains why poppers' use has rippled far beyond the anal sex or fisting encounter to the pleasures of jerking off, oral sex, making out, and dancing (Lauritsen 1993; Zmith 2021, 15).

This was not, however, the original intention in creating poppers. Amyl nitrate—the "original" poppers—was first prescribed for the management of angina in 1859 (Brunton 1867) and was available in small glass "pearls" to be crushed. Amyl nitrate remained a prescription drug from that point on in the United States until it was deregulated in 1960, although just nine years later, the Food and Drug Administration reclassified poppers as prescription drugs. The reclassification was prompted by an increase in healthy young people accessing the drug and the widespread recreational use of poppers (Romanelli et al. 2004).

In the UK, pharmacists can be "struck off" for "excessive sales" of poppers (Gay News 1976; Zmith 2021, 4–5).[10] High sales became a proxy for indicating that poppers were being used for something beyond their

"legitimate" purpose. In the latter half of the twentieth century, manufacturers of poppers around the world shifted to using isobutyl nitrate
in their production in order to fall beyond the scope of existing pharmaceutical regulations. This re-formulation would prove popular through
the 1970s in the United States, with notable success for brand names
such as Rush, which endure today. Similar re-formulations of poppers
also took place in the UK, so as to circumvent the Medicines Act 1968
that controlled amyl nitrate. This in turn led to legal challenges that
sought to apply the Medicines Act to limit the availability of poppers
to medicinal use or find other creative applications of law to constrain
access to poppers.

In 1989, there was an attempt to curb the availability of poppers by
prosecuting five men under Section 24 of the Offences Against the Person Act 1861 (OAPA) which prohibits the malicious administration of a
poison or other noxious substance, but the defendants were all cleared
(Pink Paper 1989). At this point, the possession, sale, and manufacture
of poppers were not illegal. The police who wanted to stop the use of
poppers—and they had increasingly been associated with moral panics
through the 1980s—chose to use the OAPA as a creative, albeit unsuc-
cessful, solution. Zmith identified the names of the defendants, one of
whom was the landlord of the Royal Vauxhall Tavern, a popular London
gay bar that had previously been raided by the Police (Zmith 2021, 88).
The police had seized £40,000 worth of poppers at an address in Kent.
The case cost hundreds of thousands of British pounds. Expert witnesses
(two for the prosecution and one for the defense) were also flown to
England from the United States to participate in the trial. This seems to
be the only incidence of the Offences Against the Person Act being used
in this way.

The "Zipperstore trial" in 1996 saw the Royal Pharmaceutical Society (RPS) seek to prosecute Zipperstore—what was at the time Britain's
only licensed gay sex shop—over the sale of poppers. The RPS argued
that amyl and butyl nitrate fell within the scope of the Medicines Act
1968 and thus could only be lawfully sold by pharmacies as a medicine.
Zipperstore was not a pharmacy. Historic "striking off" of pharmacies
for high volumes of poppers sales (considered indicative of abuse) had
shown the tight control that could be applied if poppers were available
only from pharmacies. These historic striking off interventions had the

intent of ending the legal availability of poppers for leisure use. A campaign against poppers accompanied the Zipperstore case. This campaign was supported by the *Sunday Times* newspaper and HIV/AIDS campaign group Positively Healthy, which argued that poppers formed part of the "unhealthy" lifestyle of drug taking that contributed to AIDS-related illness (Gay Times 1995; Pink Paper 1996).

The prosecution was only partially successful. One reporter said of the conclusion of the court proceedings that "I don't think I've ever seen a judge so angry" and went on to describe Judge Jarlath Finney QC as "cheeks ablaze"—presumably not from the use of poppers—and "fuming." Finney described the lawyers for the RPS as "sloppy" and the dragging out of the case over two years as "ineptitude." After legal wrangling, Zipperstore pled guilty to the charge in exchange for other charges to be dropped against the store owner, but the judge imposed only a nominal fine of £100 and instructed the RPS to pay their own costs—which totaled in excess of £47,000.[11] The government went on to "ban" poppers in that they became classified as a medicine—but this only applied to amyl nitrate—which as the *Gay Times* pointed out the following year was the "poppers that no one uses" following re-formulation (Hamilton 1997, 39; Northmore 1997, 2).

In the final few months of the 1990s UK Conservative Government,[12] Health Minister Gerry Malone called for a further "clampdown" on poppers in response to the Zipperstore case. No practical steps were taken and the Conservatives were then out of power for thirteen years. It would take a future Conservative government in 2016 to return to the issue of legislating poppers.

Initial health concerns relating to poppers were limited to the minor burns caused by the amyl on contact with skin (by sniffing a bottle and allowing the liquid to come into contact with the nostril). By the 1990s, concerns about poppers had become more established within the gay community itself, particularly surrounding HIV transmission (Rofes 1998, 231) and Kaposi's sarcoma (KS) (Altman 1986, 33; Evans 1981; France 2016, 37). Some studies focused on potential harm to vision (Audo et al. 2011), while other studies pointed to the link between poppers use and unsafe sexual practices, like increased instances of bareback (condomless) anal and oral sex.[13]

Most recently, the term poppers has also been applied to the "huffing" of organic solvents or propellants by men who have sex with men.

First reported as a small but growing phenomenon in Los Angeles, these "poppers" involve intense huffing (pouring the liquid on fabric or opening and placing the liquid in a bag to contain the solution for more efficient inhalation) of the solvents or propellants. Hall et al. have noted that there is growing evidence of the term poppers being applied to this practice of huffing in some online forums and pornography (Hall et al. 2015), which we can see in the popper-bating pornographic phenomenon (Mercer 2017). These evolving applications and definitions perhaps speak to the porous but persistent nature of poppers as a sociocultural artefact.

By the time the UK Psychoactive Substances Act came before the UK Parliament as draft legislation, poppers remained widely available. They were long established as a presence in English gay bars and clubs, saunas, and sex stores and available through online stores (Mercer 2017). They also continue to be sold under the name "aromas" in the UK and "room odouriser" internationally, as if an alternative to Glade or Airwick. As long ago as 1986, Lauritsen and Wilson—who formed part of the Committee to Monitor Poppers in 1981—mocked these transparent code names, particularly "room odorizor," as "marketing subterfuge." They suggested that heroin could likewise be sold as "mosquito-bite remedy ('for external use only')," or "live hand grenades could be sold as 'paperweights'" (Lauritsen and Wilson 1986, 6).

In the decades that followed, poppers received less legal attention and in the UK became a non-issue until the Psychoactive Substances Act 2016 and the queer legal praxis that followed.

Queer Legal Praxis

For LGBT people, the dominant cultural narrative in Anglo-American jurisdictions is seemingly one of incremental and then accelerated progress, anti-transgender bills and interventions notwithstanding. Progress, in turns, has come to be indexed by bestowals of rights and anti-discrimination protections. Queer theorists and queer legal theorists have increasingly asked whether this progress is a "good" thing or whether it represents an erasure or denial of identity. Queer legal praxis is in one sense momentary—an ephemeral revelation of how law interacts with queers—but can also be a practice to evaluate and understand law.

The concept of queer praxis framed by Goltz et al. has origins in performance literature and the notion of "queer decorum" as coined by Pérez and Brouwer (2010). Just as public ceremonies and performances can be viewed as offering moments of praxis (for example, a wedding), these performances are often moments in which power, as regulated and defined by law—is at play. The passing of the Psychoactive Substances Act, and the subsequent ensuing ambiguities in relation to the criminalization of poppers, act as examples of queer legal praxis in which truth(s) are revealed about contemporary queer existence and the gulf with legal assumptions or incomprehension about that existence. In the specific temporal moment of the passing of this legislation we see the willingness to enact a law that knowingly creates uncertainty about the criminalization of a substance that is often integral to the sex lives of many. The passage of this Act similarly reveals an unease and confusion about the lives that will be impacted. Lawmakers brook the possibility of criminalizing gay men more cavalierly than they would coffee or alcohol drinkers.

Queer legal praxis can therefore be defined as a revelatory moment of queer truth, a truth that appears in one's periphery vision, a snatched glance that disappears almost as quickly as one recognizes its presence. Yet, the power of such moments can be considerable and outlast the ephemeral nature of the revelation.

Foucault's 1988 interview in the French magazine *Mec* took on outsized influence given that it was not translated into English in full until 2011. While individuals had sought to secure rights from Jean Le Bitoux, who conducted the interview (Halperin 2011), and others offered their own translation of key sections, its appearance in 2011 provided a relatively rare instance of Foucault talking "on the record" about homosexuality. In the interview "the Gay Science" or "Le Gai Savouir" Foucault stated: "I believe that two homosexuals, no, two boys who are seen leaving together to go sleep in the same bed are tolerated. But if they wake up the next morning with a smile on their faces, if they hold hands and kiss each other tenderly and thereby affirm their happiness, then no one will forgive them" (Foucault 2011).

Foucault might not have clearly envisioned the change in civil and criminal legal landscape that would characterize the start of the twenty-first century, yet his understanding here of homosexuality in which sex, albeit inferred, is tolerated but intimacy is not would appear to be countered by the queer legal praxis provided by the Psychoactive Substances Act. The legislation and legislative debates over poppers reflect an enduring discomfort with the uncamouflaged pleasures of queer sex; that is, when queer sex drops its alibi of intimacy or marriage.

Happiness, or pleasure—and the expression of that joy, here in the context of poppers usage—is to reveal *affect* of the act and queer feelings. In the context of the "poppers ban" it is not merely that the legislative intervention forced legislators to confront the reality of anal sex, but to confront the fact that people, particularly men, engage in anal fucking and use poppers to enhance their pleasure. Poppers remind us not only that people engage in anal sex but that it can be joyous and pleasurable.

Kirkup has noted in the Canadian context the mistake of concluding that "the criminal law has abandoned targeting queer people altogether" (Kirkup 2020). The UK poppers ban provides a moment in which the UK government, at first through ignorance, later deliberately, and ultimately in a state of confusion, provided a new criminal intervention into the lives of queer people.

The Psychoactive Substances Act 2016 and a Moment of Queer Legal Praxis

Section 2 of the Psychoactive Substances Act (PSA) defines "psychoactive substance" as any substance that "is capable of producing a psychoactive effect in a person who consumes it"[14] and "is not an exempted substance."[15] The exemption here is important, for potentially a range of normative products could be found to fall within the scope of the legislation. Controlled drugs (within the meaning of the Misuse of Drugs Act 1971), medicinal products, alcohol, nicotine and tobacco products, caffeine, and food (includes drink)[16] provide the exceptions for the legislation.

Lyn Brown, the then Opposition Spokesperson on Home Affairs, unsuccessfully sought to amend the legislation to also exempt poppers but noted her own lack of understanding of the issue, commenting: "I know very little about drugs, apart from what I have learned hard over the past few months. I did not even know what poppers were when I first took on my brief—I had never heard of them; I thought they were the little things with the string that we had at parties."[17]

Other MPs engaged in parliamentary debate by sharing gossip about ministers and MPs who might have used poppers for health reasons in the past, notably Ernest Bevan who was a Labour Cabinet Minister during the Second World War and in the postwar period. The Labour MP Keith Vaz said of the alleged use of poppers by MPs and past Cabinet members that "this was a bit of shock for me after 28 years in this House—that Ministers have stood at the Dispatch Box having had poppers. I think that is what [the opposition spokesperson] said and it was a great surprise to the House. She obviously knows more than I do about such issues [. . .] I wonder whether they are still in use around the Cabinet table."[18]

Vaz was in fact more familiar with poppers than this parliamentary contribution would suggest. In 2016, Keith Vaz would be revealed in a national newspaper "exposé" as someone posing as a man called "Jim" during an encounter with two sex workers, claiming to sell washing machines. As part of the encounter, he asks the men to bring along cocaine and poppers, suggesting Vaz's own awareness of drugs was more proficient than he suggested in Parliament. Vaz, married to a woman and living as a straight man, arguably had some complex motivations during the debate. He would go on to note that the government had previously understood the broader value of poppers to many men, but that the government had, in the course of placing the legislation before Parliament, since changed their position. Vaz quoted previous correspondence from the government who "told us that poppers are beneficial, as if in some cases they may well be mandatory."[19] [The Minister] wrote that "the Government recognises that representations have been made to the effect that 'poppers' have a beneficial health and relationship effect in enabling anal sex for some men who have sex with men."

The interventions of one Conservative MP during the second reading of the bill would provide focus for the media reporting of what was then the potential poppers ban embedded in legislation. Crispin Blunt declared: "Sometimes a measure is proposed that becomes personal to oneself and one realises that the Government are about to do something fantastically stupid. In such circumstances, one has a duty to speak up. I use poppers—I out myself as a popper user—and would be directly affected by the bill. I am astonished by the proposal to ban them, as are very many other gay men."[20]

The intervention of Blunt did remind Parliament of the sex—specifically anal sex—element of poppers usage. However, the parliamentary debate did not linger on relaxing anal muscles. Another Conservative MP and out gay man, Mike Freer, supporting an amendment to the draft legislation and defending poppers, argued that "this is not just about the physical side of a relationship. If people want their relationship to be as intimate as possible and poppers facilitate that, they are an important element in the emotional wellbeing of that couple. Therefore, if we are talking about the medicinal benefits, we have to include the emotional and mental health benefits that the use of poppers in a relationship can bring."[21] In doing so, Freer moved the parliamentary discussion away from the seemingly more emotive aspects of gay male sex.

Yet it was Blunt's intervention that caught the attention of the media. As Zmith has noted (2021, 117), the intervention was self-serving in that Blunt noted he would be disadvantaged by any ban, but it was also a significant statement by an "out" gay Conservative MP. The front page of *The Sun*, a British tabloid, led with "Posh MP partial to partying pickled on poppers" (Cole 2016) while the BBC more soberly reported, "Tory MP Crispin Blunt 'outs himself' as popper user" (BBC 2016b). Another UK tabloid, *The Mirror*, simply reported the story as a "desperate plea to keep [poppers] legal" (Bloom 2016).

Then Conservative MP (and a junior member of the government), David Burrowes, separately observed during the passing of the legislation that "I cannot believe that those with poppers will be the main focus. We can ask that question [whether poppers are included within the scope of the legislation] in 30 months' time to, I hope, reassure ourselves. This debate will help with that, and perhaps the Minister will give us some reassurance as well. How will this be dealt with practically and properly? I hasten to say that those who consume poppers have not so much to fear; it is the people who shift the new psychoactive substances around in bulk who are causing menace."[22] In other words, poppers might fall within the scope of the legislation but since poppers were not the focus of the bill, it would not become the focus of enforcement.

Ultimately, the Government was not persuaded by these parliamentary interventions to include a poppers exemption—as it had for coffee—within the legislation. Lobbying from the National AIDS Trust, the charity Stonewall, and commercial operators *Millivres Prowler Boyz Magazine*[23] also failed to persuade the government to exempt poppers. Instead, the government offered a "review" of poppers once the legislation was passed and indicated that they would ask the ACMD for advice on whether poppers were included in the legislation (and thus needed an exemption).

Freer had suggested during the parliamentary debate that if the Home Office felt a ban was needed in light of evidence, they should consider "licensing poppers for sale through sex shops." Free argued that "that would allow some level of control, regulation and protection, without the need for an outright ban, which might lead people to be exposed to all sorts of underground drugs."[24] Yet, several years after passage of the law, poppers remain in an uncertain position legally.

Knowing that poppers provided an important means of enabling many gay men to enjoy their sex lives, and despite the long history of poppers within queer culture, the government passed legislation that might or might not have criminalized poppers, and that might or might not be enforced against the supply of poppers.[25]

The intention of Parliament during the debate was that poppers be included within the scope of the legislation. Mike Penning, the then Minister for Policing, Crime and Criminal Justice, made a favorable comparison with the Republic of Ireland where poppers were banned, and went on to suggest that there have been more than twenty deaths since 1993 that reportedly involved the use of alkyl nitrates.[26] However flawed this argument might have been, the intention of Penning, as Fortson has noted, was clear: to associate poppers with death in the minds of legislators (Fortson 2018c).

This is a key aspect of the debate. We are perhaps used to queerphobic interventions such as the 1988 law "Section 28" which banned local authorities (and local authority controlled bodies such as schools) from the "promotion of homosexuality as a pretended family relationship,"[27] or overt attempts to resist the extension of rights such as same-sex marriage or trans self-identification laws. The apparent poppers ban was not such a moment. Rather it showed a "reckless" approach to the law, with the Government—and indeed Parliament—knowing that there is a risk of criminalization and uncertainty, and proceeding with the law anyway.

With passage of the legislation, the inclusion of poppers moved from being a debate to being a matter of practical policing enforcement. Crawley Police tweeted on the first day that the ban came into force: "First day, first seizure in Crawley by PC Goater! One and only one warning given #NoSecondChance #Poppersincluded" with a photo of evidence bags filled with bottles of poppers. Within fifty-seven minutes—and after a tweet furor—they were forced to tweet "We made a mistake and apologise for it" (Lusher 2016).[28] Although the backlash temporarily heeled the police, the legal status of and enforcement against poppers remain uncertain.

* * *

In *R v. Rochester*,[29] Kirk Rochester was convicted of possession of a psychoactive substance (nitrous oxide[30]) with intent to supply, contrary to section 7 of the Psychoactive Substances Act 2016. The question before the Court of Appeal was whether a substance falls within the definition of "psychoactive substance" if it directly stimulates or depresses the central nervous system, or whether it is sufficient that it does so indirectly. The court concluded that the 2016 Act does not require a psychoactive substance to be capable of producing its effect by directly stimulating or depressing the central nervous system. Indirect effect is sufficient.

In 2016, in response to a request by the Government to provide an assessment on the harms and psychoactivity of alkyl nitrates, the ACMD commented[31] that there were three possible options for whether alkyl nitrates fell within the scope of the Psychoactive Substances Act:

a. "poppers" are caught under the definition of a "psychoactive substance" and should be controlled under the Psychoactive Substances Act 2016;

b. "poppers" are psychoactive, but should be on the list of exemptions from the Psychoactive Substances Act 2016; or

c. "poppers" are not caught by the definition of a "psychoactive substance," and the Psychoactive Substances Act 2016 therefore does not apply.

They concluded that "a psychoactive substance has a direct action on the brain and that substances having peripheral effects, such as those caused by alkyl nitrites, do not directly stimulate or depress the central nervous system."

The judgment, delivered by Lord Burnett of Maldon CJ, also turned to the question of alkyl nitrates, and drew upon the judgment in *R v. Chapman* (Sonny)[32] in which the judge noted the 2016 legislation was silent on whether a psychoactive substance was required directly or indirectly to stimulate the brain. He determined that Parliament would have distinguished between direct and indirect stimulation if it had intended to do so, and that the absence of any such distinction meant it did not matter whether the stimulation was direct or indirect. Such a distinction is however arguably important for poppers, which have been seen as constituting "indirect stimulation." If the courts are indicating that there's no distinction between direct and indirect stimulation, then poppers are criminalized.

Forston has previously noted that correspondence between the ACMD and ministers does not have the force of law, creating the original ambiguity surrounding poppers (Fortson 2018a, 2018b). Complex questions of science and the effects of poppers must now determine whether poppers fall within the scope of the legislation. Yet, other substances—notably coffee—were specifically exempted from the legislation. While poppers could simply have been added to the list of exempted substances, the Government—during the passing of the legislation—chose not to do so.

Conclusion

The central character in Andrew Holleran's fictional account of 1970s New York observed that "even if people accept fags out of kindness, even if they tolerate the poor dears, they don't want to know WHAT THEY DO" (Holleran 2019, 7). The intervening years have seen a transformed legal landscape, rooted in a shift toward the homosexual as a benign, sometimes celebrated, category of sexual identity. Particularly, since the partial decriminalization of homosexuality in England and Wales in 1967, the *what* has shifted to the *who*: from a criminal law orientated toward sexual acts, be it sodomy/buggery, importuning, or gross indecency to civil law in which LGBT people are beneficiaries of marriage rights and antidiscrimination protections. Yet in moments of queer legal praxis, we are forced to once again confront the *what* and specifically the sexual acts that define the desire at the heart of sexuality.

In these moments we see queers as sexual once more and we also see the responses to that re-sexualized identity. The UK Psychoactive Substances Act 2016 was designed to address the subject of so-called legal highs, but by including poppers in the scope of the legislation, the Act arguably also became about how the law views queer people, and particularly men who have sex with men. The legislation forced legislators to confront and debate men who have sex with men as sexual beings and as men engaging in, and enhancing the pleasure of, anal fucking.

It is arguably commonplace in queer studies that marriage politics desexualized queers to make them more respectable subjects of and for law. But perhaps, curiously, anti-sodomy reforms *also* desexualized gay subjects because the frame of reform, and the frame of gay rights politics, was really about police overreach and state-sanctioned homophobia. Poppers discourse, provoked by the 2016 legislation, leaves fewer discursive hiding places for fucking.

Writing in 1978, the San Francisco–based journalist and one-time academic, Jack Fritscher, observed that "being gay is more than sexual calisthenics energized by poppers" (Jack Fritscher, quoted in Hemry 2008, 55). We should perhaps remind ourselves that it can *also* be sexual calisthenics energized by poppers. While everyone *can* engage in anal sex, fist, and use poppers, these elements remain particularly central to gay culture and a notion of queerness that is inherently about sexual desire. Queer legal praxis—and the example provided by the treatment of poppers under the Psychoactive Substances Act—highlights the dislocation of the acts practiced by a minority identity from the identity constructed by law. This dislocation in turn raises questions about how law can and should regulate these acts, if ever.

As a moment of queer legal praxis, we see in the ambiguous "poppers ban" what is arguably a growing divergence between the lived experience of many queer people and the seemingly progressive yet ultimately normative agenda that provides the boundaries of law's imagination.

Queer legal praxis offers not only an important tool to understand these events, but a mechanism to challenge and frame future queer legal struggles.

NOTES

1 Although promoted as a "Queer Manifesto" in a 2020 major retrospective of his work by the Irish Museum of Modern Art (IMMA) and Manchester Art Gallery, the full original manifesto appeared as an appendix to Jarman's 1992 text *At Your Own Risk* and was taken from a 1991 flyer found on the floor of the club, Heaven. See also Kissane and Rehmani-White 2020.

2 Similar to the Interior Minister role in many other jurisdictions.

3 The Advisory Council on the Misuse of Drugs makes recommendations to government on the control of dangerous or otherwise harmful drugs, including classification and scheduling under the Misuse of Drugs Act 1971 and its regulations. ACMD is an advisory non-departmental public body, sponsored by the Home Office. See: www.gov.uk (last accessed October 5, 2021).

4 "ACMD Work Programme 2020 to 2022: Commissioning Letter," www.gov.uk/ (last accessed October 5, 2021).

5 *R v. Rochester* (Kirk) [2018] EWCA Crim 1936.

6 The evolving formulation of these drugs meant that they could not effectively be addressed by amendments to existing legislation, resulting instead in the broad concept of "psychoactive substance." Already prohibited drugs continue to be criminalized by the earlier specific legislation, which creates a series of "classifications" for specific drugs, with "Class A" being the most serious.

7 Unfavorable comparisons have been drawn with the Dangerous Dogs Act 1991—a piece of legislation regarded as poorly conceived and a reaction to a moral panic. See Robbins 2015. The ACMD themselves raised a number of concerns about the legislation to the Home Secretary in a letter of July 2, 2015 from the Chair Professor Les Iversen, although none of these related explicitly to poppers (see https://assets.publishing.service.gov.uk/ (last accessed October 14, 2021). Further concerns were raised in another letter on July 13, including the statement that "psychoactivity in humans cannot be *definitively* established in many cases in a way that would definitely stand up in a court of law" (see https://assets.publishing .service.gov.uk (last accessed October 14, 2021). However, in their final advice to the Home Secretary in a letter dated October 23, 2015, they reference poppers—specifically alkyl nitrates—in noting that the legislation does "cover substances the Home Office wishes to control under the Bill such as nitrous oxide and alkyl nitrates" (see https://assets.publishing.service.gov.uk (last accessed October 14, 2021). See generally Stevens et al. 2015.

8 Gay artist and filmmaker John Waters found his freezer overflowing with a lifetime supply of poppers in 2010 after being sent a consignment by the US manufacturer of Rush for featuring the brand in a painting. Waters denied to journalists that he was a "poppers pig." See Hicklin 2010. The reference to "pig" sex identities

is striking for, although poppers are arguably "mainstream," the active celebration and fetishization (for example through the use of hoods/gas masks that facilitate poppers use during sex) can be seen to transform the queer into "pig." See more generally Florêncio 2020.

9   Not all poppers are the same. Quite apart from their chemical composition, perceived strength and brand name contribute to the desirability of poppers. See for example Pasquir 2019.

10 Pharmacists in the case providing evidence had noted a significant number of sales in Brighton (an area then and now known for its large population of gay men) and the two pharmacists in question had seen "excessive" sales in the Earls Court and Notting Hill Gate areas of London (then also associated with significant populations of gay men).

11 Equivalent to around £62,000 at the time of writing. See Smith 1996, 9.

12 The Medicines Control Agency sought to prosecute QuietLynn Ltd in 2001 for distributing isobutyl nitrate as a "room odouriser" under the brands Reds, Raven, and Liquid Gold, arguing that poppers could not legitimately be regarded as a type of aroma or fragrance but were instead a sexual stimulant. The jury rejected these arguments, meaning that isobutyl nitrate is not classified as a medicine (and thus within scope of the Medicines Control Act 1968). Gerry Malone—the Conservative minister who had called for a "clampdown" on the sale of poppers—lost his Winchester seat in 1997. He challenged the result in court and won, resulting in a by-election. He lost again, this time by a landslide. This marked the end of his career in politics.

13 Shernoff 2006, 109–10. See generally Young 1994; Alcorn 1994. Debates about the safety of poppers within the queer community pre-date HIV/AIDS. See for example Kramer 1976.

14 Psychoactive Substances Act 2016 S2(1)(a).

15 Psychoactive Substances Act 2016 S2(1)(b).

16 Psychoactive Substances Act 2016 Schedule 1.

17 Hansard HC Debate Col 1445, January 20, 2016, https://publications.parliament.uk.

18 Hansard HC Debate Col 1454, January 20, 2016, https://publications.parliament.uk.

19 This is a reference to the use of poppers as a muscle relaxant for anal sex.

20 Hansard HC Debate, Col 1456, January 20, 2016, https://publications.parliament.uk.

21 Hansard HC Debate Col 1460, January 20, 2016, https://publications.parliament.uk.

22 Hansard HC Debate Col 37, October 27, 2015, https://publications.parliament.uk.

23 Freer came out as a gay man during the passing of the Marriage (Same Sex Couples) Act 2013 and would go on to marry under the legislation.

24 Hansard HC Debate, Col 1450, January 20, 2016, https://publications.parliament.uk.

25 It is important to note that the law did not criminalize possession per se (outside of custodian institutions) but by focusing on supply and possession with the intention to supply it mirrored earlier legislative interventions such as via the Medicines Act in making poppers difficult or impossible to obtain and thereby significantly restricted the ability to use them.

26 This is a long way from indicating cause—poppers might for example have been used alongside other chems during sex.
27 Local Government Act 1988, S28. The law was repealed by the Local Government Act 2003. See Baker 2022, and Colvin and Hawksley 1989.
28 The apology here appears to be that they—understandably I would suggest—were confused about whether the legislation included poppers within its scope.
29 [2018] EWCA Crim 1936.
30 Sometimes known as "laughing gas."
31 ACMD Review of Alkyl Nitrates ("Poppers") www.bl.uk (last accessed October 15, 2021.
32 [2018] 1 WLR 726.

BIBLIOGRAPHY
Alcorn, Keith. 1994. "Do Poppers Cause AIDS?" *Gay Times*, October, 22–23.
Altman, D. 1986. *AIDS in the Mind of America*. Garden City, NY: Anchor Press/ Doubleday.
Archer, Jesse. 2013. "Poppers Are Dead. Long Live Poppers." *The Advocate*, February/ March, 26–27.
Ashford, Chris. .2016. "Poppers Users Beware: A Draconian and Discriminatory Law Is on Its Way." *The Guardian*, January 21, www.theguardian.com.
Audo, I., M. E. Sanharawi, X. Vignal-Clermont, A. Villa, A. Morin, J. Conrath, D. Fompeydie, J. A. Sahel, K. Cocho-Nakashima, O. Goureaua, and M. Paques. 2011. "Foveal Damage in Habitual Poppers Users." *Archives of Ophthalmology* 129(6): 703–8.
Badge, Joshua. 2019. "Australia's Decision Not to Ban Poppers Is a Win for Sensible Drug Policy, but the Stigma Remains." *The Guardian*, January 20, www.theguardian .com.
Baker, Paul. 2022. *Outrageous! The Story of Section 28 and Britain's Battle for LGBT Education*. London: Reaktion Books.
BBC. 2016a. "What Exactly Are Legal Highs?." *BBC News*, May 26, www.bbc.co.uk.
———. 2016b. "Tory MP Crispin Blunt 'Outs Himself' as Popper User." *BBC News*, January 20, www.bbc.co.uk.
Bech, Henning. 1997. *When Men Meet: Homosexuality and Modernity*. Cambridge: Polity Press.
Bennett, Alan. 2004. *The History Boys*. London: Faber and Faber.
Berg, Charles. 1959. *Fear, Punishment, Anxiety and the Wolfenden Report*. London: George Allen & Unwin.
Bloom, Dan. 2016. "Tory MP Crispin Blunt Admits He Uses Poppers in Desperate Plea to Keep Them Legal." *The Mirror*, January 20, www.mirror.co.uk.
Brunton, T. L. 1867. "On the Use of Nitrate of Amyl in Angina Pectoris." *The Lancet* 2, 97–98.
Campbell, John. 2014. *Roy Jenkins: A Well-Rounded Life*. London: Jonathan Cape.
Chesser, Eustace. 1958. *Live and Let Live: The Moral of the Wolfenden Report*. London: Heinemann.

Cole, Harry. 2016. "Posh MP Partial to Partying Pickled on Poppers." *The Sun*, January 21.

Colvin, Madeleine and Jane Hawksley. 1989. *Section 28: A Practical Guide to the Law and Its Implications*. London: National Council for Civil Liberties.

Cory, Donald Webster. 1953. *The Homosexual Outlook: A Subjective Approach*. London: Peter Nevill.

Cossman, Brenda. 2020. "The 1969 Criminal Amendments Constituting the Terms of Gay Resistance." *University of Toronto Law Journal* 70(3): 245–62.

Coxon, A. P. M. 1996. *Between the Sheets: Sexual Diaries and Gay Men's Sex in the Era of AIDS*. London: Cassell.

Davies, Russell (ed.). 1994. *The Kenneth Williams Diaries*. London: HarperCollins.

Elaim, G., N. Macdonald, F. C. I. Hickson, Power R. Imrie, C. A. McGarrigle, K. A. Fenton, V. L. Gilbart, H. Ward, and B. G. Evans. 2008. On Behalf of the INSIGHT Collaborative Research Team, "Risky Sexual Behaviour in Context: Qualitative Results from an Investigation into Risk Factors for Seroconversion Among Gay Men Who Test for HIV." *Sexually Transmitted Infections* 84: 473–77.

Evans, A. 1981. "Poppers: An Ugly Side of Gay Business." *Coming Up!* November, http://paganpressbooks.com.

Florêncio, João. 2020. *Bareback Porn, Porous Masculinities, Queer Futures: The Ethics of Becoming-Pig*. London: Routledge.

Fortson, Rudi. 2018a. "The Psychoactive Substances Act 2016, the 'Medicinal Product' Exemption and Proving Psychoactivity." *Criminal Law Review* 3: 229–40.

———. 2018b. The Legal Status of "Poppers." www.rudifortson4law.co.uk.

———. 2018c. "Case Comment: Drug Offences: *R v. Rochester* (Kirk) Court of Appeal (Criminal Division): Lord Burnett CJ, Goos and Goose JJ; 17 August 2018; [2018] EWCA Crim 1936." *Criminal Law Review* 12: 1002–06.

Foucault, Michel, Nicole Morar, and Daniel W. Smith. 2011. "The Gay Science." *Critical Inquiry* 37(3): 385–403.

France, David. 2016. *How to Survive a Plague: The Story of How Activists and Scientists Tamed AIDS*. New York: Picador.

French R. and R. Power. 1998. "A Qualitative Study of the Social Contextual Use of Alkyl Nitrites (Poppers) Among Targeted Groups." *Journal of Drug Issues* 28(1): 57–76.

Gay News. 1976. "'Popper' Chemists Struck Off." November 18–December 1, no. 107, 1.

Gay Times. 1987. "Landlord Arrested at Vauxhall Tavern: Police Swoop on Poppers." January, 13.

———. 1995. "'Poppers' Prosecution Revived After Year's Delay." October, 36.

Goldberg, Jonathan. 1993. "Sodomy in the New World: Anthropologies Old and New." In *Fear of a Queer Planet: Queer Politics and Social Theory*, edited by Michael Warner, 3–18. Minneapolis: University of Minnesota Press.

Goltz, Dustin Bradley, Aimee Carrillo Rowe, Meredith M. Bagley, Kimberlee Perez, Raechel Tiff, and Jason Zingsheim. 2015. "Introducing Queer Praxis: Coming to Queer Love." In *Queer Praxis: Questions for LGBTQ Worldmaking*, edited by Dustin Bradley Goltz and Jason Zingsheim. New York: Peter Lang.

Hall, T. M., S. Shoptaw, and C. J. Reback. 2015."Sometimes Poppers Are Not Poppers: Huffing as an Emergent Health Concern Among MSM Substance Users." *Journal of Gay & Lesbian Mental Health* 19(1): 118–21.

Halperin, David M. 2011. "Michel Foucault, Jean Le Bitoux, and the Gay Science Lost and Found: An Introduction." *Critical Inquiry* 37(3): 371–80.

Hamilton, Angus. 1997. "Government Bans the Poppers That No One Uses." *Gay Times*, March.

Hemry M. (ed.). 2008. *Gay San Francisco: Eyewitness Drummer*. San Francisco: Palm Drive Publishing.

Hicklin, Aaron. 2010. "John Waters Is Not a Poppers Pig." *Out*, June/July.

Holleran, Andrew. 2019. *Dancer from the Dance*. London: Vintage.

Isherwood, Christopher. 2010. *The Sixties: Diaries, Volume Two: 1960–1969*. London: Chatto & Windus.

Jarman, Derek. 1992. *At Your Own Risk: A Saint's Testament*. London: Vintage

Jenkins, Roy. 1991. *A Life at the Centre*. London: Macmillan.

Kirkup, Kyle. 2020. "The Gross Indecency of Criminalizing HIV Non-Disclosure." *University of Toronto Law Journal* 70(3): 263–82.

Kissane, Séan and Karim Rehmani-White. 2020. *Derek Jarman: Protest!* London: Thames & Hudson.

Kramer, Norman D. 1976. "The Gay Man's Drug: Poppers." *The Advocate*, June 30, 22–23.

Lahr, John (ed.). 1998. *The Orton Diaries*. London: Methuen.

Lauritsen, J. 1993. "Political-Economic Construction of Gay Male Clone Identity." *Journal of Homosexuality* 24(3/4): 221–32.

Lauritsen J. and H. Wilson. 1986. *Death Rush: Poppers & AIDS*. New York: Pagan Press.

Le, Austin, Andrew Yockey, and Joseph J. Palamar. 2020. "Use of 'Poppers' among Adults in the United States, 2015–2017." *Journal of Psychoactive Drugs* 52(5): 433–39.

Leurs, Koen and Domitilla Olivieri. 2014. "Introduction." In *Everyday Feminist Research Praxis: Doing Gender in the Netherlands*, edited by Koen Leurs and Domitilla Olivieri. Newcastle upon Tyne: Cambridge Scholars Publishing.

Lusher, Adam. 2016. "Police Force Gets Legal Highs Ban Wrong—By Seizing Still Legal Poppers." *The Independent*, May 27, www.independent.co.uk.

Magee, Bryan. 1966. *One in Twenty: A Study of Homosexuality in Men and Women*. London: Secker & Warburg.

Martinez, Jacqueline M. 2015. "Human Contingency and Freedom: A Response to 'Queer Praxis.'" In *Queer Praxis: Questions for LGBTQ Worldmaking*, edited by Dustin Bradley Goltz and Jason Zingsheim. New York: Peter Lang.

Mercer, John. 2017. "Popperbate: Video Collage, Vernacular Creativity and the Scripting of the Gay Pornographic Body." *Porn Studies* 4(2): 242–56.

Northmore, David. 1997. "Ministers Overruled Report to Impose a Strict Poppers Ban." *The Pink Paper*, February 21.

Pasquir, Andrew. 2019. "Poppers: Reviewed from Best to Worst." *The Face*, August 14, https://theface.com.

Pérez Kimberlee and Daniel C. Brouwer. 2010. "Potentialities and Ambivalences in the Performance of Queer Decorum." *Text and Performance Quarterly* 30(3): 317–23.

Pink Paper. 1989. "Poppers—Case Dismissed." March 18, 3.

———. 1996. "Zipperstore Poppers Trial Date Set." January 12, 2.

Robbins, Job. 2015. "Legal Highs." *Criminal Law & Justice Weekly*, 179, 444.

Rofes, E. 1998. *Dry Bones Breathe: Gay Men Creating Post-AIDS Identities and Cultures.* New York: Harrington Park Press.

Romanelli, F., K. M. Smith, A. C. Thornton, and C. Pomeroy. 2004. "Poppers: Epidemiology and Clinical Management of Inhaled Nitrate Abuse." *Pharmacotherapy* 24(1): 69–78.

Schwartz, Cameron, Danya Fast, and Rod Knight. 2020. "Poppers, Queer Sex and a Canadian Crackdown: Examining the Experiences of Alkyl Nitrate Use Among Young Sexual Minority Men." *International Journal of Drug Policy* 77, 102670.

Shernoff, M. 2006. *Without Condoms: Unprotected Sex, Gay Men & Barebacking.* New York: Routledge.

Smith, David. 1996. "Poppers 'Ban' Cost £47,000." *Gay Times*, August.

Stevens, Alex, Rudi Fortson, Fiona Measham, and Harry Sumnall. 2015. "Legally Flawed, Scientifically Problematic, Potentially Harmful: The UK Psychoactive Substance Bill." *International Journal of Drug Policy* 26: 1167–70.

Tripp, C. A. 1977. *The Homosexual Matrix.* London: Quartet Books.

Tudor Rees, J. and Harley V. Usill (eds.) 1955. *They Stand Apart: A Critical Survey of the Problems of Homosexuality.* London: William Heinemann.

Vaccher, Stefanie. 2020. "Poppers Can Now Be Sold in Pharmacies, But Getting Them Might Not Be So Easy." *The Conversation*, February 11, https://theconversation.com.

Vaccher, Stefanie J., Mohamed A. Hammond, Adam Bourne, Toby Lea, Bridget G. Haire, Martin Holt, Peter Saxton, Brent Mackie, Joshua Badge, Fengyi Ji, Lisa Maher, and Garrett Prestage. 2020. "Prevalence, Frequency, and Motivations for Alkyl Nitrate Use Among Gay, Bisexual and Other Men Who Have Sex with Men in Australia." *International Journal of Drug Policy* 76, 102659.

Waites, Matthew. 2013. "United Kingdom: Confronting Criminal Histories and Theorising Decriminalisation as Citizenship and Governmentality." In *Human Rights, Sexual Orientation and Gender Identity in The Commonwealth*, edited by Corinne Lennox and Matthew Waites, 145–81. London: University of London Press.

Young, I. 1994. "The Poppers Story: The Rise and Fall and Rise of 'The Gay Drug.'" *Steam* 2(4). www.virusmyth.com.

Zmith, Adam. 2021. *Deep Sniff: A History of Poppers and Queer Futures.* London: Repeater Books.

10

Trans Bodies, Gay Sexuality, Dysphoria

Sexual Freedom in the Bathhouse and Beyond

IDO KATRI

Just before Tel Aviv Pride in June 2019, the Israeli police raided the new-est and internationally oriented gay bathhouse in Tel Aviv, the Sauna. Officers stormed into the club at 3 a.m., armed with flashlights and video cameras. The footage, proudly released to the media by morning, opens with a squad of officers vigorously walking toward the club, some of them wearing latex gloves,[1] as one officer prepares the others for an "aggressive and sharp entry." In the following scene, the camera pans the lower bodies of the patrons, dressed only in towels, as they are lined up and their personal belongings are searched for illicit drugs. The club was ordered to shut down indefinitely for drug trafficking. Fourteen men were detained and two club owners were arrested (Blumental 2019).

The well-established Tel Aviv gay community was outraged (Blumen-tal 2019). The CEO of the Israeli LGBT task force said the raid was a violent act against the LGBT community and declared that they "will not stay silent regarding the police actions" (Herman and Kraus n.d.). The city's Deputy Mayor and liaison to the LGBT community said: "the choice to carry out such a raid in the middle of Pride [. . .] is wrong, un-necessary and detrimental for the trust relationship between the police and the LGBT community" (Blumental 2019). Police raids aren't good for business, or for pinkwashing.[2] The police apologized, all charges were dropped, and the club reopened within 24 hours ("!?מידע מוֹדיעיני מידע מוֹדיעיני למחרת היינו פתוחים כרגיל Police Intel?! We Were Open the Next Day" 2019).

One week after the raid, on pride weekend, the Sauna made headlines again, this time for expelling Amit Shai (not a real name), who was later identified as a trans man. Amit and a friend spent almost an hour in the club, when a staff member asked them to leave because "he is a woman," and because other patrons were disturbed by his presence (Naor 2019; 09:01). The two were escorted to the locker rooms when a patron, apparently the one who complained, addressed Amit using a female pronoun and said that "her body did not look good to his eyes" (Vahash 2019).

In the following days, as queer activists on social media demanded answers from the Sauna (Landau n.d.), the Sauna clarified that Amit was expelled after violating a policy requiring all patrons to be topless. When questioned whether they asked Amit to be shirtless, the Sauna replied: "We will not ask a woman or a coccinelle[3] to undress in a gay bathhouse." The Sauna also added that Amit is still "transitioning" and when "he's done, he will be welcomed at the Sauna like everyone else" (GenderTuck Magazine 2019). The next day the Sauna issued an official response, claiming that Amit had the face and body of a woman, and that Sauna staff expelled him after many complaints from other clientele. After much consideration, the Sauna declared that it would allow any *man* to enter under the condition of having "a general male appearance without female breasts" (Sauna Tel-Aviv 2019b).[4]

The ethical duplicity of the Sauna is blatant. In their official response following the police raid, the Sauna emphasized how the police demanded patrons to undress in front of the cameras and apologized to their entire clientele for the humiliation they suffered (Sauna Tel-Aviv 2019a). Just a week later, it turned out that trans people were not part of the general clientele whose dignity and respect are to be protected. In the second incident, the Sauna took it upon itself to police queer bodies for not undressing, or for not having the ability to present a specific kind of naked masculinity. The Sauna displayed its juridical power over the sexed body first by excluding Amit in the name of an imagined collective desire to avoid seeing bodies like his, and second by asserting that his transition is incomplete, that his body is wrong.

As news of the incident broke, I reached out to Amit in my capacity as legal advisor of the Gila Project for Trans Empowerment, a mutual aid activist group based in Tel Aviv, offering to organize a legal appeal to demand an apology and a clarification of guidelines from the Sauna. However, Amit did not want to go public about the incident because, as they said, they are not a "classical FTM," and do not identify or present in a binary way. Instead of taking legal action, Amit's case prompted me to offer my own account of experimenting with trans embodiments in gay bathhouses.

Bathhouses' Mischiefs

In the summer of 2012, I attended a birthday party at the Kanal, an iconic Berlin queer space, with the person who was soon to become my partner. She told me about an action that took place in Paris, where she had been living for the past decade. Protesting the exclusion of trans men from a local gay bathhouse, a group of trans and cis gay men, including her (she was presenting as a gay boy at the time), went in together, unsettling the idea that trans bodies are not desired in the bathhouse by cis bodies. After telling this story she added that we should go to a bathhouse together sometime. My angry inner trans pedagogue came to life and I scolded her about which bodies can and cannot go into these spaces, with or without cis bodies to protect them. More than a political claim, I intuitively felt that I would be less welcomed in a bathhouse than the Paris group, as I had not medically transitioned at that time. I did not register the fact that she might be asking me to accompany her to a bathhouse not to protest, but to fuck.

We have laughed about that incident over the years. One summer morning in 2015 we found ourselves with nothing to do on Church Street in Toronto. We decided to go to Steamworks, a local bathhouse. She was still presenting as a gay boy and it had been two years since I started taking T and had top surgery. At that point, we passed as a young cis gay couple (albeit ethnically ambiguous). Nevertheless, before entering we decided to ask about their trans policy. The two people at the front desk looked confused and called the person in charge, who said: "they cannot prevent people who have M on their ID from entering the club."

We must have looked shocked, as the person added that it is "a legal issue." He explained that because it is a men's club, they cannot stop anybody who is legally male from coming in. He asked us how we felt about it. My partner told them this was outrageous, as not all people can reclassify their sex. The staff started mumbling and the man next in line shouted that we were wasting everybody's time. The people at the front desk and the one next in line were all presenting as whiter and older than we were, which could explain their unfamiliarity with trans inclusive discourse, yet their othering of trans bodies nevertheless affronted us. Feeling angry and confused we decided to leave, even though I had my health card with me which listed me as M. I am still unsure if they realized either of us is trans. It is possible they thought we were worried about the presence of trans people, and not that one of us was trans. We felt that we should have asked more pointed questions, like: Why is a gay establishment enforcing state regulations of gender? But we did not.

It took us three years to go to another gay bathhouse together. In 2018, we walked into the Tel Aviv Sauna without asking about their trans policy. The staff and patrons made us feel welcomed and desired, with their eyes and touch. Encouraged by that experience, later that year, at the end of a long weekend in Berlin, we decided to try one of the many local bathhouses. At this point my partner had feminized her upper body. Although we were let into Der Boiler, patrons pointed and laughed at us. We quickly left, resenting Der Boiler patrons for demeaning our gendered bodies.

Our bathhouse experiences confront us, and you, with broader questions: What about trans bodies within men-only erotic space awakens a need for policing, and what are the different modes of enforcement deployed? Why is a masculine chest more significant than female assigned genitals in the sexual economy of the gay bathhouse? Why can't queers (morally speaking) make space for "queers like them," i.e., cis gay men? I will consider these questions through three concurrent frameworks: the shift in the "wrong body" narratives of the administrative state—from external truth of bodies to internal truth of identity; manifestation of gay governance in low-level enforcement of gender expectations; and the tension between trans articulation of private gender and gay articulations of private sexuality.

I will fantasize answering these questions by suggesting that the negation of bodies is an integral aspect of modern gender identities and sexualities and that we need a post-dysphoric imaginary that can negate the negation of bodies and hold the interrelations of bodies, identities, and desires. Following Talia M. Bettcher (2014) and through trans encounters with gay sexual spaces, I argue that current formulation of trans "gender identity" requires negating the trans body as wrong. A recognition of self-identified gender is granted to those whose bodies are incongruent with their birth-assigned sex (identified by their genitals). The very act of public self-identification requires negating one's body as wrong, as incongruent, and specifically as incongruent with its assigned

sexual capacities. It's a recognition granted according to the logic of gender dysphoria:

> a significant distress and/or problems functioning arising from a conflict
> between the way one feels and thinks of themselves and their physical or
> assigned gender. ("What Is Gender Dysphoria?" n.d.)

But maybe trans (and non-trans) bodies go beyond this logic to find
pleasure and not just distress and/or problems in the incongruence of
physical and assigned gender. Can it be that we are all turned on by difference within ourselves and in other? By offering a lived experience of
holding together the subject and their lack, the subject and their other,
incongruence can open up space to experience the "pre-personal potentialities to differ" (Colebrook 2015, 229) that are not yet stabilized in
coherent categories of identity. A post-dysphoric imaginary offers a repertoire for reconstituting our genders and sexualities, and for opening to
a desire we had not yet felt, a playground for experiments in intimacy,
proliferation of pleasures, and curiosity. This is what's at stake for the gay
bathhouse in constituting trans bodies as wrong.

Wrong Bodies

Gay bathhouses, like many other sex-segregated institutions, are challenged by trans bodies. Incidents of excluding trans might be attempts
to maintain the bathhouse's own gender identity as spaces of coherence
where stable *gay* masculinity[5] exists. By noting "right" and "wrong"
trans bodies, a line is drawn between those deserving inclusion within
the category male and those who jeopardize the category, and thus the
bathhouse, as a male only space. In these incidents, the bathhouses are
not serving as guardians of a given category of maleness, if such a thing
exists, but rather a temporal gay manifestation of what it means to be
male. This can explain why I, as a binary presenting trans masculine
person, was welcomed at the Sauna while Amit was not. This might also
explain tensions arising from effeminate male-assigned bodies within
those same spaces.

I have elsewhere diagnosed the administrative state as suffering from
anxiety over trans bodies unsettling its own gender identity as a space

where coherent sexed bodies exist. And, like the bathhouses, the administrative state attempts to overcome its anxiety regarding gender indeterminacy through laws and policies aimed at discerning "wrong" and "right" trans (legal) bodies, those who deserve to have their sex reclassified and those who do not. The endless need for reclassification arises because birth assignment of sex is in itself an ongoing process, a reiterated citation. In this process certain genital configurations of newborns, vaginas or penises, are unified with a set of gender expectations through a differentiated legal status, M/F. These are expectations that specific gender expression will be congruent to the assignment—that those assigned "F" will be feminine and will be perceived by others as women and those assigned "M" will be masculine and perceived by others as men. Gender expectations are policed and enforced in the daily interaction with private and public actors (Spade 2008, 775).

As Paisley Currah argues, the legal classification of newborns based on visible genitals signifies a position within the reproductive process rather than reflecting actual reproductive capacity (2022, 42). Those who later reclassify their sex are expected to signify a "new" position within the reproductive order through a negation of the sexual capacities of the assigned body. But more than being required to negate sexual capacities of the body, they are required to perform a desire to negate those capacities, to *look* as if they have a certain kind of genitals.

The gender identities of those who fail or refuse this process of self-identification through a performance of self-negation are considered less "real." If you don't look like you have a penis you are less of a man, if you don't look like you have a vagina you are less of a woman (Bettcher 2014, 388). One only needs to look as if they have certain genitals rather than have them, exactly because nobody displays their genitals in public spaces, they only perform them in Butlerian terms. Genitals are invisible, not to say imagined, almost up until the moment of sexual encounter.[6]

This can explain how gender self-identification hits its political and affective boundary when a "female" breasted man or male assigned person who feminized their breast seeks entry to a gay bathhouse. From its visibility, the upper body gains its determinative power as a signifier of a position within the reproductive process, making it a conclusive marker of truth, like skin color (Hall 1997). The shape of the upper body is visible through clothes, and an exposed upper body is a sign of masculinity in most Europe-centric cultures. You don't want to be a man if you want to have tits, and you don't really want to be a woman if you desire gay sex. Negation becomes a constituting act of both self-identified gender and sexualities.

When the Berlin patrons of Der Boiler point and laugh, they displace their anxieties around gendered incoherence, suggesting that a person who has femininized their upper body and went to a gay bathhouse is less authentic than they are. When the Tel Aviv Sauna allows only those whose have a "general male appearance" and no breasts to enter, it does not simply demand one to have a different body per se, but rather a body that negates the appearance of femininity. When the Toronto Steamworks staff concedes that they cannot prevent those who legally reclassified their sex to M from entering, they link these private acts of enforcement to broader schemes of regulating gender through differentiated sex classification.

Read together as a manifestation of a desire for "right" bodies, and in relation to sex reclassification policies, the bathhouse's acts and policies constitute another site of gay governance, that is, sites in which cis gay men acquire juridical power to "conduct the conduct of men," or more precisely to conduct who can conduct themselves as men. The enforcement of birth assignment's phallocentric logic by gay bathhouses, manifested by a repudiation of breasts as the epitome of the feminine, reinforces heterosexuality at the root of their homosexuality (Butler 1997, 194). Put differently, what makes a gay bathhouse gay? The bathhouses' actions in the incidents described imply their answer: bodies *performing* cis masculinity who want and perform sex acts with other bodies *performing* cis masculinity. But must gay space, for the space to be gay, so unforgivingly police and genitalize gender?[7] What do they stand to lose?

Playing Police

Aeyal Gross builds on the concept of governance feminism to explore gay governance as "the forms whereby LGBT people and ideas get incorporated into state, state-like and state-affiliated power" (2017, 345). Gross identifies gay governance as occurring on multiple institutional levels, including: at the city level through funding of LGBT organizations; at the state level through pro-gay legislation increasing the carceral power of the state; and on the global level through the work of international financial institutions and human rights instruments to promote LGBT rights (359–61).

Gross argues that gay governance "represents a more 'respectable' politics, and queer life" (2017, 352) than previous gay attempts to intervene in public life and politics. Gross recounts queer activists' protests in 2009 against Tel Aviv's renovation of Independence Park,[8] the main cruising area in the city. Independence Park served as a main meeting site for gay men during times where homosexuality was outlawed and ousted. Until the formal revocation of the law prohibiting "unnatural sex" in 1988, the police regularly raided the park (Koka 2013). In the early 2000s, part of the broader renovation of the city included installing bright lights, uprooting thick bushes, and increasing "security" patrols (Ilany 2009). These measures effectively and intentionally ended gay cruising on site.

Queer activists objected to the renovations, claiming they would oblige people to "pay money to meet people in some club or Sauna" (Ilany 2009). The mayor's liaison to the LGBT community at the time argued that the gay community has "matured" and no longer requires or desires cruising areas. As Gross describes, the area surrounding the park has been rebranded and appropriated by consumer culture and Israeli pinkwashing politics. For example, the nearby beach was designated as the city's gay beach, whose rainbow-colored parasols, installed and maintained by city hall, regularly appear in publicity for gay tourism in Tel Aviv. In exchange, Gross explains, "for their donning a normative face," gay community representatives were "guaranteed a measure of support from the state" (Gross 2017, 350–51).

Gross's critique of the "gay deal" resonates with other accounts of the sexual citizenship of gays and lesbians which enabled limited access to life chances, specifically to legal recognition of their relationships and families. These statutory and social entitlements largely hinge on adopting heteronormative standards of self-governance (Cossman 2007, 19; Eng 2010, 27–28). The "gay deal" worked for the Tel Avivian gay elite. Recall the response of the Tel Aviv mayor's liaison for the LGBT community to the police raids on the Sauna club just a decade after the gay sanctioned expulsion of public cruising from the city. For the liaison, the raid violated the otherwise well-established "trust relationship" between the police and the gay community.

Gross casts gay radical deviance in opposition to gay governance respectability, but cis white gays in Tel Aviv and throughout the West became respectful while keeping their deviant sexual practices alive. From the bathhouse to Grindr, gay sex might be happening in private rather than public spaces, but it nevertheless is still commonly non-monogamous, anonymous, and involves multiple partners, for both married and single men (Sarson 2019, 303). These days the police are trusted with protecting these private Sodom and Gomorrahs. How can this be possible? Policing of trans bodies in gay bathhouses indicates that the political formations of respectability and deviance might be more reciprocal than conflicting. Indeed, we might even suggest that gay governance is what allows the deviant to produce a performance of respectability.

When Toronto Steamworks staff claim that they cannot prevent those who reclassified their sex from entering, they hide their political actions in the law's shadow, and affective residue, of the law. Steamworks uses the long arm of the law as an instrument for sexual play by using sex reclassification policies. In doing so, Steamworks situated the gay bathhouse within the state apparatus, employing low-level bureaucratic enforcement of gender regulations through sex classification (Spade 2008, 773). This is gay governance in action. Trans inclusion, as the staff said, "is a legal matter," and not a matter of sexual preferences, politics, ethics, or *judgment.*

Resorting to the law is a paradoxical turn for the gay bathhouse. As Joseph Fischel argued, for the purpose of identifying sexual partners in the context of legally consensual sex, the answer to the question "are you a man?" can hardly constitute a truth claim (2019, 97). Social constructions, historical contingencies, and cultural differences make such a question answerable on social and political terms, but not erotically or juridically (210, fn8). Asking about sex classification might provide a yes or no answer, but it would not solve the question of body and desire (or even of sexual consent). The M/F solution can only provide an instrument for self-governance for managing the bathhouse's sense of insecurity (Cossman 2013, 239).

By nourishing their police fetish and fantasizing that the political exclusion of trans bodies really is a "legal matter," the bathhouse reaffirms the normativity claim of the mainstream gay movement. Exactly because the bathhouse is a space of non-monogamous, multiple partner-, and anonymous sex, the pseudo-juridical acts of policing the outer limits of sex and gender allow the bathhouse to integrate itself under gay respectability politics.

In Western liberal democracies and elsewhere, the dominant discourse surrounding gay cis men has transitioned from "save our children" (Frank 2013, 127–28) to "the kids are all right" through the HIV/AIDS epidemic (Eng 2010, 27) and its legacies of activism, public mourning and the formation of wide political alliances (Schulman 2021, 153, 500). Between protecting children from gays and gay parenting, many bathhouses were shut down in the name of HIV/AIDS prevention (385). That they reopened, and many flourished, speaks to the symbiotic relationship between gay respectability and gay promiscuity.

The performance of gay governance in the bathhouse does not necessitate a direct reference to actual legal regulation. The Tel Aviv Sauna's revised policy, excluding those who do not have a male appearance and/or have a feminine upper body, also participates in the administrative regulation of gender expectations. The Sauna's revised policy enforces a *presumption* of masculinity of sexed male bodies. The pointing and laughing in Der Boiler are the lowest level of enforcement. Demarcating the contours of the "right" and "wrong" sexed bodies, by marking out those who are "wrong," enforces the gender expectations assigned at birth.

Steamworks itself has been inconsistent in its reliance on sex classification but consistent in its enforcement of gender expectations. In 2018, Justin Jolie reported being asked, "how do you identify?" when arriving at Steamworks wearing makeup and replied, "'I dunno, my ID says I'm a guy, but it's however I feel like on the day." Jolie was told that Steamworks does not allow entry to anyone wearing makeup. This time Steamworks did not think Jolie's sex classification mattered as they attempted to enforce the broader scheme of sex classification, upholding the congruence between sex assignments and the expectation of internal and external (sexual but not only) qualities, characteristics, and abilities.

Other gender nonconforming people were also turned away at Steamworks. In another incident, Torontonian DJ Scooter McCreight was turned away at the door for wearing makeup. After McCreight reported the incident over Twitter, Streamworks apologized and provided the following statement: "As a club for men, we welcome ALL men, INCLUDING Transmen or individuals who identify/present as Male "[emphasis in original] (Salerno 2018). Steamworks's statement meshes men and male, continuing the logics of birth assignment sex, as male is constituted as an identity position or attribute, that is equivalent to the category men (Butler 1994, 2). Simultaneously, "transmen" is constituted as a different position from both man and male through the compounding of trans and men and through the use of "or" distinguishing between trans men and those "who identify/present as Male."

In their statement on "ALL men," Steamworks took a similar position to the Tel Aviv Sauna adopted in 2019. And indeed, the Sauna enforces similar logic with respect to feminine gender markers. On a Friday night in June 2021, as I was revising this piece, we thought of going again to the Sauna, where we had fun in 2018. I called ahead and asked if I can come with my partner, who is a trans woman. The guy who answered the phone was lovely, but said that trans women are not allowed entry, nor is anyone else "wearing makeup." I asked if it mattered whether she had surgery, but he was insistent and said they had "many complaints" from patrons. Makeup was never mentioned in the Sauna policy statement in 2019 (allowing entry to any man presenting "a general male appearance without female breasts").

The prohibition on wearing makeup, even by those legally classified as "M" who do not identify as women, is a case in point for the performative theory of gender. Steamworks' and the Tel Aviv Sauna's policy seem to be more or less ad hoc, we-know-a-man-when-we-see-one. But since nobody knows who a man is, the rules keep changing. In this context, breasts are then something like makeup, a performative feminizing accessory.

In taking on the arbitrary enforcement of gender expectation associated with birth assignments, the gay bathhouse and its patrons participate in the reiterated citation of birth assignment. To the extent that the category men (or "ALL men") refuses and includes the category male (and "transmen"), the distinction between them performs a reduction of sex to an anatomical identity, distinct from an act or practice (Butler 1994, 4). However the subject identifies, the discriminatory impulse is triggered by markers of female reproductive capacity or by its feminine proxies (breasts or makeup).

You're Just Like You're Daddy

As a trans legal studies scholar, it is an easy go-to to blame *the gays* for running over their nonconforming siblings in their struggle for normativity. But that's just an oversimplified version of the story, and worse, it conflicts with my urge to guard the sexiness of the bathhouses and gay sexuality at large.[9] In the conflict of desires, another side of the story comes into view in which gender identity as a trope of *trans governance* is failing gender nonconforming subjects. Naming and describing trans governance requires an analysis of the power relations in which trans agents also "conduct the conducts" of others (Halley 2018b, 6).

Governance is not bad or good just by virtue of its being governance, it has its costs (Halley 2018a, xii). Lobbying bathhouses to revise their policies is a form of trans governance par excellence. There would be no controversy if trans demands had no political clout at all. This kind of lobby represents a fraction of power trans agents already hold, although trans agents still do not hold very much. Nevertheless, we can no longer say as trans agents that we are completely outsiders, and perhaps we have been negotiating with power for a long time (Stryker and Sullivan 2009, 60).

Like *the gays*, trans advocates, lawyers, and scholars have gained unprecedented access to state, state-like, and state-affiliated power in recent years. There is much to be said about what kind of trans bodies (overwhelmingly masculine, white, able) are being ushered into academic positions, government jobs, and international advocacy NGOs, and what kind of trans bodies (mostly feminine, racialized, poor) are still systemically destined to premature death. In the context of this chapter, the negotiations between trans men and gay bathhouses drives those institutions to emphasize their masculinity (whether in including or excluding trans men) through a repudiation of the feminine, the trans feminine (*and other trans masculine people* who might be faggy, femmy, etc.).

Much of the formal legal progress that provided the trans movement with access to power has been achieved through centering the idea that birth assigned sex is mutable but gender identity isn't (Currah 2014, 197). A prominent expression of this mode of trans governance is given in the definition of gender identity found in the trans-led Yogyakarta Principles on the Application of International Human Rights Law in Relation to Sexual Orientation and Gender Identity as "each person's deeply felt internal and individual experience of gender, which may or may not correspond with the sex assigned at birth." This definition and the principles on international law are understood as state obligations to: "Take all necessary legislative, administrative and other measures to fully respect and legally recognise each person's self-defined gender identity." The principles have been exported globally and contributed to numerous regulatory and legislative efforts to codify gender identity as a protected legal category.

The legal recognition of innate gender identity as a derivative of a right to privacy and autonomy makes invisible the reality in which assigned sex at birth, as a legal effect, continues to construct public spaces, interactions, and distribution of life chances. A right for private gender identity suggests that gender is just a matter of the heart and not a pivotal aspect of the biopolitical order. Susan Stryker defines gender in biopolitical terms as: "an apparatus within which all bodies are taken up, which creates material effects through bureaucratic tracking that begins with birth, ends with death, and traverses all manner of state-issued or state-sanctioned documentation practices in between" (Stryker 2014, 39).

By arguing that gender identity rather than assigned sex is immutable, trans governance upholds the immutability of gender expectations. Formulating gender identity as a legal right suggests that the congruence of birth assignment and certain gender expectations is wrong only in exceptional cases. According to this logic, in the normal course of events it is justified to expect that all those born with a penis would identify and be identifiable as men and those born with a vagina would identify and be identifiable as women. Paradoxically, the same logic that drives anti-trans violence and discrimination is reinforced through the legal codification of gender identity.

As a legal concept, gender identity allows for the ambiguity of sex as an act, identity, and apparatus of subjection to be "split into univocal dimensions in order to make the claim that the kind of sex that one is and the kind of sex that one does" belong to three segregated registries

(Butler 1994, 4). As a legal concept, private gender identity denies that gender practices are intimately interconnected to sexuality—the question of who you want to be and who you want to be with cannot be separated, psychically or politically (Stryker 2014, 39). The gayness of the trans man (like the paternity of the trans dad) exposes the co-dependent relations of gender and sexuality and the inability of privacy and autonomy to address the trapping of all legal subjects into sexed bodies. What happens when private sexual orientation and private gender identity grope each other in a dark room?

The Clash of the Deviants

The Toronto bathhouse raids of the early 1980s demonstrate how the normalization of privacy kept the bathhouses open and simultaneously facilitated the rise of gay and lesbian formal equality. Brenda Cossman shows that in resisting state violence, gay advocates argued for a broader understating of privacy that includes sexual acts between consenting adults occurring behind closed doors (2020, 259). The bathhouse is presumptively more "public" than a domestic bedroom, but it is neither strictly one nor the other, domestic or public (Cooper 2007, 244). It is possible to act privately in public, claimed gay rights activists (Cossman 2020, 260).

The broadened definition of privacy, which includes the "social making of intimacy," was a watershed success for gay and lesbian rights in Canada (Cossman 2020, 261). A right for private sexuality presumes sexual difference and an inherent difference between homosexual and heterosexual sex arising from the sexed body. The privacy afforded to gay sexuality within the intimacy of the sexual encounter is much like the privacy afforded to gender identity within the counters of the sexed body. A socially constructed private sexuality redraws the public/private lines along the dark silhouette of consenting adults groping each other; a private gender identity redraws the public/private lines along the contours of the trans body.

Both formulations of privacy presume a self-governing individual armed with an alienable right over the private property of their body and the sovereignty to act upon that property (Stryker and Sullivan 2009, 57). Both formulations reject the relationships between individual corporeality and the body politic and the constituting dependency of the individual on others: as if one just has to be left alone in a dark room to find their innate gender identity or their sexual orientation. Only when you meet someone else in the dark room (or fantasize about meeting them) could you even "know," in the biblical sense, your sexual orientation or gender identity.[10] It is never just about you. Or, as Fischel, asserts in the context of sexual deception allegations against trans people: "Gender, like sex, like sexuality, is made and remade relationally, not individually" (Fischel 2019, 115).

Thinking of sexual orientation and gender identity as a thing of the heart and not as a relational process creates a contradiction between the two formulations of privacy. Private gender identity assumes that "real sex" is determined by innate disposition rather than birth-observed genitals, and entails rejecting the sexed body. Private gay sexuality presumes the contours of the sexed body of those partaking in the sexual encounter it protects. The presumed contours of the sexed body are based on the gender expectation that those identifiable as men have penises. Thus, the autonomy of cis gay men to have sexual encounters with each other contradicts the sexual autonomy of trans and nonbinary people to not conform to normative gender expectations (Fischel 2019, 104). Seemingly, the individuated sexual deviant and the individuated gender deviant are structurally unable to enter a contractual social relationship. Can they have sex? Maybe they shouldn't even try?

Post-Dysphoric Sexy Time

I am not suggesting that cis gay men and trans people should not have sex with each other or share the same sexual spaces. I am wondering whether gender identity and sexual orientation are the proper objects to describe the interdependency of desires for a body of one's own and for the bodies of others (Long Chu 2017). We need better imagery for the encounters of bodies and selves, which the current dysphoric epistemology of gender and sexuality fails to provide—a post-dysphoric imaginary.

The post dysphoric flickers, perhaps just for a moment, in the visceral experience currently called dysphoria. What I mean is that the experience (whether dysphoric or euphoric) of incongruence "between the way one feels and think of themselves and their physical or assigned gender" is an experience of being yourself and your other. It's an experience of simultaneously having and being in psychoanalytic terms, at least as Dina Georgis (and other trans affirmative Lacanian theorists) generously reads them (Georgis 2013, 338; Gozlan 2018). And this aspect of embodiment is hot because we are all turned on by difference, even within ourselves.

I do not attempt to claim that dysphoria does not exist as a subjective feeling or that it is simply a matter of adopting a positive image of one's body. The personal incidents I described in this chapter, even the positive ones, heightened my own sense of dysphoria, as did other encounters with gay sexuality. I am suggesting that knowledge of oneself acquired through the sexed body is not only codified in terms of congruence and incongruence. The significant (social, historical, political, and juridical) distress arising from incongruence between the way people feel and think of themselves and their physical or assigned bodies fuels the drive to differentiate. The post dysphoric turns away from the drive to differentiate toward the desire for difference.

I cannot say I have attained unlimited access to this time and space, but I have visited it for a heartbeat of two (among these heartbeats some of the fastest were shared in the dark with strangers). I know other women, men, and nonbinary people who have accessed the post-dysphoric imaginary, some have birthed themselves through it. I have a feeling others have been there too. This is not to say that I think we can or should self-govern ourselves out of the necropolitics of trans lives by adopting a counternarrative of transgender congruency. Instead, I invite us to an imaginary residing beyond the distinction between "right bodies" destined to live and "wrong bodies" destined to the in-between zones of life and death (Snorton and Haritaworn 2013).

The post-dysphoric imaginary is not a vision of trans optimism or pessimism in and of itself (Gill-Peterson 2021), in the sense that it is not facing toward the future or the past to describe the here and now, but rather is a layer of the here and now. A post-dysphoric imaginary is constituted by flickering moments of transcendence (into an imminent space) beyond the ongoing symbolic chatter on the binaries of gender identities and sexed bodies. It is a space that operates outside the imperative to negate one's body or the body of another in order to become a subject, an experience of being aroused by incongruences.

Maybe gender dysphoria, like gender identity, has different (though interconnected) meanings as a subjective experience, a normative concept, a framework for governance, and as a libidinal drive. Fuck it, what if there is no personal experience of dysphoria? Maybe trans people, older gay men, and the administrative state share one dysphoric experience. Perhaps we are all just trying to deal with the difficulties of holding onto the conflicting nature of gender and sexuality, some by projecting that conflict onto trans subjects and others, including trans subjects themselves, by appealing for recognition—recognition that forever fails to deliver its promise of noncontradiction. A closed circuit of negations.

The imperative negation of the dysphoric hides the possibility for bodily becomings "extending beyond the limits of dominant corporeal and conceptual logics" (Garner 2014). An abundance of possibilities for cumming and other erotic bodily becomings are lost when the bathhouse excludes trans bodies. Maybe the spheres of (gay) sexual and (trans) gender autonomy need not be so neatly separable that they must clash against each other. Would the presence of a man with a micropenis (which can be smaller than some trans clitoris) breach the autonomy of others in the bathhouse? Would men with gynecomastia or other kinds of "man boobs" be asked to masculinize their bodies? Would a complaint that a "normal" naked body of a man assigned M at birth does "not look good to his eyes" justify expulsion from a bathhouse? The answer to these questions is most probably no.[11]

When the right to private gender identity and the right to private sexual orientation penetrate each other, a contradiction emerges in which two self-identified men have "heterosexual" sex and simultaneously two opposite birth assigned bodies have "homosexual" sex. How can anyone be gay and straight at same time through a singular act of having sex with another person? It is only possible if we clearly distinguish between identity and actions.

Trans sexuality (as all other sexualities) exceeds the either/or logics of sex as either act or identity (Long Chu 2017). Instead of focusing on either identities or actions, perhaps the bathhouse dynamics are better encapsulated though the very process of identification that "constitutes an individual as a certain kind of subject" (Cameron and Kulick 2003, 139).

Identity is not a matter of pure agency, autonomous self-determination that can be taken on and off like a piece of clothing, and identities are not simply imposed upon the subject from the outside. The subject exceeds the either/or logic of having/being but remains bound to them. The shift between external and internal identification at present holds the paradox of subjection as "the process of becoming subordinated by power as well as the process of becoming a subject" (Butler 1997, 2). The identification process constitutes the ontological status of gender identity and sexual orientation.

The external and internal aspects of identification suggest that the tension in the bathhouse cannot be answered from the private individual point of view but instead requires an acceptance of interdependence (Butler 2020, 47). The trans body in the gay bathhouse manifests the limits of the differentiation of bodies in becoming a subject through subjection by making the ambiguity unavoidable. At the same time, the sexualized trans body suggests that the indisputable either/or reproductive nature of sexuality (enabling the othering of homosexuality as that which is not "natural") and the unquestionable having/being logic of sexual difference (enacting and veiling the sex/gender distinction) are both highly disputable and questionable. To paraphrase Andrea Long Chu, within the gayness of trans masculinity, the gap between liking men and being a man is epistemologically blurred (2017).

The lived experience of trans sexuality as exceeding the either/or nature does not stop at the gay bathhouse. Long Chu analyzes the rise of anti-trans feminine TERF politics as another site of conflict between (trans) gender identity and (cis) sexuality. Chu argues that when self-identified feminist cis women choose to date men, their commitment to fighting male supremacy at the level of consciousness is questioned. In having sexual relations with men, they fail to adhere to the feminist axiom that the personal is political. In a psychic response to their conflict of desires, self-identified feminist cis women targeted lesbian trans women, arguing that their self-identification as and desire for women are acts of male supremacy.

Trans women are not a random minority target. When TERFS go after trans women by accusing them of false *identity*, that accusation is always also fueled by fear of trans *sexuality*, sexuality unmoored from, and unmooring of, gendered identity. From a trans perspective on lived experience, attempting to make the private public and the personal political is as futile as claiming they are neatly segregated. The simultaneous homo/heterosexuality of trans bodies triggers the "dread of desire's ungovernability" (Long Chu 2017). The question of who one is, and who one wants to be and to have, cannot be answered separately, either concerning gender identity or sexual orientation.

Happy Ending

In the imagined conflict between sexual orientation and gender identity, everybody's fun is killed. When fun dies a whole lot is at stake: experiments in intimacy, the proliferation of pleasures, and curiosity. When fun dies our repertoire for reconstituting our genders and sexualities, and for opening to a desire we had not yet felt, shrivels. We are all turned on by difference, which a phrase like "same-sex attraction" obscures. Gender-anxious gay men (in and out of the bathhouses) are writing off the possibility of gay desires and gay pleasures encompassing nontraditional bodies and identities, and the best part of gay culture is that it eroticizes, rather than erases, variety. Conducting the conduct of men is a rather unsexy exercise of trapping subjects into sexed bodies.

The Tel Aviv Sauna club excluded gender nonconforming bodies because of a single gay man who complained. But that incident, as all others described in this chapter, seems to be exceptional. Transness is becoming more intelligible, visible or simply desired in those spaces, including within bathhouses (Cooper 2007). Repeatedly it is a minority demand for the exclusion of trans bodies that urges institutions to adopt an anti-trans position.

But maybe there is space for empathy for the older cis gay man saying trans bodies "do not look good to his eyes." Can we hold on to his own trauma of compulsory heterosexuality, of his body also being destined to death in the HIV/AIDS pandemic and histories of criminalization? Recognizing his trauma is crucial if we claim that all deviant bodies, including his, carve the space for post-dysphoric becoming. Lovingly reminding him that the trauma of being othered is not only his own can perhaps allow him access to a post-dysphoric imaginary. This act of love can also just be too much, for both of us, but it would be an attempt to break the boundaries of external and internal policing.

What would become of a space defining itself as sexual space for gay men (or women) but allowing anybody to enter under the presumption that if they entered, they belong?[12] Maybe *bathhouses do not need rules; can they self-regulate?* But then again aren't the acts of pointing and laughing in Der Boiler or a comment like "you do not look good to my eye" at the Sauna also acts of self-regulation? Perhaps if policies are more affirmative, if trans sexuality as a matter of policy would not be suspected as false, in need of proving its inner truth, then we could allow the Tel Avivan older white men to make utterly outdated comments or permit the Berliners to point and laugh. Maybe then we can laugh back at them, talk to them about how it used to be, and ask, why am I funny? What if you were instead indifferent to me, or aroused? Why is it hard for you to get hard if I am here? Or maybe we would do nothing at all but turn away toward other eyes desiring us in heavy breaths of dark and steam. Within those breaths, inhibiting a post-dysphoric imaginary, we can refuse the command to desire a negation of the body and to desire through the negation of bodies. May the post-dysphoric imaginary offer a transitional time and space for unexpected intimacy, a repertoire for reconstituting our genders and sexualities, an opening for the desire not yet felt.

NOTES

1 During the HIV/AIDS epidemic in the United States, police routinely wore rubber gloves when handling people they perceived to be gay during arrests, searchess, and even during demonstrations, and on at least one occasion when welcoming gay delegates to the White House (see Associated Press 1995; Brandt 1986, 234; Gould 2009, 197; Yearwood 1992, 76).

2 Pinkwashing "refer[s] to states (especially, but not exclusively, Israel) using lesbian, gay, bisexual, and transgender (LGBT) rights in public diplomacy and for propaganda purposes, after state acceptability of homosexuality became a marker of liberalism" (Gross 2017, 344).

3 Derogative term in Hebrew for trans people, especially feminine people, equivalent to t****y. For the history of the term see Engelstein 2015.

4 An instructive inversion in US public indecency law: States criminalize public exposure of *genitals*, but jurisdictions are mixed when it comes to the "female breast." And some courts have struck down inclusion of the "female breast" in the law as an equal protection violation (I thank Joe Fischel for this insight).

5 Presumably the bathhouses let in some sissy boys, femme boys, etc., though these genders might also be subject to policing, as will be demonstrated.

6 Further, within gay sexuality exists the possibility of being penetrated as a man, a possibility that the trans vagina might also offer. The prevalence of penetrative sex is visible in gay porn featuring trans men who had masculinized their upper body, following the epistemology offered by the first trans masculine porn star Buck Angel, who dubbed himself "The Man with a Vagina" (Nichols 2016). On the other hand, insofar as mainstream porn sites are concerned, retaining the ability to penetrate seems to push trans women out of the categories "straight" or "gay" into a category of their own.

7 A robust (and perhaps mirror-like) debate on the inclusion of trans bodies and specifically trans feminine bodies in women-only space has been going on for decades within feminist writing. The rich political and academic debate around the trans exclusionary policy of the Michigan Womyn's Music Festival is perhaps the most notorious exemplar (see Koyama 2020; Williams 2020). In the Canadian example, the exclusion of Kimberly Nixon from the Vancouver Rape Relief Centre and the legal case that followed it raised a similar question, albeit not in a sexual space as the bathhouse or the Michigan festival, but nevertheless in relation to sexual assault (see Khan 2007). In the Canadian case, trans inclusion within women-only bathhouses has been debated and theorized on trans-affirmative terms (see Cooper 2007). The debate on inclusion of trans feminine bodies, centered around genitals and/or birth assigned sex (see Browne 2011), and hindered questions of race and class (Cooper 2007; Koyama 2020).

8 In another manifestation of historical assemblages of power, the long-time main cruising areas of both Tel Aviv and Jerusalem were located in parks named Independence Park. Both parks commemorate the 1948 war, and both are built on Palestinian cemeteries. Tel Avivian and Jerusalemite cruising (in both of which Arabic-speaking people also partake to some extent) occurred literally and metaphorically on the bodies of Palestine.

9 Notably, bathhouses and gay sexual spaces are not equally accessible to all cis gay men. While older, heavier, brown and black bodies are common patrons at bathhouses, younger, normatively attractive white men are prized in these spaces (see Han 2007, 56). The rise of Grindr and other similar "dating" apps is also a mixed blessing for many secondarily marginalized gays. While sex is more accessible, these sites also allow for direct and indirect sexual racism, ableism, and xenophobia (see Robards et al. n.d.; Shield n.d., 153–57). Similar tensions were critically documented through the debates on inclusion/exclusion of trans bodies from the Michigan Womyn's Music Festival. White middle-class post-op self-identified transsexual women appealed for inclusion through the claim that they are "just like" other women, yet this very justification hides the class and race stratification of the women-only space (see Koyama 2020, 67).

10 Butler notes, "Just as the subject is derived from conditions of power that precede it, so the psychic operation of the norm is derived, though not mechanically or predictably, from prior social operations" (1997, 21).

11 Similar questions in the context of claims of "deception" of both trans and racialized subjects were raised by Aeyal Gross (2015, 21) and others (Fischel 2019, 103;
Sharpe 2018, 83).

12 Davina Copper documented the trans affirmative policy of a Torontonian sex
party for women and trans people. The event even changed its name from
"Pussy Place" to "Pleasure Place" to reflect their trans (masculine and feminine) inclusionary policy. Anti-trans behavior was explicitly prohibited and
enforced. Further, different sexual services were provided in the space and
services providers were instructed to be impartial to potential clients, including trans women who have not accessed genital surgery. Pleasure Palace is an
example of a space in which trans inclusion was achieved by implementing
and adhering to regulations rather than a space that self-regulated through
self-identification. Still, Cooper theorizes the Pleasure Palace as a space where
different modes of feminist care were deployed with varying levels of success
(2014, 109, 121). Although feminist care was deployed foremost through rule
based obligations, these rules reflected an attempt at creating an ethical standard of choice.

BIBLIOGRAPHY

Associated Press. 1995. "White House Apologizes for Rubber Gloves." *New York Times*,
June 15, www.nytimes.com.

Bettcher, Talia Mae. 2014. "Trapped in the Wrong Theory: Rethinking Trans Oppression and Resistance." *Signs* 39(2): 383–406. https://doi.org/10.1086/673088.

Blumental, Itay. 2019. 13:47, 08.06.19. "הסאונה' על משטרתית פשיטה בתל אביב; זעם בקהילה הגאה."
Police Raids the Sauna in Tel-Aviv; Outrage in the LGBT Community." ynet. www
.ynet.co.il.

Brandt, Allan M. 1986. "AIDS: From Social History to Social Policy." *Law, Medicine and
Health Care* 14(5–6): 231–42.

Browne, Kath. 2011. "Beyond Rural Idylls: Imperfect Lesbian Utopias at Michigan
Womyn's Music Festival." *Journal of Rural Studies* 27(1): 13–23.

Butler, Judith. 1994. "Against Proper Objects. Introduction." *differences: A Journal of
Feminist Cultural Studies* 6: 1–26.

———. 1997. *The Psychic Life of Power: Theories in Subjection*. Stanford, CA: Stanford
University Press.

———. 2020. *The Force of Nonviolence: An Ethico-Political Bind*. London: Verso.

Cameron, Deborah and Don Kulick. 2003. *Language and Sexuality*. Cambridge: Cambridge University Press.

Colebrook, Claire. 2015. "What Is It like to Be a Human?" *Transgender Studies Quarterly* 2(2): 227–43.

Cooper, Davina. 2007. "'Well, You Go There to Get Off': Visiting Feminist Care Ethics
through a Women's Bathhouse." *Feminist Theory* 8(3): 243–62.

———. 2014. *Everyday Utopias: The Conceptual Life of Promising Spaces*. Durham, NC:
Duke University Press.

Cossman, Brenda. 2007. *Sexual Citizens: The Legal and Cultural Regulation of Sex and Belonging*. Stanford, CA: Stanford University Press. www.loc.gov.

———. 2013. "Anxiety Governance." *Law & Social Inquiry* 38(4): 892–919.

———. 2020. "The 1969 Criminal Amendments: Constituting the Terms of Gay Resistance." *University of Toronto Law Journal* 70(3): 245–62. https://doi.org/10.3138/utlj.2019-0058.

Currah, Paisley. 2014. "The State." *Transgender Studies Quarterly* 1(1–2): 197–200.

———. 2022. *Sex Is as Sex Does: Governing Transgender Identity*. New York: New York University Press.

Eng, David L. 2010. *The Feeling of Kinship: Queer Liberalism and the Racialization of Intimacy*. Durham, NC: Duke University Press.

Engelstein, Gil. 2015. "I Was Fed Up with Dress Up, I Just Wanted to Be: Space, Identity, and Opposition in the Life Stories of Israeli Transgender Women." *Zmanim* 131 (Summer): 34–51.

Fischel, Joseph J. 2019. *Screw Consent: A Better Politics of Sexual Justice*. Berkeley: University of California Press.

Frank, Gillian. 2013. "'The Civil Rights of Parents': Race and Conservative Politics in Anita Bryant's Campaign against Gay Rights in 1970s Florida." *Journal of the History of Sexuality* 22(1): 126–60.

Garner, T. 2014. "Becoming." *Transgender Studies Quarterly* 1(1–2): 30–32.

GenderTuck Magazine. 2019. "Facebook." www.facebook.com/GenderTuck/posts /2108598702600967.

Georgis, Dina. 2013. *The Better Story: Queer Affects from the Middle East*. Albany: State of New York Press.

Gill-Peterson, Jules. 2021. "Trans Pessimism, Part I." Substack newsletter. *Sad Brown Girl* (blog). https://sadbrowngirl.substack.com.

Gould, Deborah B. 2009. *Moving Politics: Emotion and ACT UP's Fight against AIDS*. Chicago: University of Chicago Press.

Gozlan, Oren. 2018. *Current Critical Debates in the Field of Transsexual Studies: In Transition*. New York: Routledge.

Gross, Aeyal. 2015. "Rape by Deception and the Policing of Gender and Nationality Borders." *Tulane Journal of Law and Sexuality* 24. https://journals.tulane.edu.

———. 2017. "Gay Governance: A Queer Critique." In *Governance Feminism: A Reader*, edited by Janet Halley et al. Minneapolis: University of Minnesota Press.

Hall, Stuart. 1997. "Race, The Floating Signifier." *Media Education Foundation*. www .mediaed.org.

Halley, Janet. 2018a. "Preface: Introducing Governance Feminism." In *Governance Feminism: An Introduction*, edited by Janet Halley et al., ix–xxiii. Minneapolis: University of Minnesota Press.

———. 2018b. "Where in the Legal Order Have Feminists Gained Inclusion?" In *Governance Feminism: An Introduction*, edited by Janet Halley et al., 3–22. Minneapolis: University of Minnesota Press.

Han, Chong-suk. 2007. "They Don't Want to Cruise Your Type: Gay Men of Color and the Racial Politics of Exclusion." *Social Identities* 13(1): 51–67.

Herman, Doron and Neria Kraus. n.d. "משפיל ולא רגיש': הרוחות סוערות לאחר הפשיטה על" המועדון הגאה "'Humiliating and Unsensitive': Turmoil Following the Police Raid of the Gay Club." חדשות 13. Accessed August 10, 2020. https://13news.co.il.

Ilany, Ofir. 2009. "T.A. Gay Community Says City Trying to Evict Them from Cruising Site." *Haaretz.Com*, November 23, www.haaretz.com.

Khan, Ummni. 2007. "Perpetuating the Cycle of Abuse: Feminist (Mis) Use of the Public/Private Dichotomy in the Case of Nixon v. Rape Relief." *Windsor Rev. Legal & Soc. Issues* 23: 27.

Koka, Ari. 2013. "It's In Our Gardens: The Lost Story of Independence Park [זה בגים שלנו: סיפורו האבוד של גן העצמאות]." *Mako* (blog). July 12. www.mako.co.il/pride-lifestyle /nostalgays/Article-3c9d677a8d3af31006.htm.

Koyama, Emi. 2020. "Whose Feminism Is It Anyway? The Unspoken Racism of the Trans Inclusion Debate." *Sociological Review* 68(4): 735–44.

Landau, Matan. n.d. "Facebook." Accessed June 22, 2021. www.facebook.com/Matan Landau/posts/10219401125482586.

Long Chu, Andrea. 2017. "On Liking Women." *n + 1*. November 29. https:// nplusonemag.com.

Naor, Lior. 2019. 09:01. "TLV Sauna: Trans Man Was Asked to Leave—'Patrons Were Complaining'" "סאונה ת'א': גבר טרנס התבקש לעזוב את המקום—'המבלים התלוננו'". *Walla!News*, 09:01. https://pride.walla.co.il.

Nichols, James Michael. 2016. "Buck Angel, 'The Man With A Vagina,' on the Role Sex Plays in Living Authentically." *HuffPost*, January 17. www.huffpost.com.

Robards, Brady, Bronwyn Carlson, and Gene Lim. n.d. "Grindr Is Deleting Its 'Ethnicity Filter'. But Racism Is Still Rife in Online Dating.". Accessed August 3, 2021. http:// theconversation.com.

Salerno, Bob. 2018. "Toronto Gay Bathhouse Apologizes after Refusing Entry to Men Wearing Makeup.". April 10. www.dailyxtra.com.

Sarson, Charlie. 2019. "'The Neighbourhood Cums: Ding Dong! Dick's Here!': SketchySex and the Online/Offline Cultures of Group Sex between Gay Men." *Porn Studies* 6 (3): 301–15. https://doi.org/10.1080/23268743.2019.1592698.

Sauna Tel-Aviv. 2019a. "Official Response to Police Raid." June 10. www.facebook.com /TLVSAUNA/posts/382991095655995.

———. 2019b. "Official Response to Incident on Saturday Night." June 21. www .facebook.com/TLVSAUNA/posts/388667115088393.

Schulman, Sarah. 2021. *Let the Record Show: A Political History of ACT UP New York, 1987–1993*. New York: Farrar, Straus and Giroux.

Sharpe, Alex. 2018. *Sexual Intimacy and Gender Identity 'Fraud': Reframing the Legal and Ethical Debate*. New York: Routledge.

Shield, Andrew D. J. n.d. "Grindr Culture: Intersectional and Socio-Sexual." *Ephemera* 18(1): 149–61.

Snorton, C. Riley and Jin Haritaworn. 2013. "Trans Necropolitics: A Transnational Reflection on Violence, Death, and the Trans of Color Afterlife." *Transgender Studies Reader* 2: 66–76.

Spade, Dean. 2008. "Documenting Gender." *Hastings Law Journal* 59(4): 731–842.

Stryker, Susan. 2014. "Biopolitics." *Transgender Studies Quarterly* 1(1–2): 38–42.

Stryker, Susan and Nikki Sullivan. 2009. "King's Member, Queen's Body: Transsexual Surgery, Self-Demand Amputation and the Somatechnics of Sovereign Power." In *Somatechnics: Queering the Technologisation of Bodies*, edited by Nikki Sullivan and Samantha Murray, 249. Oxon, UK: Ashgate.

Tyler, Michael and Leslie Kane (eds.). 2009. *Siddur Sha'ar Zahav*. San Francisco: Congregation Sha'ar Zahav.

Vahash, Nofar. 2019. "גבר טרנס הוצא מהסאונה בתל אביב: "התקבלוֹ תלונות" Trans Man Was Taken Out of the Tel-Aviv Sauna: 'We Received Complaints.'" *TimeOut*, June 20. https://timeout.co.il/טרנס-הוצא-מהסאונה/.

"What Is Gender Dysphoria?" n.d. Accessed October 5. https://web.archive.org.

Williams, Cristan. 2020. "The Ontological Woman: A History of Deauthentication, Dehumanization, and Violence." *Sociological Review* 68(4): 718–34.

Yearwood, Douglas L. 1992. "Law Enforcement and AIDS: Knowledge, Attitudes, and Fears in the Workplace." *American Journal of Police* 11(2): 65–84.

"מידע מודיעיני?! למחרת היינו פתוחים כרגיל" Police Intel?! We Were Open the Next Day." 2019. Walla!News. June 11. https://pride.walla.co.il.

11

"I Would Kiss a Man Whenever I Want, Let Some Fucker Hit Me"

Queering Narratives of Incarceration, Sexuality, and Offending

MATTHEW BALL

The recent development of queer criminology as an area of scholarly inquiry has brought attention to the experiences of sexually and gender-diverse communities in a criminal justice context. Much of this work seeks to address historical oversights in criminology, wherein sexually and gender-diverse communities have largely been excluded from collective understandings of offending, victimization, the actions of criminal justice agents, and the operation of criminal justice institutions. These oversights exist even though there has long been attention paid to issues of queer criminality and victimization in other disciplines such as sociology, and even in popular culture and media. As Peterson and Panfil (2014, 6) point out, "criminological and criminal justice research has typically been heteronormative, assuming traditional sex-based gender roles and heterosexual orientation." This means that in criminology and criminal justice, "'non-normative' sexual orientation, gender identity, and/or gender expression remain relatively unrecognized and certainly under-examined," and thus the needs of sexually and gender-diverse people are not always effectively understood, acknowledged, or responded to in criminal justice policy (ibid.). Queer criminological research is also motivated by a social change agenda, seeking to enhance justice for sexually and gender-diverse communities and ensuring more responsive criminal justice policy (Ball 2016).

Queer criminology has opened a space for criminologists to ask new research questions that challenge existing orthodoxies, utilizing methods and tools not often adopted within the field. In this chapter, I will explore and reflect on how the use of queer archival materials in a criminological context unsettles several dominant narratives relating to offending and the experiences of incarceration for sexually and gender-diverse people. Specifically, building on emerging queer criminological research (Carr et al. 2020), my research: queers dominant narratives about sexual subjectivities under conditions of carceral governance; highlights the role that the prison plays in producing sites for pleasure, forming intimacies, and performing, creating, and maintaining sexual subjectivities; and contributes insights into the relationship between sexuality and offending. Queer archival materials, this chapter concludes, unsettle criminological narratives, generate new forms of criminological knowledge, and energize criminology's disruptive potential.[1]

Encountering the Archive

To date, many studies under the aegis of queer criminology have sought to enhance the representation of queer people in criminal justice–related research and criminological theory. This has been achieved by implementing several methods: sampling strategies that ensure the inclusion of queer people; research design that utilizes nonbinary demographic categories and allows for data collection that meaningfully reflects queer experiences; and projects specifically targeted at queer communities and their needs (Ball 2020; Ghaziani and Brim 2019; Meezan and Martin 2009; Woods 2014). While these strategies begin to queer criminology, they underline the dominance of positivistic research paradigms in the discipline. To further queer criminological research and better represent queer lives and experiences, new methods must be employed. In this chapter, I suggest that this is possible using queer archives. Queer archives can be a rich source of material to deepen criminologists' understandings of the impacts of criminal processing systems and agents in the lives of queer people. As I also show, queer archives dislodge dominant criminological narratives more generally.

In recent decades, queer archives have grown and, in some cases, even become institutionalized, enhancing the ways that queer lives and stories are made visible and memorialized. The "archival turn" (Arondekar et al. 2015) that has drawn the attention of some queer theorists fills the gap left by many "official" or established archives, which either fail to fully encapsulate the histories of queer communities or hold records that demonize queer people (such as records or reportage of arrests during the period when homosexuality was criminalized). Queer archives tell different stories, containing voices from queer communities that challenge official archives' descriptions and representations (Cvetkovich 2003; Halberstam 2005; Kumbier 2014; Kunzel 2008; Loftin 2012; Love 2007; Marshall et al. 2015; Stone and Cantrell 2015). Beyond a simple repository of information in the form of documents, queer archives are also "archives of feeling" (Cvetkovich 2003)—the "ephemeral objects" (Kumbier 2014) they house serve as memorials to pain and trauma as well as resilience, strength, and community.

The archival materials utilized in this project (referred to as "the Collection" throughout) were drawn from a queer historical archive in North America (unidentified here for ethical reasons discussed below). The Collection contains correspondences between sixteen incarcerated people (fifteen cisgender men, most of whom identified as gay, bisexual, or pansexual, and one transgender woman) and a single member of the gay community outside of prison (who also subsequently donated the letters to the archive). The correspondences span the early 1990s through to the late 2000s. The correspondents were serving sentences ranging from several months to thirty years, for offenses including murder, assault, computer fraud, robbery, shoplifting, and sexual assault. Several of the sexual assault convictions entail offenses against children and young people. The length and content of the correspondence differs for each person—some last over years, discussing a variety of topics, while others occur for a short time, are more transactional, and end abruptly.

It is unlikely that a collection of this kind is unique. Similar collections are sure to exist in countless personal papers around the world, given the way in which such correspondence between members of the queer community and incarcerated people has historically featured in gay and lesbian political movements. The historical criminalization of queer people has produced a long history of solidarity, activism, and community building in and around prison spaces, and LGBTQ activism has involved a broad political effort to dismantle the prison as a system of oppression, while supporting those subjected to its harshest treatment (Kunzel 2008). Solidarity of this kind was not solely driven by a view that such incarceration was unjust but was also informed by a keen awareness among LGBTQ people that they (or someone they knew) could be arrested and imprisoned because of their sexuality or gender nonconformity. Moreover, LGBTQ people knew that should they be imprisoned, and their family had rejected or disowned them, they may have a limited support network outside of prison. One prominent avenue for solidarity with and support for gay prisoners involved sustained campaigns, particularly among gay men outside of prison, to write letters to those incarcerated. The purpose of letter writing was to exchange information about injustices and forms of maltreatment occurring inside prison and to build community; these letter-writing campaigns are ongoing (Kunzel 2008; Spade 2011).

The Collection is notable for at least three reasons. First, it includes correspondences with multiple incarcerated people. The single community member who undertook (and subsequently donated) this correspondence was writing to several people across the United States at the same time and not just a single incarcerated person. This means that the correspondence contains a breadth of experiences. Second, the Collection contains lengthy correspondence (in some cases, lasting more than eight years). This means that over the course of the (sometimes) years of letter-writing, the correspondents offer richly detailed narratives about their lives in prison, their lives prior to imprisonment, the offenses for which they are imprisoned, their future plans, and their sexuality and/or gender identity. They discuss many other topics too, such as their family, thoughts on politics, and tastes in music, offering a rich picture of their lives. Third, and finally, the letters were not written by people incarcerated for homosexual-related offenses. The subjects of this research are therefore distinguishable from those who emerge in standard queer histories and narratives, as the stories of queer people who have committed serious and/or violent offenses rarely get heard. Because of the depth of some of the correspondence, the broad group of people, offenses, and experiences represented in the Collection, and the relative paucity of such accounts in criminology, an analysis of the Collection holds significant value for queer criminology and for queer histories more generally. Exploring this queer archive offers several ways of queering narratives relating to sexual subjectivities in prison, the role of prison in producing sites of pleasure, and the relationship between sexuality and offending.

I offer two caveats about the following analysis—methodological and ethical. Methodologically, because I am interested in the prisoners' self-understanding of their experience in prison and their relationship with the correspondent outside of prison, I am not concerned with the truth or falsity of any claims that they make. Thus, I have not sought to confirm their accounts using court or police records. It is possible that these letters are performative, wherein correspondents present a more socially desirable picture of themselves and their lives and thereby embellish or gloss over aspects of their stories. However, such accounts are themselves valuable precisely because they give voice to the experiences of the correspondents while they were in prison. Moreover, as we will see below, concerns about the accuracy of such correspondence are offset by just how honest and open the correspondents appeared to be about most of the issues they discussed.

In terms of ethical considerations, there are concerns both with using personal correspondence in research (Dever et al. 2009; MacNeil 1992) and with research involving incarcerated queer people, given their vulnerability to violence and secondary forms of marginalization and exclusion (Cowburn 2017; Ellem et al. 2008; Meezan and Martin 2009). To undertake this research, I received a waiver of consent from my institution's research ethics review committee.[2] This was granted on the basis that gaining consent was impractical in the circumstances, that any risks to the correspondents was low (given that court records are generally already publicly accessible, the letters were written to a stranger, they were potentially subject to screening by prison authorities, and are already in a publicly accessible archive), and that there was a protocol in place to reduce the risk of any further marginalization to the incarcerated correspondents. It is for these reasons that no identifying details of the correspondents or the archive itself are provided in this chapter.

Queering Narratives of Incarceration and Sexuality

A core focus of queer criminology is the experiences of incarcerated LGBTQ people. There is a significant body of research on sexuality, sexual relations and violence, HIV and AIDS, and masculinity and homophobia in prison environments (see Buist and Lenning 2016; Butler et al. 2012; Kunzel 2008; Miller 1999; Mogul et al. 2011; Rollins 2004; Sabo et al. 2001; Simpson et al. 2016; Stanley and Smith 2011).

Much of the discussion is focused on what Sykes terms the "pains" of imprisonment—LGBTQ peoples' experiences of violence, sexual assault, and harassment in prison, the need to remain closeted for their safety, and, for trans people, the numerous issues that arise as a result of extreme vulnerability and being forced to live in institutions so solidly built on a gender binary (Carr et al. 2016; Mann 2006; Mogul et al. 2011; Spade 2011; Stanley and Smith 2011; Sylvia Rivera Law Project 2007). Often such research is animated by a desire to highlight the injustices produced by incarceration. There has been concomitant research interest in sex in prison and the sexual identities of those incarcerated. One specific topic of interest is whether incarcerated people have a "preformed" gay identity prior to entering prison, or whether they engage in "situational homosexuality" and are simply "gay for the stay" without their same-sex sexual activity in prison signifying anything about their "true" sexual identity (Blackburn et al. 2014; Kunzel 2008). This binary continues to structure research and discourse in the field, despite, as Kunzel (2008, 102) identifies, the notion of "situational homosexuality" being a "rhetorical maneuver by which midcentury social scientists sought to contain the disruptive meanings of sexual acts apparently unlinked to, and therefore unsettling of, sexual identity."

Studies highlighting these experiences are important, however the extant scholarship, with few exceptions, mainly describes imprisonment as characterized by threats, violence, sexual assault, and the closeting of one's sexuality (but see Carr et al. 2020; Kunzel 2008). This means that comparatively little focus is given to the more mundane realities of prison life for incarcerated LGBTQ people, and the multiple ways that sexual and gender subjectivities are maintained and performed under carceral governance beyond being repressed or closeted. Studying the correspondence from the Collection offers insights that develop and shift the queer criminological literature. The incarcerated correspondents recount their boredom with prison life, their occasional fulfillment through the work they do (like organizing the prison library or helping fellow inmates with their legal cases), and the intimate (and, importantly, not always sexual or coercive) relationships they form with their cellmates.

Correspondents reflect upon their sexual and gender identities under conditions of carceral governance. They recount that, in their

experience, the prison environment has not forced them to remain closeted, and they do not experience overt repression of their sexuality or
gender. In many cases, correspondents wrote about what appears to be
a tolerance for their sexual identities in prison, even though they were
still cautious about how they performed or expressed their sexuality,
spoke about it, and how openly they sought intimacy and sex. Their
experiences suggest that they were neither embraced nor particularly
reviled by fellow inmates or officers. While some of the correspondents
were not "out" in prison, even those who were did not report feeling as
though they were in constant danger of violence. One correspondent,
for example, wrote that he was not particularly concerned with (or could
handle) any negative response he might receive should he express same-
sex attraction: "I would kiss a man whenever I want, let some fucker hit
me" (C5).[3] Another indicated that, if a guard or another inmate saw gay
reading material in his cell, he could "just tell a white lie" about it (C3).
This correspondent felt that such a response would be sufficient to deal
with the issue and would not expose him to further scrutiny or harassment. Another correspondent noted that "I am pretty much as 'out' as I
can be in here, with the respect of most of the guards who matter" (C8).

It is not clear why the correspondents did not experience the threats,
violence, and harassment in the same way or apparently to the same
extent as reported in other research. It could be due to the nature of the
institutions in which they were incarcerated. It could be because they
were not particularly visible as "queer" in prison. Or it could simply be
that they did not wish to reflect on these issues in their letters (although
this would be surprising given the broad range of topics that they did
discuss as well as the detailed picture of prison life they provide).

There is significant research confirming that same-sex sexual activity is common within prison environments (see Marcum and Castle 2014). This was supported by some correspondents, one of whom
noted that "so much sex goes on here, their [other prisoners'] wives
should be shocked" (C5). Another pointed out that some inmates were
even "married" and lived in the same cell (C6). Some sexual and intimate relationships of this kind are understood within the literature as
"situational"—that is, emerging because of the prison environment and
often for companionship, protection, or mutual exchange, not as an in-
dicator of same-sex attraction or gay identification. The correspondents

did not ponder whether others' same-sex sexual activities and relationships were orientational or situational, but they apparently understood themselves and their partners as gay.

Other correspondents noted that while they did not feel at risk because of their sexuality, the prison was not the place for an overt expression of gay identity. They indicated their life was one of caution—of cautious expression of sexuality and of some suspicion toward other inmates. So, while they did not always deny or hide their sexuality, they did not make a big deal of it either. While one indicated that they knew of only six other openly gay inmates (C6), it is clear from the letters written by other correspondents that they knew of (and were connected to) networks of gay prisoners in their own or other prisons, through which they shared resources and information (C14). Some noted that while they felt they had to limit their movements and expressions, they had not seen or heard of any sexual assaults or what one referred to as "sexual power plays" (C6). In contrast to some of the views mentioned above, some correspondents noted that not much sex happened—that while they might enjoy "chasing boys on the yard" (C16), and that "some might think that there's lots of sexual activity in prison . . . there really isn't" (C16). Yet another correspondent indicated that "in prison 95% of the guys have a mask on [i.e., were closeted] and has [sic] to portray a hard tough role, because if you're weak, you'll get taken advantage of" (C9).

Interestingly, correspondents' expressed anxieties did not focus on exposure to violence because of their sexuality. Instead, they usually focused on the violent and traumatic nature of the prison environment more generally. The correspondents witnessed significant trauma while incarcerated, including violence from prison guards, the capricious enforcement of the prison rules, extended lockdowns, and the suicide or attempted suicide of their fellow inmates (C4; C7). As one correspondent noted, "I could go on and on [talking about life under lockdown and the violence of guards] but it really is unhealthy for me now. We have lost so much and there is no end in sight. They just keep taking the few privileges we have" (C12). Another pointed out that "I'm dealing with stupid rookie guards (no more cute ones), frustrating property officers, too much work and too little pay, too few hugs and too many fences, and a mountain of time to cope with" (C8). For many correspondents, these issues commanded their attention and their anxiety over and above their sexuality.

What the experiences of these correspondents illustrate is that prison is not the environment characterized by totalizing homophobic violence and vulnerability that it is often taken to be. This is not to suggest that such violence and vulnerability are absent from prison or that reports of such are overblown. Rather, these examples simply indicate that there is potentially more depth to the experiences of imprisonment which are not fully drawn out in research on the experiences of violence and vulnerability in incarceration (Carr et al. 2020). My engagement with these correspondences offers a deeper insight into life in prison and its quotidian, nonsexual modes of violence, and offers a way of further queering some of our orthodox assumptions about offending and about prison for queer people. These complexities need to be accounted for further within queer criminology.

Incarceration and Correspondence: Producing Pleasure

The preceding discussion highlights the range of experiences that correspondents had expressing sexual subjectivities in prison. In all, relatively few reported that their sexual identities and sexual desires, or those of others, were overtly expressed in prison. This contrasted to the correspondence itself, where sexuality and sexual desires and fantasies were discussed quite freely. It became apparent that this correspondence offered a way for the incarcerated correspondents to produce, maintain, and perform sexual subjectivities under conditions of carceral governance. Moreover, the way that sex and sexuality emerged here was unique to the format of correspondence itself. We largely apprehend prison sexuality either through positivistic reports that document sexual conduct in prison, or through critical analysis that focuses on the way that sexual activity is restricted or coerced in prison. These correspondences offer an alternative way to perceive prison sexuality. They also allow us to recognize how prison produces pleasure—specifically, how the quotidian spaces and experiences of prison life allow for pleasure to be constituted in unexpected forms and places (for a similar discussion in the context of heterosexual relationships, see Comfort 2007; see also Amin 2017).

Correspondents indicated that because of the complexities of expressing sexual identity and desire in prison, the correspondence with the community member outside prison became vital in the expression of their sexual subjectivity. Their correspondence provided a space to claim a gay identity, develop and engage in sexual fantasies, be part of the gay community, and share these identities, fantasies, and experiences with another person (for a history of such interactions, see Kunzel 2008). Many of the correspondents relied on the community member to send them gay-related material, whether fiction or community magazines, that allowed them to keep up to date (or become acquainted) with the gay scene. As one correspondent noted to the community member, "I cannot have relations in here so therefore I live vicariously through the literature you provide" (C3). Often, the incarcerated correspondents would recount past sexual encounters or their sexual fantasies in vivid detail. Sometimes, these letters also seemed to blur the boundaries between fantasy and reality. For example, in one of the letters, an inmate recounts having sex with another inmate in a prison bathroom and describes it explicitly in a way that borrows somewhat from the tropes of pornography or erotic fiction (including with embellishments that strain credibility), making it not entirely clear whether the event happened or is fantasy (C9). As this correspondent wrote:

> as I was walking down the company this Spanish dude was on his hands and knees in the shower area eating out this gay guy who has breast[s], while one of his legs was posted on a chair opened wide. They both seen me, but I didn't stop I kept walking and my dick got hard as hell, but I chilled. So on my way back, only the black gay guy with tits was in the shower alone. So I walked right in the shower pulled my long black eal [sic] out + put it deep inside his brown eye and moved nice + slow [']til I was able to release all this white lava deep inside his tight ass hole—wow! He used his wash rag to wipe off my "magic stick" [. . .] and tucked him back inside my pants + I left his company a happy camper.

Some correspondents shared their own pornographic novels and art in their letters. One such correspondent, who had a keen interest in photography, compiled a book of photos of mostly naked men in which he not only explained his desire for those men, but also commented on the artistic composition of the photographs and the technical details of the cameras, lenses, and lighting effects (C12). He had also been able to access gay pornography on a computer in prison and print the images, using the blank side of those pages as the stationery on which he wrote many of his letters. Interestingly, the relative absence of sexual activity in prison life recounted by the incarcerated correspondents contrasts quite starkly to the explicit, and abundant, descriptions of sexual activity and sexual fantasies in their letters.

Building on Elena Vasiliou's (2020) and Carr et al.'s (2020) recent work that draws attention to what Vasiliou terms the "perverse plea- sures," and not just the pains, of imprisonment, the Collection highlights the way that such correspondence offers a space for the creation, main- tenance, and performance of sexual and gender subjectivities. In this sense, inmates' correspondence produced new spaces for, and forms of, pleasure and desire, allowing incarcerated people to create and experi- ence pleasure even within the confines of the prison. This move from strictly focusing on prison "pains" to thinking about the original and creative (and perverse) ways the prison produces pleasure is important for furthering queer thought in the criminological literature. In addi- tion, by looking at these letters and other sites as spaces for the perfor- mance of sexual subjectivities, we can begin to think about sexuality in prison beyond simply who does what to or with whom.

While the Collection extends our ways of thinking about sexuality in prison, it is also worth paying attention to the very act of reading such correspondence, and accounting for that act within such research. While reading the letters is sometimes disturbing given their content detailing prison life and serious offending, it is also pleasurable. Clearly, some of the letters were written with the aim of arousing the recipient (and potentially the writer). As these letters are incredibly personal, and the correspondent had no reason to believe that their thoughts or fantasies would ever be read by anyone apart from the community member to whom they wrote, what is today's reader of these letters supposed to make of their own potential arousal when reading them? At times, the reader feels they are intruding on an intimate, sometimes sexual, rela- tionship, especially when the content is clearly intended to arouse. Yet there is a perverse pleasure in sharing in personal correspondence in this way—as an observer or, effectively, a voyeur (and even as a partici- pant, despite not being the addressee). Even though you are separated from those whose lives you are observing, protected by your temporal and physical distance from them, you still feel exposed as someone who is reading material you should not. And yet, the existence of these letters as archival objects *encourages* an engagement with them, continuing to exert a pull on the researcher. By producing pleasure in the reader, the letters allow the reader to become entangled (and participate) within the unique form of prison sexuality they produce. In these circumstances, the researcher is being made both a voyeur and a participant. Does this make every reader of this chapter a voyeur and participant as well? And is this a problem or a productive mode of engagement from a queer point of view? These questions speak to Kathryn Bond Stockton's queer description of reading as "promiscuous, penetrating, pleasurable, vibrant, and estranging"—as a process whereby "we are being penetrated by an author's sequencing of sensuous dildos we call words," and in which "we are consenting to what we can't control, to a kind of transport we cannot predict" (Stockton 2015). Queer criminology could reflect more on embodiment, attachment, and affect in research processes, queering not only what we know about incarceration, but also *how* we know it. It could also further explore these new and unexpected sites through which pleasure is produced, particularly by thinking through the queer act of reading.

Queering Offending: Identity, Agency, and Crime

My research can also contribute to a queering of dominant narratives of offenders found in much of the literature. Of particular interest here are questions about the relationships between queer identity and offending. My nascent research suggests that it might be time to reevaluate the queerness of the queer offender now that queerness is no longer synonymous with criminal deviance.

Exploring the issue of queer offending is an emerging direction for queer criminology. Historically, the gaze of criminology was clearly locked on queer offenders. Queer people were, by virtue of the criminalization of their sexualities or genders, *always already* offenders. However, after the decriminalization of homosexuality, and despite the growing interest in queer victimization as an object of criminological inquiry, criminology maintained a curious silence about queer offenders (Woods 2015; Woods 2014). As such, it is only recently that queer criminologists themselves are turning to the question of how we should understand and engage with the figure of the queer offender. It is particularly important for us to consider how to talk about the role that their sexuality or gender identity may or may not have played in their offending now that we no longer assume their *inherent* deviance.

For example, Nicole Asquith, Angela Dwyer, and Paul Simpson (2017) have outlined the structural and social factors that lead to what they term a "queer criminal career." This work aligns with existing critical criminological research that identifies the structural influences on criminal behavior, and that which explores the intersecting inequalities such as race and socioeconomic status that increase the likelihood that some queer people will be exposed to policing and carceral governance (see generally, DeKeseredy and Dragiewicz 2018). The factors that Asquith, Dwyer, and Simpson identify include family exile, societal homophobia, and transphobia that might push young LGBTQ people into survival crimes, which in turn lead to greater contact with the justice system. Placing (some) queer offending in its social context in this way is important, as it draws attention to the unique confluence of circumstances that (some) queer people experience that enhance their likelihood of offending. Doing so does not situate offending in a queer identity, but points to the ways that queer identity may be relevant to understand offending. Equally important is the need to account for individual agency. Vanessa Panfil has sought to foreground agency in her work on gay gang members (2017). As Panfil notes, recognizing the agency of LGBTQ people— that they are "citizens with the same capabilities for control and (or, and thus) crime" as non-LGBTQ people (2014, 104)—is important and will only enhance our understanding of queer offending. Again, this does not adhere offending to queer identity, but shows how queer identity is, again, relevant to offending behavior. Without recognizing agency, we are likely to continue to see queer people as either victims of crime or victims of circumstance.

While these antihomophobic approaches position offending apart from queer identity, it is not clear how queer criminologists ought to respond to those cases where there is, or might be, a connection between the two. How do queer criminologists respond to queer criminals without assuming the inherent deviance of queer people and activating those stereotypes? For some, a discussion of (particularly serious) offending committed by queer people might not sit comfortably with a progressive view that queer communities ought to play up the respectable and palatable (read: homonormative) aspects of queer lives and play down messy issues of (sometimes quite serious) offending. Of course, avoiding a discussion of such offending merely reinforces the place of already privileged queers as the objects of queer criminological inquiry and as the subjects of rights.

At least eight of the correspondents in the Collection committed sexual offenses against children and minors and spoke openly about their offending and its connection (or otherwise) to their sexuality. While these were not the only offenses committed by the correspondents in the Collection, these sex offenses offer a clear opportunity to consider how to navigate these issues of exploring offending without assuming the deviance of queer people and activating queerphobic stereotypes.

Understandably, this topic puts a queer researcher into a difficult position, given that the modern liberal gay rights movement is built fundamentally on, and partly legitimated by, its renunciation of intergenerational desire, relationships, and sex. Queer communities have long fought against any view that would interpret their desire to achieve greater social acceptance for sexually diverse people as extending to include sex offenders, and child sex offenders in particular (McDonald 2016; Walker and Panfil 2017; for extended discussions, see also Amin 2017; Fischel 2016; Kunzel 2008; Lancaster 2011). This makes the work to balance issues of recognizing context, agency, and avoiding harmful stereotypes even more urgent. While the inclusion of the voices and experiences of sex offenders (who self-identified as gay, bisexual, or unsure) in this project might be considered controversial, queer criminologists already interrogate these sensitive questions in disciplinary debates over who constitutes the "subjects" of queer criminology. Scholars such as Dave McDonald (2016) and Allyn Walker and Vanessa Panfil (2017) push queer criminology to consider who might fall under the label "queer." They have done so by arguing that the subjects of "queer criminology" should not solely be LGBTQ people, but that the insights from queer theory can be used to understand and think in new ways about the experiences of sex offenders and minor-attracted people. These scholars explore the legal and criminal regulation of sex beyond LGBTQ identities and toward those sexualities still rendered violent (McDonald

2016; Walker and Panfil 2017). This example therefore invites us to take seriously how the offender understands his sexual identity in relation to his criminal sexual conduct.

In the context of this correspondence, most of the sex offenses involved what is often referred to in the United States as "statutory rape" (Burrow et al. 2020; Koon-Magnin and Ruback 2013). In most of the cases, there was not a significant difference in age between the perpetrator and victim, though the victim was still younger than the legal age of consent. In this context, these cases involved young men (in their early twenties) incarcerated for offenses involving victims who were in their mid-teens when the offending occurred. Statutory cases also focus on the nonforcible nature of the offenses. According to the accounts in the correspondence, the sexual activity that constituted the offenses was described by the correspondents themselves as consensual.[4] In this vein, several of the incarcerated correspondents reported that they had been in relationships with the victims for a relatively long period of time. In each of these cases, as discussed below, the correspondent indicated that the victim was mature enough to consent to the relationship. In some cases, these relationships even occurred with the knowledge of families and friends of the victims, who made no attempts to stop it (C3).[5]

Key to understanding how queer identity intersected (or not) with the offending of the correspondents is to consider the identification of these offenders with the gay community. Through their correspondence, they reached out to a member of the gay community outside prison. Two identified as being homosexual or gay, one identified as bisexual, and one was unsure, saying that their sexuality shifted across time and place. However, at no point did any of the correspondents suggest that being gay *explained* their offending. Some noted that their attraction was not toward minors specifically, but that for a range of reasons they developed a relationship with someone below the legal age of consent. This story was common for those cases where there was not a large age gap between the offenders and victims: The correspondent had been involved with a community or sporting group or attended events at which there were young people, they had few other friends (and often knew no one in the gay community), and they had little to no experience with relationships. They developed a close friendship, and subsequently relationship, with one of the young people with whom they interacted (C3; C15). Some correspondents with similar stories indicated that they had not considered themselves as gay prior to their arrest. They described confusion as to their sexuality and suggested that this confusion explained their offending. In this sense, they understood their offending as being out of character for themselves and simply an unfortunate outcome of exploring their own sexuality (C3).

For several of these correspondents, reaching out to a member of the gay community outside prison was a way to explore their own sexuality and stake a claim on a particular identity (see Kunzel 2008 for an historical discussion of the role the gay community outside prison played in modeling "normative" homosexual relations for those incarcerated, particularly for those who had committed sex offenses). Importantly, though, they understood their offending as wrong and something they did not wish to repeat. That is, they did not suggest that an attraction to young people was part of their gay identity. They indicated no specific sexual attraction to children, viewed their behavior as morally and criminally wrong, and often engaged with programs that were available to them through which they could change that behavior (C3; C8). One correspondent notably thanked the community member for sending them LGBTQ-themed material which, in their view, offered a way of moving past what they had done and toward understanding who they felt they really were (see Kunzel 2008). Their correspondence also offered them a path out of offending and toward a community they wanted to be a part of and that they felt could model healthy and non-criminal relations (C3; C8). Moreover, none of these correspondents expected the community member to excuse their offending, and neither did they assume that he would sympathize with their experience.

In contrast, there were several correspondents who were clearly comfortable with their attractions to minors and expressed no remorse about their histories of sex offending. One labeled himself as a "non-predatory paedophile" (C12), despite describing what amounted to clearly predatory and grooming behaviors toward young people. Another said that they were "all sexual," being attracted to every gender and all ages but with a preference for children under fourteen years old (C14). In these cases, the offending usually involved significant age gaps between the offenders and victims. This also points to an apparent contradiction between these two groups of men. Though there is a limited number of correspondents to draw any more meaningful conclusions, it seems that the men who engaged in behavior that might be considered less objectionable appeared to be more contrite and ashamed about their offenses. Those who had engaged in clearly assaultive, manipulative, or exploitative behavior displayed less contrition or none at all.

Notably, none of the offenders who expressed no remorse about their offending overtly identified as gay. While these offenders generally did not engage in any self-interrogation to explain their own offending, one did reference their significant history of abuse as a child. He had been sexually abused by his brother at age five, then by two men a couple of years later, and again violently raped at age fourteen. His own pattern of offending and the way he describes his own attractions appear to reflect the abuse he experienced (C11). Again, the men in this group of offenders did not expect the correspondent outside of prison to excuse their offending. At times, they appeared to assume the community member was at least comfortable discussing their offending. Some may have even thought he was at least ambivalent about their sexual offenses, to the point that, several times, the community member had to adamantly remind the correspondents that he did not find their offending acceptable and urged them to seek help for it.

Exploring these uncomfortable stories, which form just a handful of those in the Collection, provides insights into how some offenders navigate and reconcile their offending and identity—in this case, their sex offending history and their sexual identity. These stories also point to the political tension that exists at the heart of the modern gay rights movement, which, on the one hand, has protested against the criminalization of (some) forms of sex (i.e., sodomy) *as* offenses, while at the same time reserving the right to criminalize other forms of sex (i.e., between age-discordant partners) as part of a claim to societal respectability (see Fischel 2019; Kunzel 2008; Lancaster 2011). While the inclusion of such stories is certainly controversial, it is due to their disruptive potential and their unique perspectives on the links between offending and identity, and the complexity that they add to these narratives, that makes them, and other stories like them, so important. These stories are valuable precisely because, among other reasons, they manifest arenas of queer experiences, reflection, and pleasure that have been railroaded by the social triumph of gay rights and marriage equality.

Conclusion: Engaging the Archive in Queer Criminology

This brief exploration suggests the potential benefits of using prisoners' correspondence and other archival materials for future queer criminological research. The use of archival material in queer criminological research provides rich and detailed information about incarceration and many other issues that research methods like interviews cannot. Correspondence, particularly over the span of years, offers deeper and contemporaneous insights on issues and events that are more difficult to capture through interviews, which rely on participant recall and may be distorted by various inequalities of power within the prison environment and between interviewer and interviewee. While such correspondence does not necessarily provide us with an unmediated or more objective truth of queer experience or queer life in prison, analyzing correspondence offers greater agency to those incarcerated over the stories they tell about themselves and how they tell them, and an avenue of more open reflection. Analyzing the correspondence of incarcerated people centers their subjectivities and allows the complexity of those stories and experiences to emerge. More dimensional understandings of incarceration have the potential to benefit incarcerated LGBTQ people through improved criminal justice policy and service provision (Buist and Lenning 2016; Panfil 2014). Such research also contributes to scholarship beyond queer criminology, detailing the lives of individuals rarely featured in lesbian and gay history. Politically, the archives of queer criminology multiply the number of queer voices in broader public discourse, as well as the kinds of queer voices that are heard there.

Archival records such as correspondence offer an advantage to many other criminological research methods in that they humanize offenders, even those who have committed heinous crimes. As desire for social change motivates much queer criminology, the humanizing of those subjected to the harshest aspects of the criminal justice system is important. As an artifact of a social relationship, the correspondence is imbued with emotion—it expresses emotion and produces emotion in the reader. It is impossible to avoid "feeling" the letters in some way and being moved by them, sharing in the joy of an approaching release date, the frustration toward the tangle of policies and bureaucracy and violence that governs their lives, and the antipathy toward capricious guards and authority figures who implement harsh policies. Conversely, some letters push the reader away, generating feelings of disgust and aversion given the nature of the crime at issue, and the indifferent or even arrogant attitudes of some correspondents. However, overall, the letters inculcate reader empathy. They allow the reader to empathize with aspects of the situation of those incarcerated—their separation from loved ones, their lack of freedom, and the burden of living with the consequences of a mistake that they made. Reading these stories in the words of incarcerated persons themselves, without the usual institutional gatekeeping through which meaning is made of their lives (such as media reporting, trial records, or prison authorities) reinforces the empathetic connection. Queer criminologists can enhance such approaches within criminology more broadly and, in so doing, thoroughly queer dominant narratives in a range of other contexts.

Put most broadly, this research offers new insights into what we think we know about prisons. It contributes to our understanding of the creation, maintenance, and performance of sexual subjectivities under conditions of carceral governance. It shows that prison life for queer people is characterized by far more than violence. The regulation of sexuality in prison also carves new avenues for pleasure and for the performance and exploration of sexual subjectivities in the form of correspondence. My research gestures to several ways in which offenders draw or refuse to draw connections between their sexual identities and their sex offending. Finally, the queer criminological archive beseeches us to embrace discomfort as we encounter and make sense of the plethora of queer life and queer experience.

NOTES

1 The foregoing discussion deploys the term 'queer' in multiple ways. 'Queer' is used as an umbrella term referring in some way to non-normative sexualities and genders (such as queer people, or a queer archive), and as a verb to describe a process of disruption and deconstruction (queering) drawing on queer theory. For more detail on the ways that 'queer' has been used in criminological discourse, and particularly how 'queer criminology' can draw from both approaches, see Ball (2016).

2 QUT UHREC approval number 1700000847, in line with the *Australian National Statement on Ethical Conduct in Human Research*.

3 Quotes from individual correspondents will be referenced using (C), followed by a number indicating the specific correspondent.

4 As mentioned, this research focuses on the narratives of those incarcerated. I have not gained access to other records such as court reports to verify the ages of those involved, the status of consent, the existence of relationships, or any other such details.

5 The circumstances of these offenses also draw attention to a related, and difficult, set of questions that have long been debated in the gay movement about the nature of these offenses. Should these offenses be considered offenses? Are their "victims" actually victims? Were these men prosecuted because these cases involved same-sex sex? Would they have been prosecuted had they involved heterosexual sex, even when similar age differences existed? (For an extended discussion of such questions, see Fischel 2016; Lancaster 2011.) The answers to these questions, which space here precludes me from investigating further, may reveal that discriminatory laws and the homophobic state are the key problem in this context. These answers may suggest that the minds and desires of the incarcerated correspondents differ very little from the minds and desires of gay men outside of prison. If this is the case, then the questions about whether those who have committed these offenses ought to be accepted into the queer community seems to misdirect from a necessary structural critique.

BIBLIOGRAPHY

Amin, Kadji. 2017. *Disturbing Attachments: Genet, Modern Pederasty, and Queer History.* Durham, NC: Duke University Press.

Arondekar, Anjak, Ann Cvetkovish, Christina B. Hanhardt, Regina Kunzel, Tavia Nyong'o, Juana María Rodríguez, and Susan Stryker. 2015. "Queering Archives: A Roundtable Discussion." *Radical History Review* 122: 211–31.

Asquith, Nicole L., Angela Dwyer, and Paul Simpson. 2017. "A Queer Criminal Career." *Current Issues in Criminal Justice* 29(2): 167–80.

Ball, Matthew. 2016. *Criminology and Queer Theory: Dangerous Bedfellows?* Basingstoke: Palgrave Macmillan.

———. 2020. "Queering Criminology Globally." In *Oxford Research Encyclopedia of Criminology and Criminal Justice*, 1–28. United Kingdom: Oxford University Press.

Blackburn, Ashley G., Shannon L. Fowler, and Janet L. Mullings. 2014. "Gay, Lesbian, Bisexual, and Transgender Inmates." In *Sex in Prison: Myths and Realities*, edited by Catherine D. Marcum and Tammy L. Castle, 87–111. Boulder, CO: Lynne Rienner.

Buist, Carrie L. and Emily Lenning. 2016. *Queer Criminology.* London: Routledge.

Burrow, John, Deena A. Isom Scott, and Toniqua Mikell. 2020. "No Man's Land: The Denial of Victimisation in Male Statutory Rape Cases." *Journal of Sexual Aggression* 26(3): 316–33.

Butler, Tony, Juliet Richters, Lorraine Yap, and Basil Donovan. 2012. "Condoms for Prisoners: No Evidence that They Increase Sex in Prison, but They Increase Safe Sex." *Sexually Transmitted Infections* 89(5): 377–79.

Carr, N., S. McAlister, and T. Serisier. 2016. *Out On the Inside: The Rights, Experiences and Needs of LGBT People in Prison*. Irish Penal Reform Trust Research Report.

———. 2020. "Sexual Deviance in Prison: Queering Identity and Intimacy in Prison Research." *Criminology and Criminal Justice* 20(5): 551–63.

Comfort, Megan. 2007. *Doing Time Together: Love and Family in the Shadow of the Prison*. Chicago: University of Chicago Press.

Cowburn, Malcolm. 2017. "Researching Sex Crimes and Sex Offenders: Some Ethical and Epistemological Considerations." In *Research Ethics in Criminology: Dilemmas, Issues, and Solutions*, edited by Malcolm Cowburn, Loraine Gelsthorpe, and Azrini Wahidin, 115–32. New York: Routledge.

Cvetkovich, Anne. 2003. *An Archive of Feelings: Trauma, Sexuality, and Lesbian Public Cultures*. Durham, NC: Duke University Press.

DeKeseredy, Walter S. and Molly Dragiewicz. 2018. *Routledge Handbook of Critical Criminology*. 2nd edition. Oxon: Routledge.

Dever, Maryanne, Sally Newman, and Ann Vickery. 2009. *The Intimate Archive: Journeys through Private Papers*. Canberra: National Library of Australia.

Ellem, Kathleen, Jill Wilson, Wing Hong Chui, and Marie Knox. 2008. "Ethical Challenges of Life Story Research with Ex-Prisoners with Intellectual Disability." *Disability and Society* 23(5): 497–509.

Fischel, Joseph J. 2016. *Sex and Harm in the Age of Consent*. Minneapolis: University of Minnesota Press.

Ghaziani, Amin and Matt Brim (eds.). 2019. *Imagining Queer Methods*. New York: New York University Press.

Halberstam, Judith. 2005. *In a Queer Time and Place: Transgender Bodies, Subcultural Lives*. New York: New York University Press.

Koon-Magnin, Sarah and Barry R. Ruback. 2013. "The Perceived Legitimacy of Statutory Rape Laws: The Effects of Victim Age, Perpetrator Age, and Age Span." *Journal of Applied Social Psychology* 43: 1918–30.

Kumbier, Alana. 2014. *Ephemeral Material: Queering the Archive*. Sacramento, CA: Litwin Books.

Kunzel, Regina. 2008. *Criminal Intimacy: Prison and the Uneven History of Modern American Sexuality*. Chicago: University of Chicago Press.

Lancaster, Roger N. 2011. *Sex Panic and the Punitive State*. Berkeley: University of California Press.

Loftin, Craig M. (ed.). 2012. *Letters to One: Gay and Lesbian Voices from the 1950s and 1960s*. Albany: State University of New York Press.

Love, Heather. 2007. *Feeling Backward: Loss and the Politics of Queer History*. Cambridge, MA: Harvard University Press.

MacNeil, Heather. 1992. *Without Consent: The Ethics of Disclosing Personal Information in Public Archives*. Lanham, MD: Scarecrow Press.

Mann, Rebecca. 2006. "The Treatment of Transgender Prisoners, Not Just an American Problem—A Comparative Analysis of American, Australian, and Canadian Prison

Policies Concerning the Treatment of Transgender Prisoners and a Universal Recommendation to Improve Treatment." *Law and Sexuality* 15: 91–133.

Marcum, Catherine D. and Tammy L. Castle (eds.). 2014. *Sex in Prison: Myths and Realities*. Boulder, CO: Lynne Rienner.

Marshall, Daniel, Kevin P. Murphy, and Zeb Tortorici (eds.). 2015. "Queering Archives: Intimate Tracings." *Radical History Review* 15 (full issue).

McDonald, Dave. 2016. "Who Is the Subject of Queer Criminology? Unravelling the Category of the Paedophile." In *Queering Criminology*, edited by Angela Dwyer, Matthew Ball, and Thomas Crofts, 102–20. Basingstoke: Palgrave Macmillan.

Meezan, William and James I. Martin (eds.). 2009. *Handbook of Research with Lesbian, Gay, Bisexual, and Transgender Populations*. New York: Routledge.

Miller, Teresa A. 1999. "Sex & Surveillance: Gender, Privacy & the Sexualization of Power in Prison." *George Mason University Civil Rights Law Journal* 10(2): 291–356.

Mogul, Joey L., Andrea J. Ritchie and Kay Whitlock. 2011. *Queer (In)justice: The Criminalization of LGBT People in the United States*. Boston: Beacon Press.

Panfil, Vanessa R. 2014. "Better Left Unsaid? The Role of Agency in Queer Criminological Research." *Critical Criminology: An International Journal* 22(1): 99–111.

———. 2017. *The Gang's All Queer: The Lives of Gay Gang Members*. New York: New York University Press.

Peterson, Dana and Vanessa R. Panfil. 2014. "Introduction: Reducing the Invisibility of Sexual and Gender Identities in Criminology and Criminal Justice." In *Handbook of LGBT Communities, Crime, and Justice*, edited by Dana Peterson and Vanessa R. Panfil, 3–13. New York: Springer.

Rollins, Joe. 2004. *AIDS and the Sexuality of Law: Ironic Jurisprudence*. New York: Palgrave Macmillan.

Sabo, Don, Terry A. Kupers, and Willie London (eds.). 2001. *Prison Masculinities*. Philadelphia, PA: Temple University Press.

Simpson, Pauk, Joanne Reekie, Tony Butler, Juliet Richters, Lorraine Yap, and Basil Donovan. 2016. "Sexual Coercion in Men's Prisons." In *Queering Criminology*, edited by A. Dwyer, M. Ball, and T. Crofts, 204–28. Basingstoke: Palgrave Macmillan.

Spade, Dean. 2011. *Normal Life: Administrative Violence, Critical Trans Politics, and the Limits of Law*. New York: South End Press.

Stanley, Eric A. and Nat Smith (eds.). 2011. *Captive Genders: Trans Embodiment and the Prison Industrial Complex*. Oakland, CA: AK Press.

Stockton, Kathryn Bond. 2015. "Reading as Kissing, Sex with Ideas: 'Lesbian' Barebacking." www.lareviewofbooks.org.

Stone, Amy L. and Jaime Cantrell (eds.). 2015. *Out of the Closets, Into the Archives: Researching Sexual Histories*. Albany: State University of New York Press.

Sylvia Rivera Law Project. 2007. *'It's War in Here': A Report on the Treatment of Transgender and Intersex People in New York State Men's Prisons*. New York: Sylvia Rivera Law Project.

Vasiliou, Elena. 2020. "Penitentiary Pleasures: Queer Understandings of Prison Paradoxes." *Criminology and Criminal Justice*. doi: 10.1177/1748895820939147.

Walker, Allyson and Vanessa R. Panfil. 2017. "Minor Attraction: A Queer Criminological Issue." *Critical Criminology* 25(1): 37–53.

Woods, Jordan B. 2014. " 'Queering Criminology': Overview of the State of the Field." In *Handbook of LGBT Communities, Crime, and Justice,* edited by Dana Peterson and Vanessa R. Panfil, 15–41. New York: Springer.

———. 2015. "The Birth of Modern Criminology and Gendered Constructions of Homosexual Criminal Identity." *Journal of Homosexuality* 62(2): 131–66.

PART IV

Queer Feels

12

Thinking with Care

A Critique of Love across Interdisciplines

JENNIFER C. NASH

Care is ubiquitous—or at least its radical promise is. Care is heralded as an "anti-institutional" form of relationality and life sustenance (Crawley 2020, 24). It is a response to the harm—spectacular and ordinary—of the world we inhabit, and it is an insistence on another way of being, one that embraces mutual regard, tenderness, and love. In Black studies, care has come to be the keyword of a moment marked by the intersections of Black Lives Matter and COVID-19. Christina Sharpe's *In the Wake*—a text that has become the field's manifesto—asks, "How can we think (and rethink and rethink) care laterally, in the register of the intramural, in a different relation than that of the violence of the state?" (2016, 20). In placing care as the central "problem for thought" (5), Sharpe tethers care to a practice of tending to dead and dying Black people. These are, at times, deaths captured on police officers' bodycams; they are also "slow deaths" at the hands of poverty (Berlant 2007), institutionalized cruelty, and state neglect. Care, Sharpe reminds her readers, is also a practice of tending to Black life, which is always lived in the face of the deadly "weather" of antiBlackness and always lived with a deep proximity to the Black dead (2016, 103). In another manifesto—this one, explicitly described as such—Joshua Chambers-Letson hails care as necessary for minoritarian survival. Chambers-Letson writes, "Under conditions like these, survival isn't merely a drive; it's an imperative. It is a command to stay close to each other and take care of each other because we need each other in order to stay alive with each other. What we've got, when there's nothing else, not even the feeling of freedom, is our flesh, life, and each other. We can't afford any more losses. We need More Life" (2018, 77). In Chambers-Letson's exploration of queer of color life "after the party," it is care that ensures collective survival. There is only the commons—the brown commons, drawing from José Muñoz's work (2020)—that can create structures of mutual regard that provide a shelter, even if ephemeral, from the persistence of state violence.

In some ways, the notion of care as an urgent and life-saving practice is an enduring preoccupation of Black feminist thought, from Audre Lorde's reminder that "caring for myself is not self-indulgence. It is self-preservation, and that is an act of political warfare" (2017, 130) to Alice Walker's conception of the womanist as a figure who retreats periodically "for health" (2004, xi). The idea of self-care as a radical act has circulated beyond the academy to become a mantra for Black women's self-maintenance in the face of an antiBlack and misogynistic world. Evette Dionne writes, "Many of us [Black women] are poor, many of us are working ourselves into early graves. And so saying that I matter, that I come first, that what I need and what I want matters I think is a radical act because it goes against everything that we've been conditioned to believe" (2015). The notion of Black women's premature death has come to be evidence of the need for a Black intramural ethic of care, and even for an ethic of retreat (Geronimus 1992). In this vein, care is a form of maintaining the self, a radical insistence on the need for time, attention, slowness, respite, and a recognition of the ordinary and regularized violence that the demands of the present inflict.

Even as care is hailed as "something white supremacist capitalist patriarchy cannot give nor withhold, even when it tries to privatize care as an industry that is primarily about making money and exploiting workers. Care is not private property, it only exists when it is shared" (Crawley 2021), there is also a new attention to care work as commodified, exploited, and devalued feminized labor. This attention to commodified care—refueled by COVID-19—considers both the centrality of reproductive labor to the maintenance of life and the devaluation of care work precisely because it is feminized. COVID-19 has fueled a new awareness of the "crisis" of care work: This critical attention to who is asked to perform care work was combined with a new interest in the gendered dimensions of care work as women generally, and mothers specifically, became the "shock absorbers" navigating the demands of caring for the young, the sick, the old, the vulnerable, and increasingly stepping out of the labor force to deal with the no-end-in-sight pandemic (Grose

2020). Care work is once again revealed to be a gendered burden on women's bodies, a kind of contemporary "problem that has no name" as women labor in homes that are also offices, childcare centers, and doctor's offices; as we home school, meet for telemedicine visits, and feed and nourish children (Friedan 1963). And even care work performed outside of the house—still gendered, still essential, still performed by the most vulnerable—remains unprotected by the state, underpaid (and sometimes unpaid). How, feminists have asked again and again, can care be essential to the maintenance of the self, the household, the community, and be treated with such explicit disregard?

There are, then, two competing views of care and its work. There is the care that Black and Brown communities offer each other, and there is commodified care or extracted care. There is a vision of care advanced by Black studies—one that has also been advanced by queer of color theorists including Martin Manalansan and Joshua Chambers-Letson—and a vision of care advanced by feminist studies. How might we square these two visions, and how might we think with care to trouble the notion of care's certainty, of either the romantic investment in care or the need to wholly divest from it? This chapter elects to *think with* care *about* care rather than posing a critique or staging a celebration. This chapter instead stages a conversation between Black studies and feminist theory, and thinks with care in three different contexts. First, I put care next to another keyword in Black studies—refusal—and think about what it might look like for Black studies to consider the refusal of care (work) rather than the embrace of it as engendering a new form of futurity. How might we understand how Black studies both hails care *and* refusal simultaneously, and how might Black studies think with feminist studies' long-standing investment in thinking about the refusal of housework—broadly defined—as a kind of freedom? Second, I consider the *where* of care, probing why some geographies are thought to be venues of radical care—particularly Black intramural care—and others are presumed to be ripe with the extraction of care. Here, I ask why certain *locations* and *geographies* are imagined to engender radical forms of care and others are imagined to extract care from bodies, particularly women's bodies. In the final section, I return to an archive of work that is uncomfortable for Black studies: critical race feminist work that embeds care in the state, precisely the site that has been hailed by many who advocate care's virtues as the preeminent site of violence. I ask what might happen if Black studies refused to disavow the juridical, and instead sat—even if uneasily—with a body of Black feminist scholarship that imagines a caring juridical practice. Ultimately, this chapter attempts to think with care as an object worthy of scrutiny and refuses the romance of care as a site of Black liberation or patriarchal violence. Instead, I treat care as a dense site of Left political desire and even fantasy.

Caring Work, Refusing Work

Christina Sharpe recognizes both the force of the antiBlack "weather" and the necessity for a Black intramural ethic of tenderness and love. For Sharpe, this practice of care is always understood as "work" even as work remains an undertheorized portion of the care her book advocates. She develops the term "wake work" to describe an urgent form of care and attention that is necessary for individual and collective survival. Sharpe's manifesto underscores the labor of *staying* in the wake, sitting with the work, even as it describes the task of staying and sitting in myriad ways. Sharpe writes, "To tend to the Black dead and dying: to tend to the Black person, to Black people, always living in the push toward our death? It means work. It is work: hard emotional, physical and intellectual work that demands vigilant attendance to the needs of the dying, to ease their way, and also to the needs of the living" (2016, 10). Work, she reminds us again and again, is required. As Sharpe notes, "We must be (and we already are) about the work of what I am calling wake work as a theory and praxis of the wake; a theory and a praxis of Black being in diaspora" (19). If "work" is central to Sharpe's plea for care, it is also central to how she argues scholars must reshape and reimagine the project of writing, theorizing, and studying, to how we engage in Black study. She reminds her readers, "We must become undisciplined. The work we do requires new modes and methods of research and teaching; new ways of entering and leaving the archives of slavery, of undoing the 'racial calculus and . . . political arithmetic that were entrenched centuries ago' and that live into the present" (13, quoting Hartman 2008, 6). This call for "undisciplined" scholarship that is also "enfleshed work" requires the labor of challenging academic mores and standards of valuation, upending prevailing notions of what constitutes scholarly writing. It also requires, as Sharpe says, the act of writing the self into scholarly work. This kind of writing is taxing even as it is rewarding. As Patricia J. Williams notes, "Writing for me is an act of sacrifice, not denial. . . . I deliberately sacrifice myself in my writing. I leave no part of myself out, for that is how much I want readers to connect with me. I want them to wonder about the things I wonder about, and to think about some of the things that trouble me. What is 'impersonal' writing but denial of self?" (1991, 92). Yet Williams's own reflections reveal the cost of writing as sacrifice: Williams learns, for example, that her colleagues report that "all this emotional stuff just leaves me cold" (19). And when Williams "go[es] back to my computer to find a way of saying it just for him [one of her critics]," she is engaged in work that is intellectual, psychic, spiritual (20). It is a form of care for the self, the spirit, the mind, and it is also demanding labor.

For Sharpe, the term "work" is an acknowledgment of care as labor, yet the book maintains little analysis of the gendered demands of work, particularly caring work; and little analysis of how it is so often women who perform caring work, or how often this work is extracted from women's bodies, even as they receive far too little care. Keguro Macharia warns, "There might be something *theoretically uninteresting* about care. It is feminized work, so devalued. It is also, frequently, tedious, repetitive, unglamorous work: feeding the vulnerable, cleaning up shit and puke, washing bedpans, changing nappies, cooking, cleaning, medicating. Repeat. And repeat" (2018). Macharia's investment in the banality of care, the sheer repetitiveness required to maintain life, reveals how little attention has been paid to the "unglamorous" nature of care work. What does it mean for Black feminists to engage care as the "problem" and solution for Black thought—a necessary and urgent practice of tending to the Black intramural—with little regard for the labor required of care, for putting one's body on the line? Where is a Black feminist engagement with how so often the work of caring, holding communities together, making food, arranging visits is women's work? Indeed, as I have argued elsewhere, Black care work for the Black dead is so often Black women mourning Black men and boys, leaving the deaths of Black women and girls largely invisible and leaving Black women's own pain—at the hands of the state, antiBlack violence, and Black patriarchy—unnoticed (Nash 2016).

If care has become a keyword for Black studies, refusal has as well. Tina Campt describes "practicing refusal" as "the urgency of rethinking the time, space, and fundamental vocabulary of what constitutes politics, activism, and theory, as well as what it means to refuse the terms given to us to name those struggles" (2019, 80). Campt emphasizes that the practices of refusal that interest her are everyday rather than spectacular, embedded in ordinary practices of life, and that they are "neither utopic nor autonomous, and neither pessimistic nor futuristic. It functions instead through relationality and adjacency, and its power lies in its ability to engage negation as generative" (81). The celebration of refusal is not autonomous to Black studies; feminists have long called for various forms of work refusal, perhaps most notably in the context of household work. Silvia Federici's now-canonical "Wages Against Housework" treats the household and its relentless demands of reproductive, sexual, and affective labor as a key site through which the production of normative gendered roles is secured. She argues for the importance of organizing for a wage for housework so that women can see themselves as workers and the household as a factory, and can begin to refuse the work itself. As she notes, "We say: stop celebrating our exploitation, our supposed heroism. From now on we want money for each moment of it, so that we can refuse some of it and eventually all of it" (1975, 6). What refusal makes possible is not only making visible the unrecognized and wholly essential labor of housework—which for Federici includes not simply the tasks of reproducing life but the affective work too, the "smile," the tenderness, the care, sex, intimacy—but also refusing gendered roles entirely. I want to linger in the centrality of the refusal of affective labor to Federici's vision, which underscores both how much emotion, care, tenderness, and love are extracted from women's bodies, but also how much this labor has clouded and obscured women's capacity to see or imagine what love might be, what sexuality might be, what desire might be. She writes, "[W]e want to call work what is work so that eventually we might rediscover what is love and create our sexuality, which we have never known" (8). The notion that labor has colonized love, so deeply and profoundly, that we can now no longer discern love from work, suggests the need for an affective revolution that allows women to reclaim their "smiles," their tenderness, their care.

So we find ourselves sitting at the incommensurability of two traditions—Black studies' investment in care as the necessary and urgent work of sustaining Black life and a feminist tradition that insists on underscoring how care is taken, stolen even, from women's bodies, that calls for the refusal to be a housewife, the refusal to perform care, as the necessary form of revolution. In placing these traditions side by side, I suggest the importance of thinking robustly about *what it might mean to refuse to perform care*. In making this claim, I am not advocating an embrace of harm (although all sociality includes harm and I insist that we cannot free ourselves from vulnerability to harm). But what we might accomplish—theoretically—if we think un/care in the face of the gendered demand to "wake work," or if we think the work of "wake work" is precisely what Federici might argue women need to avoid in a quest to get free. At the very least, she would suggest that we think about the extraction of labor with critical attention, that we rigorously consider how the extraction of care gets taken up as *love* and not as *labor*. What if a practice of carefully tending to the Black living and the Black dead is also a form of demanding, exacting, and exhausting labor, and how might we offer an account of that work *as work*, as something that takes a toll on bodies? Most important, this critical juxtaposition—of Sharpe and Federici—suggests the urgency of staging conversations between Black studies and feminist theory, conversations that ask how we might be simultaneously called on to care more, and more vigorously, and to divest from labor, particularly emotional labor.

The *Where* of Care

Care marks geographies, and competing conceptions of care suggest that it is the *where* of care that can make it either a form of tenderness or a form of exploitation. For Sharpe, care is performed in the world: Care is a doing, a reading practice, a tactic for "keeping and putting breath back in the body" and for "the ways we must continue to think and imagine laterally, across a series of relations in the hold, in multiple Black everydays of the wake" (2016, 113). Yet, unlike other Black feminist scholarship that elevates the household, the domestic, and the interior as crucial sites of care, Sharpe's conception of care seems to move apart from space, from geography. Instead, she calls for interpretative work, a mode of seeing, reading, thinking, studying, and attending to. As she writes, "we yet reimagine and transform spaces for and practices of an ethics of care (as in repair, maintenance, attention), an ethics of seeing, and of *being* in the wake as consciousness; as a way of remembering an observance that started with the door of no return, continued in the hold on the ship and on the shore" (131). This version of care suggests the need for care across time and space because antiBlack violence, the "weather," has suspended ideas of time and space. In other words, the "door of no return" has ruptured logics of time and space so that we continue to live in and with that threshold, in what Saidiya Hartman terms the "afterlife of slavery" (2008, 13).

Yet Black studies has also advanced the argument that care performed in the household, in the space of the domestic, is particularly urgent because of its capacity to affirm Black life in the space of a sanctuary. This body of work—indebted to Black feminist scholars like bell hooks who offered a radical vision of the Black domestic in her articulation of "homeplace"—imagines a Black private sphere as a site of world-making and self-preservation. Dani McClain's work on Black mothering in the age of Black Lives Matter emphasizes the radical nature of Black domesticity. She writes, "It's true that I've retreated into private life. I've slowed way down, turned inward. I've long been interested in nutrition, but now my research on the topic and the food prep I do as a result feels all-consuming" (2019, 29). Her attention to the banalities of maternal life reveals the political labor of the Black quotidian because even small actions are about Black survival: what is eaten, where one shops, how one accesses information, what music is heard. As McClain indicates, it is crucial to guard the "protected space in our home and in the small orbit in which she moves, an oasis where she as a Black girl can feel free and empowered and dignified. That's meant the right books and the decision not to spank and all the organic, whole foods, and on and on" (160). These practices of noting, making time, giving attention are, for McClain, practices of Black maternal freedom even as they are forms of domestic labor. As she notes, "I am claiming for myself and my child time that was historically denied Black women and children who wanted and needed to bond. I am taking the time that so many Black women before me could not, because they were caring for someone else's child or cooking someone else's food or toiling away in someone else's field" (31).

Here, a mother's care for her child is about making a world for a Black child, one marked by safety, security, reassurance, that works against the tendency of the world to violate Black children, to refuse them the privilege of the construction of childhood innocence. This is a kind of care work that is thought of not just as care for Black children but as care for Black communities, with Black mothers acting as vessels for Black life more generally. This is part of a tradition of work that sees the Black domestic, the Black interior, as sanctuary, as radical, as necessary for the preservation of Black life.

Yet feminist scholarship suggests the necessity of attention to the locations where care is performed, revealing that care's geographies contain information about how care exploits. Indeed, for feminist theorists, it is care work performed in the household that remains most troubling, most exploitative. Federici writes, "No matter how well trained we are, few are the women who do not feel cheated when the bride's day is over and they find themselves in front of a dirty sink." It is the "dirty sink," the call to "raise his [her husband's] children, mend his socks, and patch up his ego" that constitutes the "peculiar combination of physical, emotional and sexual services that are involved in the role women must perform for capital that creates the specific character of that servant which is the housewife, that makes her work so burdensome and at the same time invisible" (1975, 8). Here, the household is problematic because it shields labor from public view, from recognition *as* work. As Federici observes, "To say that we want wages for housework is to expose the fact that housework is already money for capital, that capital has made and makes money out of our cooking, smiling, fucking. At the same time, it shows that we have cooked, smiled, fucked throughout the years not because it was easier for us than for anybody else, but because we did not have any other choice. Our faces have become distorted from so much smiling, our feelings have got lost from so much loving, our over-sexualization has left us completely desexualized" (8). What the household makes invisible is that "cooking, smiling, [and] fucking" are not separate from the workings of capital but integral to it.

This notion of the household as a locus of exploitation has led feminists to analogize forms of feminized, degraded work to housework even if they unfold outside of the domestic sphere. Dale Bauer's work on academic labor in women's studies as the "domestic work of academe" reveals how feminist academics all too often perform a "second shift" of academic labor in women's studies (1999, 246). She writes, "Thus, the analogy of Women's Studies Programs to the conventional heterosexual marriage assures that whatever we do in 'private'—that is, in programs—is our own business, as long as Women's Studies professors do the 'home' work in departments (which often turns out to be the department's housekeeping, such as formal and informal mentoring, work with students rather than in research, social events)" (247). Bauer's analogizing of feminized academic labor to housework—of women's studies to the household—reveals a long-standing feminist investment in spotlighting how invisibility works to hide labor as love.

Staging a conversation across Black studies and feminist studies reveals the centrality of geography to conversations about care, the ongoing collective notion that care performed in certain locales is either radical or repressive, freeing or subordinating. Yet, if care comes into stark view as a problem during the ongoing pandemic, so too does the question of geography. As work becomes home, becomes school, becomes doctor's office, as we "work from home" and home becomes work, the once more rigid boundaries between private and public become far more porous and permeable, making clear that it is impossible to map care's radical possibility or regressive underpinnings by examining where care is staged, performed, and enacted.

Care's Other Archives

Part of Black studies' celebration of care has been a call to embrace its anti-institutional logic. Perhaps no institution is thought to embody violence, injustice, and unfreedom more than the US state, increasingly described—in all of its iterations—as fundamentally carceral, as oriented toward punishment, retribution, and anti-Black violence whether ordinary or spectacular. Amplified calls for abolition—of prisons, of the police—alongside calls for mutual aid instead of state "charity" (and in the face of state neglect) reveal the extent to which a desire to jettison the carceral institution has become central to a US Left agenda. But there is another archive of care—another Black feminist archive of care—rooted in the juridical. This archive emerging from critical race feminism finds a cohort of Black feminist and women of color feminist legal scholars exhibiting what I can only call a reluctant faith in law and in its possibilities, even as they reckon with law as a site of anti-Black violence, what Patricia J. Williams terms "spirit murder." Perhaps their impossible faith in the possibilities of the juridical is manifested in their own formal experimentations, their "alchemical writing" style that fuses memoir, poetry, allegory, fiction, and legal analysis. These writings refuse the lure of objectivity and manifest the radical possibility of dreaming. Black studies' current articulation of care's parameters would require that we disavow these thinkers, that we un-see their faith in law, that we un-write them from our canons precisely because of their sustained refusal to disavow law, their continued investment in law's promise. Yet I suggest that this archive of Black feminist scholarship offers us a chance to see care's multiple itineraries, complicating and deromanticizing where care is now. These texts suggest that care might move in uncomfortable ways, in uncomfortable places, even in legal doctrine, and that care might perform its most radical work through its fierce commitment to dreaming even in seemingly impossible ways.

Patricia J. Williams's stunning *Alchemy of Race and Rights* is a book that refuses categorization. The book traverses multiple genres and performs its refusal to be pinned down even in its final note, when Williams refers to Harvard University Press's "struggle" with the Library of Congress over how to classify the book. She writes, "The librarians think 'Afro-Americans—Civil Rights' and 'Law Teachers' would be nice. I told my editor to hold out for 'Autobiography,' 'Fiction,' 'Gender Studies,' and 'Medieval Medicine'" (1991, 249). But if law itself rests on the project of categorization and classification, what might it mean to invest in the juridical while undoing its foundational premises, while resisting categorical thinking?

Indeed, Williams reveals that she invests in law through her intellectual and political commitment to the concept of rights. She articulates this investment in a moment in which critical legal studies was arguing for the displacement of rights, their false promise, perhaps even the "cruel optimism" invested in them (Berlant 2011). Yet Williams refuses to abandon rights, instead inflecting them with a deep valence of care. She argues that rights have been politically limited because we have failed to imagine what might happen if we *give* them away," to objects, ideas, concepts, time (1991, 165). What would happen, she asks, if we give rights away to the natural world, if we assume that trees, air, history, and rocks have a right to something—or somethings—including freedom, autonomy, respect, integrity. What would happen if we assumed the past had rights, that water has rights, that the table has rights, and what would it do to imagine ourselves embedded in a world of obligations, and what Adrienne Rich calls "responsibility" and "accountability"? (1986). Williams's articulation of the radical power of rights—their capacity to embed us in the world and to attach us to each other—is rooted in an ethic of care, in the capacity of care to unleash new forms of vulnerability. Yet Williams explicitly decides to root this radical vision, this notion of an unleashed care, in law and in the language of rights, imagining law as a crucial space for staging an exploration of the possibility of rights. Even as Williams gestures to this radical possibility, she also recognizes law's non-imagination, or constrained imagination, its unwillingness to treat vulnerability and witnessing as ethics. Her capacious conception of rights can never be met by conventional juridical thinking, yet Williams refuses to cede the territory of law, insisting instead on dreaming in a juridical lexicon, in thinking rights as a radical technology of living otherwise.

If Williams's work suggests the possibility of juridical care, we might also think of Kimberlé Crenshaw's highly traveled concept of intersectionality as, at least in part, a plea for law to see one of its constitutive absences: discrimination and violence against Black women. Law, Crenshaw argues, has been constructed to un-see Black women's experiences of harm. For Crenshaw, this is most visible in the context of employment discrimination where Black women experience violence that is seen as too specific, too general, or too unknowable to be redressed (1989). Instead, it is simply rendered invisible. Intersectionality is, at least in part, a creative experiment, a speculative endeavor, that asks what it might mean for law to take seriously what it has been constructed to ignore. It is an endeavor that asks for a model of juridical care, that includes Black women in neither a doctrinal structure modeled around their constitutive absence nor one that thinks redress simply. Instead, intersectionality asks what law might look and *feel* like if it took seriously Black women's experiences of injury and reckoned with how law itself produces the experiences of vulnerability that constitute the subjectivity of the multiply marginalized.

Intersectionality, then, asks what it might mean to imagine a juridical structure, to dream a juridical form, that could see Black women's injuries, and that could recognize how social structures—including law—render some bodies particularly vulnerable to harm, to injury, to pain, to trauma. Crenshaw's vision, like Williams's conception of rights, imports a model of care to the juridical by imagining a legal grammar that can be attentive to witnessing antiBlack and misogynistic harm, that can respond to that harm in a form other than disavowal or strategic containment.

While I highlight Williams and Crenshaw and their shared commitment to constructing an ethic of care *within* law, we might think of how both practice what Williams has termed a "jurisprudence of generosity," one that reimagines the possibilities of law and invests in a faith in the juridical as a site that can unleash new forms of relationality. This is not an anti-institutional vision of care. Instead, it is a vision of care that is wedded to institutional structures, even institutions that are imagined as carceral, as violent, as antiBlack. My investment in this archive is in how scholars in Black studies might carefully attend to the visions of care amplified by these scholars. These are visions of care that embrace rather than reject law, even as they recognize law's limits, its failures, its elisions and blind spots. These are visions of care that imagine that law might be a necessary grammar for forging a lexicon of freedom, that insist that we cannot afford to disavow the framework of the juridical.

Thinking with and against Care

This chapter has aspired to stage a conversation between Black studies and feminist studies on the question of care, an object that has been romantically hailed as the way to survive the conditions of the present and as a locus of women's oppression. I end with a turn to the legal archive—perhaps even a queer turn to the legal archive—because I am curious about when care moves in archives that are deemed troubling, unconventional, or difficult. These are difficult moments because they disrupt the notion of Black feminism's anti-institutional longings and demands. They suggest the importance of treating care as a fraught object rather than as a site of political certainty. It is my hope that if we follow care's complex genealogies—including into an archive that embraces rather than rejects law, finding in the juridical the possibility of certain forms of freedom dreams—we can jettison the ongoing tendency to relegate certain archives, methods, and fields as inherently regressive.

BIBLIOGRAPHY

Bauer, Dale. 1999. "Academic Housework and Second Shifting." In *Women's Studies On Its Own: A Next Wave Reader in Institutional Change*, edited by Robyn Wiegman. Durham, NC: Duke University Press.

Berlant, Lauren. 2007. "Slow Death (Sovereignty, Obesity Lateral Agency)." *Critical Inquiry* 33(4): 754–80.

———. 2011. *Cruel Optimism*. Durham, NC: Duke University Press

Campt, Tina. 2019. "Black Visuality and the Practice of Refusal." www.womenandperformance.org.

Chambers-Letson, Joshua. 2018. *After the Party: A Manifesto for Queer of Color Life*. New York: New York University Press.

Crawley, Ashon T. 2020. *The Lonely Letters*. Durham, NC: Duke University Press.

———. (@ashoncrawley). 2021. https://twitter.com/ashoncrawley/status/1360626435396956162.

Crenshaw, Kimberlé. 1989. "Demarginalizing the Intersection of Race and Sex: A Black Feminist Critique of Antidiscrimination Doctrine, Feminist Theory, and Antiracist Politics." *University of Chicago Legal Forum* 1: 139–67.

Dionne, Evette. 2015. "For Black Women, Self-Care Is a Radical Act." www.ravishly.com.

Federici, Silvia. 1975. *Wages Against Housework*. London: Falling Wall Press.

Friedan, Betty. 1963. *The Feminine Mystique*. New York: W.W. Norton.

Geronimus, Arline T. 1992. "The Weathering Hypothesis and the Health of African-American Women and Infants: Evidence and Speculations." *Ethnicity & Disease* 2(3): 207–21.

Grose, Jessica. 2020. "Mothers Are the 'Shock Absorbers' of Our Society." www.nytimes.com.

Hartman, Saidiya. 2008. "Venus in Two Acts." *Small Axe* 26: 1–14.

Lorde, Audre. 2017. *Burst of Light & Other Essays*. New York: Ixia Press.

Macharia, Keguro. 2018. "Black (Beyond Negation)." https://thenewinquiry.com/blog/black-beyond-negation/.

McClain, Dani. 2019. *We Live for the We: The Political Power of Black Motherhood*. New York: Bold Type Books.

Muñoz, Jose Esteban. 2020. *The Sense of Brown*. New York: New York University Press.

Nash, Jennifer C. 2016. "Unwidowing: Rachel Jeantel, Black Death, and the 'Problem' of Black Intimacy." *Signs* 41(4): 751–74.

Rich, Adrienne. 1986. "Notes Toward a Politics of Location." In *Blood, Bread, and Poetry: Selected Prose, 1979–1985,* 210–31. New York: W.W. Norton.

Sharpe, Christina. 2016. *In the Wake: On Blackness and Being.* Durham, NC: Duke University Press.

Walker, Alice. 2004. *In Search of Our Mothers' Gardens: Womanist Prose.* New York: Harcourt.

Williams, Patricia J. 1991. *The Alchemy of Race and Rights.* Cambridge, MA: Harvard University Press.

13

Sexual Innocence in Crisis-Justice Movements

A Political Theology

NOA BEN-ASHER

In September 2020, two seemingly unrelated articles appeared in the mainstream press. The first, *How Shouting, Finger-Waving Girls Became Our Conscience* (Mishan 2020), examines the rise of female adolescents, such as Greta Thunberg, to the role of social justice orators. The other, *QAnon Goes to Washington* (van Zuylen-Wood 2020), investigates the popularity of QAnon (millions of followers in the United States and elsewhere) and documents the entry of QAnon believers into political positions of power. Greta Thunberg is an international symbol of justice, outrage, purity, and generational innocence; QAnon, a bizarre conspiracy theory about an evil cabal of pedophilia rings run by Hillary Clinton and others, received heightened international attention in the wake of the US Capitol Insurrection of January 6, 2021 (Barry et al. 2021). The public images and representations of both Thunberg and QAnon reflect a disturbing reliance of crisis-driven social justice movements, on the right, and left, on Christian theology. Christian theology and its vision of sexuality underwrite contemporary crisis-justice politics.

Times of crisis generate dramatic, often ecstatic, tales about justice. This chapter identifies a particular type of crisis-justice narrative that involves two key characteristics. First, the narrative recycles and relies on myths about human sexuality, especially regarding the sexual purity of children.[1] Second, it incorporates central elements of Christian theology. This crisis-justice narrative has emerged both on the political right and on the political left. This double appearance across the political divide is a fascinating and telling occurrence of political theology in the twenty-first century. The narrative is "political" in the sense that both the perceived crisis and the perceived social justice solutions are in the domain of public affairs, as opposed to private ones; and it is "theological" because it embodies Christian theological themes to make and shape political claims.[2] I analyze Greta Thunberg and QAnon side-by-side for three reasons. First, they both generated passionate, public engagement among millions of people in the United States and abroad. Second, they emerged in close time proximity to each other but for seemingly opposite audiences, one for liberals and the left (Thunberg), and one for the far right (QAnon). Third, and relatedly, they both seem at first glance to be utterly dissimilar. They are not.

This chapter warns future social justice movements about the pitfalls of crisis-justice and the theological and sexual tropes upon which crisis-justice relies. But more than just a warning, this chapter also complicates one of the leading contemporary narratives about American society: the one about political and social polarization. Across disciplines, many have observed and tried to explain the growing polarization in the United States between liberals and conservatives.[3] This chapter shows that despite polarization on *policy* issues such as reproductive rights, gun rights, immigration, climate change, LGBTQ rights, and pandemic measures, there are some surprising convergences between the political right and left when it comes to issues of *ethics*, *morality*, and *affect*. To illustrate this, the chapter briefly examines three overlapping plot lines in the QAnon and Thunberg narratives. First, they both rely, albeit in entirely different ways, on the presumptive innocence and sexual purity of children. QAnon is a conspiracy theory that seeks to "save the children" from a liberal cabal of pedophiles. Thunberg's climate justice activism seeks to save a present generation of children from the immorality of current adults, and her iconic imagery, as several have noticed, is enhanced by her pre-sexual, white female child status. Second, both QAnon and Thunberg declare an apocalyptic war of good against evil. QAnon's war is against liberal and leftist pedophile elites represented by Hillary Clinton and others. Thunberg's war is against profit and power-driven climate destroyers. Third, QAnon and Thunberg posit themselves as truth-tellers and truth revealers in a world run by conspiring elites and evil corporations.

* * *

The twenty-first century has already proved crisis-rich. From 9/11 to the climate crisis to the coronavirus pandemic, US politics and culture have been shaped by—and in response to—public crisis. And yet, by its third decade, there is a noteworthy shift in *how real or perceived crises shape social justice movements and claims.* Our sources of knowledge have changed, and with it, knowledge itself. Social media networks disseminate information based on algorithmic calculations that consider factors such as geography, social circles, education, and consumer data.[4] Whereas in the not so far past (e.g., 9/11), public understanding of an event was shaped by relatively similar news sources (even if from varying political angles), public understanding is now finessed and fractured by algorithms. As many have observed, when news consumption is channeled through social media networks, the story you are told is highly dependent on your demographic background and digital biography. If you happen to live in Brooklyn or Portland, you are a more likely consumer of Greta's environmentalist message. You will also be offered a Green toxic-free mattress called Avocado (seriously). If you live in Missouri or Tennessee, QAnon is a presumed better fit for you, and you will more likely be offered guns rather than package-free soap. The messages of QAnon and Greta cannot be separated from their forms of dissemination. Greta followers hear about QAnon as a tale of caution about the fanatic right, and QAnon followers will most likely never hear about Greta. It is therefore no surprise that the real or perceived crisis they both respond to and the solutions they offer are so different.

I am not the first to notice religious-Christian elements in Greta Thunberg or in the QAnon following.[5] Conservative-leaning writers tend to emphasize climate activism religiosity while liberal-leaning writers emphasize QAnon's. Revealing the religiosity behind what initially manifests as non-religious has long been a way of casting doubt. That is not the main purpose of this chapter. Instead, in putting these two samples of current claims for social justice side-by-side, I ask the reader to interrogate what it is about Greta (if you are a Greta fan) or QAnon (in the unlikely event that you are reading this) that appeals to your sense of justice, and why it is that when a similar tale appears on the opposite end of the political spectrum you are likely appalled. Might it strike you as odd to dismiss one story out of hand and embrace another that is so similarly structured?

A preliminary note to the reader. Placing QAnon and Greta Thunberg under one conceptual umbrella may be startling. QAnon is a ridiculous conspiracy theory, and Greta Thunberg, the 2019 Times Person of the Year, is addressing arguably the most significant challenge of our times. How dare I suggest similarities? It is my hope that by the end of the chapter you will realize, or at least be more sympathetic to my contention, that Thunberg's and QAnon's popularity and message are shaped by recycled Christian theology and attendant myths about sexuality. More important, it is striking and perhaps disappointing that in the third decade of the twenty-first century, social justice still depends on Christianity and myths about sexuality.

Two Crisis-Justice Movements on the Political Right and Left

It is undisputed that both Greta Thunberg and QAnon have generated robust social engagement of millions of people across the globe. They have offered messages that triggered massive protests in physical and virtual streets. These protests involve calls for justice to the planet, endangered species, future generations (Greta), and abused and trafficked children (QAnon). This chapter treats them as movements for social justice. The driving question here is the following: What are the material and conceptual conditions that lead millions of people (on the right or left) to perceive something as an injustice worth fighting against? The social justice fight is generated by the perceived absence of justice, injustice. And that injustice is often constructed by or around a messenger, in this case QAnon and Greta Thunberg.

Greta Thunberg's Climate Activism

The reports on climate change are alarming, and governments must act now.[6] In September 2019, sixteen-year-old Swedish climate activist Greta Thunberg addressed the United Nations Climate Action Summit at UN headquarters in New York City.[7] She delivered a powerful, political, educational, personal, and raging speech. She waved her finger, shouted, and prophesied our well-deserved mass extinction—a consequence of financial greed, inter alia. I feel empathy for Thunberg, but saddened by the delivery of the message and by its uncritical reception by many liberals and leftists. "How dare you?" she accused, "You have stolen my dreams and my childhood with your empty words . . . entire ecosystems are collapsing. We are in the beginning of a mass extinction and all you can talk about is money and fairytales of eternal economic growth. How dare you?" (Thunberg 2019a, 0:52). Science is on her side, she told us,[8] and yet affirmed that we are ignorant, not evil: "if you really understood the situation and still kept on failing to act, then you would be evil and that I refuse to believe" (2:10).[9] She promises on behalf of young people (are there young people for whom the Swedish, white, privileged, Greta cannot speak?[10]): "if you choose to fail us, I say we will never forgive you. We will not let you get away with this, right here, right now, is where we draw the line" (4:23). Greta announces a great awakening.[11] On behalf of her generation, she accuses governments of non-action, declares a forthcoming mass extinction, identifies greed, ignorance, and immaturity as primary causes of catastrophe, threatens non-forgiveness, and calls for a worldwide awakening. About four million people participated in the September 2019 global climate strikes that Thunberg inspired (Marchese 2020).

At the Vatican, Thunberg was greeted by a huge crowd chanting, "Go Greta, save the planet!" (McKie 2020). In Greta's alarming yet comforting message, many Westerners have found good causes to fight for (reducing carbon footprint, resisting greed) and evil to fight against (nations, corporations, and individuals who recklessly and shamelessly contribute to and profit from the warming of the planet). She offers practical tools to feel moral. If you reuse objects or drive a tiny car or walk, bicycle, or canoe, you are on the way to redemption. There are entities that manufacture Greta's image, brand, and message, and profit from it (Chua 2019). She says time is running out and we must repent. After a physically and emotionally strenuous two weeks at sea,[12] she arrives to the shore of New York in a sailboat with its hortatory imprint, "Unite Behind the Science." A young enthusiastic white female student welcomes Greta to the United States and thanks her for "bringing the future to America." It seems indeed that a storm propels America, united behind science, while a "pile of debris before [it] grows skyward"; the storm "is what we call progress" (Benjamin 1968).[13]

What bewilders me about the Thunberg effect is not that a sixteen-year-old girl would invoke familiar tropes and preach with conviction.

We have all preached J. D. Salinger or Ayn Rand or Nirvana or whomever rocked our excitable young hearts. I am bewildered when these strange words resonate with millions of adults who nod and wipe tears of repentance. How is Thunberg's message resonating with millions? *I* am the heretic, I know. I whisper only to one or two people I really trust that Thunberg's message sounds a bit simple, and am reminded of the beautiful, kind, heart-breaking Prince Mishkin, who knew what real love without barriers means (Dostoevsky 2003). Being simple *like that* can be a sign of grace or wisdom.

Thunberg's self-professed autism is central to deciphering the crisis-justice narrative that has emerged around her. Thunberg identifies as autistic and views this as among her greatest strengths (Grossman 2020). She views herself as a truth-teller with a strong moral compass who can distinguish right from wrong and is unafraid (partly due to her disability) to speak the truth. Her self-perception aside, Thunberg's style of simple, direct, moral, pathos-filled speech makes her an ideal spokesperson for wide audiences, including nations and corporations. I will return to the significance and problematic aspects of the representation of Thunberg's autism.

QAnon's Conspiracy Theory

Who wouldn't want to find secret meaning in the spectacle called Donald Trump? QAnon has a theory: A cabal of Satan-worshipping Democrats, Hollywood celebrities, and billionaires runs the world while engaging in pedophilia, human trafficking, and the harvesting of a supposedly life-extending chemical from the blood of abused children. This is a fascinating tale of good and evil.[14] Donald Trump is secretly battling against this cabal and is planning a day of reckoning—"The Storm" or "The Great Awakening"—in which members of the cabal will be arrested. Trump is acting strange, in other words, because he is secretly trying to save children from abuse.

QAnon first appeared in October 2017 in a post on the image board 4chan by "Q,"[15] who claimed to have access to classified information involving the Trump administration and its opponents. Q has since accused liberal Hollywood actors, Democratic politicians, and high-ranking officials of being members of a cabal and alleged that Trump feigned conspiracy with Russians to enlist Robert Mueller to join him in exposing the sex-trafficking ring and preventing a coup d'état by Barack Obama, Hillary Clinton, and George Soros (Stanley-Becker 2018). QAnon is not one theory, but a combination of many. Some followers believe that JFK junior is still alive and is himself Q. Some believe that Trump is the Messiah and was elected to put an end to horrors perpetrated against children. Some believe the coronavirus is a Democratic hoax designed to prevent a second term for Trump (Rosza 2019). Most believe that in "The Storm" thousands of members of the cabal will be arrested and possibly sent to Guantanamo Bay. Then there will be salvation and utopia on earth (Ross 2021). In an interview with Chloe, a suburban mom, she cries as she talks about the children that she believes President Trump is saving from pedophile rings (Today 2020). She says a lot of her fellow neighbors in the Pittsburg suburbs are also Q followers. Professor Alice Marwick, a QAnon researcher, observes that "getting involved in something that purports to help children is very appealing to a great deal of women" (Marwick 2020).

The precursor to the QAnon theory has come to be known as "pizzagate," which emerged in October 2016 after a Twitter account posting white supremacist material claimed that the NYPD had discovered a pedophilia ring linked to members of the Democratic Party (Silverman 2016). What followed was a social network storm in which proponents of the theory interpreted emails hacked and published by WikiLeaks from the account of John Podesta, Hillary Clinton's campaign manager. They alleged that the emails contained code words for pedophilia and human trafficking, and that a pizzeria called Comet Ping Pong pizzeria was a meeting ground for satanic ritual abuse (Aisch et al. 2016). The theory gained momentum on Twitter and Facebook and took on the meme #PizzaGate. One day a young man arrived at Comet Ping Pong pizzeria and fired a rifle; he then surrendered after finding no evidence of child slaves being held there (Domonoske 2016).[16]

QAnon became known worldwide and earned its place in history books when, on January 6, 2021, many of its members proudly and filled with rage stormed the US Capitol along with other far right groups such as the Proud Boys (Leatherby et al. 2021). That historic episode occurred after the perceived savior, then-President Donald Trump, refused to concede his loss of the presidential election to Joe Biden, and instead promoted another conspiracy theory—"stop the steal"—according to which he had actually won the 2020 elections. With prayers to Jesus the Lord, a well photographed horn, and other religious symbols, QAnon supporters stormed the Capitol in a fight against forces of evil. But even before that day, QAnon was far from a fringe movement.[17] By the fall of 2020, it had gained a large following of believers and spreaders. The FBI had classified it as a potential domestic terror group, Facebook has banned it across platforms (Collins and Zadrozny 2020), and the House voted to condemn it (Davis 2020). Still, a national survey concluded that "an astounding 50% of President Trump's supporters say they believe top Democrats are involved in elite child sex-trafficking rings, and an even higher percentage of Trump supporters believe the president is diligently working to dismantle these rings" (Beer 2020; Romano and Dickson 2020). There was clearly something appealing about QAnon's founding fantasy of the good savior Donald Trump fighting the evil cabal of sex traffickers.

Sexual Purity of Children

The cultural representations of QAnon and Greta Thunberg reveal familiar anxiety about sexual purity and innocence of real or imagined children. Thunberg is portrayed in popular culture, news, and social media as pure, virginal, and pre-sexual; and the fantasized children allegedly abducted for sex, trafficking, blood drinking, and murder by Hillary Clinton, Jews, and Hollywood collaborators are portrayed as victims in need of Donald Trump, their alleged savior. In narratives on both the right and left, adults are typically portrayed as possessing sexual desire and agency, while children by contrast are situated as victims of sexual abuse (QAnon) or planetary ruin (Thunberg). And this is not a side characteristic of these movements. It is the core. Purity, virtue, and innocence of children *are the lynchpins for judgment and condemnation* of the impurity, corruption, and guilt of adults.[18]

Pure Greta

"The Pure Spirit of Greta Thunberg Is the Perfect Antidote to Donald Trump," declared a writer for the New Yorker in late 2019 (Kormann

2019). Accompanying this proclamation is a close-up silhouette-style photograph of the seventeen-year-old's facial profile. The only light in this mostly dark photograph outlines Thunberg's skull as she gazes upward. Greta is portrayed as a virginal saint.[19] Like Joan of Arc, her public image is that of a pre-sexual teen.[20] Her prophetic iterations can be angry without condemnation. She is a visionary. This public image of a pure messenger of truth interestingly involves a complex combination of her gender, age, race, and autism.

Greta's public image and professed self-perception are that of a young girl. Although already seventeen years old at an interview, she claims that finding solutions to climate change is "not up to us children to do. That would be strange" (Marchese 2020), and "technically and legally I am a child [. . .] when I turn 18 I'm going to switch to describing myself as an adult. That's a very autistic way of seeing things . . . I'm autistic, and I say things the way they are" (Marchese 2020). In fact, Thunberg underscores her advocacy for climate justice as that *of a child* when she admits, "I don't think I have any specific wisdom. I don't have much life experience. One thing I do have is the childlike and naïve way of seeing things. We tend to overthink things. Sometimes the easy answer is, it is not sustainable to live like this" (Marchese 2020). It is children and not adults, according to Thunberg, who can save the world.

Prevailing beliefs about autistic youth as less sexual or asexual add an important layer to Thunberg's self-perception and her public perception. In recent years, literature has emerged that connects autism with the asexual spectrum (Bush et al. 2020).[21] Thunberg echoes these studies when she professes lack of social and sexual interest in her peers (Marchese 2020). She describes herself as someone who does not know or socialize with people her age. For pleasure, she says, "I do jigsaw puzzles. I watch lots of documentaries, and I read a lot. I am with my dogs" (Marchese 2020). Consciously or not, her asexual or pre-sexual image has been utilized to emphasize the innocence of childhood and to promote climate justice activism. Her public image is that of a female-child prophet. Her rage is perceived as holy and prophetic, not catty, nasty, deceitful, or self-interested.[22] You can't trust women. But you can trust Greta![23]

Figure 13.1. Greta Thunberg: angelic and prophetic. Photo by Luis Filipe Catarino/4See/Redux.

QAnon's War on Pedophilia

A bizarre exchange took place between reporter Savannah Guthrie and President Trump in a Town Hall aired on NBC on October 15, 2020, less than three weeks before the general elections (Bump 2020).

> GUTHRIE: Let me ask you about QAnon. It is this theory that Democrats are a satanic pedophile ring and that you are the savior of that. Now, can you just once and for all state that that is completely not true and disavow QAnon in its entirety?
>
> TRUMP: I know nothing about QAnon—
>
> GUTHRIE: I just told you.
>
> TRUMP: I know very little. You told me. But what you tell me doesn't necessarily make it fact, I hate to say that. I know nothing about it. I do know they are very much against pedophilia. They fight it very hard, but I know nothing about it. If you'd like me to—
>
> GUTHRIE: They believe it is a satanic cult run by the deep state.
>
> TRUMP: —study the subject. I'll tell you what I do know about: I know about antifa and I know about the radical left. And I know how violent they are and how vicious they are. And I know how they're burning down cities run by Democrats, not run by Republicans.
>
> . . .
>
> TRUMP: Let me just—let me just tell you, what I do hear about it, is they are very strongly against pedophilia. And I agree with that. I mean, I do agree with that. And I agree with it very strongly.
>
> GUTHRIE: But there is not a Satanic pedophile cult being run by—
>
> TRUMP: I have no idea. I know nothing about it.
>
> (Bump 2020)

While Trump, the alleged savior, claims to know "nothing" about QAnon, he does somehow know that "they are very strongly against pedophilia" and he "agree[s] with it very strongly." As one QAnon follower attests, QAnon's appeal is that it is not "boring" like the regular news cycle: You actively participate in the breaking down and revealing of huge child trafficking networks (van Zuylen-Wood 2020). You help save the children. QAnon is situated in a popular genre in American culture that involves catching and condemning pedophiles.[24] Queer and feminist theorists have extensively studied the construction of the child in American culture as a site of innocence and purity, and the related moral condemnation of pedophilia.[25] Allegations of sexual child abuse, no matter how absurd or grounded in facts, are a sure recipe to generate a moral panic.[26]

QAnon and its popularity can be seen as a backlash through ironic mimicking of #MeToo, a movement that revealed many instances of sexual violence and structures of injustice. Since the fall of 2017, public attention to sexual exploitation of women and children has intensified, with wide media coverage of abuses of power and of criminal prosecutions of celebrities such as Harvey Weinstein and Jeffrey Epstein.[27] In many of these cases, real men, women, and children were abused by powerful men (and occasionally women).[28] It is no surprise and yet still quite ironic that Q would mobilize key themes of the #MeToo movement—abuse-of-power, trauma, and sexual innocence of children—still fresh in the public zeitgeist to launch an apocalyptic battle against an imaginary cabal of Satan worshippers who allegedly abused imaginary children. In the event known as "The Storm," harasser-in-chief Donald Trump will allegedly reveal the cabal, punish its members, and save innocent children from sex abuse (Locke 2017).

Greta's climate justice message and her popular image as a prophet of doom are inseparable from her public image of sexual purity and innocence; the fictitious children that Donald Trump will allegedly save from predators such as Clinton (a white woman), Obama (a Black man), and Soros (a wealthy Jew) are also perceived by QAnon followers as pure and innocent. Whether the child is the messenger of doom (Greta) or the actual (yet nonexistent) victim of doom (in QAnon), both movements demonstrate how some of the most powerful justice claims in the twenty-first century (still) depend on innocence and purity of children.

Apocalyptic Genre

Around the year AD 50, Paul wrote a letter to the Thessalonians in which he advised them to prepare for the Last Judgment, which will be imminent and sudden.[29] Paul did not invent the apocalyptic genre or the idea of the end of times (Boyarin 1994).[30] He inherited the genre from early apocalyptic texts dating at least from the third century BCE.[31]

Early apocalyptic narratives involved a mystifying veneer and an angel appearing to explicate the meaning and implication of the vision.[32] Since then, apocalyptic writings have taken a variety of forms. As historian of religious thought Michael Stone summarizes:

> Two general categories [of apocalyptic literature] seem, however, to be particularly prominent. The first is eschatology. Apocalyptic eschatology is permeated by the expectation of the imminent end and, for it, the advent of the end does not depend upon human action. The second type of material, here called the speculative, is the revelation of heavenly or similar secrets. The secrets revealed may include matters of cosmography and uranography, angelology and meteorology, calendar and cosmogony, and more. A third, less prominent subject appears in a number of cases, a pietistic, moral preaching. (Stone 1984, 383–84)

In the following section, I demonstrate how these subgenres of apocalyptic thought have become central in social justice narratives on both ends of the political spectrum: Greta Thunberg and other climate justice activists on the one end and QAnon and other far right conspiracy theories on the other.

Eschatology and Moral Reckoning

We are already in the midst of a sixth extinction, Greta tells us. Environmentalist writing and activism has long embraced eschatological apocalyptic narratives,[33] and it is prominent throughout Thunberg's speeches. "Our house is on fire . . . I want you to panic. I want you to feel the fear I feel every day" (Thunberg 2019b); "Entire ecosystems are collapsing. We are in the beginning of a mass extinction."[34] Eschatology is the crux of Greta's message and persona. What is the point of going to school if the world is ending? Greta does not provide new data. Her role as an orator is to deliver the message of science that the world as we know it is over.

Greta's eschatological pronouncements about a looming planetary disaster come with moral accusations about the bad deeds that have caused this climate catastrophe. She does not offer herself as a savior who can solve the problem (she says only scientists can), but she situates herself as a prophet, a sage, and a martyr who suffers the consequences of the sins of others. In a presentation entitled *Averting a Climate Apocalypse*, her moral demand on world leaders and businesses is clear:

> Our emissions have to stop . . . We demand at this year's World Economic Forum participants from all companies, banks, institutions, and governments immediately hold all investments in fossil fuel exploration and extraction, immediately end all fossil fuel subsidies, and immediately and completely divest from fossil fuels. We don't want these things done by 2050, or 2030, or even 2021. We want this done now. . . . Our house is still on fire. Your inaction is fueling the flames by the hour. And we are telling you to act as if you loved your children above all else. (Thunberg 2019b)

QAnon followers believe that in the event known as "The Storm," thousands of members of the cabal will be arrested and possibly sent to Guantanamo Bay, and there will be salvation and utopia on earth (Ross 2021). When the coronavirus began to spread in early 2020, Q issued a round of important clues. "Nothing Can Stop what is Coming," Q tweeted, "The Great Awakening is Worldwide," and "God Wins" (LaFrance 2020). The pandemic provided new and exciting material for the apocalyptic messaging of the QAnon community (Argentino 2020). After calling it a "hoax" (following the lead of the alleged savior) and accusing the media and Democrats for inducing panic aimed at stopping Trump rallies and undermining economic gains of his presidency, the narrative shifted to viewing the pandemic as a promised coming of the Kingdom of God.[35] Like Greta, Q delivers an eschatology, but of a different sort. It is a defeat of evil forces by good forces. As summarized by a reporter for *The Atlantic*, "The eventual destruction of the global cabal is imminent, Q prophesies, but can be accomplished only with the support of patriots who search for meaning in Q's clues . . . One of Q's favorite rallying cries is 'You are the news now.' Another is 'Enjoy the show' . . . *When the world as we know it comes to an end, everyone's a spectator*" (LaFrance 2020).

Truth-Telling/Secret-Revealing

One of the founders of Critical Autism Studies, philosopher Ian Hacking, warns against misleading stereotypes about autism that emerge out of popular culture narratives (Hacking 2009, 514). Common perceptions about autism, he writes, "can encourage the image of the autist as gifted with secret knowledge or wondrous powers. It can lead to sliding from a genuine fact to a foolish fiction" (514). In other words, viewing insight and truth-telling *as necessarily derivative of* autism can be misleading. Relatedly, disability scholars have discussed the phenomenon of the "supercrip,"[36] a disabled person (Christopher Reeve, the actor best known for "Superman," who later became disabled through an accident, is a prominent example) who overcomes tremendous obstacles and achieves fame and success through strength and perseverance *despite* their disability.[37] The supercrip is often celebrated as a hero and a spokesperson, even if their life or view does not represent or do justice to other disabled people who are subjected to discrimination in an ableist society (Clare 2017).

The notion that Thunberg's autism makes her a prophet and a truth-teller is central to her self-narration and public image. A supercrip narrative has emerged in which Thunberg's neurological difference authorizes her as the prophet of climate justice. She describes herself and is presented as a truth-teller who stands up to a culture of lies, interest, and deception (Grossman 2020). Those who are not neurodiverse, she implies, are more likely to be complicit in planet destruction because they are deferential to power. "To get out of this climate crisis," she says, "we need a different mindset from the one that got us into it. People like me—who have Asperger's syndrome and autism, who don't follow social codes—we are not stuck in this social game of avoiding important issues. We dare to ask difficult questions. It helps us see through the static while everyone else seems to be content to role-play" (McKie 2020).

Q presents himself as a truth-revealer and a prophet by claiming a position of insider authority. He is allegedly an intelligence officer or military official with Q clearance. Based on his access to government secrets, Q has dropped clues about "the truth" and offered prophecies.[38] Q's prophecies and "truth-telling" have shifted through different conspiracies—involving the Satanic cabal, the coronavirus as a hoax,[39] and the stolen 2020 elections—all portraying Donald Trump as the savior fighting the deep state.

Conclusion

The structural parallels of these two late-modern social justice movements are clear. They both rely on myths about sexual purity and innocence of children, apocalyptic battles of good and evil, a savior, suspicion of lies, and deception by power elites. But still, you may wonder, should it not matter that QAnon is fantasy and Greta's story is true? Of course it should. And it shouldn't. Consider the following thought experiment. Step 1: Separate the factual claims of these two social justice movements from the general moral-political-normative implications offered by them. Step 2: Assume that each of these sets of facts, in turn, is verifiable as true. Step 3: Would the moral-political-normative implications of that movement be sensible to you? Step 4: Assume that each set of facts is verifiable as false. Step 5: Would the moral-political-normative implications of that movement be sensible to you?

For most readers the answer to step 3 is "yes" and the answer to step 5 is "no." This is simply because, should these facts be true, it is sensible that some course of action should be taken that more or less fits what these movements are calling for. If we assume for a moment that all the facts offered by QAnon *and* Greta Thunberg activism are true (Hillary Clinton and Barack Obama are running a satanic cabal, trafficking in

TABLE 13.1. The premises and proscriptions of two crisis-driven social movements.

	QAnon	Greta Thunberg
Alleged Facts	Democratic and liberal elites traffic in and abuse children. Donald Trump is secretly acting to save the children from this conspiracy of elites.	Planet is rapidly warming, mostly due to human action. Climate disasters are already occurring and will continue to do so with increasing frequency.
Moral-Political-Normative Theory	End child trafficking; support Donald Trump; pursue criminal legal action against Hillary Clinton and other Democrat child abusers.	End carbon emissions through national and international policy reforms; make individual lifestyle changes, including reducing carbon footprint.

children, drinking their blood, together with key characters in Holly-wood, and Donald Trump is fighting this evil cabal in order to save the children; the earth is headed towards a sixth extinction in which only the rich elites will survive with comfort and the rest will die or suffer, and if we follow Greta's path and sail to our destinations, we could delay or prevent the magnitude of the extinction), we can see two social justice theories that are actually the same tale of Christian salvation. The significant difference between these two movements is that one is based on scientific facts that we can test and verify (climate change); while the other is based on fantasy. But from a commonsense perspective, fact verification is the significant difference between these two movements. And yet, although they support inapposite political goals, they are both social justice movements that utilize Christian values and myths and rely heavily on the sexual purity of children.

Contemporary social justice movements tell Christian tales that are sometimes supported by science (Thunberg) and sometimes not (QAnon). Critical and queer theory cannot stop at verification or falsi-fication of facts. Science, of course, sorts and verifies facts, and scientific expertise ought to guide our understanding of climate change, pandemics, and many other such issues. But reliance on medical science and expertise ought not to blind us to how justice and morality are produced and manufactured. Scientific data, as many have observed (Ronell 2008), has become a primary way of understanding the world. But Christianity and myths about sexuality, pedophilia, and danger still shape leading perceptions of social justice in the West. Although Greta's message is science adjacent and QAnon's is pure falsehoods, both theories of justice deserve close attention and scrutiny. It may be that for you, as long as social justice movements are based on true facts, it does not matter that they follow a Christian trajectory or sexual mythology. If you expect something more from social justice, however, then "I want you to panic" (Thunberg 2019b).

NOTES

1 For a discussion of how innocence as a key ethical-moral concept, from its classic figures such as the child, the refugee, the trafficked victim, and the animal, has come to structure ideas about politics in the contemporary Euro-American context, see Ticktin 2017, 571–730.

2 See generally Sullivan and Vries 2006; Varghese et al. 2021, 1–10.

3 For a representative text, see Klein 2020.

4 See, for example, Orlowski 2020.

5 See, for example, Graves and Fraser-Rahim 2021; Green 2019; Luo 2021; Vargic 2019.

6 For representative and influential texts see, for example, Klein 2014; Wallace-Wells 2019.

7 For full speech, see Thunberg 2019a.

8 "For more than 30 years, the science has been crystal clear" (Thunberg 2019a).

9 "The popular idea of cutting our emissions in half in ten years only gives us a 50 percent chance of staying below 1.5 degrees and the risk of setting up irreversible chain reactions beyond human control . . . With today's emissions levels, that remaining CO_2 that entire budget will be gone is less than 8 and a half years." (Thunberg 2019a).

10 For critique of the lack of racial awareness in Thunberg's message see, for example, Peach 2019.

11 "The world is waking up and change is coming whether you like it or not!" (Thunberg 2019a).

12 See Grossman 2020.

13 "a storm is blowing in from Paradise; it has got caught in [an angel's] wings with such a violence that the angel can no longer close them. The storm irresistibly propels him into the future to which his back is turned, while the pile of debris before him grows skyward. This storm is what we call progress" (Benjamin 1968, thesis IX).

14 See generally Roose 2021 and Rosza 2019.

15 "Q" is a reference to the Q clearance used by the US Department of Energy.

16 For an elaborate reporting of the role of social media in #pizzagate, see Orlowski 2020.

17 "more and more of these ideas are becoming mainstream, we are starting see political candidates running on QAnon platforms and ideas more palatable the to the average person seep into daily life" (Marwick 2020).

18 Several have offered feminist and queer critique of the centrality of the image of the innocent child in American culture. See, for example, Kincaid 1998 (critically examining the legacy of Victorian sexuality in modern American culture, in which children and images of youth are idealized, fetishized, and eroticized); Fischel 2016a (arguing that the figures of the sex offender and the child enable fictions that allow the concept of consent to thrive in late modern sexual politics). See also Fischel 2016b (synthesizing critiques of the myth of "childhood innocence" with scholarship on the racialization of innocence, and pointing to the complexity of "innocence" as a political idiom for the promotion of social and sexual welfare).

19 "The form of Greta Thunberg's protest is familiar to any student of medieval Europe, the civilization that produced the Children's Crusade and Joan of Arc. The content of her protest is deliquescence of Protestantism into narcissistic terror" (Green 2020).

20 *See also* Mishan 2020.

21 Existing research suggests that people with Autism Spectrum Disorder (ASD) are more likely than those without ASD to self-identify as asexual, or as being on the asexual spectrum (Bush et al. 2020).

22 Rebecca Traister has nicely articulated the role of the rage of women in social justice movements (Traister 2018).

23 For critical analysis of overlapping stereotypes about asexuality and disability, see for example, Clare 1999.

24 See generally Fischel 2016b.

25 See, for example, Fischel 2016b; Edelman 2004.

26 See, for example, Jarecki 2003 (covering the criminal investigation, conviction, and suicide of Arnold Friedman, who pleaded guilty to multiple charges of sodomy and sexual abuse of children, after he was caught with a collection of child pornography); Kincaid 1998.

27 See, for example, Bryant 2020.

28 See generally Ben-Asher 2020. *Leaving Neverland* (2019), for instance, is a heart-wrenching documentary film presenting two young men who were sexually abused as young boys by Michael Jackson, which presumes and emphasize the trauma of its protagonists and the conviction that children do not (and cannot) have sexual desire or agency.

29 "To the end he may establish your hearts unblameable in holiness before God, even our Father, at the coming of our Lord Jesus Christ with all his saints" (1 Thess. 3:13); "For the Lord himself shall descend from heaven with a shout, with the voice of the archangel, and with the trump of God: and the dead in Christ shall rise first: Then we which are alive and remain shall be caught up together with them in the clouds, to meet the Lord in the air: and so shall we ever be with the Lord" (1 Thess. 4:16–18).

30 See also Dunn 1990.

31 See generally Boyarin 2012. Before the apocalyptic texts there were the major prophets of the Old Testament, such as Jeremiah, who announced the destruction of Jerusalem and the Temple. Jeremiah began giving prophecies of Jerusalem's coming destruction in 626 BC by invaders from the north. This was a punishment for worshiping the idols of Baal, burning children as offerings to Moloch, and deviating from God's laws. Jeremiah prophesized that the nation of Judah would suffer famine, foreign conquest, plunder, and captivity in a land of strangers.

32 See generally, Stone 1984, 383.

33 See, for example, Kolbert 2014 and Wallace-Wells 2019.

34 For full speech see Thunberg 2019b.

35 David Hayes, an influencer in the QAnon community, reassured his viewers in a March 14, 2020 livestream that they may not be affected by the "spiritual warfare" because only those who have not been chosen by God will be affected (Argentino 2020). The person known as Q pushed a conspiracy theory about COVID-19

being a Chinese bioweapon and that the virus release was a joint venture between China and the Democrats to stop Trump's re-election by destroying the economy.

36 As disability scholar David T. Mitchell wrote, "He's [Reeve] the good guy—the supercrip, the Superman, and those of us who can live with who we are with disabilities, but who cannot live with, and in fact, protest and retaliate against the oppression we confront every second of our lives are the bad guys" (quoted in Goggin and Newell 2004). See also McRuer 2006.

37 Another example of this can be found in the documentary film *Murderball* (Rubin and Shapiro 2005) (portraying quadriplegics, who play full-contact rugby in wheelchairs and overcome unimaginable obstacles to compete in the Paralympic Games). In the case of Christopher Reeve, the critique of disability scholars was that he used his power, wealth, and supercrip status to advocate for *cure* for people with spinal injuries rather than address discrimination against people with disabilities. For critique of the "cure" narrative, see Clare 2017.

38 His first was that Hillary Clinton will be arrested imminently.

39 In April 2020, a "Q drop" alleged a coordinated propaganda effort by Democrats, Hollywood, and the media to promote "mass hysteria" about the coronavirus: "What is the primary benefit to keep public in mass-hysteria re: COVID-19? Think voting. Are you awake yet? Q" (LaFrance 2020).

BIBLIOGRAPHY

Aisch, Gregor Jon Huang and Cecilia Kang. 2016. "Dissecting the #PizzaGate Conspiracy Theories." *New York Times*, December 10, 2016. www.nytimes.com.

Argentino, Marc-André. 2020. "QAnon Conspiracy Theories about the Coronavirus Pandemic Are a Public Health Threat." *The Conversation*, April 8. https://theconversation.com.

Barry, Dan, Mike McIntire, and Matthew Rosenberg. 2021 "'Our President Wants Us Here': The Mob That Stormed the Capitol." *New York Times*, January 10. www.nytimes.com.

Beer, Tommy. 2020. "Poll: Half of Trump Supporters Believe Baseless Child Sex-Trafficking QAnon Claims." *Forbes*, October 20. www.forbes.com.

Ben-Asher, Noa. 2020. "Trauma-Centered Social Justice." *Tulane Law Review* 95: 95–142.

Benjamin, Walter. 1968. "Theses on the Philosophy of History." In *Illuminations*, edited by Hannah Aredt, translated by Harry Zohn, 253–64. New York: Schocken Books.

Boyarin, Daniel. 1994. *A Radical Jew: Paul and the Politics of Identity*. Berkley: University of California Press.

———. 2012. *The Jewish Gospels: The Story of the Jewish Christ*. New York: New Press.

Bryant, Lisa, dir. 2020. *Jeffrey Epstein: Filthy Rich*. Netflix. www.netflix.com.

Bump, Philip. 2020. "Rather than Condemn the QAnon Conspiracy Theory, Trump Elevates Its Dangerous Central Assertion." *Washington Post*, October 15. www.washingtonpost.com.

Bush, Hillary, Lindsey Williams, and Eva Mendes. 2020. "Brief Report: Asexuality and Young Women on the Autism Spectrum." *Journal of Autism and Developmental Disorders* 51(2): 725–33. https://doi.org/10.1007/s10803-020-04565-6.

Chua, Jasmin Malik. 2019. "Is Your Greta Thunberg T-Shirt Contributing to Climate Change?" *Fashionista*, October 24, 2019. https://fashionista.com/

Clare, Eli. 1999. *Exile and Pride: Disability, Queerness, and Liberation*. Cambridge: SouthEnd Press.

———. 2017. *Brilliant Imperfection: Grappling with Cure*. Durham, NC: Duke University Press. https://doi.org/10.1515/9780822373520.

Collins, Ben and Brandy Zadrozny. 2020. "Facebook Bans QAnon across Its Platforms." *NBC News*, October 6. www.nbcnews.com.

Davis, Susan. 2020. "House Votes to Condemn QAnon Conspiracy Theory: 'It's a Sick Cult.'" *NPR*, October 2. www.npr.org.

Domonoske, Camila. 2016. "Man Fires Rifle Inside D.C. Pizzeria, Cites Fictitious Conspiracy Theories." *NPR News*, December 5. www.npr.org.

Dostoevsky, Fyodor. 2003. *The Idiot*, translated by Richard Pevear and Larissa Volokhonsky. New York: Vintage.

Dunn, James. 1990. *Jesus, Paul, and the Law: Studies in Mark and Galatians*. Louisville, KY: Westminster/John Knox Press.

Edelman, Lee. 2004. *No Future: Queer Theory and the Death Drive*. Durham, NC: Duke University Press.

Fischel, Joseph J. 2016a. "Pornographic Protections? Itineraries of Childhood Innocence." *Law, Culture and the Humanities* 12(2): 206–20.

———. 2016b. *Sex and Harm in the Age of Consent*. Minneapolis: University of Minnesota Press.

———. 2019. *Screw Consent: A Better Politics of Sexual Justice*. Oakland: University of California Press.

Goggin, Gerard and Christopher Newell. 2004. "Fame and Disability: Christopher Reeve, Super Crisp, and Infamous Celebrity." *M/C Journal* 7(5). https://doi.org/10.5204/mcj.2404.

Graves, Melissa and Muhammad Fraser-Rahim. 2021. "The U.S. Needs Deradicalization—for Christian Extremists." *Foreign Policy*, March 23. https://foreignpolicy.com.

Green, Dominic. 2019. "The Apotheosis of St. Greta." *Spectator UK*, September 24. https://www.spectator.co.uk/.

Grossman, Nathan, dir. 2020. *I Am Greta*. Hulu. www.hulu.com.

Hacking, Ian. 2009. "How We Have Been Learning to Talk about Autism: A Role for Stories." *Metaphilosophy* 40(3–4): 499–516. www.jstor.org.

Jarecki, Andrew, dir. 2003. *Capturing the Friedmans*. HBO Documentary Films.

Kincaid, James. 1998. *Erotic Innocence: The Culture of Child Molesting*. Durham, NC: Duke University Press.

Klein, Ezra. 2020. *Why We're Polarized*. First Avid Reader Press hardcover edition. New York: Avid Reader Press.

Klein, Naomi. 2014. *This Changes Everything: Capitalism vs. The Climate*. New York: Simon & Schuster.

Kolbert, Elizabeth. 2014. *The Sixth Extinction: An Unnatural History*. New York: Henry Holt.

Kormann, Carolyn. 2019. "The Pure Spirit of Greta Thunberg Is the Perfect Antidote to Donald Trump." *New Yorker*, December 13. www.newyorker.com.

LaFrance, Adrienne. 2020. "The Prophecies of Q." *The Atlantic*, June. www.theatlantic.com.

Leatherby, Lauren, Arielle Ray, Anjali Singhvi, Christiaan Triebert, Derek Watkins, and Haley Willis. 2021. "How a Presidential Rally Turned Into a Capitol Rampage." *New York Times*, January 12. www.nytimes.com.

Locke, Kaitlyn. 2017. "Gloria Steinem Calls Trump the 'Sexual Harasser in Chief.'" *Boston Globe*, December 7. www.bostonglobe.com.

Luo, Michael. 2021. "The Wasting of the Evangelical Mind." *New Yorker*, March 4. www.newyorker.com.

Marchese, David. 2020. "Greta Thunberg Hears Your Excuses. She Is Not Impressed." *New York Times Magazine*, October 30. www.nytimes.com.

Marwick, Alice. 2020. "QAnon Researcher: 'If we can't agree on what's true, how can we agree on anything else?'" Interview by David Crabtree. *WRAL News*. October 15. Video, 4:42. www.wral.com.

McKie, Robin. 2020. "Greta Thunberg: 'Only people like me dare ask tough questions on climate.'" *The Guardian*, October 11. www.theguardian.com.

McRuer, Robert. 2006. *Crip Theory: Cultural Signs of Queerness and Disability*. New York: New York University Press.

Mishan, Ligaya. 2020. "How Shouting, Finger-Waving Girls Became Our Conscience." *New York Times*, September 30. www.nytimes.com.

Orlowski, Jeff, dir. 2020. *The Social Dilemma*. Exposure Labs. Netflix. www.netflix.com.

Peach, Charlie. 2019. "Greta Thunberg, a Rich White Girl from One of the Whitest Places on Earth, Is NOT a Victim. #Climate Change." *Medium*, September 24. https://politicspeach.medium.com.

Romano, Andrew and Caitlin Dickson. 2020. "New Yahoo News/YouGov poll: Half of Trump Supporters Believe QAnon's Imaginary Claims." *Yahoo News*, October 20. www.yahoo.com.

Ronell, Avital. 2008. *The Test Drive*. Urbana: University of Illinois Press.

Roose, Kevin. 2021. "What Is QAnon, the Viral Pro-Trump Conspiracy Theory?" *New York Times*, March 4. www.nytimes.com.

Ross, Alexander Reid. 2021. "How the Fascist-friendly Pro-Trump QAnon Conspiracy Theory Led to Insurrection." *Ha'aretz*, January 14. www.haaretz.com.

Rosza, Matthew. 2019. "QAnon Is the Conspiracy Theory That Won't Die." *Salon*, August 18. www.salon.com.

Rubin, Henry Alex and Dana Adam Shapiro, dirs. 2005. *Murderball*. MTV Films.

Silverman, Craig. 2016. "How a Completely False Claim About Hillary Clinton Went from a Conspiracy Message Board to Big Right Wing Blogs." *BuzzFeed*, December 5. www.buzzfeed.com.

Stanley-Becker, Isaac. 2018. "'We Are Q': A Deranged Conspiracy Cult Leaps from the Internet to the Crowd at Trump's 'MAGA' Tour." *Washington Post*, August 1. www .washingtonpost.com.

Stone, Michael E. 1984. "Apocalyptic Literature." In *The Literature of the Jewish People in the Period of the Second Temple and the Talmud, Volume 2 Jewish Writings of the Second Temple Period*, edited by Michael E. Stone, 383–441. Boston: Brill.

Sullivan, Lawrence Eugene and Hent de Vries (eds.). 2006. *Political Theologies Public Religions in a Post-Secular World*. 1st edition. New York: Fordham University Press.

Thunberg, Greta. 2019a. "Speech to the UN" (speech). Filmed September 2019 in New York, NY. PBS. www.pbs.org.

———. 2019b. "'Our House Is on Fire'" (speech). Filmed January 2019 in Davos, Switzerland. www.theguardian.com.

Ticktin, Miriam. 2017. "A World without Innocence." *American Ethnologist* 44(4): 571–730.

Today. 2020. "QAnon Spreading in the Suburbs: Inside Look at How Conspiracy Theories Are Taking Hold." YouTube. October 15. Video, 5:43. www.youtube.com.

Traister, Rebecca. 2018. *Good and Mad: The Revolutionary Power of Women's Anger*. First Simon & Schuster hardcover edition. New York: Simon & Schuster.

van Zuylen-Wood, Simon. "QAnon Goes to Washington." *New York Magazine*, September 28. https://nymag.com.

Varghese, Ricky, Fan Wu, and David K. Seitz. 2021. "Introduction: Queer Political Theologies." *GLQ* 27(1): 1–10.

Vargic, Hrvoje. 2019. "The New Religion of Greta Thunberg." *Ethica Politica*, December 11. https://ethikapolitika.org.

Wallace-Wells, David. 2019. *The Uninhabitable Earth: Life After Warming*. New York: Tim Duggan Books.

14

An Interview on *Feeling Queer Jurisprudence: Injury, Intimacy, Identity*

SENTHORUN SUNIL RAJ, JOSEPH J. FISCHEL, AND
BRENDA COSSMAN

In *Feeling Queer Jurisprudence: Injury, Intimacy, Identity* (2020), Sentho-run Sunil Raj undertakes an expansive, careful, and caring examination of emotion across an array of late twentieth, early twenty-first-century "pro-LGBT" cases and legislative reforms. Surveying flashpoints of political and legal contestation for LGBT people, Raj tracks how dis-gust, hate, anger, fear, and love ricochet and shapeshift among litigants, judges, activists, and scholars. Such emotions, explains Raj, have been indispensable for advancing the legal recognition of LGBT lives and relationships. At the same time, the "jurisprudential crystallization" of emotion risks devaluing and therefore endangering non-normative genders, sexualities, and intimacies. The *Enticements* editors interviewed Raj about the arguments, methods, and proposals of *Feeling Queer Jurisprudence*.

JOSEPH FISCHEL: I love the emotions diary entry that are the first two
    pages of *Feeling Queer Jurisprudence*; what an entreaty of vulner-
    ability for your readers! You relay that while you were drafting
    the manuscript, Australia undertook a public opinion survey on
    same-sex marriage. "I was furious," you confess, that the state was
    subjecting human rights to popular vote. But your fury immediately
    competes with your "lament" for the social justice issues marginal-
    ized by marriage politics, lament followed by "relief" at the survey
    results, relief then attenuated by reflective "frustration" before being
    fully capsized by "rage" against legislative exemptions to nondiscrim-
    ination mandates.

My hunch is that a lot of right-minded, left-thinking queer folks identify with kaleidoscopic feelings when it comes to mainstream gay rights questions and gay rights cases. As the late great Lauren Berlant used to ask, *what do we lose when we win?* And yet you make a methodological decision, one that seems right but opaque, to focus on a *single* emotion for each chapter of the book, an emotion you then read through a subset of gay rights cases (about sodomy, nondiscrimination, hate crimes, immigrant asylum, marriage, and so forth). What are the advantages, you think, in concentrating your analytic energy upon a single emotion through a subset of gay rights cases, rather than observing the many emotions that collide or complement one another? If we focus, say, on the circulation of *fear* in LGBT asylum cases, might we overlook the political and jurisprudential operations of other emotions in these cases? Or perhaps you are excavating what you take to be the most salient emotion in a line of cases in order to teach us how those emotions shape the juridically possible?

SENTHORUN RAJ: A kaleidoscope is such an apt metaphor to describe the emotions that underpinned writing the book. When I began thinking about what I wanted to write about for my dissertation, which the book is based on, I found myself reflecting on LGBT topics that felt salient to me personally. I began storyboarding blogs and articles I had written, law reform proposals I had worked on when I was a policy advisor, and human rights campaigns I had participated in as a student activist. In doing this exercise, I was trying to find a coherent narrative to distill my "views" on LGBT rights. Instead, I found myself identifying the different emotional registers of the work I had done. For example, I had worked on a reform proposal to amend an Australian state law that would allow same-sex couples to adopt children. When meeting politicians and drafting parliamentary submissions, I found myself trying to ease the anxieties of homophobic politicians by talking sweetly about "productive" and "respectable" gay couples who were already caring for children but were denied the ability to legally formalize a "traditional" parental relationship. Yet I was writing elsewhere about what could be possible if Australian family law expanded conceptions of parenting to allow for legal recognition of more than two parents. At times, the split in my legislative and intellectual labors felt disingenuous. As you say, I think queer activist-scholar-lawyers can relate to what I am saying in relation to that feeling.

But I also think these affective conflicts are quite generative. I began to wonder what might be possible if, instead of foregrounding contested "rights" or "issues" in a depersonalized sense, I foregrounded feelings on my storyboard about "LGBT progress." How might paying greater attention to emotions reveal what we focus on when we pursue LGBT rights, and what fades away from view?

I started with a kaleidoscope of emotions and began to parse each of them in relation to specific LGBT law reform issues. I would take a particular subject—such as relationship recognition—and begin to trace how particular actors (politicians, judges, activists, lawyers, myself) articulated their feelings about it. I then considered how those emotions were produced or mediated by the register of their articulation (parliamentary speeches, judgments, tweets, blog posts, legal briefs). My storyboard began to spiral again, returning to that kaleidoscope of feelings I started with. I felt in awe of the scale of the project that was emerging on the horizon.

I had to find a way, then, to concentrate my analytic energy, to focus on something specific within that horizon. As Mariana Valverde (2015) reminds us, legal scholarship has default objects (norms, rules, regulations) that are framed or analyzed within particular jurisdictional scales (local, state, federal, transnational). I realized that emotion could be both a legal object and legal frame. Contrary to what was taught to me in law school, emotion is central to more conventional forms of legal analysis. For example, colonial laws criminalizing "gross indecency" and "carnal intercourse against the order of nature" operationalize disgust to criminalize socially "contaminating" or "deviant" sexual practices that range from consensual gay sex to child sexual abuse. In international refugee law, those who seek asylum are legally mandated to prove "a well-founded fear of persecution." Emotion is not marginal. It is named directly in law. I took this insight as an opportunity to undertake more conventional forms of legal analysis (i.e., analyzing homosexuality criminalization cases within particular jurisdictions) by taking emotion as a legal object while "queering" the legality of that analysis by using emotion as my analytic frame. In doing so, I was attempting to take part in a common law discourse that organizes around judicial precedents (which name emotion) while also speaking to critical queer sensibilities by reading precedents through emotion. This is why I focused on the most salient emotion that structured a set of legal cases. I felt that approach, while opaque and selective, made it possible to render something clear and meaningful to judges, lawyers, activists, and scholars. This is not to say that analyses of conflicting and complementary emotions are not useful. That analysis is essential.

To return to the late great Lauren Berlant, there seemed to be something more pedagogically useful about using emotions selectively as part of an analytic strategy to understand how socio-legal norms are produced and secured. Their *Cruel Optimism* (2011) is a good example of this. Berlant excavates optimism in popular culture texts to show how it binds us to social fantasies that inhibit our flourishing. Sara Ahmed also inspired me to think about the political consequences of emotion. In *The Cultural Politics of Emotion* (2004), Ahmed coupled specific emotions with political case studies to show how emotion operates as political or social glue that holds together troubling norms. In my book, I adapted this approach to look at how emotions function as legal glue that hold together different ideas of injury, intimacy, and identity in relation to LGBT people.

I also want to share a personal anecdote. A decade ago, as an undergraduate student, I presented a paper at a Gender Studies seminar at the University of Sydney about fear and LGBT people who seek asylum. Lauren Berlant was a visiting fellow at the time and prompted me to think about the judicial emotion expressed through the legal texts I was writing about, rather than trying to diagnose or isolate the emotions of the people seeking asylum. In many ways, my book is a response to Berlant's generous pedagogic invitation.

I try to use emotion as an analytic tool to better understand how legal recognition of LGBT rights is structured without trying to make some formal or authoritative claim about the exclusivity of emotion, or authenticating the emotions of those who participate in these decisions (judges, lawyers, activists). I am not sure how methodologically robust this approach might seem to social scientists or doctrinal scholars, but it makes political and pedagogic sense to me.

JF: A related question—why do you think when we travel from criminal law to public law in *Feeling Queer Jurisprudence*, we move from disgust and hate to anger, fear, and love?

SR: This is a fascinating question and one, I must admit, I do not address sufficiently in the book. I think the different emotions speak to different purposes of those subdisciplines of law. Criminal law regarding sexual minorities, probably unsurprisingly to most people, organizes around contempt, disgust, and hate. If I were to caricature the purpose of criminal law in a way that would be familiar to people who watch legal dramas, I would say that it proscribes conduct which is deemed harmful or destructive to society. In that sense, what society finds gross or loathsome is easily associated with what is criminal. When discussing hate crimes in my book, for example, I note how there is a palpable redirection of legislative expressions of hate and disgust from LGBT people who are stigmatized as socially contaminating (and once criminalized as such) to homo/transphobes who are now marked with that criminal stigma through hate crime laws for their refusal to "tolerate" diversity.

In contrast, public law addresses the authorized conduct of the state (as manifested in the actions of state officials) rather than the (bad) behavior of private individuals. When it comes to LGBT people, several "progressive" governments articulate LGBT rights through discourses of dignity, protection, and respect. Anger emerges in state condemnations of discriminatory action that inhibits the rights of some LGBT people to work freely or access services. Fear manifests in state concern about the return of some LGBT people to situations where they might be tortured or killed for existing. Love materializes in how the state proclaims the dignity of some LGBT families who are denied the security of relationship recognition. I qualify those sentences with "some" because those emotions circumscribe the limits of recognition. For queer people who seek asylum, they must not make decision-makers fearful they are trying to injure the integrity of the immigration system with a "bogus claim" of being gay. For same-sex couples who want to marry, they must appeal to a romantic conjugal notion of intimacy or risk state denial of their relationship. For LGBT people who endure discrimination, they must not make too many demands for accommodation, particularly when it comes to religious or purportedly religious institutions, or they will not solicit the angry condemnation of the court.

As I mentioned earlier, we do not travel in a linear direction by jumping from one emotion to another. While I focus each chapter on a particular emotion, I also gesture to how those emotions connect with others. If anything, emotions travel together across different areas of law. Sometimes those emotions cleave apart to create different routes (such as when gay intimacy moves from abject criminalization to loving celebration) but sometimes they entangle together and make it difficult for us to see the direction we are traveling (such as when compassion opens up the space for protecting LGBT refugees alongside fear and anxiety that confines protection to those who are "authentic").

JF: In nearly every chapter of *Feeling Queer Jurisprudence*, you track the itinerary of a powerful emotion, say anger or fear, within or proximate to a set of LGBT legal cases. I found this move on your part—descriptive but also expositive and so prescriptive—to be both terrifically compelling and also humbling. For example, in your discussion of *Romer v. Evans* (517 U.S. 620 (1996)), the US Supreme Court decision invalidating an amendment to Colorado's state constitution that would have barred a host of antidiscrimination protections to lesbian, gay, and bisexual people, you show how *anger* ricochets across stakeholders and decision makers. The majority opinion expresses judicial anger at the purported anger or animus of Colorado voters; meanwhile, in his famous dissent, Justice Scalia is righteously angered by the majority's anger that the demos are driven by anger. For another example: You describe how hate crime legislation redirects hatred historically reserved for homosexuals onto homophobes instead. I say this sort of analysis is humbling because it reveals that however profoundly felt one's political feeling, that feeling may be just as deeply felt, and as readily deployed, by one's opponent. Of course, your point is not something like moral or affective relativism; but then, what is your point? What do queers learn when we see our emotions mirrored back to us by legal actors, whether LGBT-antagonistic or LGBT-accommodating?

SR: I think an affective analysis can be humbling and necessary. And you are right, I am not making a moral or relativist claim about emotions. Rather, I am trying to create analytic space to hold different articulations of emotion together so we might better respond to LGBT people's material injuries, intimacies, and identities.

Right now, if I might focus on trans rights in the United States for a moment, we are witnessing considerable public anxiety toward young trans people accessing gender-affirming healthcare. Some conservative state governments, bolstered by a queer alliance of homo/transphobic groups and some self-described feminist and gay groups, have repudiated medical care for trans kids. Anxiety, I think, offers a useful lens to understand what exactly is at stake in this protracted debate about trans existence. For young trans people, denial or delay of medical care induces great anxiety. Young trans people have spoken extensively about how medical affirmation alleviates their anxieties associated with unwanted pubertal changes. Contrastingly, some gay groups express anxieties that gay/lesbian children are being coerced into "gender change" to avoid accepting their homosexuality (an assumption which ignores the fact that many trans people are also gay, lesbian, and bisexual). Some feminists note their anxieties about how clinicians promote medical transition for gender non-conforming children who might come to "regret" their medical transitions. Anti-LGBT groups express anxieties at how children are "indoctrinated" into "ideologies" that deny what they believe to be a child's immutable sex. These differentiated anxieties crystallize and contour the scope of what is possible with trans law reform. Those of us committed to laws that enable the flourishing of trans children need to take seriously the way these anxieties are solidified in public debates and recognize the socio-political consequences of their refraction in legislation or jurisprudence. In doing so, we can navigate the role anxieties play in (limiting) access to trans healthcare. By seeing those emotions refracted back at us, we can address them in a critically, politically therapeutic way—one that does not diminish the depth of conflicted feelings manifested but also refuses to countenance transphobia.

In an analytic sense, more broadly, our emotions direct our attention toward certain objects or spaces while obscuring or covering over others. We need to map out what emotional enactments are doing across different registers of law if we are to get a more precise understanding of what is imaginable or thinkable in the context of law reform.

BRENDA COSSMAN: On that point, your treatment of anger suggests it is a more fertile emotion than, say, hate or fear. Your analysis of the ways in which anger has enabled pro-LGBT intervention toward the exposure of injury and the recognition of intimacies/identities is powerful. I found your argument about the need for activists and lawyers to "make space for LGBT people's anger when facing discrimination to accommodate their identities and intimacies," as well as the ways in which the judicial accommodation of anger risks marginalizing non-normative sexual subjects, to be persuasive. Attention to anger strikes me as so important in recognizing how injustice and harm feel, and how subjects and their injuries have been produced in part through this anger. But I wondered whether your approach to anger was too pastoral. Anger is a volatile, potentially destructive emotion. It equally divides progressive communities. As Audre Lorde (1984) remarked long ago on the productive uses of anger, we need to—but have yet to—develop tools to disagree angrily but collaboratively with our comrades. Judith Butler asks, "[w]hat can be done with rage? We don't always think about that, because we view rage as an uncontrollable impulse that needs to come out in unmediated forms. But people craft rage, they cultivate rage, and not just as individuals. Communities craft their rage" (quoted in Terry and Butler 2020). In my own work, I have been increasingly thinking about the role of anger within and between progressive communities, and how we might craft it to better uses (Cossman 2021). What do you see as the role of anger for queer actors, activists, claim-making and so on?

SR: What a prescient analysis of anger. You are right to suggest that my analysis of anger is pastoral. I think this is where I need to acknowledge how my own impulse to "resolve" the messy, divisive dimensions of anger may have romanticized my gloss. The question you ask, citing Lorde, about the need to develop tools to engage with others angrily but collaboratively is vital. I do not have a clear answer to this question. For me, harnessing the power of rage requires us to register the terms of "our" rage. Is it an individual feeling? Is it a collective articulation? Where does it focus our attention? Why do we feel it? Does it seek to punish? Does it attempt to heal?

We know from the work of queer and feminist scholars that anger enables us to register the "texture" of inequality or discrimination, and anger is also a resource to dismantle structures that enable such inequality while building solidarities among those who experience (overlapping forms of) discrimination. Yet, as social psychologists remind us, anger can also function as a projection of insecurity in a way that undermines social conditions that are necessary for interpersonal relationship building. Anger is volatile and destructive. Anger is also generative and revealing. In the book, through my reading of public accommodation cases like *Romer v. Evans* (1996) and *Boy Scouts of America et al. v. Dale* (2000), I try to show that how we make use of anger needs to be differentiated, and that such affective differentiation gives us a better sense of the consequences of the claims made by parties, activists, lawyers, and judges.

Making space to register the anger of those who experience discrimination (such as those denied access to a social or commercial service) requires scholars and activists to countenance that anger and to develop tools to deal with productive disagreement (for example, when public denials of social or commercial services are justified along religious lines). For activists and lawyers who seek to harness anger to illustrate specific unlawful acts of discrimination or conflicts between rights, we need conceptual and organizational tools to register anger that neither pathologize anger as a universalizing "authentic" representation of the discrimination claim nor fetishize anger (to borrow a concept from Wendy Brown's *States of Injury*, 1995) in a way that obscures the political conditions that underpin the discriminatory conduct.

Judges must parse and assess the parties' different articulations of anger; articulations that take shape through judicial condemnation of the party that discriminates against a marginalized individual or the party seeking to unreasonably "impose" itself on a "vulnerable" institution. Communities might then angrily respond to those legal decisions because they think the decisions went too far or not far enough.

Developing a conceptual framework for registering, differentiating, and responding to anger is important if we are to take anger seriously and make space for it as an analytic resource that allows us to productively conflict together. It is a provocation without a simple answer.

JF: I would just add that anger's objects are especially slippery and prone to projection—a phenomenon likely overdetermined by historical materialism (see Bernstein 2010) and psychodrama (see Brown 2001). What I mean is: When the left eats its own, I wonder if that appetite is sometimes whetted by our sense of impotence against Big Daddy (the state, the court, the university . . .).

Despite or maybe in syncopation with the relatively free flotation of powerful emotions that you describe across pro-LGBT legal cases, one of your main objections to such cases is the "judicial crystallization of emotion"; indeed, you mentioned "crystallization" several times earlier in our interview. Your concern, if I am reading and listening to you correctly, is that rigid and righteous attachments to emotions like disgust, fear, anger, or even love "obscures" or "occludes" a wider array of injuries and inequalities experienced by sexual and gender minorities. The "crystallization of hate . . . produces punitive legal parochialism," for instance, by focusing juridical and political attention onto the allegedly evil homophobe and away from state and structural violence and neglect. *Love*, as expressed in and judicially emblematized by the couple form, cabins conceptions of freedom, equality, dignity, rights-worthiness.

The idiom you reach for as your preferred antidote to "crystallization" is "loosening": You ask us, and you ask lawyers, judges, scholars, and activists, to loosen our attachments, maybe our fidelity, to powerful emotions like fear and love in order to "make space for queer intimacies and identities." "Loosening the emotional tether[s]" of disgust and love, for example, might cultivate both social sympathy for as well as legal protections to kinky folks and poly folks, respectively.

To put my question provocatively: Are you emotional about emotions? Or less provocatively: Is crystallization of collective feeling always a problem for sexual and social minorities, and is loosening our attachments to strong emotions always the answer? For as you just acknowledged, the activation and amplification of *anger* has been elemental to queer activism (of course, you also suggest anger is distinctive in this regard from the other emotions you canvass).

SR: I do get emotional about emotions! Your provocative and less provocative questions are precisely the kind of musings I hoped my book would cultivate. Some jurisprudence scholars, such as Lon Fuller (1969) and Ronald Dworkin (1986), have written at length about how judicial attachments to purposive interpretations of legislation and procedural norms are key to "good law." LGBT legal scholars, such as Kenji Yoshino (2015) and Lisa Bower (1994), have written about how a more critical fidelity to ideas of dignity and equality can generate "good law." Queer legal scholars, like Eddie Bruce-Jones (2020) and Katherine Franke (2015), have encouraged us to be suspicious of legal attachments to (hetero)normative ideas of the "good," including progressive ideas like dignity, equality, and human rights. Different traditions of legal scholarship draw attention to the attachments that make possible the legal recognition of LGBT people, whether progressive or not. By drawing out the fidelities generated by emotion, we (as activists, scholars, lawyers, judges) can hold space to loosen our attachments without necessarily letting them all go.

Let me illustrate what I mean with an example from the book. In the chapter on marriage equality, I follow closely the queer commitment to recognize non-dyadic, kinky, non-sexual forms of intimacy. I use *love* as the lens in my reading of cases like *Obergefell v. Hodges* (2015) to expose how romantic, individualized notions of liberty (such as the right to express your commitment through marriage) combine with social hopes for equality (such as the freedom to live without discrimination from society) and expectations of respectability (such as the aesthetic of monogamy) to create the affective conditions within US constitutional law that let gay and lesbian people marry.

These attachments are generative, but their articulation also harnesses emotions like love in a way that diminishes the possibility of recognizing intimacy in other forms. Monogamous love is one form of intimacy worthy of legal recognition; it need not restrict recognition for messier, kinkier intimacies. Loosening our attachments to that specific form of love might enable us to pursue a queerer, decolonial feminist vision of love that foregrounds community solidarities instead of romantic partnerships (see Raghavan 2017).

Loosening attachments, then, is a structural intervention that relates to creating critical distance to the type of subjects that come before the law and the types of recognition that law affords those subjects. This analytic and political maneuver is not about eschewing emotions or recognition. Anger plays an important role in highlighting harm, fear reveals the potential for injury, disgust exposes that which contaminates, and love illustrates our capacities for connection and community. Loosening our attachments to emotions in law is about opening out modes of recognition for queers who are currently excised by the emotional frame of reference, "LGBT progress."

BC: So much queer legal analysis has an underlying anti-regulatory impulse. Yours does not. I love how your analysis, while revealing the multiple paradoxes, costs, and exclusions of a strategic turn to law, does not eschew law altogether. Rather, you embrace it, and channeling José Muñoz (2009), urge us to think harder about these paradoxes to build "a better future for LGBT people." What constitutes Sen Raj's queer regulatory imaginary? Is there a police force in the queer state? Prisons? Criminal law?

SR: That is such a difficult and important question. As someone who has worked within the legal system to secure material changes for LGBT people, I have always been wary of queer engagements with law that eschew regulation entirely. What I find so powerfully moving about José Muñoz's work is that it imagines a future unbound by the temporality of heterosexual reproduction and privatized domesticity. Queer potentiality takes the affectivity of the present moment that many queers experience, particularly feelings of shame and deficiency, to "cruise" a future where failure is accepted alongside virtuosity and generosity. It is at this juncture that I see my contribution to queer legal analysis. A queer jurisprudence of emotion enables scholars, activists, lawyers, and judges to take seriously the emotions that circumscribe the (legal) reality for LGBT people while also analytically opening avenues for scholarship, activism, litigation, and decision-making that support the well-being of LGBT people.

I'll try to contextualize what I mean with an example from the book. When writing about hate crime laws, I found myself ambivalently hateful throughout the research and writing process. I remember reading the case of trans man Brandon Teena, who was viciously assaulted and killed in Nebraska. I was repulsed by the cis men who had killed Teena. But I was also repulsed by the way in which local police dealt with Teena's complaints about sexual violence prior to the murder. I found my sense of loathing toward both the state (scaled narrowly here as the local police) and the perpetrators made me question what, if anything, could be done to hold everyone involved accountable. Is justice even possible in such a situation? This question is not new, and I have to say my thinking on this topic has evolved as I have engaged more with the work of Angela Davis (2003) and other abolitionist scholars who see our future free of police and prisons. In the book, I write about the value of criminal law (murder convictions for Teena's killers) alongside civil remedies (tort claims against the police) as a way of maintaining a differentiated but also robust form of accountability in response to transphobic violence. Yet, I now think that a regulatory framework that pursues accountability in a non-carceral form might be better placed to address the structural (rather than just interpersonal) conditions that make transphobic violence possible in the first place. Heeding Annalise Acorn's advice (2004), I do not wish to romanticize restorative justice remedies for violence. However, it is possible to reject police and prisons while also creating conditions of public governance that can respond to homo/transphobic violence in a way that secures accountability, safety, and rehabilitation. Davina Cooper (2019) has recently written about social groups withdrawing from formal state intervention as an invitation to "play" with alternative modes of governance. I find this idea of state play politically seductive and need to think more about how this might work in relation to the questions raised in my book.

So, I do not think I am able to articulate what my queer regulatory imaginary might be at the moment because I think that imaginary takes shape in response to the particular area of law or policy we are talking about and the particular intervention we might wish to make. But if my book can help extend the work of other queer legal scholars and activists to reimagine governance better, I will consider the book a success.

JF: Let's turn to the vexing question of religion and religious rights. You write, "By loosening jurisprudential anger . . . it is possible to acknowledge how LGBT people can be accommodated by religion, not in spite of it." If one looks to *Masterpiece Cakeshop* (2018) and *Fulton* (2021), US Supreme Court cases that carve out religious exceptions to LGBT antidiscrimination ordinances, one would be forgiven for assuming that not only is the polarization between religious rights and gay rights complete, but also that religion is winning.

Yet your work documenting the political foreclosures attendant to the judicial enactment of emotion militates against decrying these cases as pure losses. Whether or not some claims to religious freedom are pretexts for sexism and homophobia, I think we cannot be so dismissive of our opponents' injuries—and you might even nominate some of these opponents "queer." So I think my question is not: Who should win, or what are better strategies for progay litigation, but: How might attention to emotion, and intense emotions especially, soften polarity between religious citizens and queers, between claims of freedom and equality?

SR: I do not find the binary approach to how we, as an LGBT community, often talk about legal "wins" and "losses" to be useful. We need to be honest about how we are simultaneously winning and losing depending on our social metrics. This is also true in a narrow legal sense because a "bad outcome" for one party might be accompanied by progressive expansion of legal doctrine, while a "good outcome" for a party might be situated in confusing jurisprudence.

As with so much litigation around gay equality and religious freedom, it isn't so much that one triumphs and the other is defeated. Rather, it is about how each claim is emotionally positioned by both political and legal actors (it is impossible to separate the imbrication of law and partisan politics here). I think it is accurate to say that dominant legal and political articulations of religious freedom assume the homophobic position that being gay is incompatible with being religious. You are right to say this polarization is acutely evident in the United States with a conservative-led Supreme Court, where restrictions on LGBT people's access to public spaces is becoming more jurisprudentially entrenched.

Even if we think more transnationally about the "conflict of rights" issue, we see how courts are compelled to "balance" the anger of LGBT people who are denied goods or services (such as buying a wedding cake or adopting kids) against the anger of religious individuals or organizations who claim being LGBT is "incompatible" with their religious convictions. Rendering the sense of injury expressed through anger requires careful attention to what the purported harms to each legal actor are. If we take seriously the depth of feeling of those who angrily oppose greater accommodation of LGBT people in public, we can push back against it by first recognizing, and then attending to, the affective logic of their anger. Equally, when LGBT people angrily (and understandably) dismiss religious objections to their existence, we must recognize whether that repudiation also erases the existence of religious queers whose claims for freedom do not reside in judicial distinctions between public (secular) and private (religious) space but exist in the interstices of both. As such, religious queers may seek a (legal) claim of freedom that is unique, and which cannot be achieved by indexing their existence against some formal benchmark of equality that is secured through a legal separation of public/private space. Foregrounding their anger at being erased from (non-religious) queer communities and (homo/transphobic) religious communities might offer a way to bridge the polarization that not only limits anti-discrimination protections for LGBT people but also limits solidarity between divided communities.

BC: I am fascinated (perhaps obsessed) with the question of queer theory/queer legal theory's subject and object. Lauren Berlant and Michael Warner wrote, more than twenty-five years ago, that "queer theory is not the theory *of* anything in particular" (1995). Many have contested, in Judith Butler's language, the "proper objects" of queer theory (1994). Queer theory/queer legal theory has an ambivalent relationship with all things LGBT. If it had an essence, which is of course a very unqeer thing, it might be its anti-identitarian imperative. Much queer legal theory swirls around non-normative sexualities and genders. Yet, you are refreshingly unapologetic in your focus on "pro-LGBT cases" which you carefully delineate. What would you say of the proper and improper objects of queer legal theory?

SR: I take Butler's essay you reference as my cautionary queer academic tale against prescribing the "proper objects" of queer legal theory. Also, taking notes from Robyn Wiegman (2012), I prefer to ask what we might learn about the grammar of queer legal scholarship by attending to its analytic strategies, strategies honed to troubling our investments both in legal structures and in modern sexual taxonomy. Some queer legal scholars might name my continuing strategic investments in law and legal strategies as "improper" because I refuse to eschew taxonimizing structures like law that have, and continue to, marginalize sexual and gender minorities. They might query whether "pro-LGBT cases" could ever be queer. Yet, in legal theory circles, my choice of using emotion as an object of study and mode of analysis would be deemed "improper" given law school dispositions to valuing objectivity, neutral rules, and clear norms. Indeed, even writing about my emotions in legal scholarship would be "queer."

I enjoy playing in this space of impropriety. I'm probably too queer for "proper" legal scholars. I'm probably too normative for "proper" queer scholars. Yet, my contribution to queer legal theory emerges from a commitment to using law, as Muñoz might say, to cruise a fabulously queer future while pursuing that commitment by faithfully attending to conventional legal objects (like legislation and judgments). Developing an analytic framework that captures the emotional grammar of law is queer legal scholarship.

BC: I want to think with you finally about the methodological sensibilities of queer legal theory. It seems that a common approach/theme/ critical disposition is to illustrate the paradoxical ways in which the legal inclusion of marginalized sexualities simultaneously risks reinforcing heteronormative—and subsequently homonormative— identities and intimacies, marginalizing those who do not fit its norms and practices. Your analysis extends this method to the realm of emotions, describing how emotions deployed in the pro-LGBT cases include some identities and intimacies at the cost of injuring others. Does this tell us something about the way queer method travels to law, with close and paradoxical readings of legal discourse?

SR: When I was writing the book, it was important to clarify the different articulations of queer, and how those articulations travel into law and legal scholarship. While I could not hope to cite the rich range of theorizing on *queer*, I will try to crudely paraphrase a few usages that were critical to the project. I start with locating *queer* in terms of individuals who express and experience sexual and gender non-conformity. I also look at political uses of *queer* as a form of resistance to normalizing modes of social governance that promote heterosexuality, reproduction, monogamy, domesticity, and privatization. Alongside those individual and political registers, I lastly consider the analytic use of *queer* as a lens to understand and deconstruct the organization of social norms that produce ideas of what is "normal" and disciplinary expectations of what is "acceptable."

In the book, I bring these different articulations of *queer* together through the lens of emotion to think about what queerness does in and through cases that purport to protect the rights of LGBT people. In parsing each of those different articulations of *queer* through my reading of "LGBT cases," we begin to see how legal protections for queer people may nevertheless entail foreclosure. For example, when judges review LGBT asylum claims, their expressions of fear and anxiety crystallize to both affirm "authentic" queer people in need of protection from persecution while repudiating "queer" claims of intimacy and identity that cannot be authenticated against (hetero)normative ideas of sexuality. Judicial worries about accepting "bogus" individuals who are pretending to be gay or judicial anxieties about overstretching definitions of what it means to be a refugee militate against political articulations of queerness that move to dismantle normative categorizations and institutions. In other words, emotion is a queer analytic lens that shows us how jurisprudence forecloses capacious understandings of queer intimacies and identities that might undermine the integrity of the refugee adjudication system, even as judicial recognition extends to protect some queers who seek asylum. Queer travels to law through different experiential, political, and analytic trajectories, and those trajectories often conflict.

JF AND BC: Thank you Sen for sharing your reflections here, and for your excellent intervention on law, sexuality, and emotions.

BIBLIOGRAPHY

Acorn, Annalise E. 2004. *Compulsory Compassion: A Critique of Restorative Justice*. Vancouver: University of British Columbia Press.

Ahmed, Sara. 2004. *The Cultural Politics of Emotion*. Edinburgh: Edinburgh University Press.

Berlant, Lauren. 2011. *Cruel Optimism*. Durham, NC: Duke University Press.

Berlant, Lauren and Michael Warner. 1995. "What Does Queer Theory Teach Us about X?." *PMLA* 110: 343–49.

Bernstein, Elizabeth. 2010. "Militarized Humanitarianism Meets Carceral Feminism: The Politics of Sex, Rights, and Freedom in Contemporary Antitrafficking Campaigns." *Signs* 45(Autumn): 45–71.

Bower, Lisa C. 1994. "Queer Acts and the Politics of Direct Address: Rethinking Law, Culture and Community." *Law & Society Review* 28(5): 1009–33. https://doi.org/10.2307/3054022.

Brown, Wendy. 1995. *States of Injury: Power and Freedom in Late Modernity*. Princeton, NJ: Princeton University Press.

———. 2001. *Politics Out of History*. Princeton, NJ: Princeton University Press.

Bruce-Jones, Eddie. 2020. "Death Zones, Comfort Zones: Queering the Refugee Question." In *The Queer Outside in Law: Recognising LGBTIQ People in the United Kingdom*, edited by Senthorun Raj and Peter Dunne, 49–78. Cham: Springer International.

Butler, Judith. 1994. "Against Proper Objects. Introduction." *differences: A Journal of Feminist Cultural Studies* 6: 1–26.

Cooper, Davina. 2019. *Feeling Like a State: Desire, Denial, and the Recasting of Authority*. Durham, NC: Duke University Press.

Cossman, Brenda. 2021. *The New Sex Wars: Sexual Harm in the #MeToo Era*. New York: New York University Press.

Davis, Angela Y. 2003. *Are Prisons Obsolete?* New York: Seven Stories Press.

Dworkin, Ronald. 1986. *Law's Empire*. Cambridge, MA: Belknap Press.

Fischel, Joseph J. 2019. *Screw Consent: A Better Politics of Sexual Justice*. Oakland: University of California Press.

Franke, Katherine M. 2015. *Wedlocked: The Perils of Marriage Equality: How African Americans and Gays Mistakenly Thought the Right to Marry Would Set Them Free*. New York: New York University Press.

Fuller, Lon L. 1969. *The Morality of Law*. Rev. edition. New Haven, CT: Yale University Press.

Lorde, Audre. 1984. *Sister Outsider: Essays and Speeches*. Trumansburg: Crossing Press.

Muñoz, José Esteban. 2009. *Cruising Utopia: The Then and There of Queer Futurity* New York: New York University Press.

Raghavan, Anjana. 2017. *Toward Corporeal Cosmopolitanism: Performing Decolonial Solidarities*. London: Rowman & Littlefield International.

Raj, Senthorun Sunil. 2020. *Feeling Queer Jurisprudence: Injury, Intimacy, Identity*. Abingdon; New York: Routledge.

Terry, Brandon and Judith Butler. 2020. "The Radical Equality of Lives." *Boston Review*, January 7.

Valverde, Mariana. 2015. *Chronotopes of Law: Jurisdiction, Scale, and Governance*. New York: Routledge.

Wiegman, Robyn. 2012. *Object Lessons*. Durham, NC: Duke University Press.

Yoshino, Kenji. 2015. *Speak Now: Marriage Equality on Trial: The Story of* Hollingsworth v. Perry. 1st edition. New York: Crown.

Afterword

JANET HALLEY

In October and November 2005, Eve Kosofsky Sedgwick gave three lectures at Harvard Law School, "The Weather in Proust" (in two parts) and "Melanie Klein and the Difference Affect Makes." Along with the lecture series she showed artworks under the title "Works in Fabric, Paper, and Proust" at the Radcliffe Institute. You can read the essays and see reproductions of some of the artworks in *The Weather in Proust*, the posthumous, beautifully produced publication of Sedgwick's last works, edited by her friend Jonathan Goldberg (Sedgwick 2011).

I organized all these events. When it was all over, Eve gave me the mock-up for "Adjective Game," one of several of her works in cloth and paper that she classified as an "Artist's Book" (Eve Kosofsky Sedgwick website). Floating on an 8 × 11 softly figured background in a rosy tangerine color is a yellow page with a paragraph from Marcel Proust's *In a Budding Grove*, translated into English, printed on it. All the adjectives, and the first parts of all the adverbs that end in "-ly," are missing from the page itself, leaving gaps where they once appeared. But Eve has supplied each of them as a separate cut-out word, lightly fixed to the yellow page with Velcro. They beckon the viewer to move them around.

The paragraph itself is voluptuous, the adjectives even more so, and there are seemingly (not actually) infinite possibilities that open up because you can move the words around. There is a temporal dimension to this mounting multiplicity, moreover. I have been moving the words around for years now. To write this afterword I found the passage in *In a Budding Grove* and restored all the Velcro'd words to their original positions, restoring too the pleasure of the shape-shifting perceptions of Proust's narrator. But fingers just itch to move the little Velcro'd words again. I want to hear the little rip of the word coming loose; I want to undergo the surprise when an adjective that never becomes an adverb by adding -ly nevertheless does so: a nonce word. Even stuck to the page in the "right" places, the words are slightly akimbo to the printed line: It is almost impossible to get them to align perfectly with the printed letters. It all makes an iconic masterpiece of Western literature into the very emblem of lush, even louche, proliferating possibility. Which it already was.

I think of this construction as a queer hypothesis about the world. So different from the hypothesis we get from Catharine MacKinnon's famous summation of her argument about sexuality as the eroticization of male domination and female subordination, "Man fucks woman, subject verb object" (1982, 541). There is no way out of that sentence. Male and female are pitched as pure opposites; one owns all the world's power and privilege, the other all its abjection and victimization. Sedgwick's mock-up, like her famous list of just some of the dimensions—none including m or f—along which people's sexuality differs,[1] asks us to look at the world not through the lenses of a binary but through glasses that can take in unpredictable and possibly innumerable variation (Sedgwick 1990, 25–26).

Even when she saw very strong patterns, Sedgwick was intent on staying alert to their mobility and capacity to sustain multiplicity. Consider table A.1 of *Epistemology of the Closet*:

TABLE A.1. Models of Gay/Straight Definition in Terms of Overlapping Sexuality and Gender. From Eve Kosofsky Sedgewick's *Epistemology of the Closet*.

	Separatist	Integrative
Homo/hetero*sexual* definition	*Minoritizing*, e.g., gay identity, "essentialist," third-sex models, civil rights models	*Universalizing*, e.g., bisexual potential, "social constructionist," "sodomy" models, "lesbian continuum"
Gender definition	*Gender separatist*, e.g., homosocial continuum, lesbian separatist, manhood initiation models	*Inversion/liminality/transitivity*, e.g., cross-sex, androgyny, gay/lesbian solidarity models

Source: Eve Kosofsky Sedgwick, *Epistemology of the Closet*, 1990, 2008 by The Regents of the University of California. Published by the University of California Press. Figure 2. "Models of Gay/Straight Definition in Terms of Overlapping Sexuality and Gender," p. 88.

This is a classic example of what I will call chiasmatic critique. Let's take homo/heterosexual definition first. However narrowly any one person, group, or social movement might assert a minoritizing identity (some versions would be "born that way," essentialist, and "immutable characteristics"), somewhere in the political landscape, and even in the ambivalent self, beats the thrumming heart of a universalizing identity (the bisexual potential of every single human, the universal propensity to act, Adrienne Rich's idea that all women share a place on a lesbian continuum and that their "choice" to be heterosexual was made under coerced circumstances that cast deep doubt on it). Sedgwick emphasizes again and again the *incoherence* of this collision of models: One may be in the ascendency but neither gets the last word; neither has any necessary, fixed relationship to liberation or oppression; no one is sufficiently "above the fray" to say which is true.

At the same time and layering onto the question of homo/heterosexual definition, gender definition is divided on parallel lines. Gender separatist models abound: buff men, straight and gay, celebrate masculinity on a homosocial continuum; lesbian separatists split off from radical feminism to form communes that welcome only womyn. To update Sedgwick's sampling a bit is to see the leakage of minoritizing thinking into the gender space: essentialist, born that way, anima muliebris forms of trans identity insist on the ultimate reality of one's male or female destination gender.

Meanwhile, gender is *also* saturated with celebrations of inversion, liminality, and transitivity: not he or she as the destination gender but transition with no destination; they, them, theirs; nonbinary identity. And again, the universalistic tendencies of Sedgwick's analysis of homo/heterosexual definition are leaking into this quadrant of gender experience: LGBTQ+ itself is an assertion of continuum that knows no stopping place. Sedgwick's examples feel a bit dated: butch lesbians, pansies, androgyny, and the occasional flourishing of strong gay/lesbian cross-identification. However much one of these formations might be the key to survival for any individual, that could change: At a later stage in the same life, or next door in a different life, the seemingly opposite one is what's needed. Again, incoherently, they are both latently available, and both can be, depending on the circumstances, the key to survival or a deep threat.

What makes this chiasmatic is frequent crossing *across* the grid as a gender model seeks its homo/heterosexual model or vice versa. Here's Sedgwick (1990, 89):

> Gender-*separatist* models like [Adrienne] Rich's or [Benedict] Friedlän-der's [that is, respectively, lesbian and gay-male separatist models], seem to tend toward *universalizing* understanding of homo/heterosexual potential. To the degree that gender-integrative inversion or liminality models, such as [Magnus] Hirschfeld's "third-sex" model, suggest an alliance or identity between lesbians and gay men, on the other hand, they tend toward gay-*separatist*, minoritizing models of specifically gay identity and politics.

We certainly see the latter today in the intense rights orientation, strong essentialist claims, and minoritizing political positioning emerging from the nonbinary segment of the trans landscape.

This chiasmatic move brings the degree of systematic incoherence to an almost fever pitch. When one is being intellectually lazy, it's easy to wrap one's self in the flag of minoritizing or universalizing sexual identity claims. "That's me," we say. But when they make sense because of one's distinctivist (so close to minoritizing) and transitivity-celebrating gender ideas (so close to universalizing), we begin to see that voting one's way out of this complex system is not going to be an option.

So we have from Sedgwick two modes of critique: One is the refusal of boundary in the willingness to see a series that could extend even to infinity. I will call this the "and others" queer sensibility, invoking a series of essay and book titles that Sedgwick and Jonathan Goldberg and Michael Moon, her housemates during her years at Duke University (1988–97; Eve Kosofsky Sedgwick website), all used to point the way to lush interconnectedness and extension without closure (Sedgwick 1993, 167–76; Moon 1998).[2] And the other is the mobile, contradictory holding together of opposites in an unstable but systematic discourse of diacritical differences that can shift and even flip over time. I will call that "openness to charismatic critique."

Both modes of critique are visible again and again across the full length of this remarkable book.

* * *

"And others" moments abound. Take Zachary Herz's chapter, "The Epistemology of the Courthouse: Classical Antiquity in American LGBT-Rights Litigation." Herz collects instances in which anti-gay and pro-gay litigants seek to trace answers to today's questions to classical antiquity, and praises queer historians who have substantiated the "radical inapplicability of arguments from history and called their audiences to think in different terms" (chapter 1). Martha Nussbaum, for instance, countered anti-gay arguments that ancient Greek moral thought condemned what we understand to be homosexuality by substantiating "the weirdness, the foreignness, and the fundamental contingency of that morality" (chapter 1). The very next chapter, Ratna Kapur's "The Sexual Subaltern and Law: Postcolonial Queer Imaginaries," manifests the spiritual yearning for liberation through a radical search for alterity that one sees so often in her work. Kyle Kirkup's "Queer Risk Knowledge" offers a learned genealogy of sex-affirmative strategies and conceptions of risk devised to deal with COVID-19, tracing them back to the queer activism of the HIV precursor epidemic: The constant morphing of old strategies into new ones has the feel of Nietzschean genealogy, a telling of the past leading to the present not through logic or repetition but through constant creative transformation. Evelyn Kessler brings a specifically Sedgwickian hypothesis to her chapter "Oversexed, Undersexed, 'No Sex': Queer Subjects and the Anti-Chinese Movement in the Age of Capital," where she displays in rich historical detail the radically unstable and ever-shifting representation of the sexuality, gender, family economics, and labor of Chinese immigrants into the United States during the latter half of the nineteenth century. What she finds are the "dissonances and resonances, lapses and excesses of meaning" that Eve placed at the heart of her "and others" critique (Sedgwick 1993, 8; quoted in chapter 6). Matthew Ball's "'I Would Kiss a Man Whenever I Want, Let Some Fucker Hit Me': Queering Narratives of Incarceration, Sexuality, and Offending," urges scholars to follow the "turn to the archives" in studies of queer incarceration in an effort to "and others" the contemporary emphasis on the sheer violence of life in state custody: "The queer criminological archive beseeches us to embrace discomfort as we encounter and make sense of the plethora of queer life and queer experience" (chapter 11).

Finally, the reticence of some contributors to use the slogan LGBTQ or LGBTQ+—both Kapur and Matthew Waites reserve Q for deeply transitive and universalizing modes of thought and leave LGBT to refer to minoritized identities made to resemble one another as much as possible—cracks the acronym to create an "and others" opening at its close.

* * *

Instances of chiasmatic critique are also plentiful—a remarkable fact given that this is a pretty fancy hypothesis. Libby Adler's analysis of Unitedstatesean and Cuban rivalry in the Cold War and after the Fall of the Wall shows them locked in a diacritical contest, full of the will to "not be" the other. And yet she reveals a massive and uncanny repetition: both the tight linkage of the Lavender Scare to the Red Scare in US Cold War ideology and the deep rejection of Cuban colonial-resort-prostituted-homosexuality by the Revolution pivot in a pro-gay direction in the official ideology of both rivals. In the United States, the pivot is to rights; in Cuba, to public health, including gay-affirmative sex education in Cuba. Wow.

Ummni Khan limns a political contest over depictions and mocking re-enactments of morally bad sex, using the Hulu television series *The Handmaid's Tale* and parodic Halloween costumes and lingerie based on it as a focal point. Khan stages an encounter between "feminist killjoy" condemnations of, and a "kinky brat" sensibility willing to relish and get turned on by depictions of, the ritual rape scene in season one of the show. But she also "demonstrates how brat and killjoy perspectives can be complementary as well as conflicting" and even ends the essay with her own killjoy judgments on *The Handmaid's Tale* for the racial political incorrectness of its casting. This is a complex diacritic that is constantly teetering on the verge of flipping, and then doing so.

Ido Katri, Matthew Ball, and Noa Ben-Asher diagnose paradoxes of moral judgment in the domain of sexual identity and advocacy for victims of sexual predation. For Katri, in "Trans Bodies, Gay Sexuality, and Dysphoria," the vexed site is the gay male bathhouse: victim or victimizer? Katri opens with the drug enforcement police raid of a Tel Aviv gay male bathhouse, quickly decried as homophobic by official pinkwashers and retracted by representatives of the police. The very next week the very same club escorted a trans patron to the door, explaining that his presence was disturbing patrons. LGBT governance in both cases, one public and the other private. The tension between the two episodes sets up the terms in which Katri assesses his own several visits to gay bathhouses with his partner as they maneuver their bodily differences against and alongside a "temporal gay manifestation of what it means to be male" (chapter 10). The result is a series of morally delicate reflections in which Katri both condemns and extends empathy to gay male trans-excluders. What will it mean to bring into existence "trans governance" in which we cannot always embrace wayward desire and secure complete inclusion?

Ball's chapter reads letters "between 16 incarcerated people (15 cisgender men, most of whom identified as gay, bisexual, or pansexual, and one transgender woman) and a single member of the gay community outside of prison (who also subsequently donated the letters to [an] . . . archive)" (chapter 11). The letters date between 1990 and 2010. At one point, Ball zeroes in on the eight correspondents who were convicted of committing sexual offences against minors, including some children. He has placed himself in a morally vexed position: He feels empathy for people incarcerated for forms of sexual deviance which the official LGBT community has denounced, and even for conduct that "disgust[s]" him. And he discovers a remarkable instance of moral tension in that subset of the collection. Letter writers imprisoned for statutory rape had sex with persons close to themselves in age, perceived their sex partners as consenting, denied being attracted to younger people per se, suffered intense remorse for their acts, and used their correspondence with the community letter-writer to explore the implications of their moral fault for their pathway to a healthy sexual identity. They were open, moreover, to gay identification. Meanwhile, the correspondents who described themselves as oriented to minors had had sex with people significantly younger than themselves. They denied being predators but described their own conduct in ways that convinced Ball that they had groomed and preyed upon minors. They were adamantly not gay. He drew the tentative conclusion that, compared with the first set of letter-writers, the second group, "who had engaged in clearly assaultive, manipulative, or exploitative behaviour[,] displayed less contrition or none at all" (chapter 11). Ball gives us a complex nest of nexuses: offense, moral value, responsibilization (that seems profoundly askew), and identity.

Noa Ben-Asher, in an astonishing comparison of the political performances of Greta Thunberg and QAnon, gives us two instances of moral panic over the violation of sexual innocence and its capacity to mobilize social justice movements. Both instances invoke massive conspiracy theories, both place the violation of childhood sexual innocence at the heart of their "crisis-justice narrative," both refuse all responsibility for finding political solutions to the crisis they point to, both pose as truth-telling prophets and bring an apocalyptic narrative of the nigh end of times that Ben-Asher traces back to Christian eschatology. How should we think about a demagogue for a cause we believe in? About outrage over the sexual injury of innocents used as a fulcrum for changing the world?

Finally, Mary Anne Case and Jennifer C. Nash engage chiasmatic critique in assessing the moral value of despair over, and refusal of, law's capacity to deliver a more just world. In "Donorsexuality after *Dobbs*," Case reflects on the rights to reproductive freedom, if any, enjoyed by men who convey their fresh sperm directly to intended parents, on a massive scale and entirely outside of the regulated space of sperm banks. Staggering over the rubble left by *Dobbs v. Jackson Women's Health Organization* (2022), Case surveys the substantive due process landscape and wonders—as do we all—how many of the landmark cases there will fall now that *Roe v. Wade* (1973) is overruled. But she correctly notes that no amount of cleaning out the Augean stables of substantive due process precedents will touch *Skinner v. Oklahoma* (1942), the Supreme Court case that declared the right to procreate to be fundamental, invented the term strict scrutiny, framed an equal protection problem in Mr. Skinner's sanction of sterilization for stealing chickens when white-collar offenders like embezzlers were not subject to that punishment, applied strict scrutiny to that equal treatment problem because a fundamental right was at stake, and concluded that Skinner's constitutional rights had been violated. In a chiasmatic critique of rising and falling rights to sexual freedom, *Skinner* read this way looks like a safe haven, however small, for rights. But in her closing pages, Case rightly notices that equal protection outcomes are radically unstable: The equal protection problem in *Skinner* could just as logically be solved by exposing all property-crime offenders to sterilization. This dreadful flip, if it happens, could permit a dysphoric world of vast regulation of what is, even under *Dobbs*, the space of sexual freedom. This is a chiasmatic critique of rights walking the dark, dark side.

If Case's flip of her legal diacritics is nasty and scary, Nash's is encompassing and benign. Her project in "Thinking with Care" is to piece together theoretical and normative resources for a Black-affirmative understanding of care. From Black studies she adduces the work of Christina Sharpe and Joshua Chambers-Letson (and others) for "evidence of the need for a Black intramural ethic of care, and even for an ethic of retreat" (chapter 12). It is a necessary antidote to pervasive state violence. But she also adduces from feminist studies a vision of care, as extracted from low-income workers and women and as exploitative and soul-destroying. The high point of the latter is the famous manifesto *Wages Against Housework*, in which Silvia Federici (1975) calls upon all women to boycott care until they are paid fairly for it. This creates a double diacritics: care as redemptive specifically *from* the state and care as exploitation; care embraced and care refused. Each has its own vision of the household, moreover. Black studies houses arguments that the Black household is a vital sanctuary for Black life, while feminist studies houses arguments that the household is capitalism's hyper-exploited space. The flip comes when Nash turns to Patricia J. Williams's *Alchemy of Race and Rights* (1991) for a specifically Black embrace of legal rights as the aspirational language for deep, indeed spiritual respect—care— for all persons and things that exist as a "necessary grammar for forging a lexicon of freedom" (chapter 12). She closes: "It is my hope that if we follow care's complex genealogies—including into an archive that embraces rather than rejects the law, finding in the juridical the possibility of certain forms of freedom dreams—we can jettison the ongoing tendency to relegate certain archives, methods, and fields as inherently regressive" (chapter 12). She asks us to temper the intense anti-statism found in some segments of the contemporary anti-racist left by "*thinking with* care *about* care."

* * *

In her 2005 lecture on "Melanie Klein and the Difference Affect Makes" at Harvard Law School, Sedgwick twice indicated to the audience—mostly made up of law professors and law students, including graduate students studying for a doctorate in law—that we would never find a home for her critical insights in our work because they were profoundly athwart the commitments to reason, balance, symmetry, and correctness that belonged to law. Twice Philomila Tsoukala, then one of those graduate students, raised her hand to disagree: *We* were the crits, she said; *we* inherited the irrationalist branch of legal realism; *we* were the queers of law. It made me sad to think that Eve never really understood what Philo was saying; especially because, after Eve's death, Philo said it in writing with astonishing insight into the erotics of intellectual gratitude (Tsoukala 2010). This collection is a fourth hand raised to insist that being queer in law is not merely possible but a highly productive thing to do.

NOTES

1 See also Sedgwick's mocking list of all the dimensions along which one's sexuality is "supposed" to "line up" according to the dictates of the binary in *Tendencies* (1993, 7). In the latter, every ridiculous mandate casts the long shadow of the variations it seeks to banish from existence.

2 I want to capture for you the "and others" sensibility in a remarkable passage from Sedgwick's essay "Willa Cather and Others." The last sentence of Sedgwick's essay is an anagrammatic spinoff of the last sentence of Cather's novel *The Professor's House*, "He thought he knew where he was, and that he could face with fortitude the *Berengaria* and the future" (Cather 1973, 282–83); The *Berengaria* was the ship bringing the protagonist's wife and family back home). Sedgwick closes her essay: "Underneath the regimented grammatic f-f-fortitude of the heterosexist ordering of marriage, there are audible in this alphabet the more purely semantic germs of any vital possibility: *Berengaria*, ship of women: the {green} {aria}, the {eager} {brain}, the {bearing} and the {bairn}, the {raring} {engine}, the {bargain} {binge}, the {ban} and {bar}, the {garbage}, the {barrage} of {anger}, the {bare} {grin}, the {rage} to {err}, the {rare} {grab} for {being}, the {begin} and {rebegin} {again}" (1993, 176).

BIBLIOGRAPHY

Cather, Willa. 1973. *The Professor's House*. New York: Vintage Books.

Dobbs v. Jackson Women's Health Organization, 597 U.S. ___ (2022).

Eve Kosofsky Sedgwick Website, https://evekosofskysedgwick.net/.

Federici, Silvia. 1975. *Wages Against Housework*. London: Falling Wall Press.

MacKinnon, Catharine A. 1982. "Feminism, Marxism, Method, and the State: An Agenda for Theory." *Signs* 7(3): 515–44.

Moon, Michael. 1998. *A Small Boy and Others: Imitation and Initiation in American Culture from Henry James to Andy Warhol*. Durham, NC: Duke University Press.

Roe v. Wade, 410 U.S. 113 (1973).

Sedgwick, Eve Kosofsky. 1990. *Epistemology of the Closet*. Berkeley: University of California Press.

———. 1993. *Tendencies*. Durham, NC: Duke University Press.

———. 2003. *Touching Feeling: Affect, Pedagogy, Performativity*. Durham, NC: Duke University Press.

———. 2011. *The Weather in Proust*, edited by Jonathan Goldberg. Durham, NC: Duke University Press.

Skinner v. Oklahoma, 316 U.S. 535 (1942).

Tsoukala, Philomila. 2010. "Reading a Poem Is Being Written: A Tribute to Eve Kosofsky Sedgwick." *Harvard Journal of Law and Gender* 33: 339–47.

Williams, Patricia. 1991. *The Alchemy of Race and Rights: Diary of a Law Professor*. Cambridge, MA: Harvard University Press.

ACKNOWLEDGMENTS

Joe and Brenda got to know each other editing this book, not in the *you really get to know someone when you work together* sense but in the sense that we only knew each other through our work before we agreed to collaborate on *Enticements*. Fan-crushing on Brenda and upon meeting her for the very first time, Joe proposed that we jointly edit the volume. Brenda hesitated, but only for five minutes. And so the project was born, as was our friendship. We hope that friendship is evidenced in the volume. We found in one another a shared sense of intellectual and political generosity toward all things *sex* and *regulatory*. Neither of us feel comfortable in queer theory camps that are constitutionally *against*. We invested in a project that retained queer criticality but also prescriptive possibility.

We started in 2019 with grand visions of workshopping the draft chapters in various locations across Canada and the United States. The pandemic had other plans, relocating our workshops to Zoomland. Our contributors were generous and gracious, patient and engaged. We held multiple zoom sessions, in which our contributors offered wise, constructive feedback for each other's drafts. We are so grateful to each of our contributors who, despite (and because of) a global pandemic, ongoing brutality against Black lives, the ascendence of far-right leaders, and on and on, showed up for one another and for our collective endeavor.

We would also like to thank several other colleagues and comrades who contributed their intellectual time and energy. Gratitude to Paisley Currah and Lara Karaian for their interlocution. We appreciate the participants at the Law and Society Association Conference 2021, who joined us online to learn from and instruct us on the project. Thank you to our anonymous readers, who saved us from our worse ideas and made the collection that much stronger. Special thanks to our research assistants, Charlotte Butler, Caroline Monahan, and Katie Lawless, for their meticulous work.

Our respective institutions provided generous support along the way: the Women's, Gender, and Sexuality Studies Program at Yale University and the Faculty of Law at the University of Toronto. During and partially for this project, Joe received a master's degree from Yale Law School, and is especially indebted to Reva Siegel and Gerald Torres for their mentorship.

We would also like to thank Ilene Kalish, our editor, for encouraging this project from the beginning, as well as Yasemin Torfilli and the New York University Press editorial staff.

This volume is a labor of queer love for queer law. We hope you are enticed.

LIBBY ADLER is Professor of Law and Women's, Gender, & Sexuality Studies at Northeastern University in Boston. She is the author of *Gay Priori: A Queer Critical Legal Studies Approach to Law Reform*.

CHRIS ASHFORD is Professor of Law and Society at Northumbria University. He is co-editor (with Alexander Maine) of Edward Elgar's *Research Handbook on Gender, Sexuality and the Law*.

MATTHEW BALL is Associate Professor in the School of Justice, Queensland University of Technology, Australia. He is the author of *Criminology and Queer Theory: Dangerous Bedfellows?* and the editor of *Queering Criminology*.

NOA BEN-ASHER is a Professor of Law at St. John's University School of Law. They are the author of *Secular-Christian Social Justice*.

MARY ANNE CASE is Arnold I. Shure Professor of Law and a member of the board of the Center for the Study of Gender and Sexuality at the University of Chicago. While diverse interests include German contract law, theological anthropology, and the First Amendment, her scholarship to date has concentrated on the regulations of sex, gender, sexuality, religion, and family, and on the early history of feminism.

JANET HALLEY is Eli Goldson Professor of Law at Harvard Law School. A scholar of feminist legal theory, critical legal studies, sexuality and law, and family law, she is the author of *Split Decisions: How and Why to Take a Break from Feminism*, and co-author of *Governance Feminism: An Introduction*.

ZACHARY HERZ is Assistant Professor of Classics at the University of Colorado–Boulder. His research explores how law shaped and was shaped by the political and ethical culture of the Roman Empire.

RATNA KAPUR is Professor of International Law at the School of Law, Queen Mary University of London, and Senior Faculty at the Institution of Global Law and Policy, Harvard Law School. She is the author *Gender, Alterity and Human Rights: Freedom in a Fishbowl.*

IDO KATRI is Assistant Professor at Tel Aviv University School of Social Work in Collaboration with the Faculty of Law. He teaches and researches in the fields of Trans Studies and Critical Theory, as well as Public, Administrative, and Poverty Law.

EVELYN KESSLER is a PhD candidate in History at the University of Chicago. She studies the intellectual, legal, and cultural history of consent in American life.

UMMNI KHAN is Associate Professor in Legal Studies at Carleton University. She is the author of *Vicarious Kinks: SM in the Sociolegal Imaginary* and is completing her first novel, *Office Hours.*

KYLE KIRKUP is Associate Professor at the University of Ottawa Faculty of Law (Common Law Section). His research examines the regulation of gender and sexuality across the fields of constitutional law, human rights law, and criminal law.

JENNIFER C. NASH is Jean Fox O'Barr Professor of Gender, Sexuality, and Feminist Studies at Duke University. She is the author of *Birthing Black Mothers* and *Black Feminism Reimagined: After Intersectionality.*

SENTHORUN SUNIL RAJ is Reader in Human Rights Law at Manchester Law School. His research focuses on the relationship between emotion, law, and LGBTIQ rights. He is the author of *Feeling Queer Jurisprudence: Injury, Intimacy, Identity* and co-editor of *The Queer Outside in Law: Recognising LGBTIQ People in the United Kingdom.*

MATTHEW WAITES is Reader in Sociology in the School of Social and Political Sciences at University of Glasgow. He is the author of *The Age of Consent: Young People, Sexuality and Citizenship*, and co-editor, with Corinne Lennox, of *Human Rights, Sexual Orientation and Gender Identity in the Commonwealth: Struggles for Decriminalisation and Change*. He has authored articles concerning sexuality, human rights, and decolonizing in journals such as *Social and Legal Studies, International Sociology, International Review of Sociology*, and the *Journal of Genocide Research*.

ABOUT THE EDITORS

JOSEPH J. FISCHEL is Associate Professor of Women's, Gender, & Sexuality Studies at Yale University. He is the author of *Screw Consent: A Better Politics of Sexual Justice* and *Sex and Harm in the Age of Consent*.

BRENDA COSSMAN is the Goodman-Schipper Chair and Professor of Law at the University of Toronto. She is the author of *The New Sex Wars: Sexual Harm in the #MeToo Era* and *Sexual Citizens: The Legal and Cultural Regulation of Sex and Belonging*.

INDEX

Page numbers in italics indicate Figures and Tables

QAnon on, 326, 333–35, 338n35, 339n39; sexual risk and, 213–15, 223–27
Cowell, Simon, 35
Crawley, Karen, 150
Crenshaw, Kimberlé, 316–17
crime, 90, 99–102. *See also* offenses, criminal
criminalization, 20, 96–104, 125, 137, 281, 295; colonial, 15, 88–95, 345; COVID-19, 224–27; HIV nondisclosure, 214, 217, 221–22; of homosexuality, 42–43, 65; of poppers, 234, 240; pornography, 144; of same sex sexual acts, 86–95, 100; of sex, 13, 18–19; of sodomy, 38, 62–63, 67
criminal law, 1, 19, 222–23, 224–27, 246–47, 347
criminology, queer, 279–83, 290–91, 296–97, 297n1
crisis-justice narratives, 21, 320–21, 323–27, 370
Critical Autism Studies, 334
critical legal studies, 9, 11–12, 22, 90, 315
critical race feminism, 21, 314–15
critical race theory (CRT), 3, 11–12, 22
critique, queer, 60–62, 67–72, 337n18
"cross-dressing," 89
CRT. *See* critical race theory
Cruel Optimism (Berlant), 346
Cuba, 16, 115–18, 122–26, 368; US compared to, 109–11, 127–29
The Cultural Politics of Emotion (Ahmed), 346
Currah, Paisley, 259
currencies, dual, 125–26
custody of children, 194, 198
customary law, 2, 15, 85–87, 90–94; in Kenya, 15, 87, 95–103
Cvetkovich, Ann, 140

Daigle, Megan, 116
Daily Mail (media), 35–36
Daughters of Bilitis, 129n4

Davis, Angela, 355
death/s, 35, 51, 61, 65, 194, 196, 244, 265; of Black people, 305–6, 308–9, 311; HIV related, 118, 272; suicide, 286, 338n26; of transgender people, 355
decolonial studies/politics, 86–87, 90–91, 96
decriminalization of homosexuality, 64, 76n5, 76n8, 88–91, 101, 246, 290; in Cuba, 122–23, 128
dehumanization, 151–52
Deleuze, Gilles, 147–48
D'Emilio, John, 112
dental dams, 220–21
Der Boiler (gay bathhouse), 160, 257, 273
Deroy, Pere, 89
desire, 3, 142, 260, 268; sexual, 152, 247, 287, 327, 338n28
deviance, sexual, 16, 369
diaries, prison, 2
difference, 174–75; sexual, 51, 267, 271
dimorphism, sexual, 67
Dionne, Evette, 306
disabilities, 179n3; "supercrips" and, 334, 339nn36–37
discrimination, 66, 125, 146, 205n16, 298n5, 316; anger and, 351–52; based on sexuality, 32, 62–63; against Chinese immigrants, 162; gender identity and, 23; against homosexuals, 41–43; LGBT, 75n2, 347–48; racial, 112, 116; sexual orientation, 32, 95, 122; against transgender people, 64, 264–65; against women, 60. *See also* antidiscrimination protections
diseases, communicable, 189–90, 195, 217–18. *See also* COVID-19 pandemic; HIV/AIDS epidemic
disgust, 21–22, 42, 136, 149, 345, 347, 352, 354, 369
distancing, physical/social, 213, 223
divorce, 112, 116–18, 190, 199
Doan, Laura, 34

www.ingramcontent.com/pod-product-compliance
Lightning Source LLC
Chambersburg PA
CBHW020531030426
42337CB00013B/799